Bad∞End∞Night
~インセイン・パーティー~

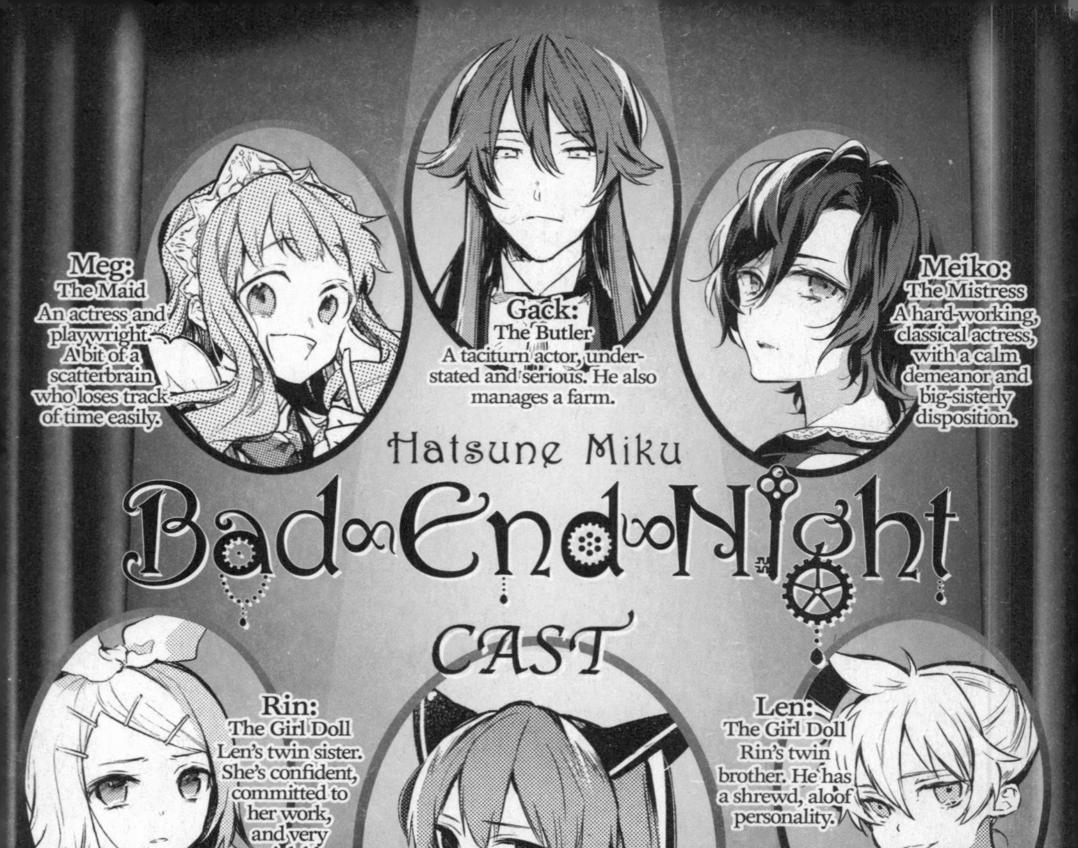
Meg:
The Maid
An actress and playwright. A bit of a scatterbrain who loses track of time easily.
Gack:
The Butler
A taciturn actor, under-stated and serious. He also manages a farm.
Meiko:
The Mistress
A hard-working, classical actress, with a calm demeanor and big-sisterly disposition.
Hatsune Miku
Bad∞End∞Night
CAST
Rin:
The Girl Doll
Len's twin sister. She's confident, committed to her work, and very socialable.
Len:
The Girl Doll
Rin's twin brother. He has a shrewd, aloof personality.
Luka:
The Young Miss
As star actress and a model. Despite her aloof attitude, she's actually quite kind.
Miku:
The Villager
A novice actress who was cast as the play's leading lady. She's normally very meek, but when she's on the stage, her acting abilities memerize the audience.
Kaito:
The Young Miss
The mediator of the group. He's kind, gentle, and a little bit of an airhead.

STORY

Novice actress Miku is cast in the role of a lifetime as the main character of the legendary playwright Burlet's lost play, Crazy Night. But the night after their first performance, Miku is drawn into a mysterious mansion as the sound of a buzzer signifies the start of a play. The mansion is identical to the one described in Crazy Night, and for some reason, the other seven actors are there, calling each other only by their characters' names. In order to find a way back to reality, Miku searches for a page that was stolen from the script, hoping to find a happy end...

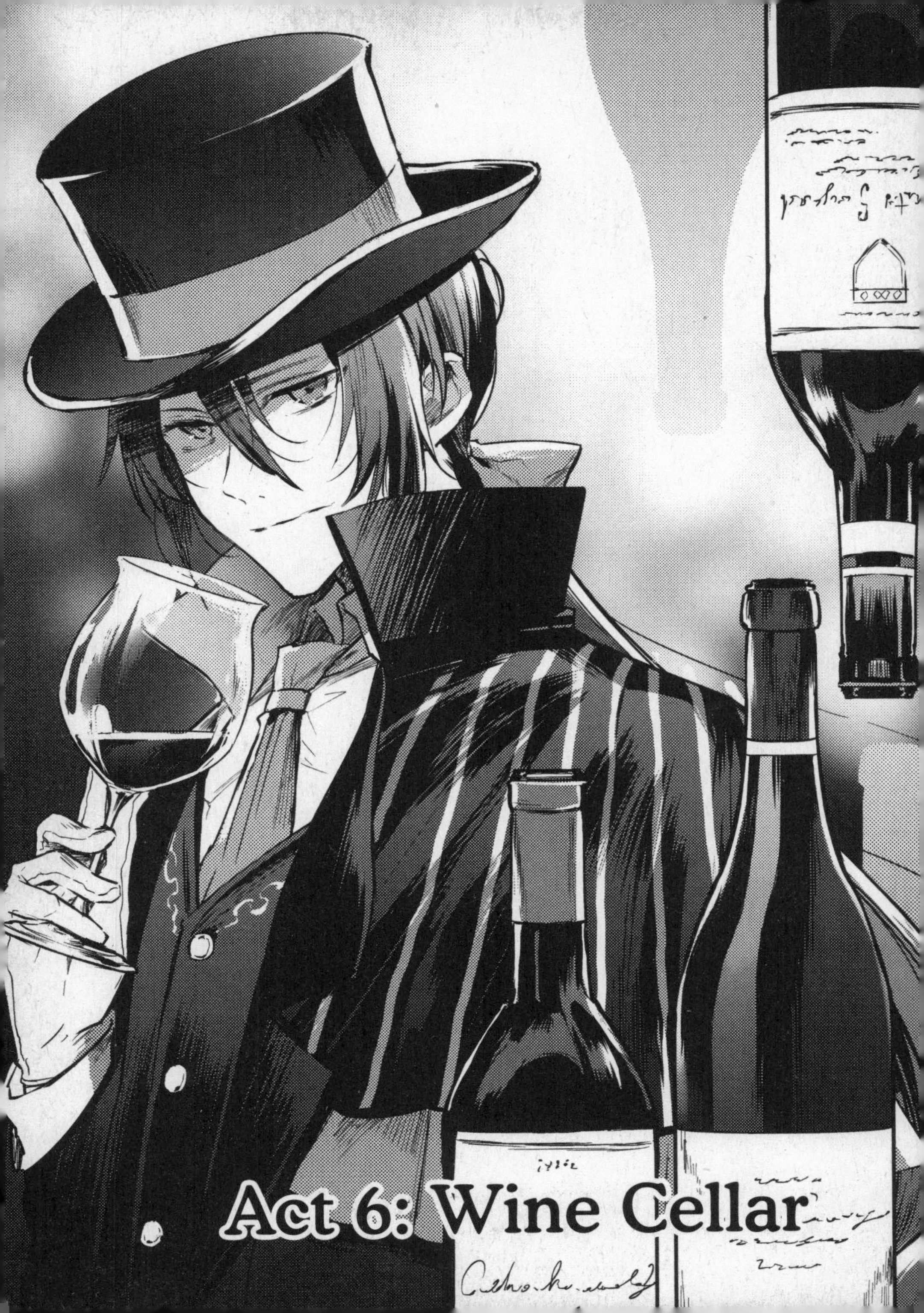
Act 6: Wine Cellar

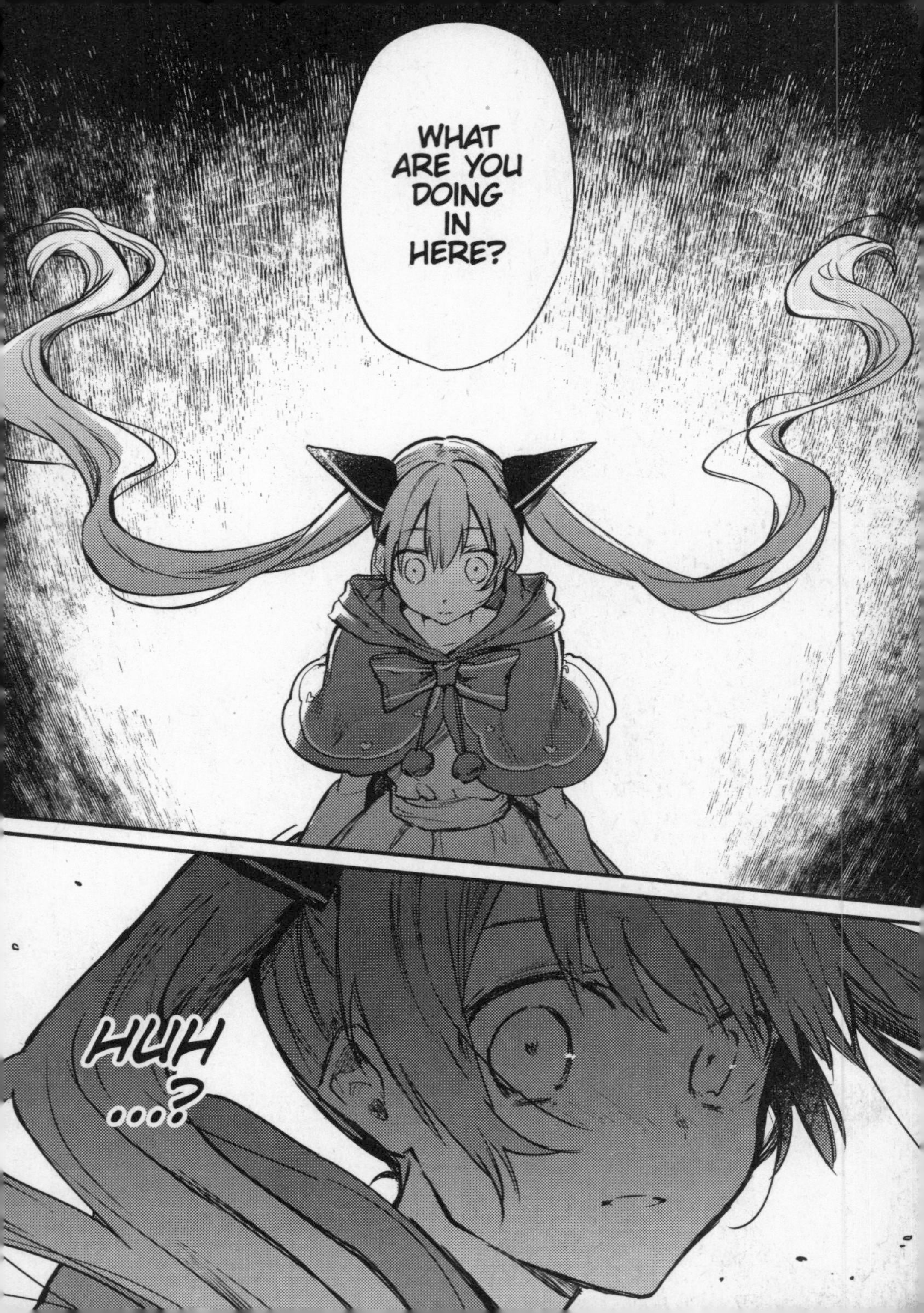
WHAT ARE YOU DOING IN HERE?
HUH ...?

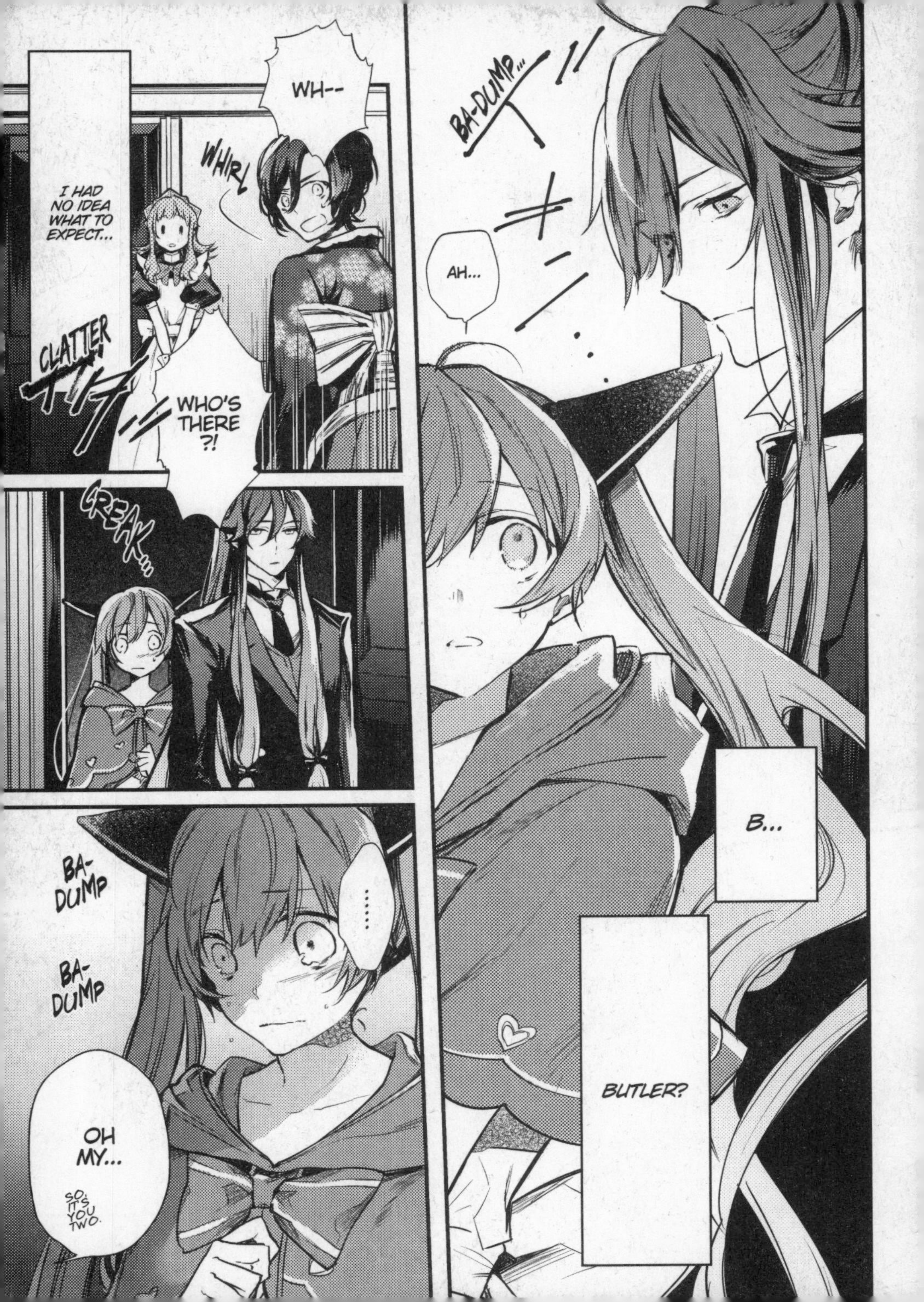
BA-DUMP...
AH...
B...
BUTLER?
WH--
WHIRL
I HAD NO IDEA WHAT TO EXPECT...
CLATTER
WHO'S THERE?!
CREAK...
BA-DUMP
BA-DUMP
......
OH MY...
SO, IT'S YOU TWO.

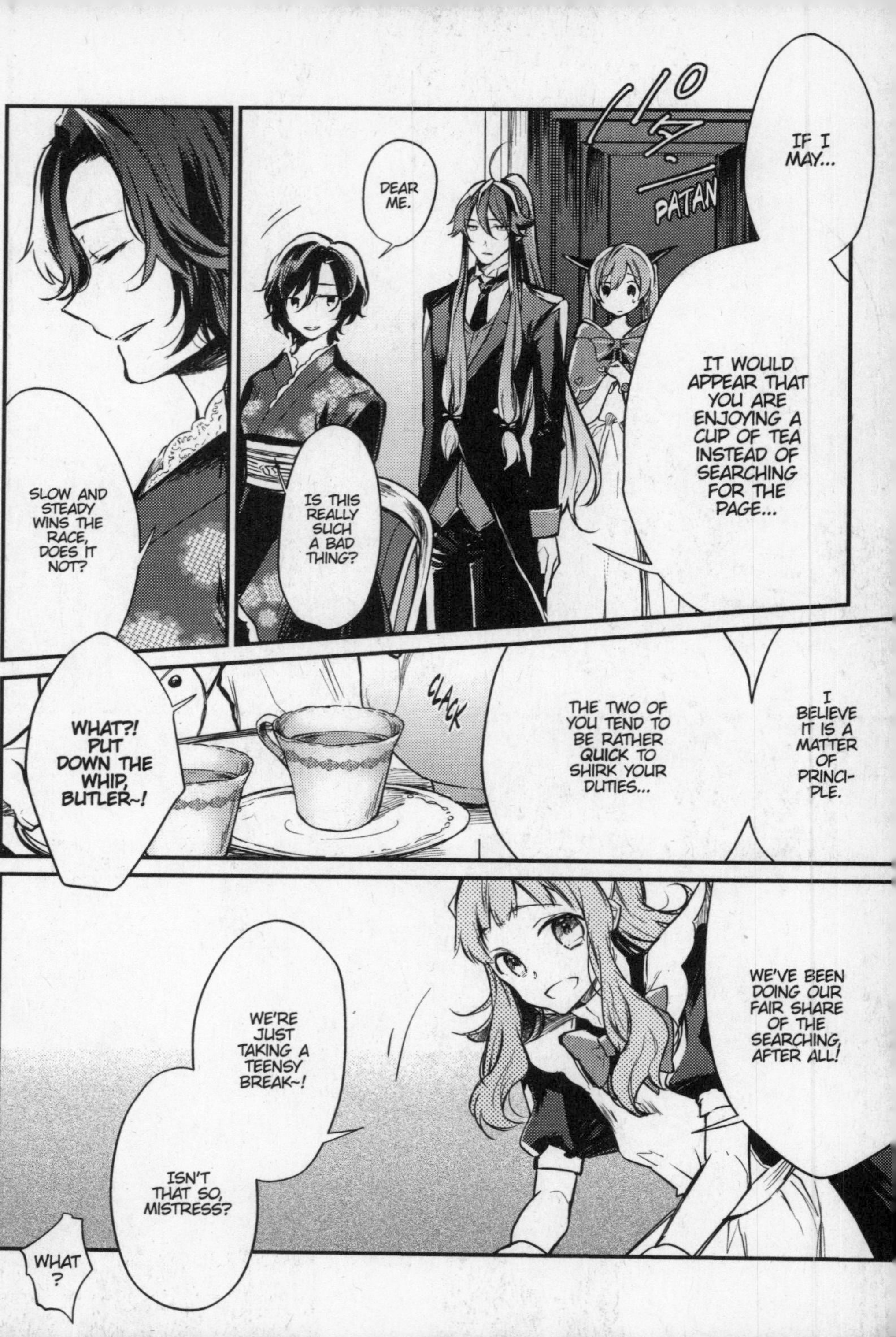
IF I MAY...
パタ
PATAN
DEAR ME.
IT WOULD APPEAR THAT YOU ARE ENJOYING A CUP OF TEA INSTEAD OF SEARCHING FOR THE PAGE...
IS THIS REALLY SUCH A BAD THING?
SLOW AND STEADY WINS THE RACE, DOES IT NOT?
I BELIEVE IT IS A MATTER OF PRINCIPLE.
THE TWO OF YOU TEND TO BE RATHER QUICK TO SHIRK YOUR DUTIES...
CLACK
WHAT?! PUT DOWN THE WHIP, BUTLER~!
WE'VE BEEN DOING OUR FAIR SHARE OF THE SEARCHING, AFTER ALL!
WE'RE JUST TAKING A TEENSY BREAK~!
ISN'T THAT SO, MISTRESS?
WHAT?

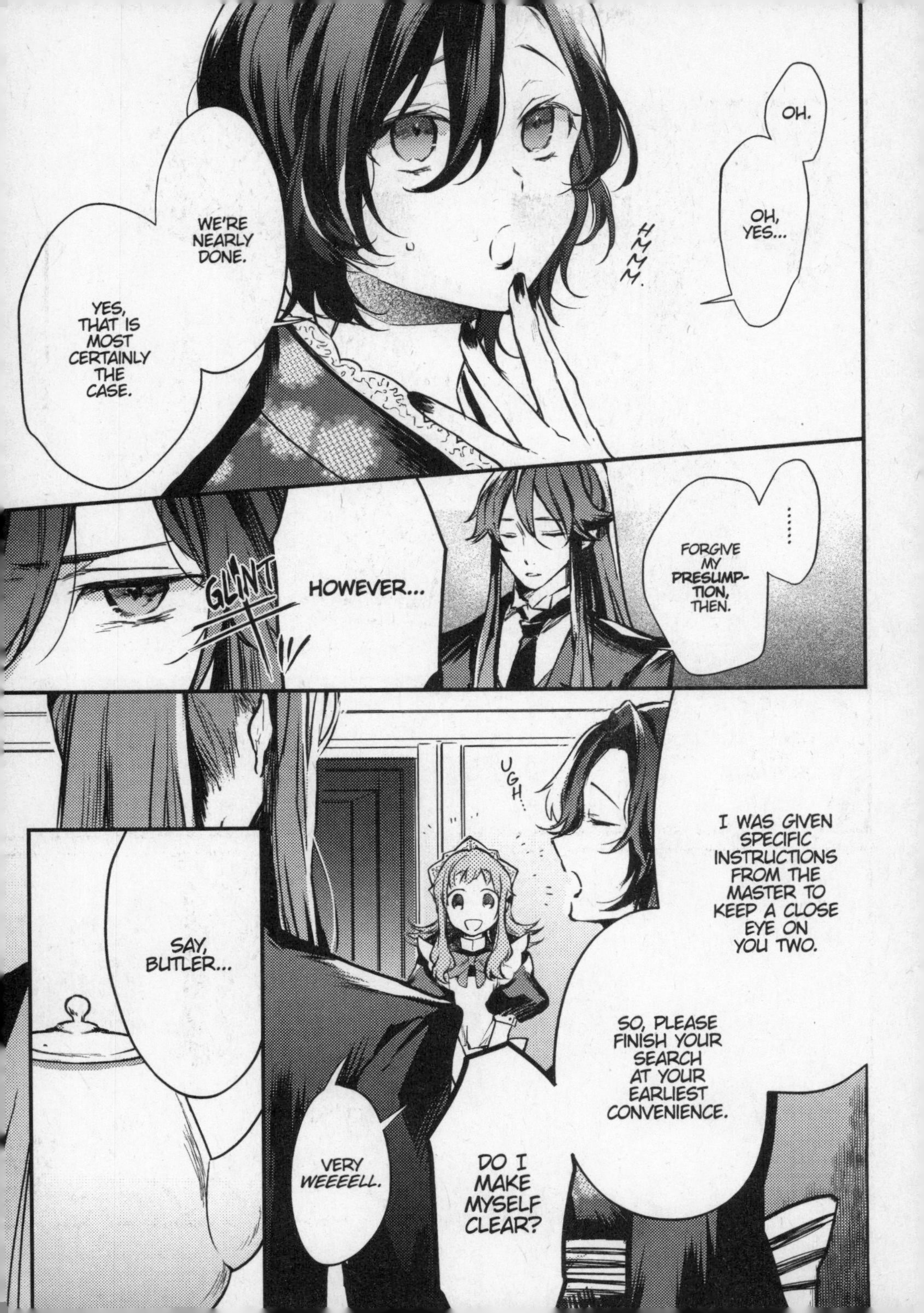
OH.
OH, YES...
HMMMM.
WE'RE NEARLY DONE.
YES, THAT IS MOST CERTAINLY THE CASE.
......
FORGIVE MY PRESUMPTION, THEN.
HOWEVER...
GLINT
I WAS GIVEN SPECIFIC INSTRUCTIONS FROM THE MASTER TO KEEP A CLOSE EYE ON YOU TWO.
UGH...
SO, PLEASE FINISH YOUR SEARCH AT YOUR EARLIEST CONVENIENCE.
DO I MAKE MYSELF CLEAR?
VERY WEEEELL.
SAY, BUTLER...

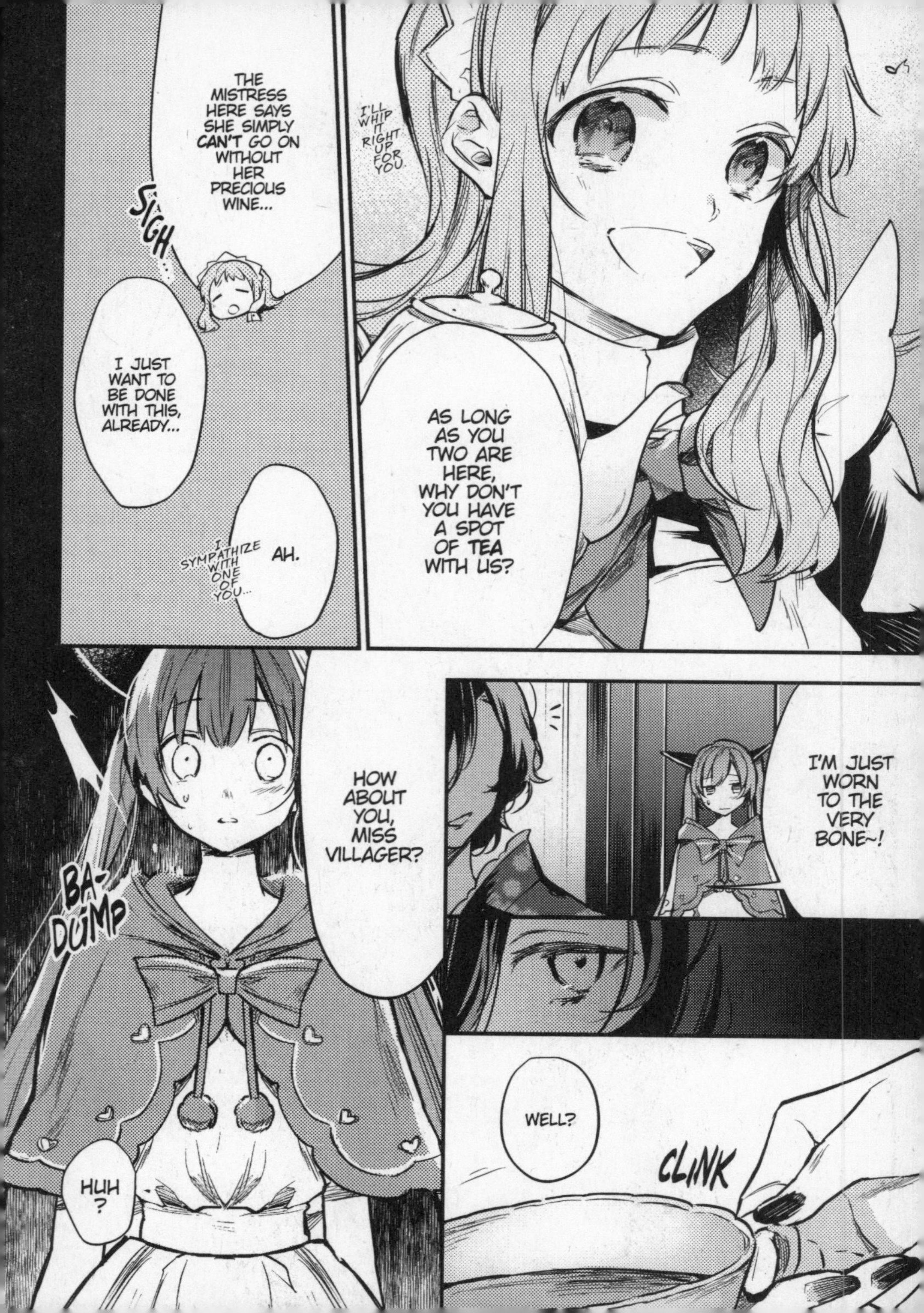
I'LL WHIP IT RIGHT UP FOR YOU.
AS LONG AS YOU TWO ARE HERE, WHY DON'T YOU HAVE A SPOT OF TEA WITH US?
THE MISTRESS HERE SAYS SHE SIMPLY CAN'T GO ON WITHOUT HER PRECIOUS WINE...
SIGH
I JUST WANT TO BE DONE WITH THIS, ALREADY...
AH.
I SYMPATHIZE WITH ONE OF YOU...
I'M JUST WORN TO THE VERY BONE~!
WELL?
CLINK
HOW ABOUT YOU, MISS VILLAGER?
BA-DUMP
HUH?

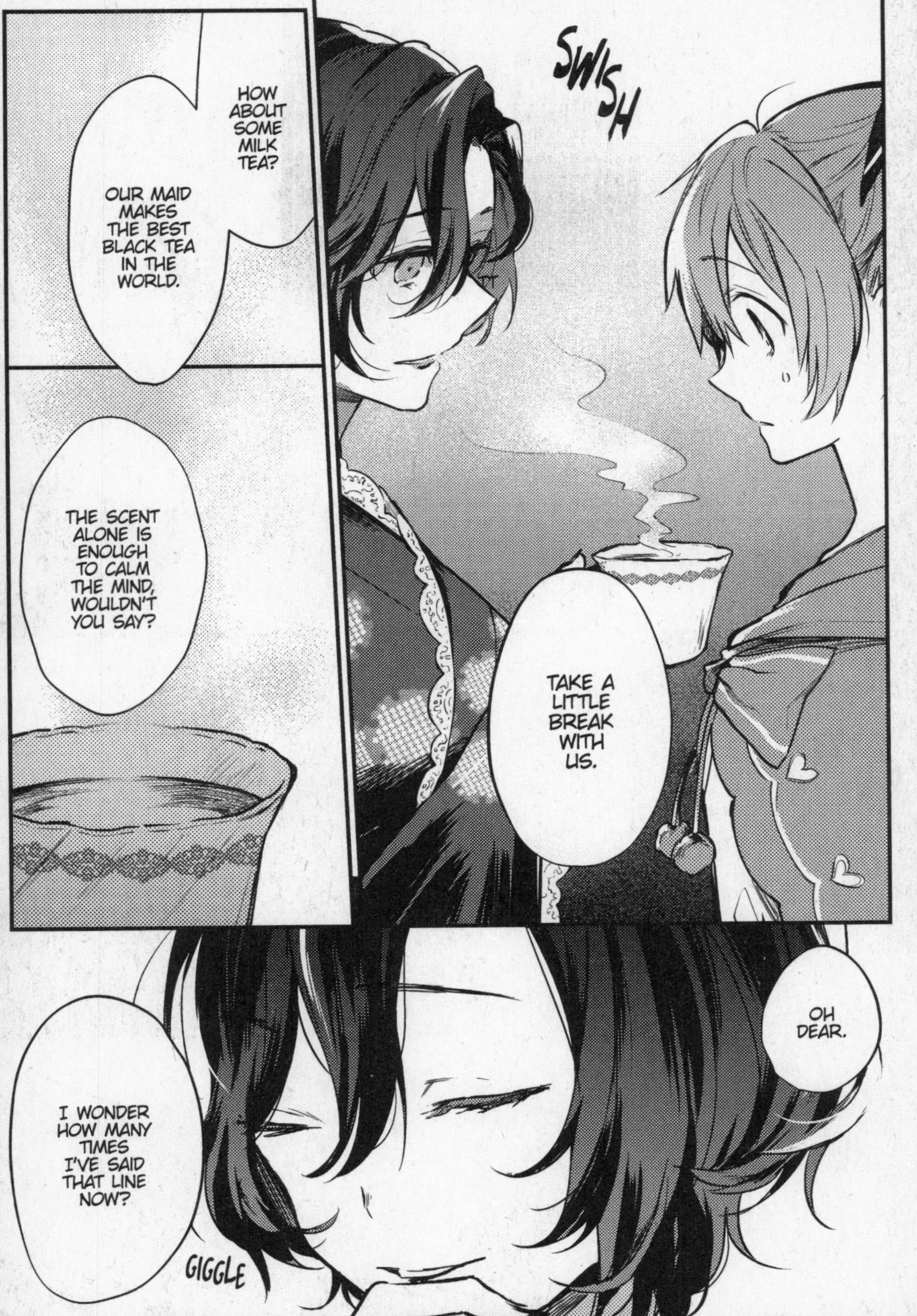
SWISH
TAKE A LITTLE BREAK WITH US.
HOW ABOUT SOME MILK TEA?
OUR MAID MAKES THE BEST BLACK TEA IN THE WORLD.
THE SCENT ALONE IS ENOUGH TO CALM THE MIND, WOULDN'T YOU SAY?
OH DEAR.
I WONDER HOW MANY TIMES I'VE SAID THAT LINE NOW?
GIGGLE

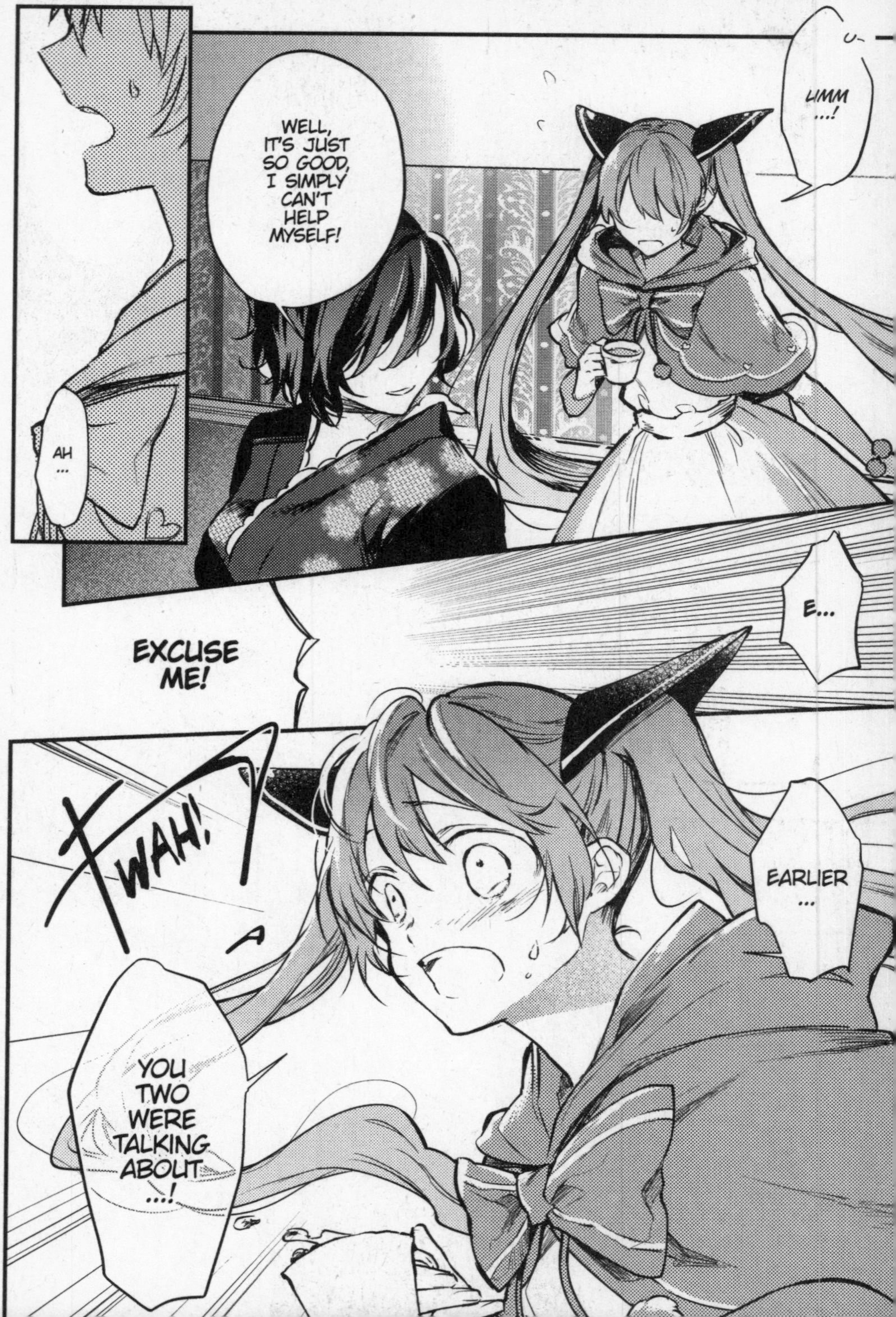
U–
UMM ...!
WELL, IT'S JUST SO GOOD, I SIMPLY CAN'T HELP MYSELF!
AH ...
E...
EXCUSE ME!
EARLIER ...
FWAH!
YOU TWO WERE TALKING ABOUT ...!

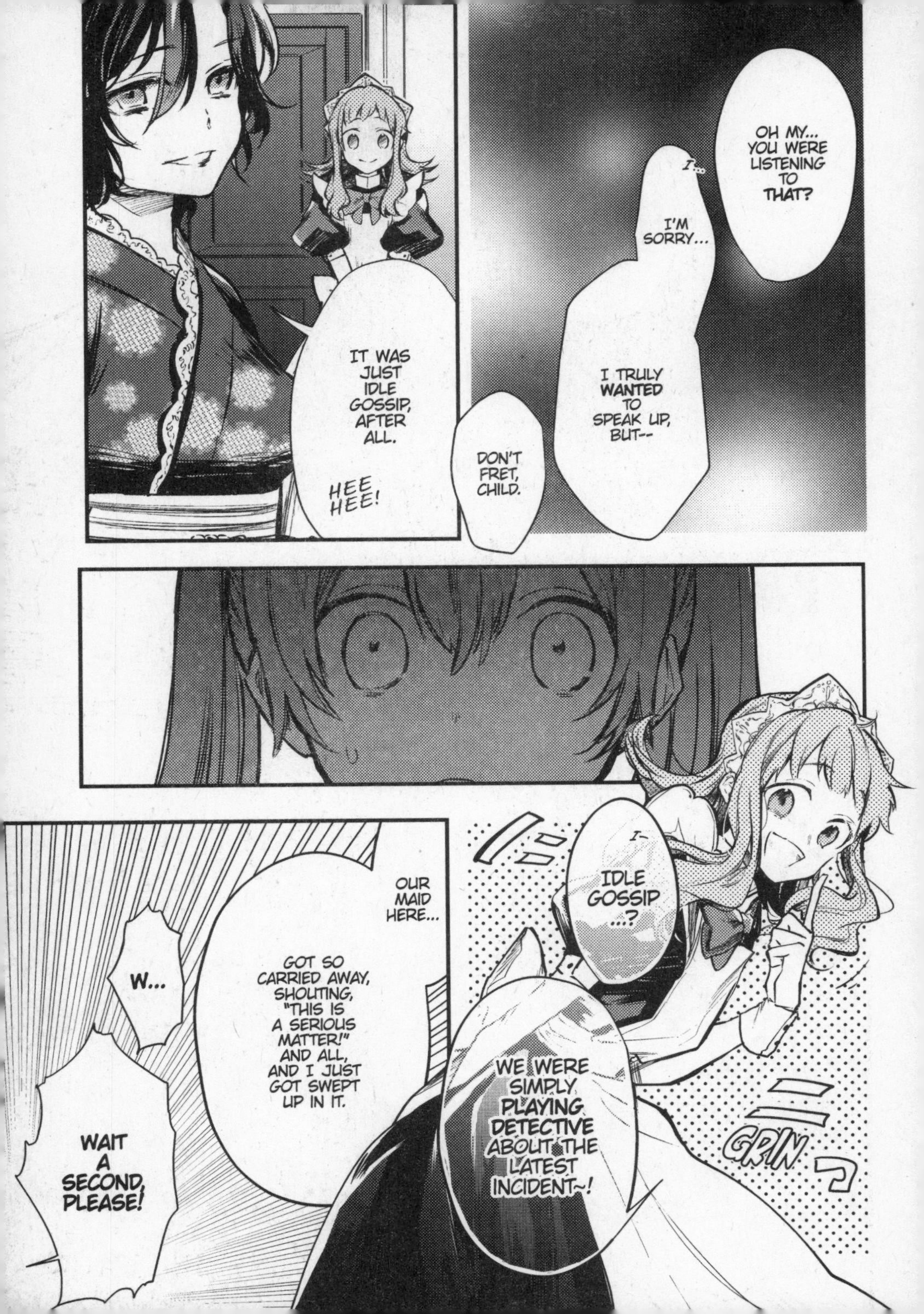
OH MY... YOU WERE LISTENING TO THAT?
I...
I'M SORRY...
I TRULY WANTED TO SPEAK UP, BUT--
DON'T FRET, CHILD.
IT WAS JUST IDLE GOSSIP, AFTER ALL.
HEE HEE!
I- IDLE GOSSIP ...?
OUR MAID HERE...
GOT SO CARRIED AWAY, SHOUTING, "THIS IS A SERIOUS MATTER!" AND ALL, AND I JUST GOT SWEPT UP IN IT.
WE WERE SIMPLY PLAYING DETECTIVE ABOUT THE LATEST INCIDENT~!
GRIN
W...
WAIT A SECOND, PLEASE!

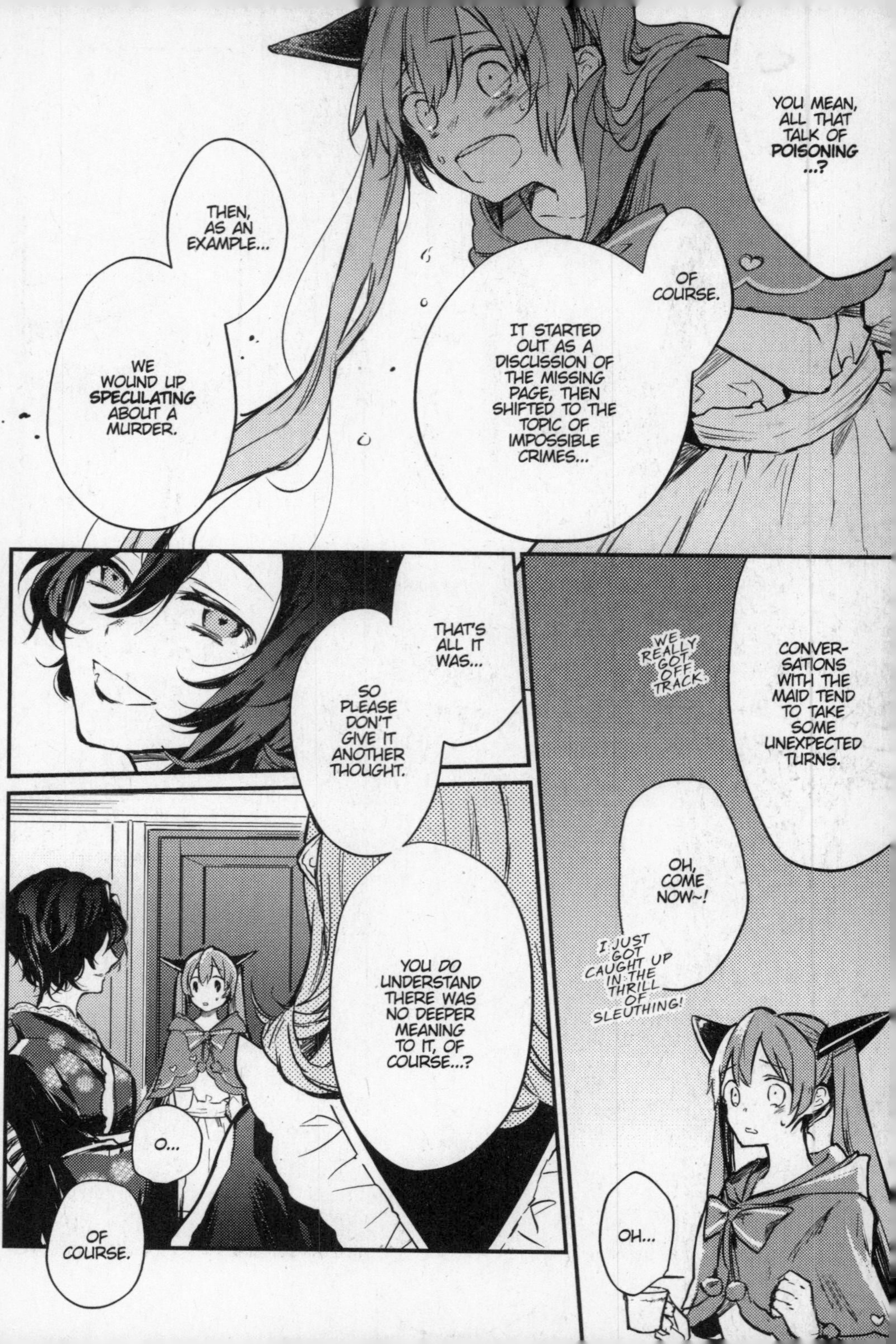
YOU MEAN, ALL THAT TALK OF POISONING ...?
OF COURSE.
IT STARTED OUT AS A DISCUSSION OF THE MISSING PAGE, THEN SHIFTED TO THE TOPIC OF IMPOSSIBLE CRIMES...
THEN, AS AN EXAMPLE...
WE WOUND UP SPECULATING ABOUT A MURDER.
CONVERSATIONS WITH THE MAID TEND TO TAKE SOME UNEXPECTED TURNS.
WE REALLY GOT OFF TRACK.
OH, COME NOW~!
I JUST GOT CAUGHT UP IN THE THRILL OF SLEUTHING!
OH...
THAT'S ALL IT WAS...
SO PLEASE DON'T GIVE IT ANOTHER THOUGHT.
YOU DO UNDERSTAND THERE WAS NO DEEPER MEANING TO IT, OF COURSE...?
O...
OF COURSE.

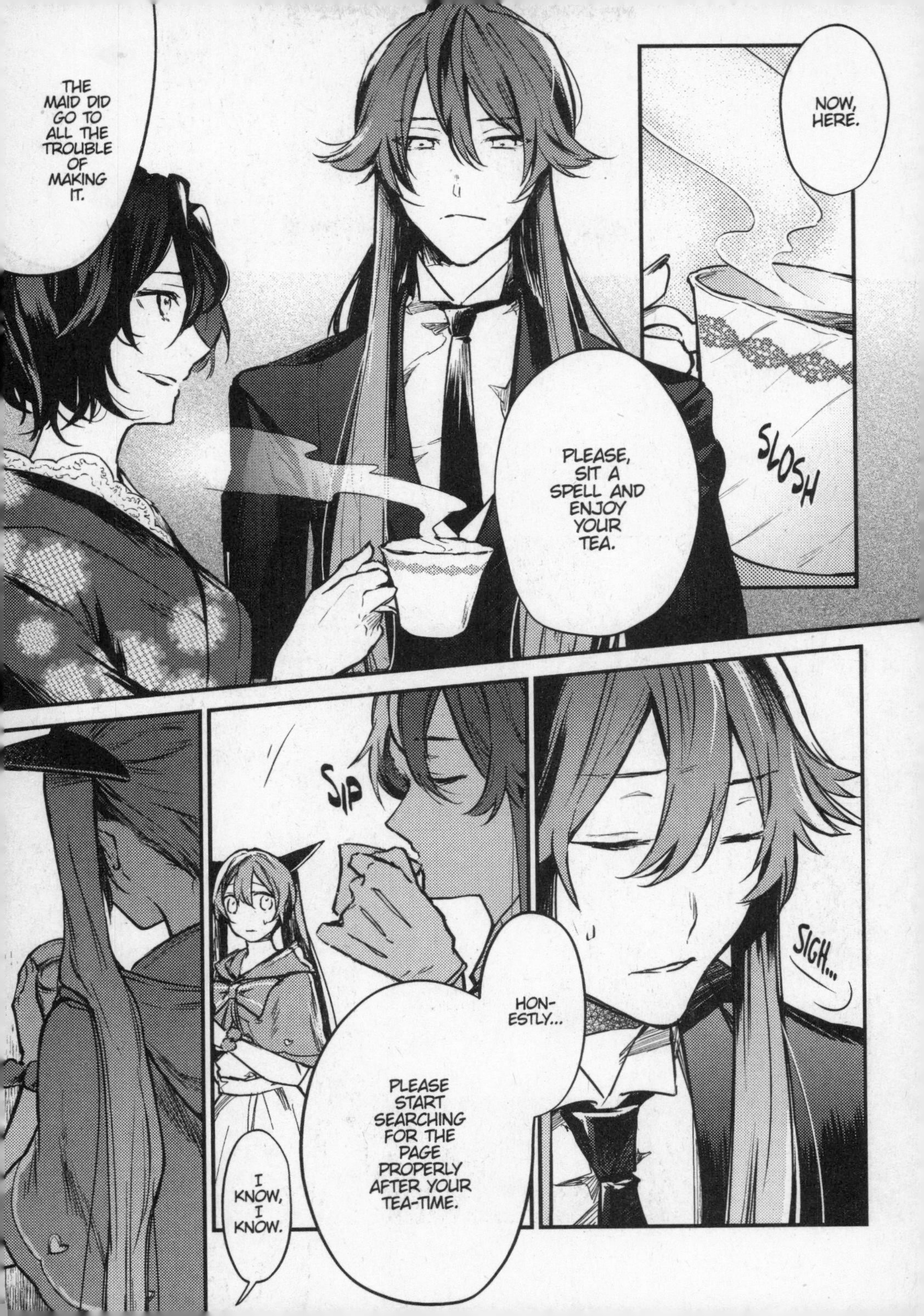

NOW, HERE.
SLOSH
PLEASE, SIT A SPELL AND ENJOY YOUR TEA.
THE MAID DID GO TO ALL THE TROUBLE OF MAKING IT.
SIGH...
HON-ESTLY...
PLEASE START SEARCHING FOR THE PAGE PROPERLY AFTER YOUR TEA-TIME.
SIP
I KNOW, I KNOW.

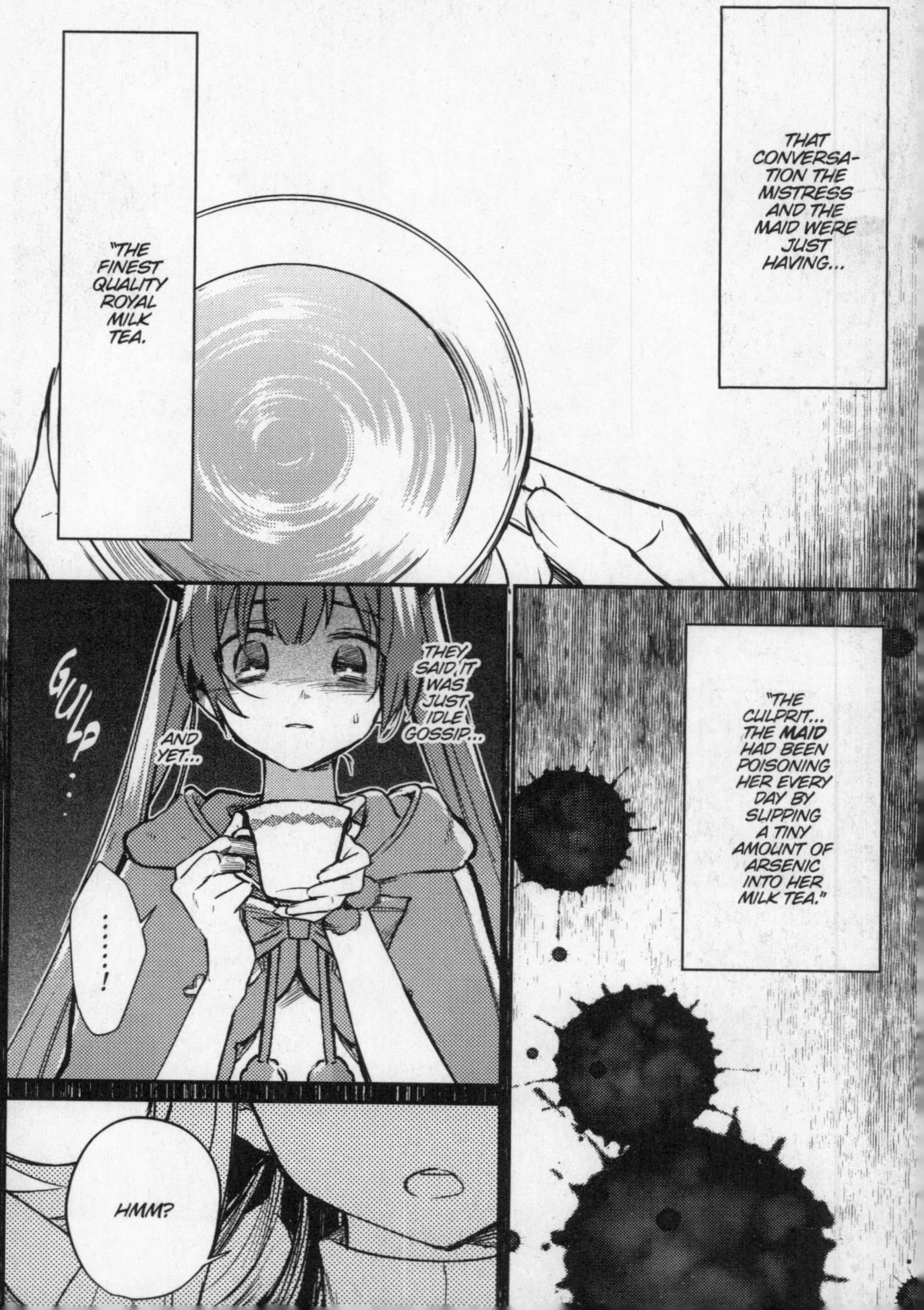
THAT CONVERSATION THE MISTRESS AND THE MAID WERE JUST HAVING...
"THE FINEST QUALITY ROYAL MILK TEA.
"THE CULPRIT... THE MAID HAD BEEN POISONING HER EVERY DAY BY SLIPPING A TINY AMOUNT OF ARSENIC INTO HER MILK TEA."
THEY SAID IT WAS JUST IDLE GOSSIP...
AND YET...
GULP...
......!
HMM?

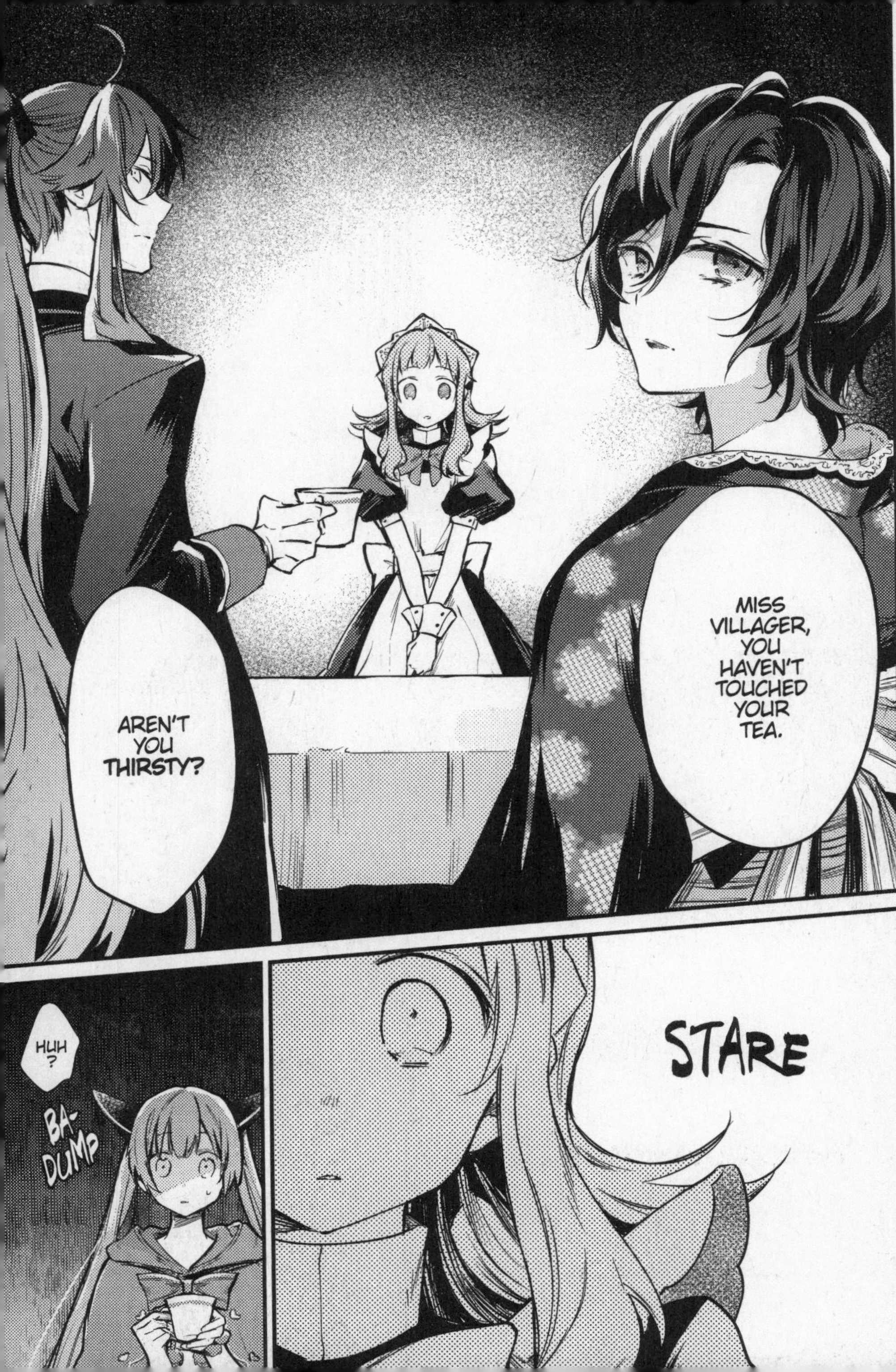
MISS VILLAGER, YOU HAVEN'T TOUCHED YOUR TEA.
AREN'T YOU THIRSTY?
STARE
HUH?
BA-DUMP

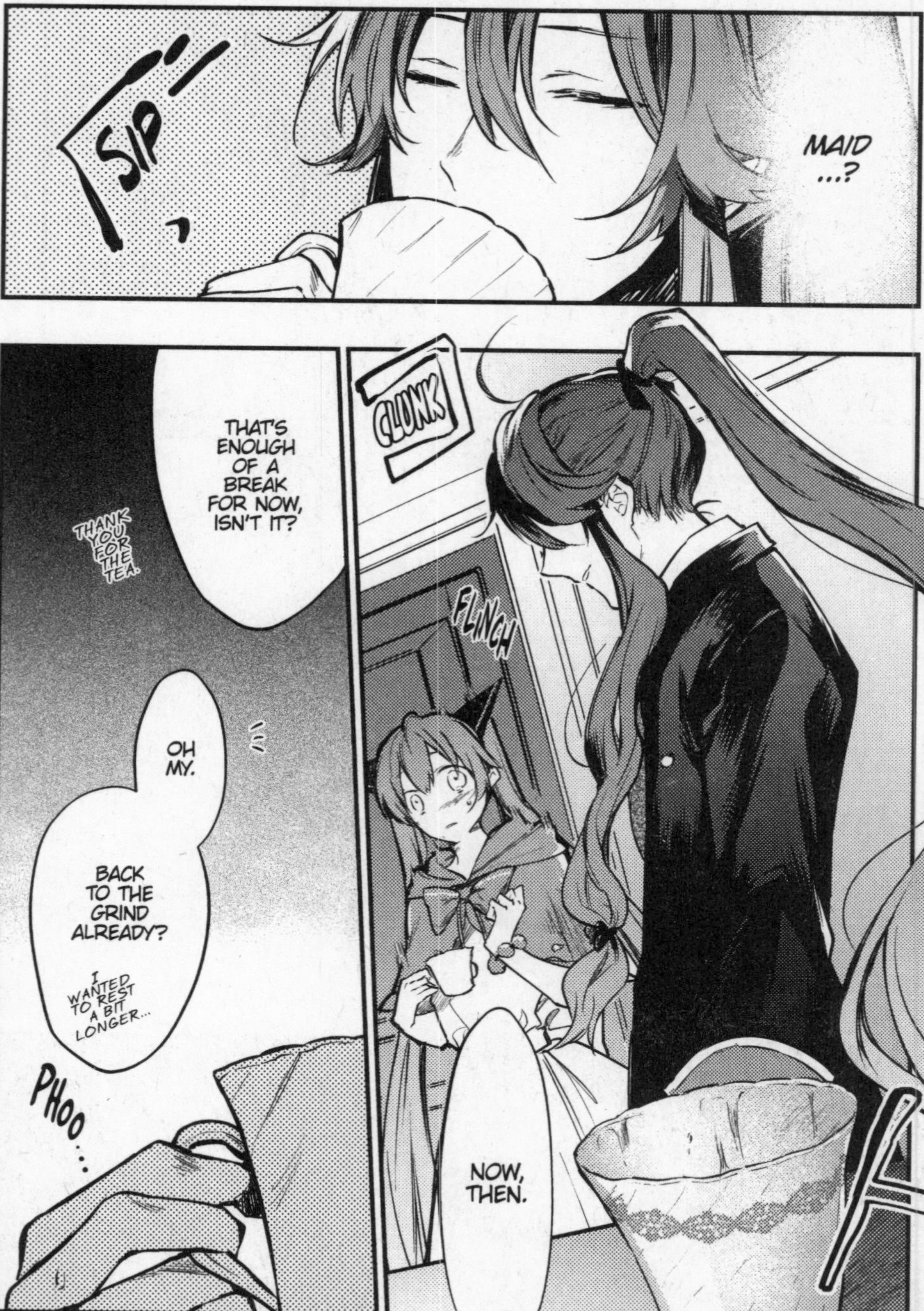
MAID ...?
SIP
CLUNK
FLINCH
NOW, THEN.
THAT'S ENOUGH OF A BREAK FOR NOW, ISN'T IT?
THANK YOU FOR THE TEA.
OH MY.
BACK TO THE GRIND ALREADY?
I WANTED TO REST A BIT LONGER...
PHOO...

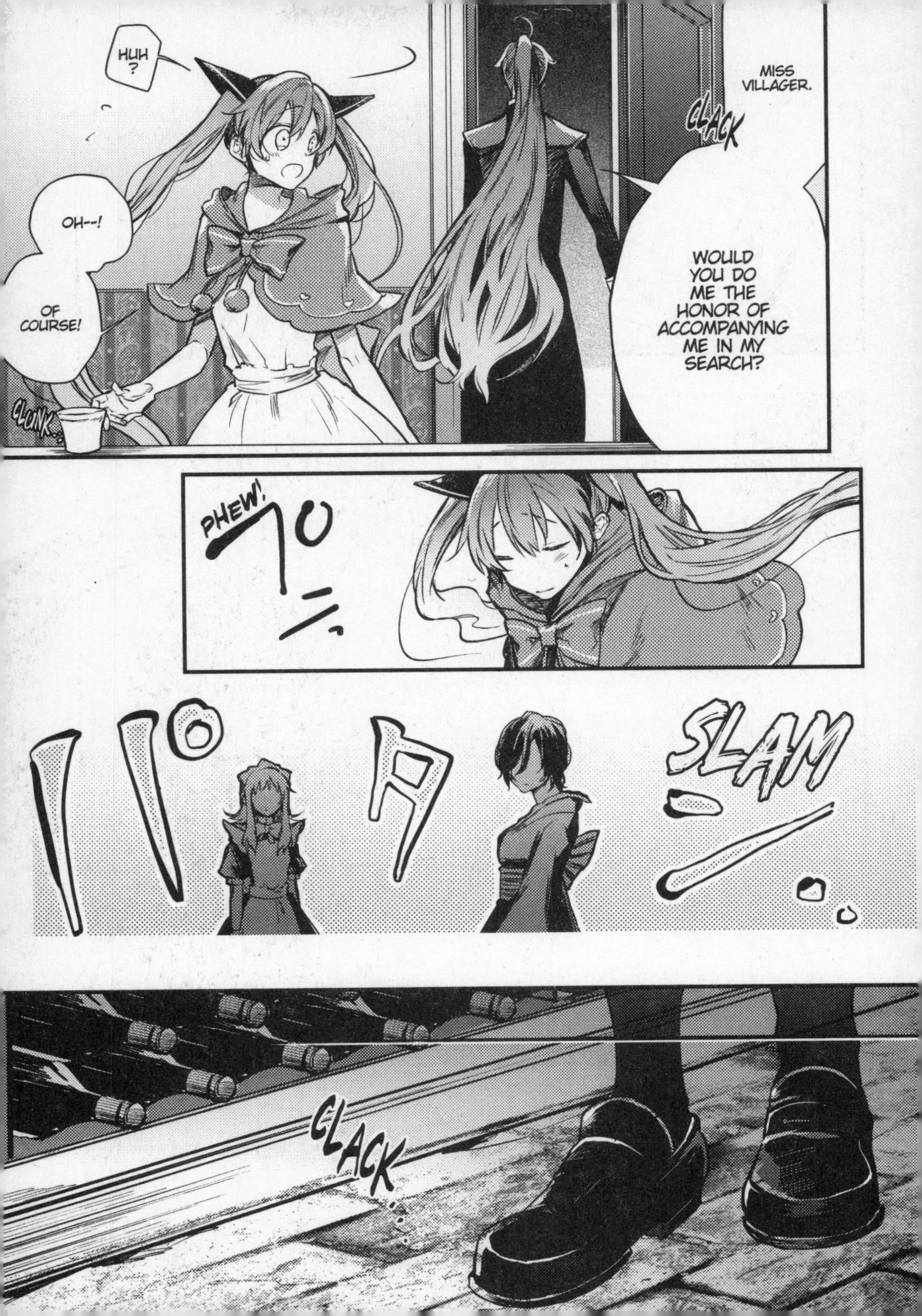
MISS VILLAGER.
CLACK
WOULD YOU DO ME THE HONOR OF ACCOMPANYING ME IN MY SEARCH?
HUH?
OH--!
OF COURSE!
CLONK...
PHEW!
SLAM
CLACK

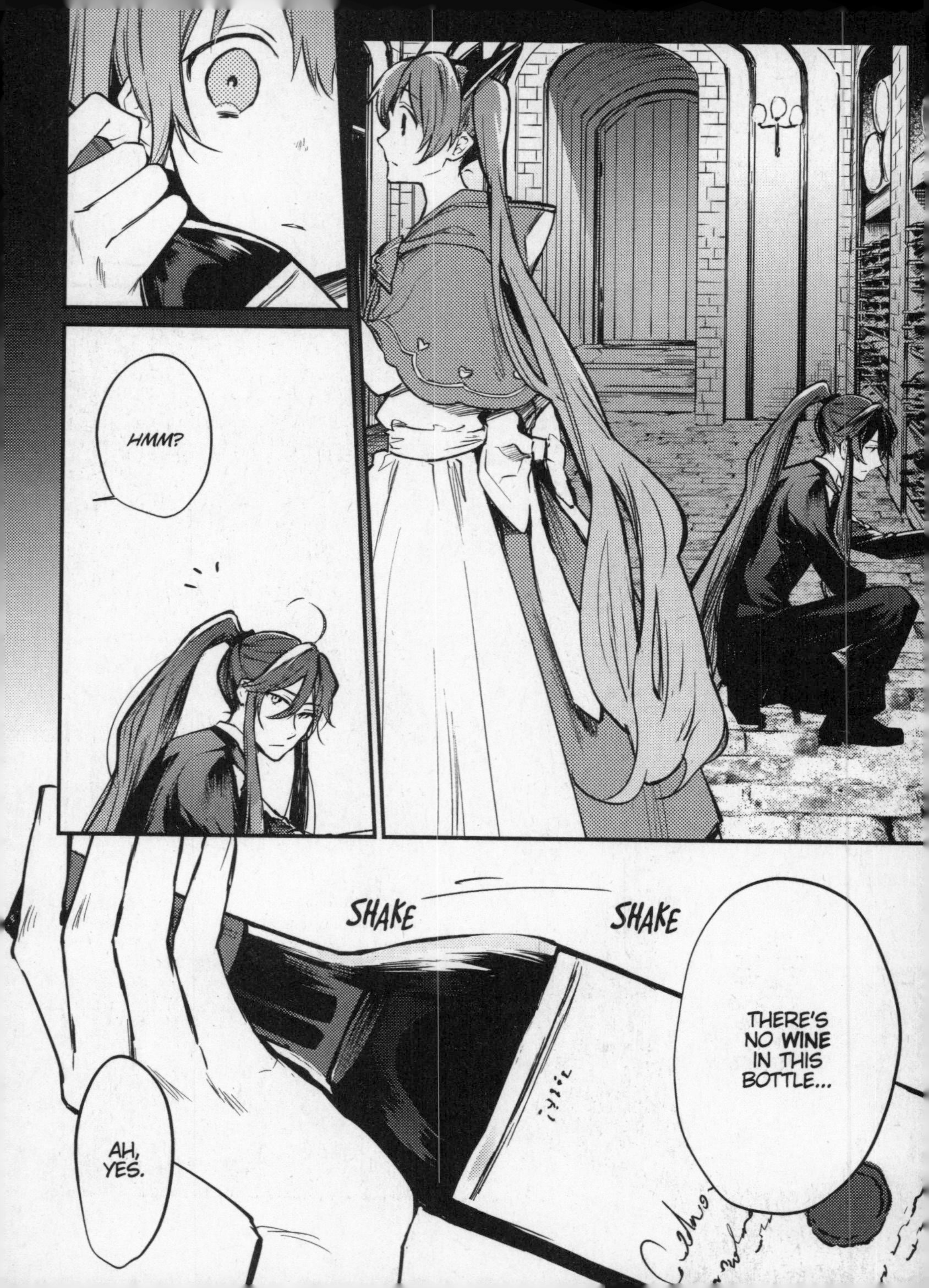
HMM?
SHAKE
SHAKE
THERE'S NO WINE IN THIS BOTTLE...
AH, YES.

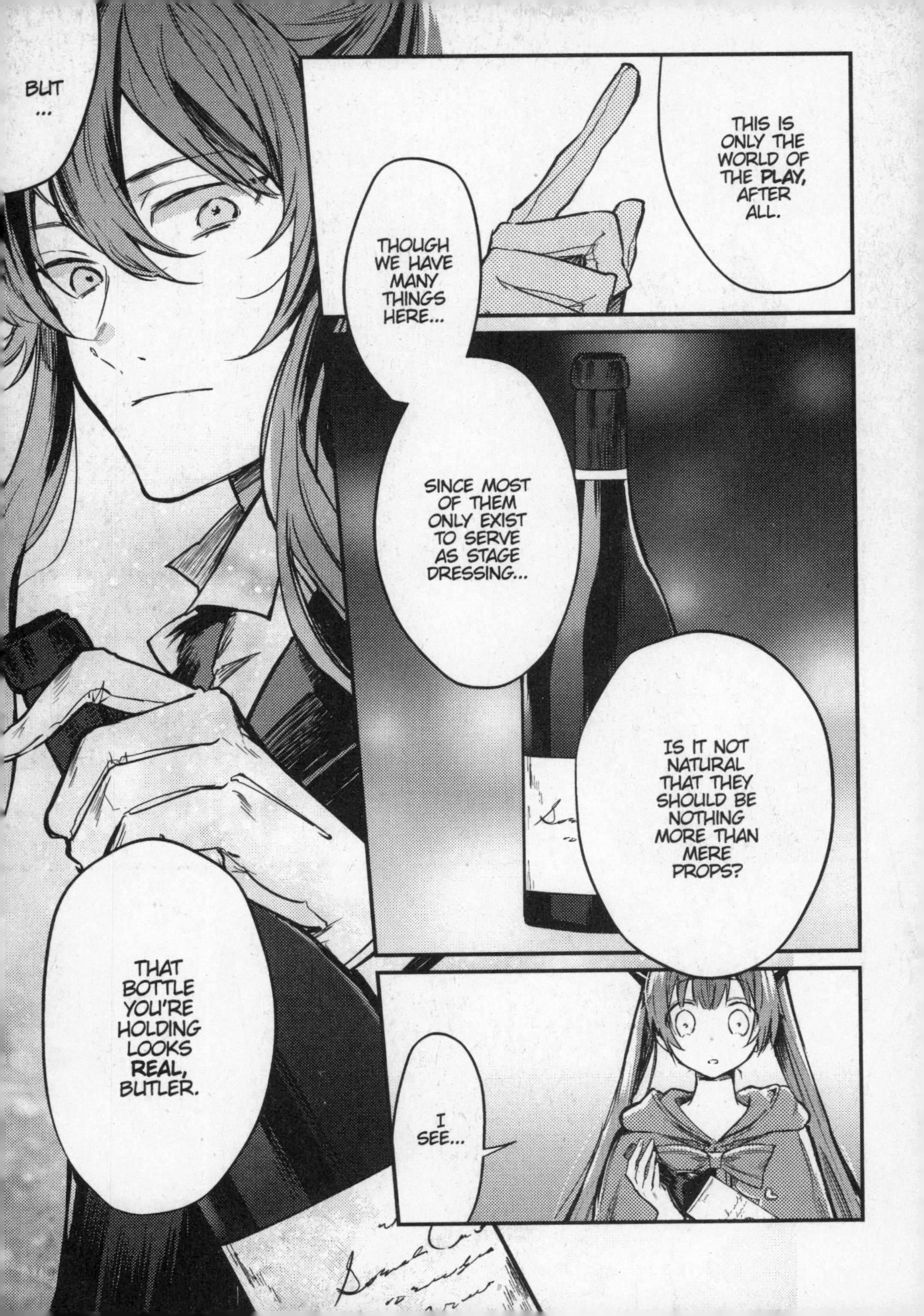
THIS IS ONLY THE WORLD OF THE PLAY, AFTER ALL.
THOUGH WE HAVE MANY THINGS HERE...
SINCE MOST OF THEM ONLY EXIST TO SERVE AS STAGE DRESSING...
IS IT NOT NATURAL THAT THEY SHOULD BE NOTHING MORE THAN MERE PROPS?
I SEE...
BUT ...
THAT BOTTLE YOU'RE HOLDING LOOKS REAL, BUTLER.

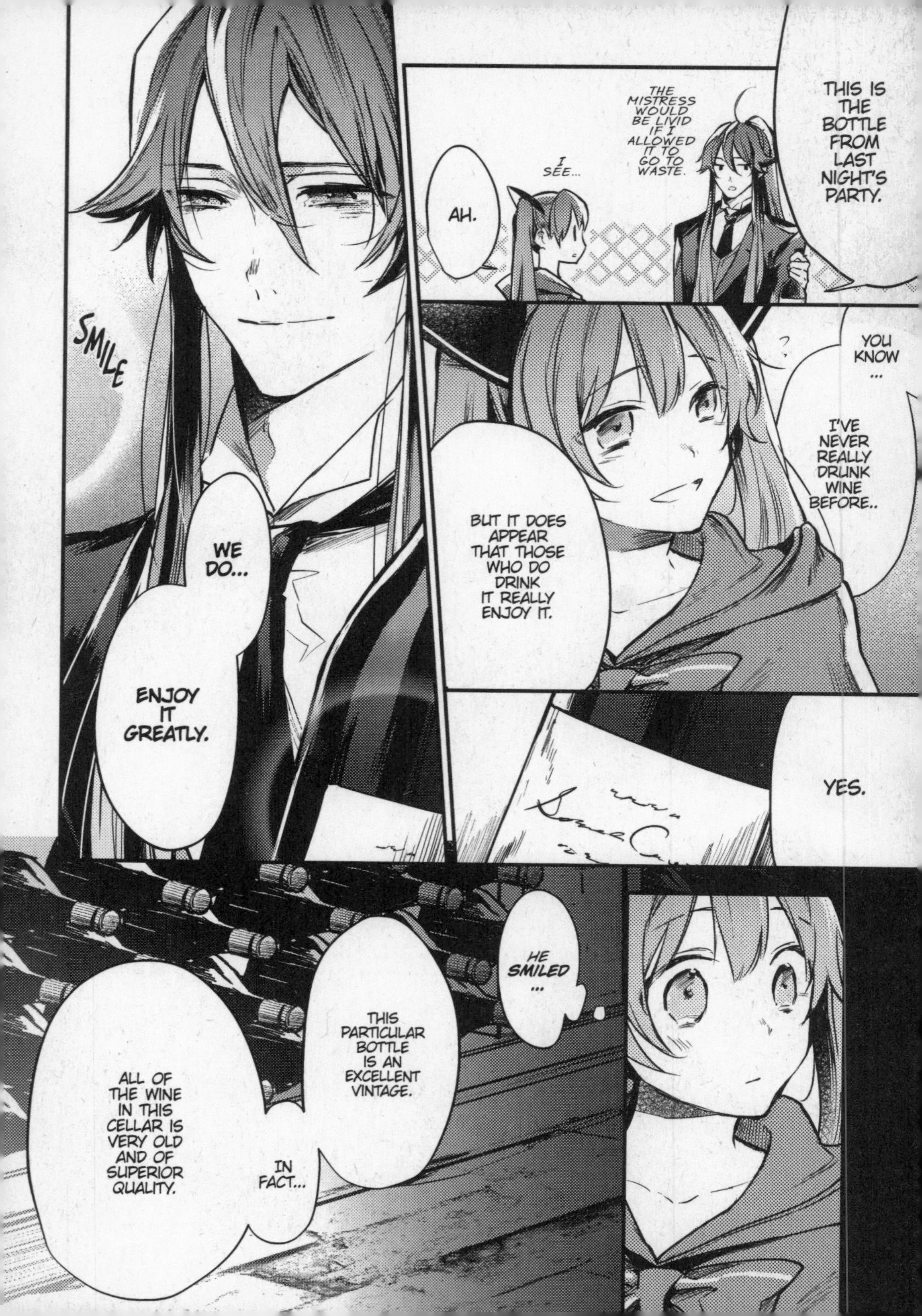
THIS IS THE BOTTLE FROM LAST NIGHT'S PARTY.
THE MISTRESS WOULD BE LIVID IF I ALLOWED IT TO GO TO WASTE.
I SEE...
AH.
YOU KNOW... I'VE NEVER REALLY DRUNK WINE BEFORE..
BUT IT DOES APPEAR THAT THOSE WHO DO DRINK IT REALLY ENJOY IT.
YES.
SMILE
WE DO...
ENJOY IT GREATLY.
HE SMILED...
THIS PARTICULAR BOTTLE IS AN EXCELLENT VINTAGE.
IN FACT...
ALL OF THE WINE IN THIS CELLAR IS VERY OLD AND OF SUPERIOR QUALITY.

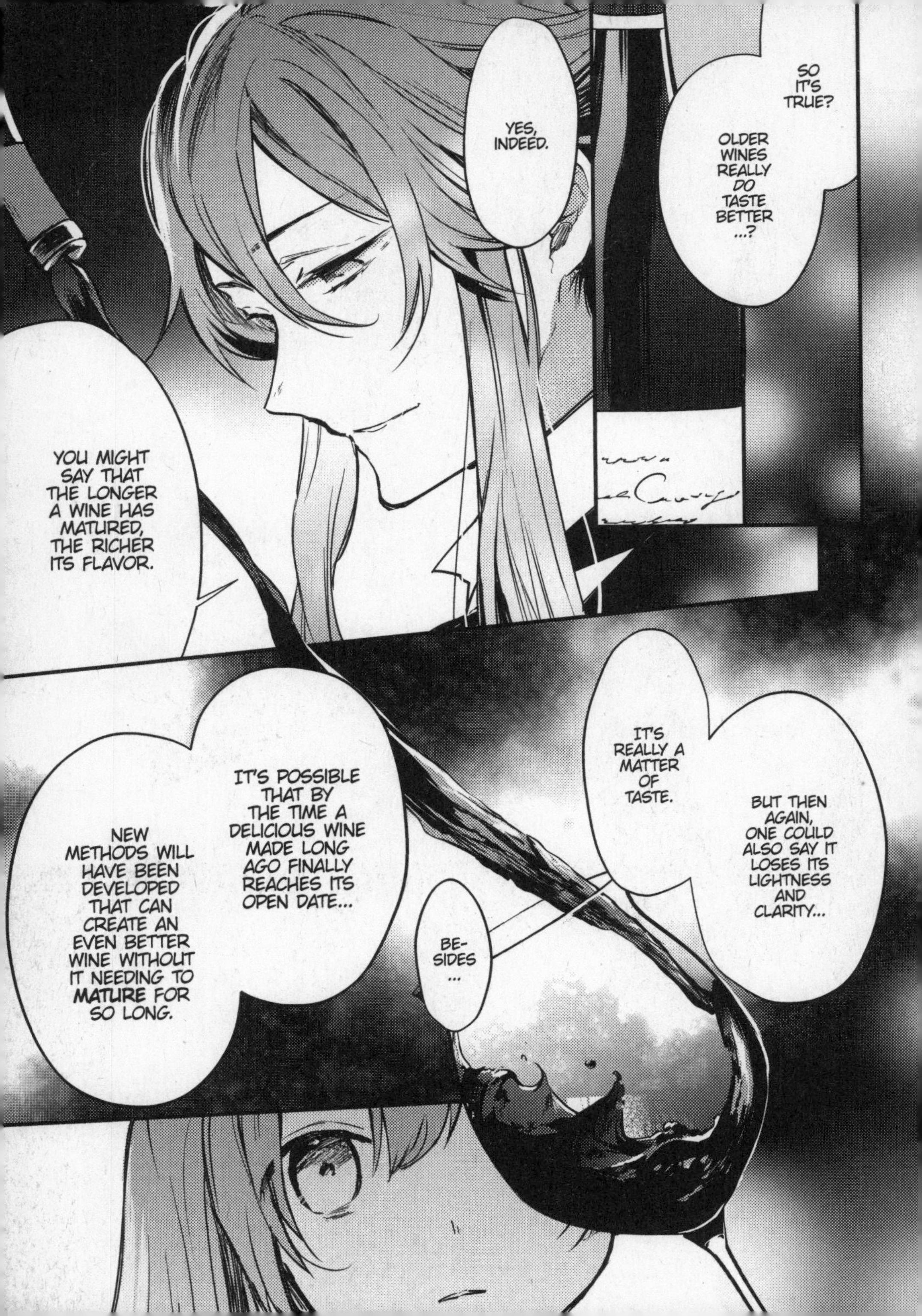
SO IT'S TRUE?
OLDER WINES REALLY DO TASTE BETTER ...?
YES, INDEED.
YOU MIGHT SAY THAT THE LONGER A WINE HAS MATURED, THE RICHER ITS FLAVOR.
BUT THEN AGAIN, ONE COULD ALSO SAY IT LOSES ITS LIGHTNESS AND CLARITY...
IT'S REALLY A MATTER OF TASTE.
BE-SIDES ...
IT'S POSSIBLE THAT BY THE TIME A DELICIOUS WINE MADE LONG AGO FINALLY REACHES ITS OPEN DATE...
NEW METHODS WILL HAVE BEEN DEVELOPED THAT CAN CREATE AN EVEN BETTER WINE WITHOUT IT NEEDING TO MATURE FOR SO LONG.

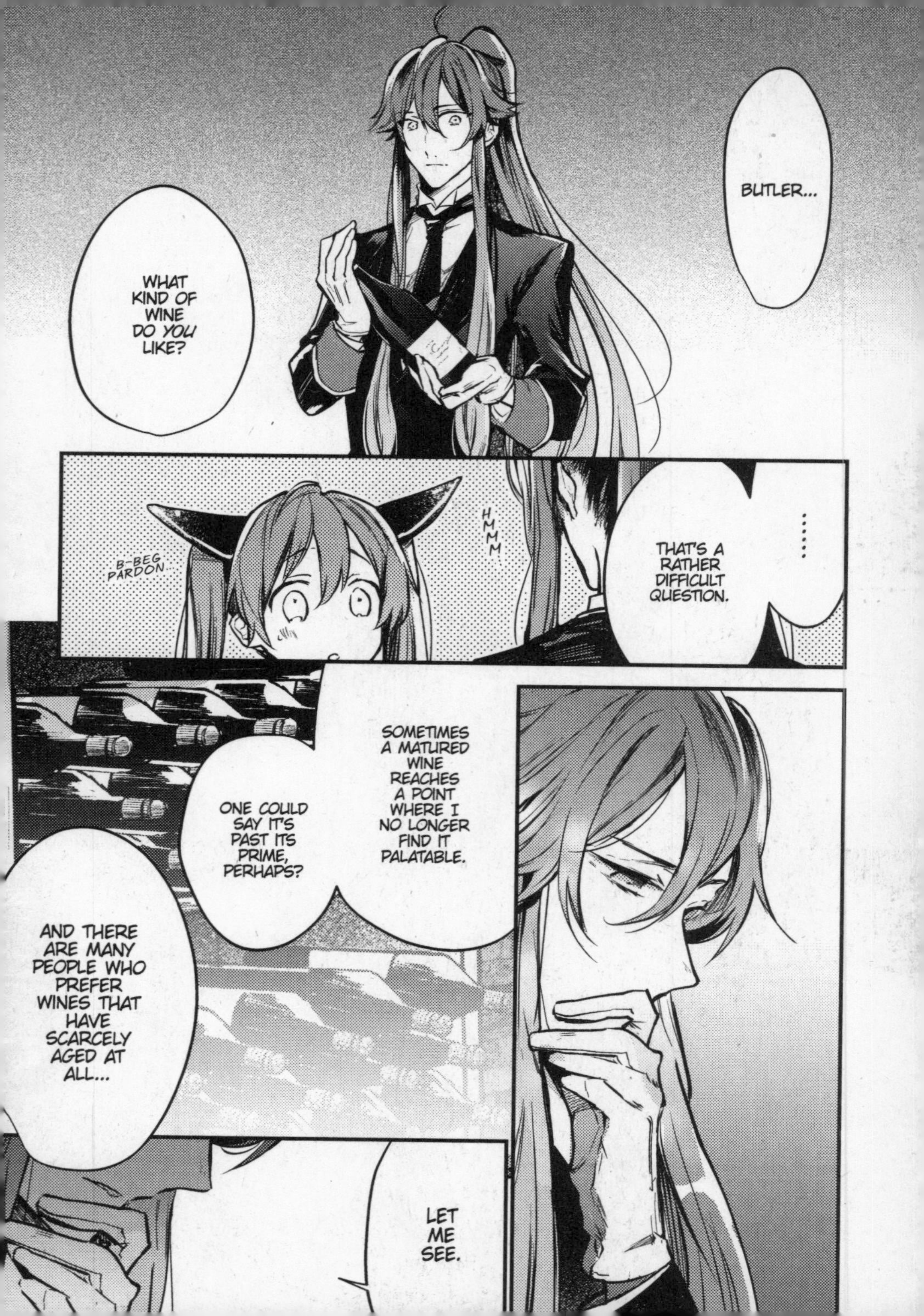
BUTLER...
WHAT KIND OF WINE DO YOU LIKE?
...... THAT'S A RATHER DIFFICULT QUESTION.
HMMM
B-BEG PARDON...
SOMETIMES A MATURED WINE REACHES A POINT WHERE I NO LONGER FIND IT PALATABLE.
ONE COULD SAY IT'S PAST ITS PRIME, PERHAPS?
AND THERE ARE MANY PEOPLE WHO PREFER WINES THAT HAVE SCARCELY AGED AT ALL...
LET ME SEE.

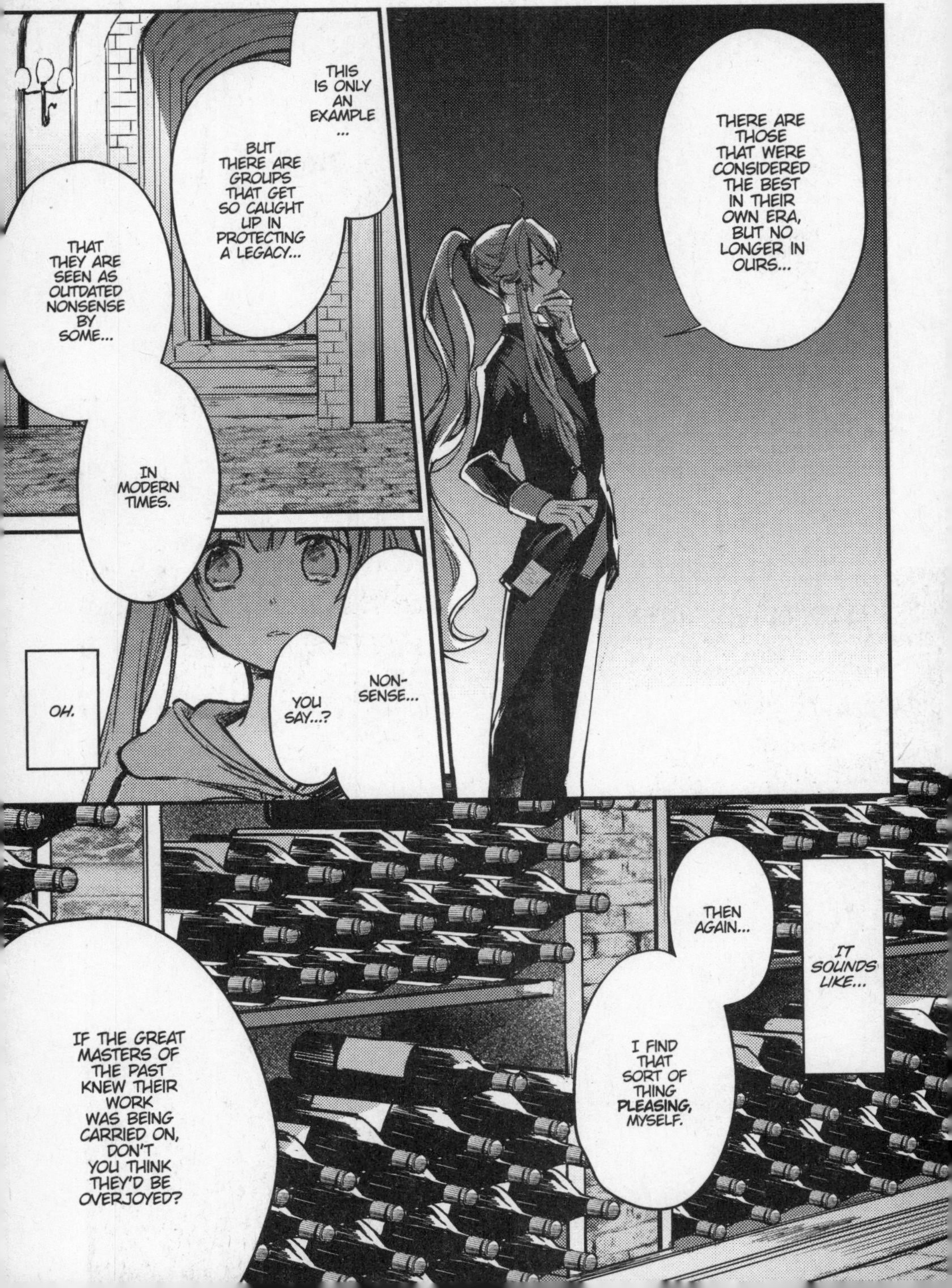
THERE ARE THOSE THAT WERE CONSIDERED THE BEST IN THEIR OWN ERA, BUT NO LONGER IN OURS...
THIS IS ONLY AN EXAMPLE ...
BUT THERE ARE GROUPS THAT GET SO CAUGHT UP IN PROTECTING A LEGACY...
THAT THEY ARE SEEN AS OUTDATED NONSENSE BY SOME...
IN MODERN TIMES.
NON-SENSE...
YOU SAY...?
OH.
IT SOUNDS LIKE...
THEN AGAIN...
I FIND THAT SORT OF THING **PLEASING,** MYSELF.
IF THE GREAT MASTERS OF THE PAST KNEW THEIR WORK WAS BEING CARRIED ON, DON'T YOU THINK THEY'D BE OVERJOYED?

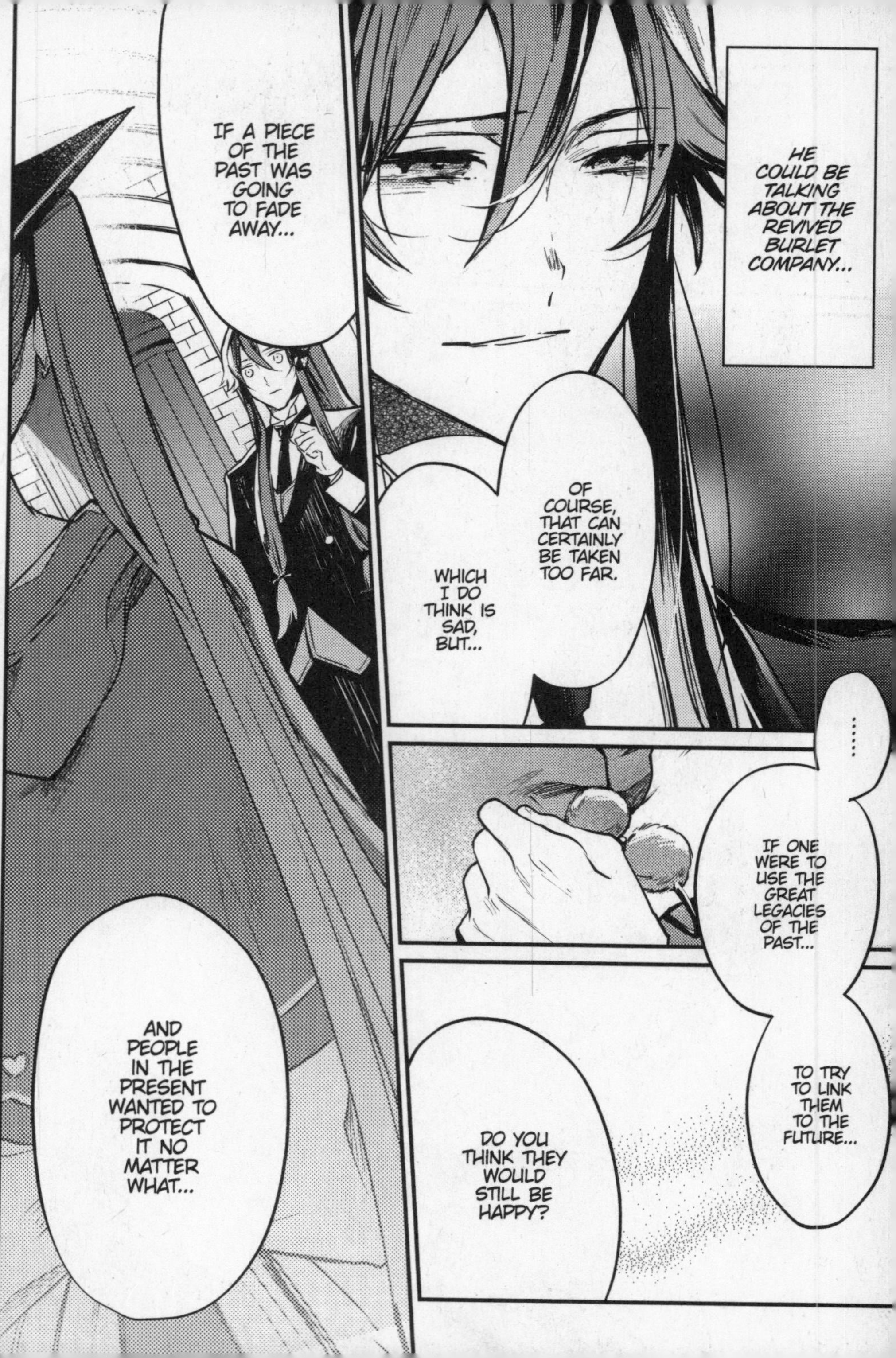
HE COULD BE TALKING ABOUT THE REVIVED BURLET COMPANY...
OF COURSE, THAT CAN CERTAINLY BE TAKEN TOO FAR.
WHICH I DO THINK IS SAD, BUT...
......
IF ONE WERE TO USE THE GREAT LEGACIES OF THE PAST...
TO TRY TO LINK THEM TO THE FUTURE...
DO YOU THINK THEY WOULD STILL BE HAPPY?
IF A PIECE OF THE PAST WAS GOING TO FADE AWAY...
AND PEOPLE IN THE PRESENT WANTED TO PROTECT IT NO MATTER WHAT...

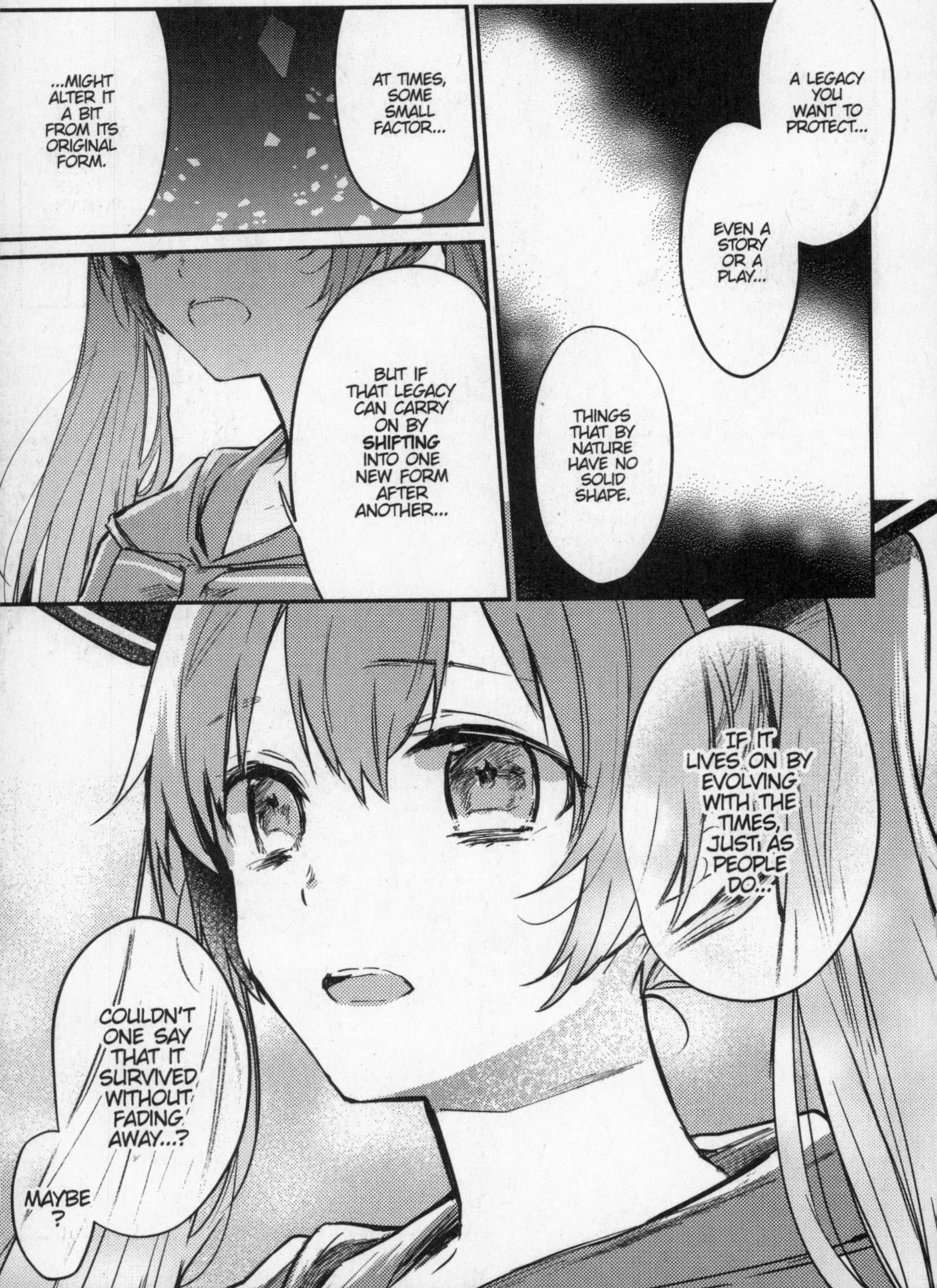
A LEGACY YOU WANT TO PROTECT...
EVEN A STORY OR A PLAY...
THINGS THAT BY NATURE HAVE NO SOLID SHAPE.
AT TIMES, SOME SMALL FACTOR...
...MIGHT ALTER IT A BIT FROM ITS ORIGINAL FORM.
BUT IF THAT LEGACY CAN CARRY ON BY **SHIFTING** INTO ONE NEW FORM AFTER ANOTHER...
IF IT LIVES ON BY EVOLVING WITH THE TIMES, JUST AS PEOPLE DO...
COULDN'T ONE SAY THAT IT SURVIVED WITHOUT FADING AWAY...?
MAYBE?

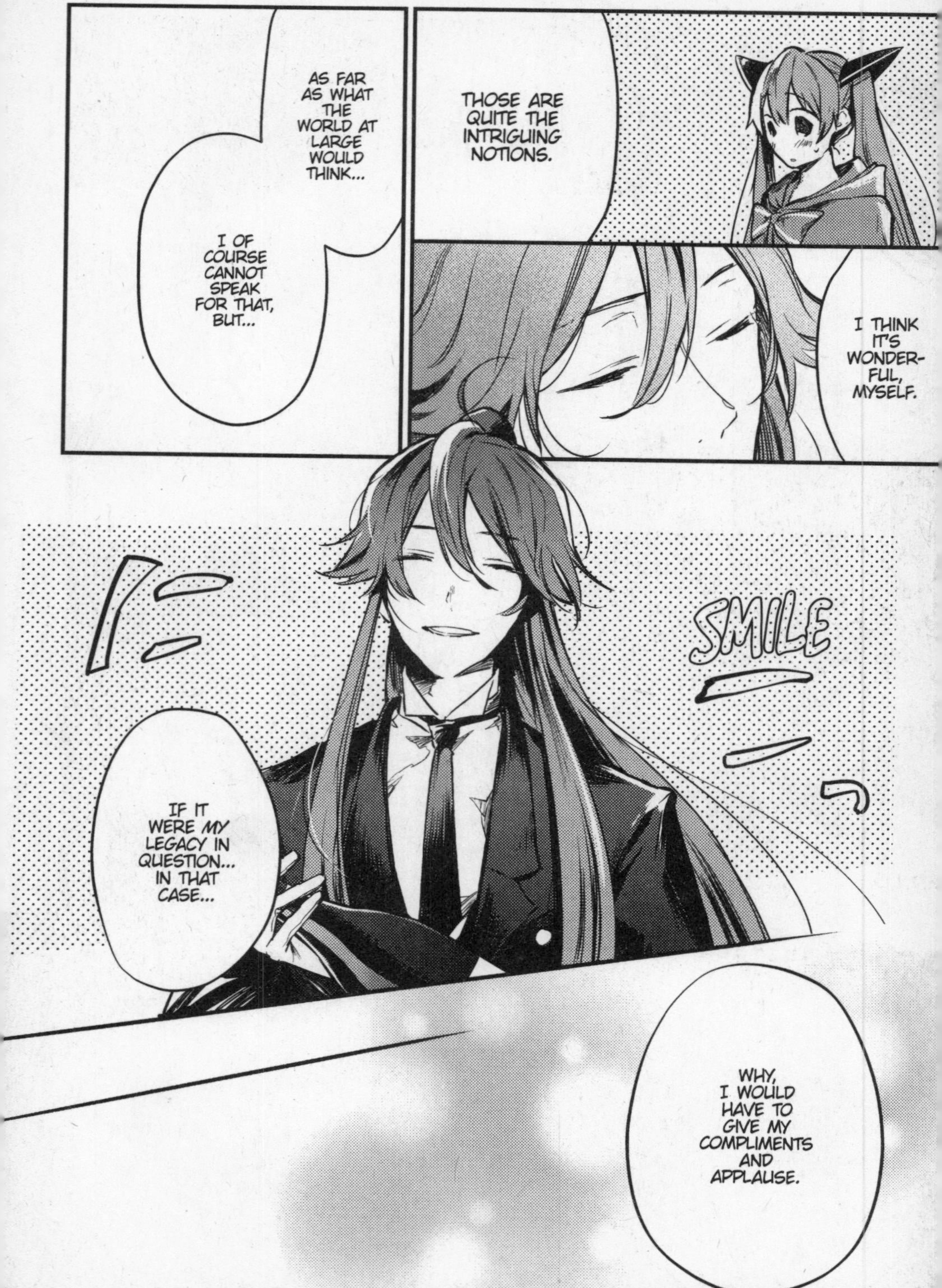
THOSE ARE QUITE THE INTRIGUING NOTIONS.
I THINK IT'S WONDER-FUL, MYSELF.
AS FAR AS WHAT THE WORLD AT LARGE WOULD THINK...
I OF COURSE CANNOT SPEAK FOR THAT, BUT...
SMILE
IF IT WERE *MY* LEGACY IN QUESTION... IN THAT CASE...
WHY, I WOULD HAVE TO GIVE MY COMPLIMENTS AND APPLAUSE.

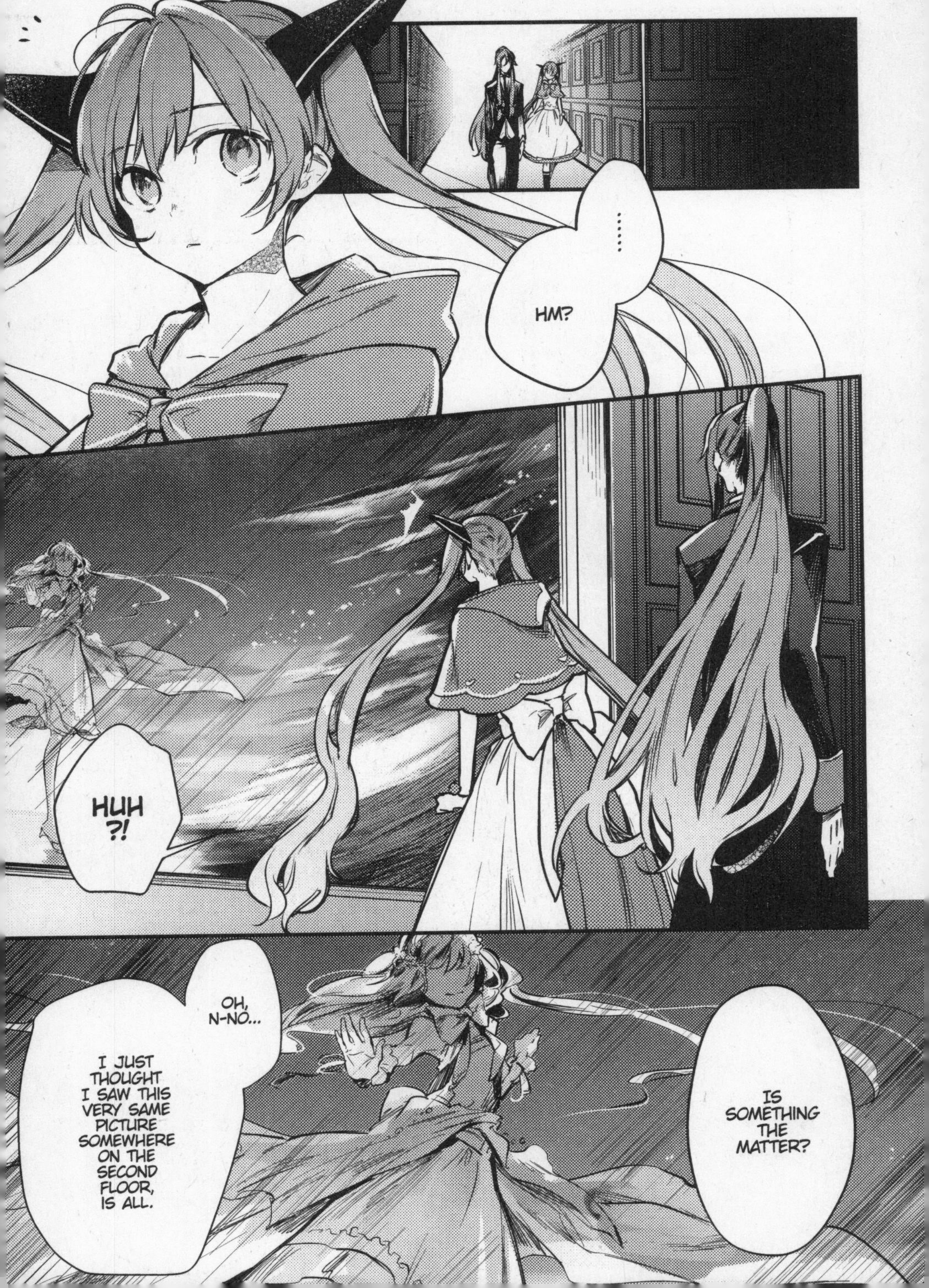
......
HM?
HUH ?!
IS SOMETHING THE MATTER?
OH, N-NO...
I JUST THOUGHT I SAW THIS VERY SAME PICTURE SOMEWHERE ON THE SECOND FLOOR, IS ALL.

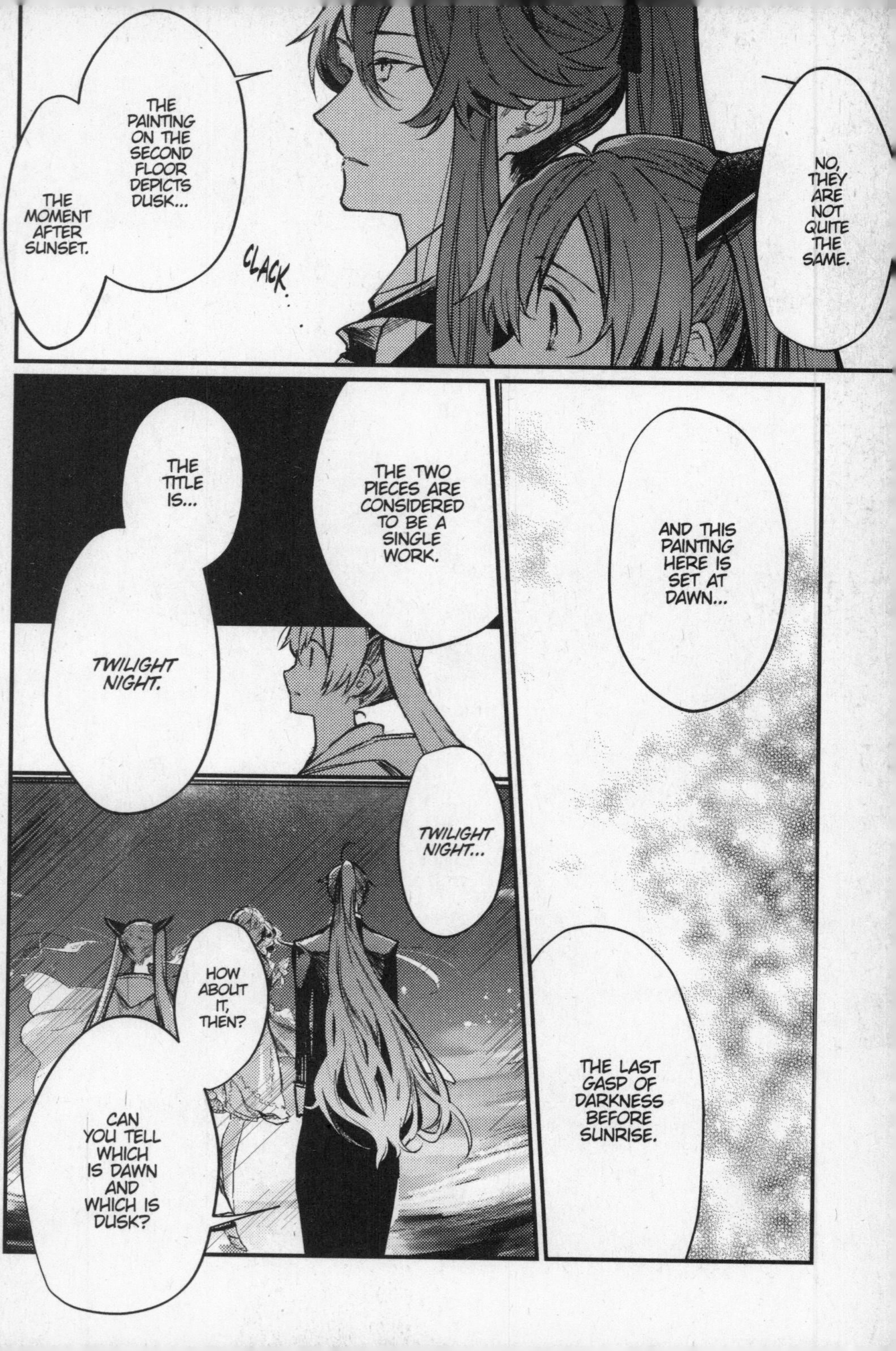
NO, THEY ARE NOT QUITE THE SAME.
THE PAINTING ON THE SECOND FLOOR DEPICTS DUSK...
CLACK
THE MOMENT AFTER SUNSET.
AND THIS PAINTING HERE IS SET AT DAWN...
THE LAST GASP OF DARKNESS BEFORE SUNRISE.
THE TWO PIECES ARE CONSIDERED TO BE A SINGLE WORK.
THE TITLE IS...
TWILIGHT NIGHT.
TWILIGHT NIGHT...
HOW ABOUT IT, THEN?
CAN YOU TELL WHICH IS DAWN AND WHICH IS DUSK?

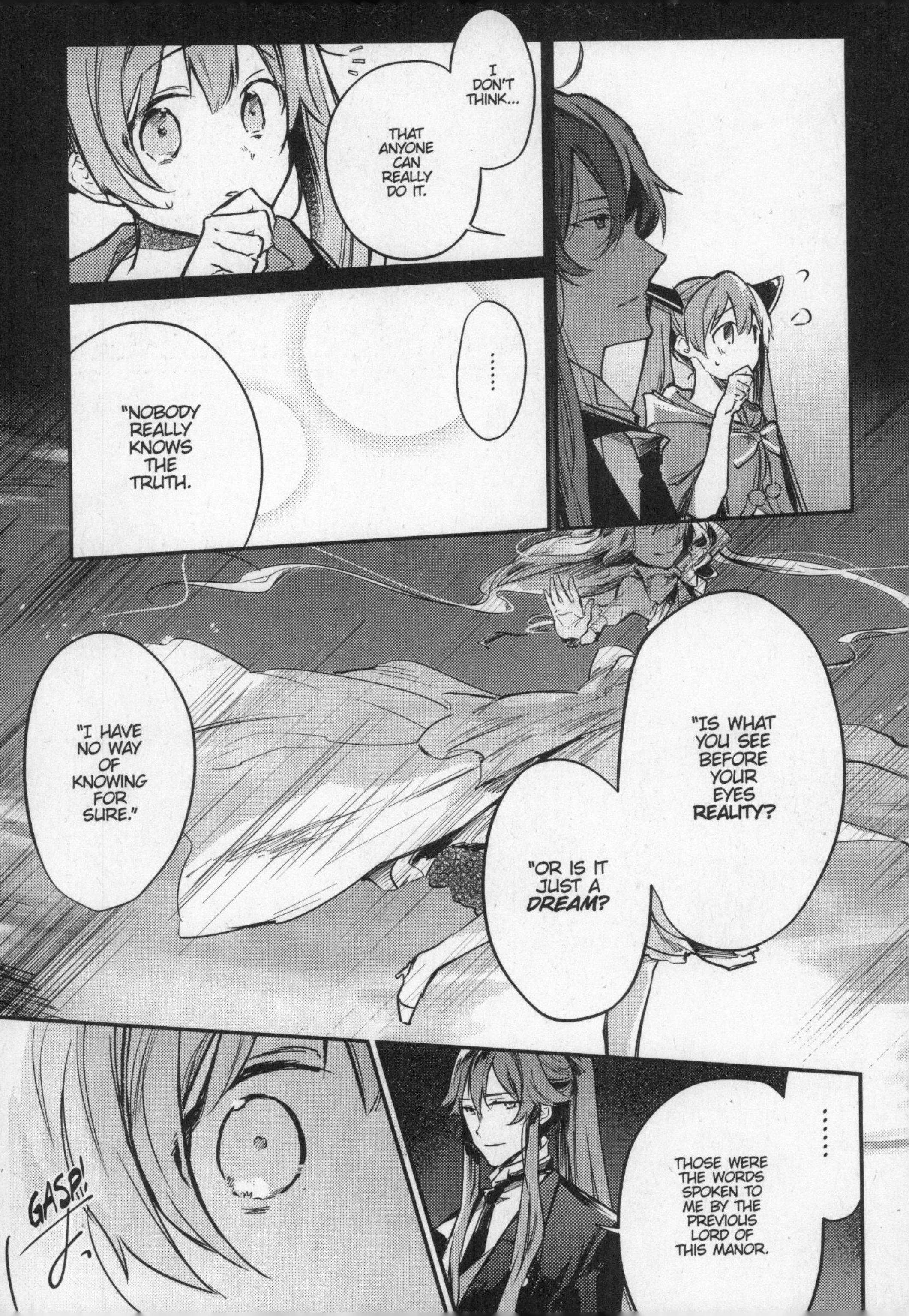
I DON'T THINK...
THAT ANYONE CAN REALLY DO IT.
......
"NOBODY REALLY KNOWS THE TRUTH.
"IS WHAT YOU SEE BEFORE YOUR EYES **REALITY?**
"OR IS IT JUST A ***DREAM?***
"I HAVE NO WAY OF KNOWING FOR SURE."
......
THOSE WERE THE WORDS SPOKEN TO ME BY THE PREVIOUS LORD OF THIS MANOR.
GASP!

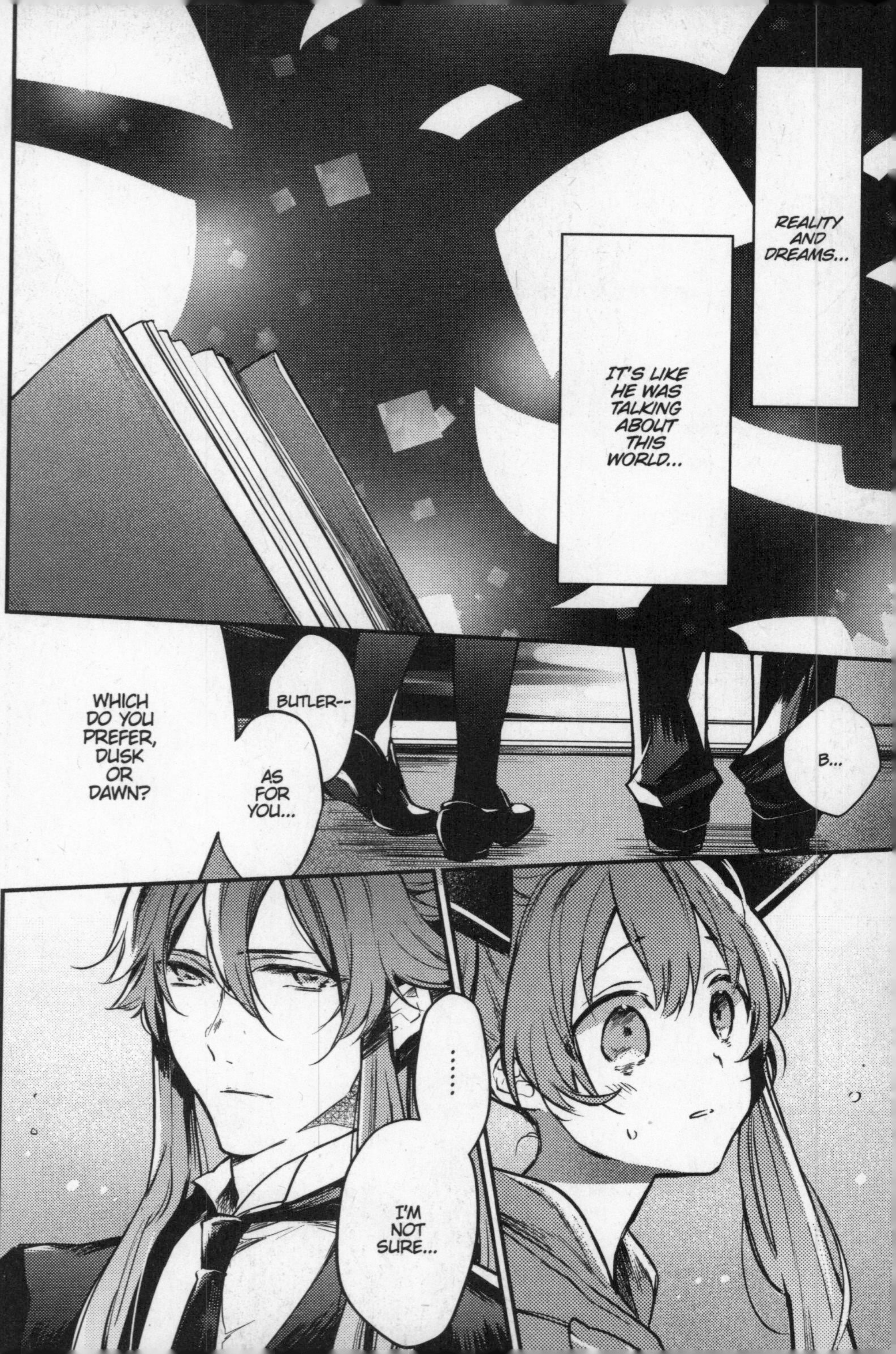
REALITY AND DREAMS...
IT'S LIKE HE WAS TALKING ABOUT THIS WORLD...
B...
BUTLER--
AS FOR YOU...
WHICH DO YOU PREFER, DUSK OR DAWN?
......
I'M NOT SURE...

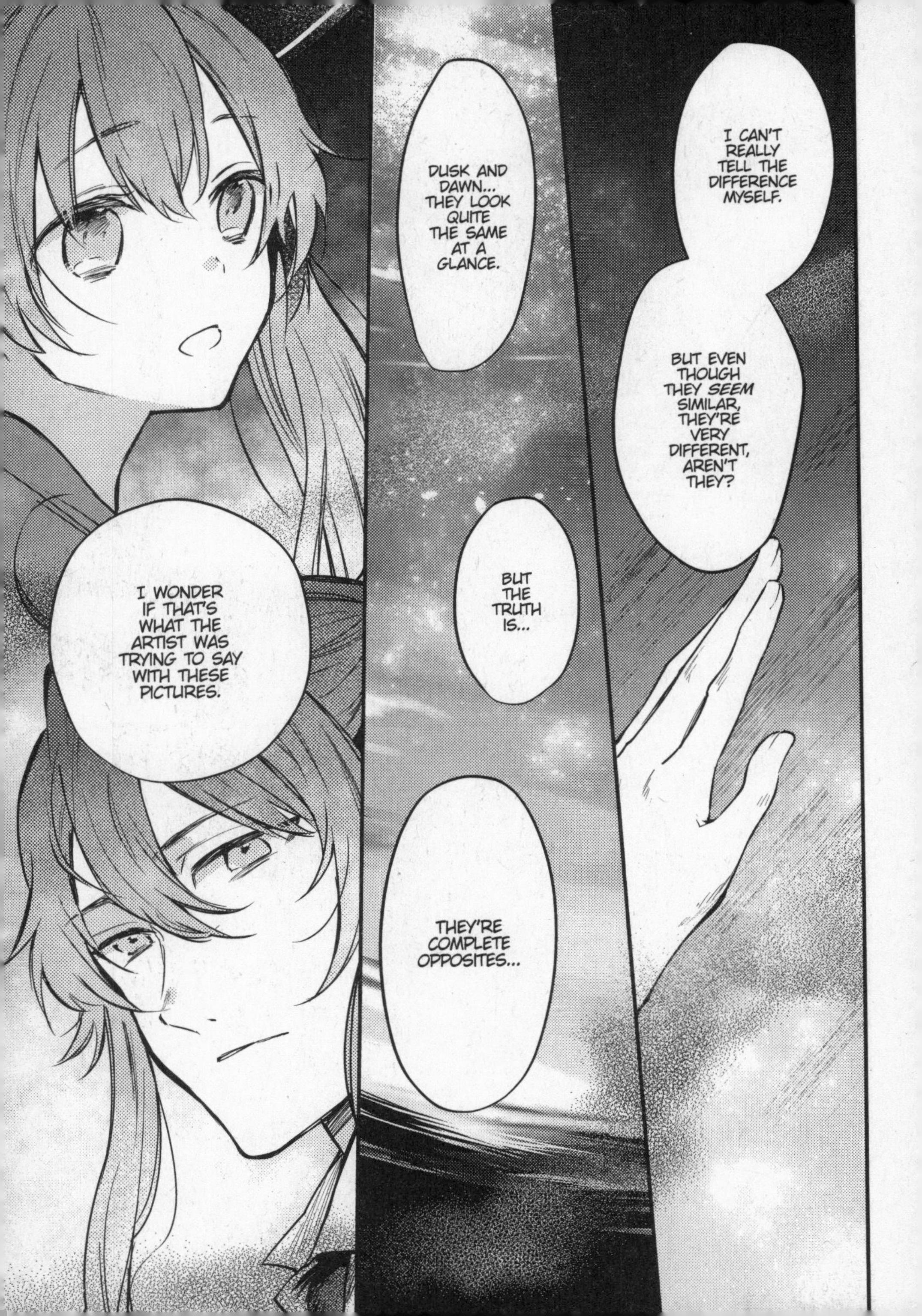
I CAN'T REALLY TELL THE DIFFERENCE MYSELF.
BUT EVEN THOUGH THEY *SEEM* SIMILAR, THEY'RE VERY DIFFERENT, AREN'T THEY?
DUSK AND DAWN... THEY LOOK QUITE THE SAME AT A GLANCE.
BUT THE TRUTH IS...
THEY'RE COMPLETE OPPOSITES...
I WONDER IF THAT'S WHAT THE ARTIST WAS TRYING TO SAY WITH THESE PICTURES.

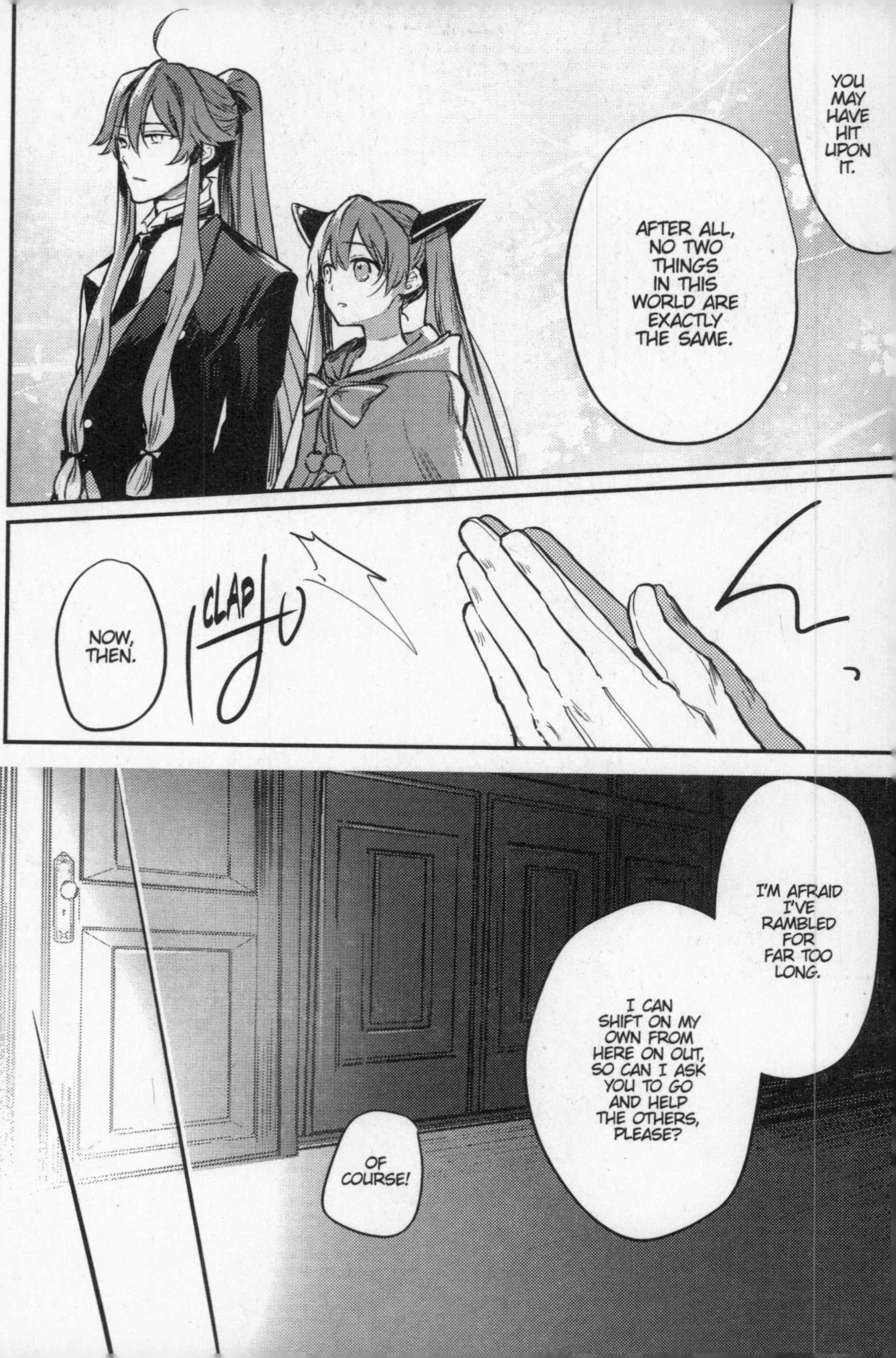
YOU MAY HAVE HIT UPON IT.
AFTER ALL, NO TWO THINGS IN THIS WORLD ARE EXACTLY THE SAME.
CLAP
NOW, THEN.
I'M AFRAID I'VE RAMBLED FOR FAR TOO LONG.
I CAN SHIFT ON MY OWN FROM HERE ON OUT, SO CAN I ASK YOU TO GO AND HELP THE OTHERS, PLEASE?
OF COURSE!

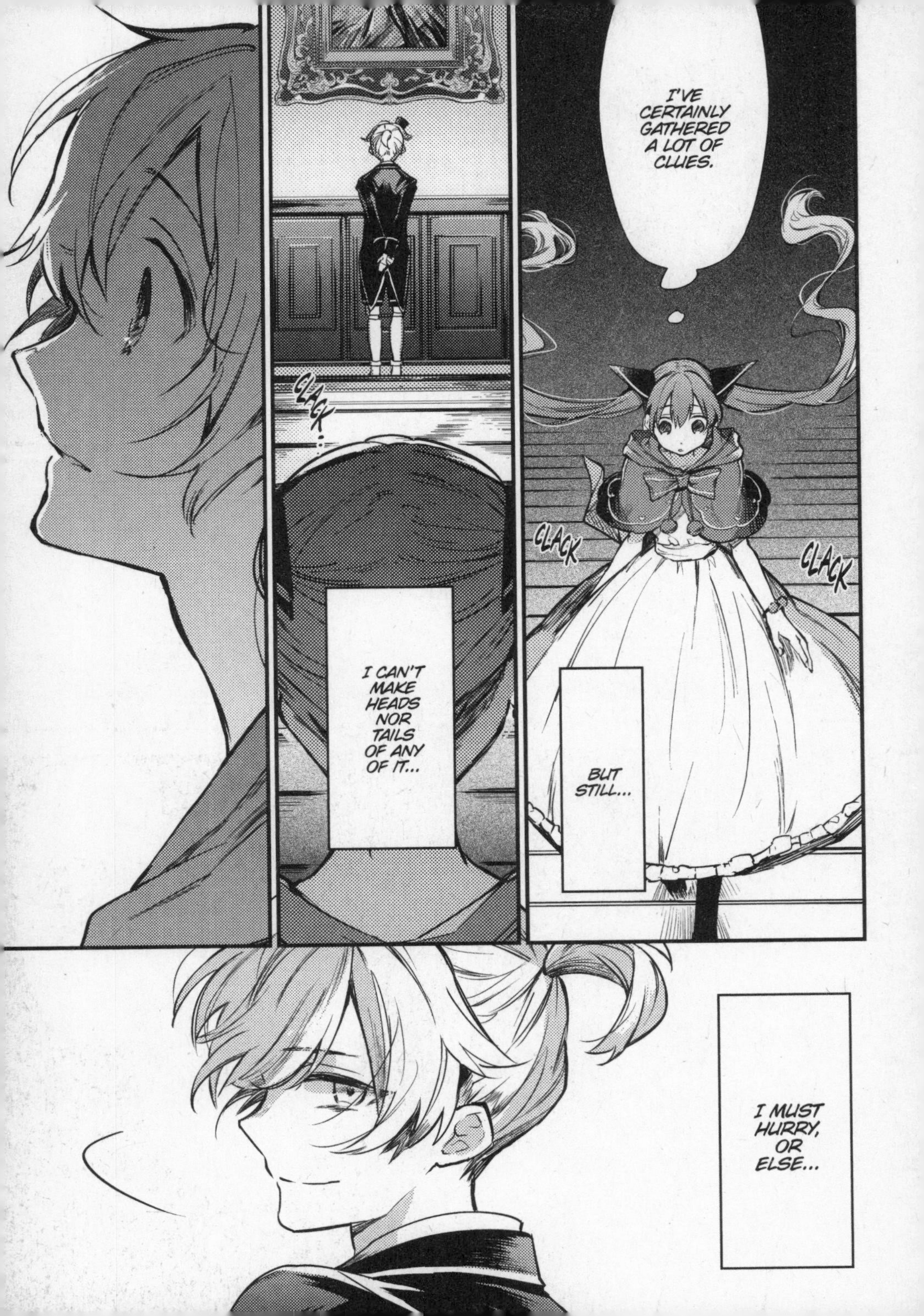
I'VE CERTAINLY GATHERED A LOT OF CLUES.
CLACK
CLACK
BUT STILL...
CLACK...
I CAN'T MAKE HEADS NOR TAILS OF ANY OF IT...
I MUST HURRY, OR ELSE...

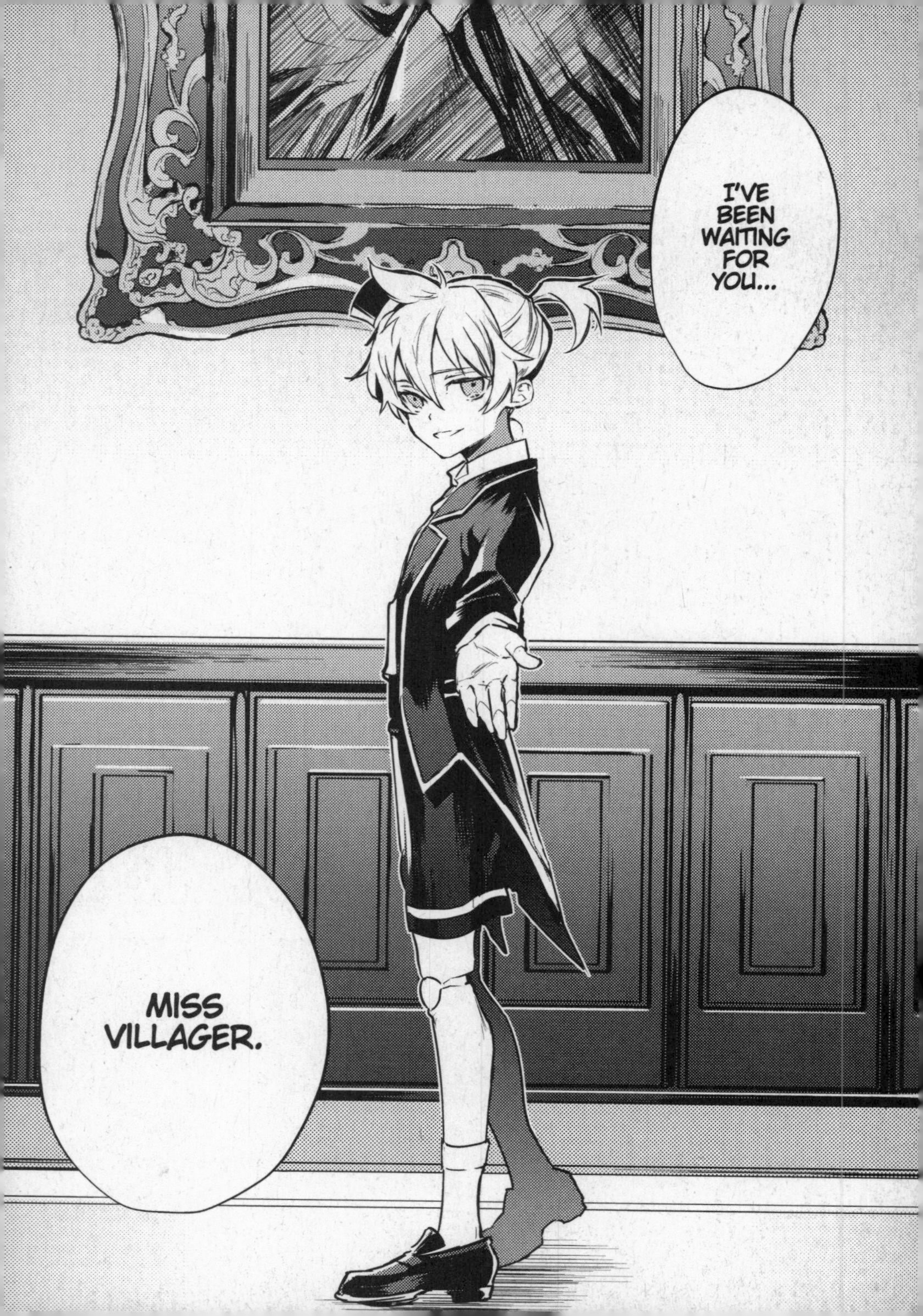
I'VE BEEN WAITING FOR YOU...
MISS VILLAGER.

Bad∞End∞Night

～インセイン・パーティー～

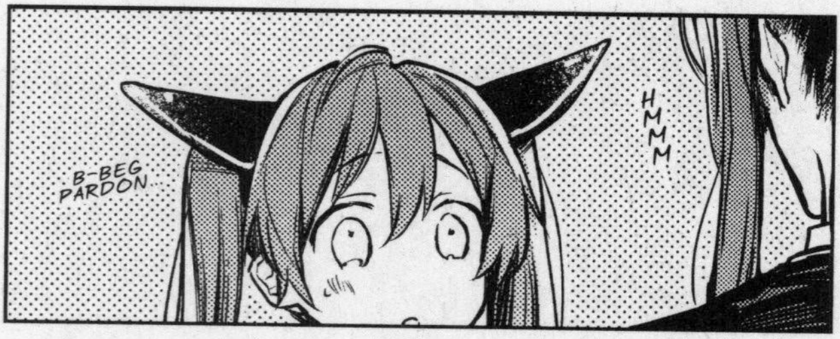
HMMM
B-BEG PARDON...

Act 7: The World's Secret

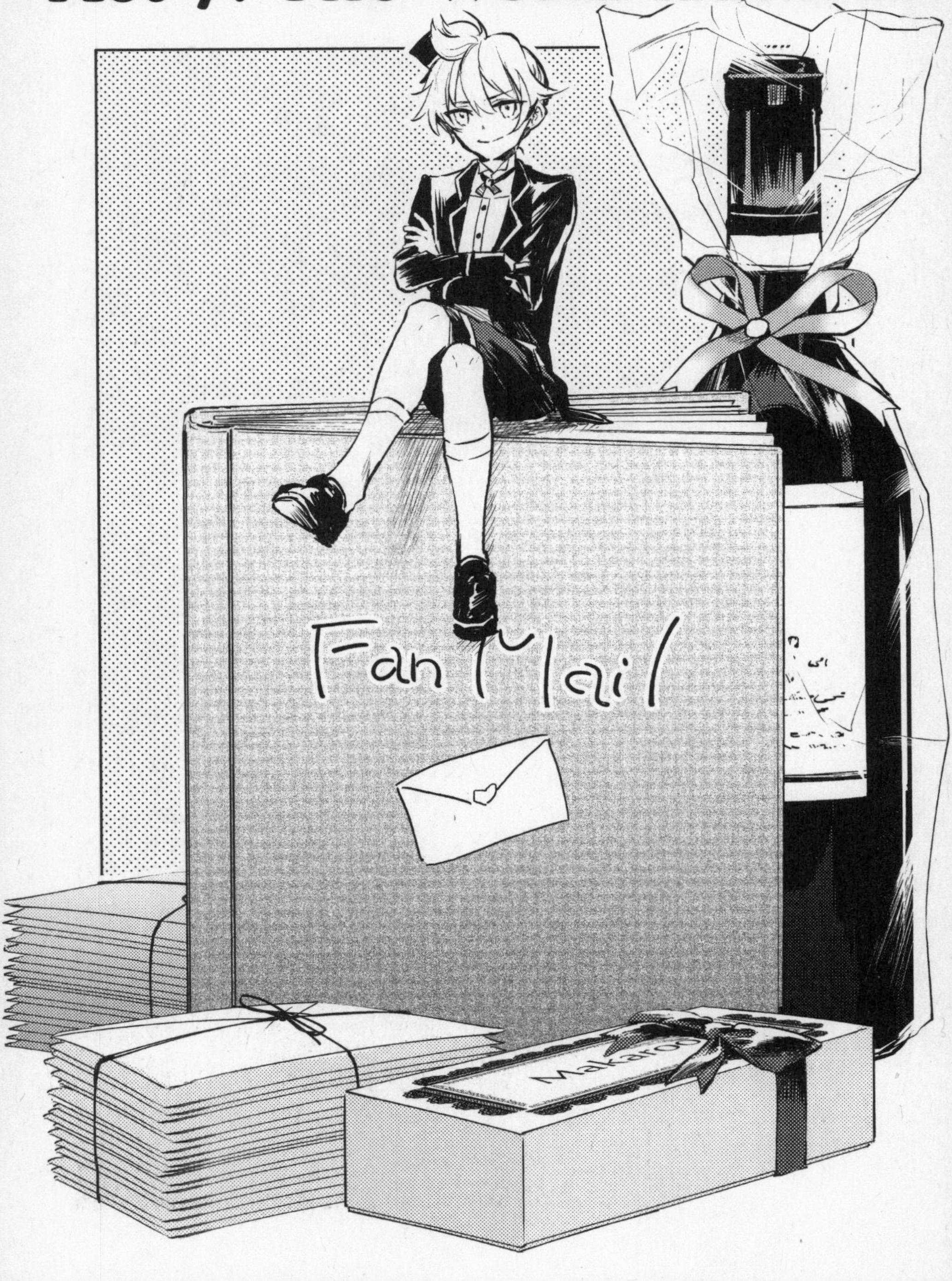
Fan Mail
Makaroo

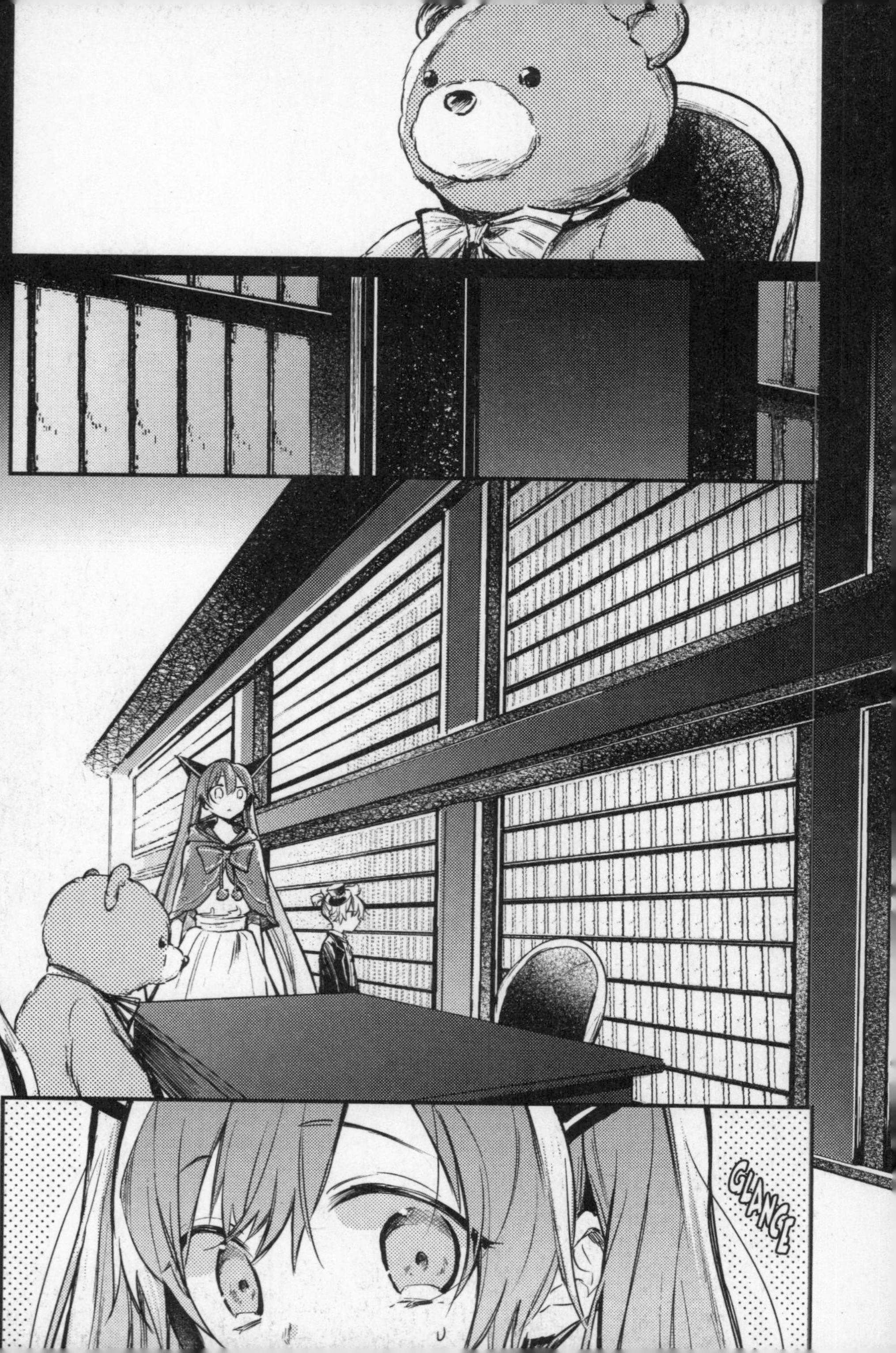
GLANCE

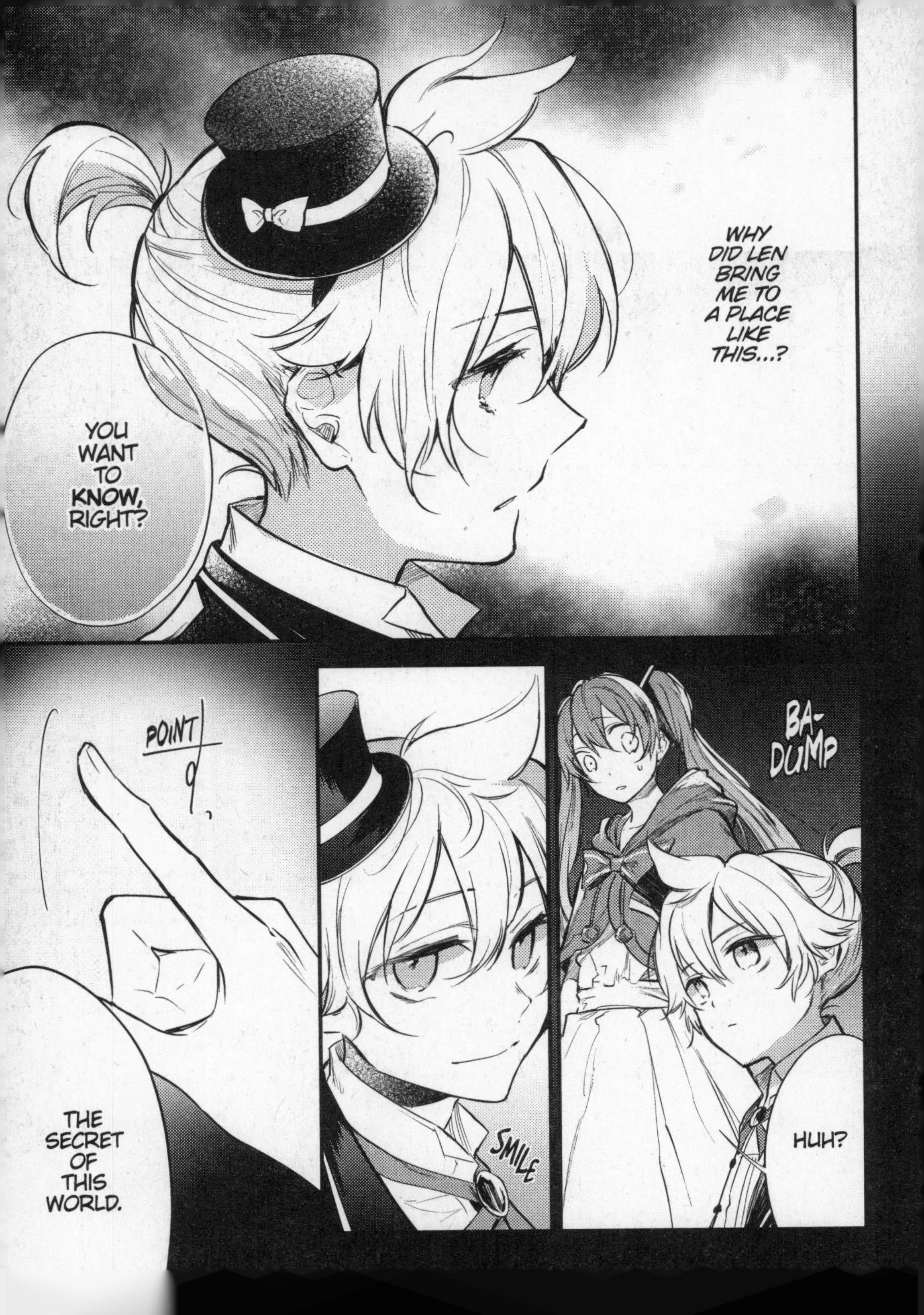
WHY DID LEN BRING ME TO A PLACE LIKE THIS...?
YOU WANT TO KNOW, RIGHT?
BA-DUMP
HUH?
SMILE
POINT
THE SECRET OF THIS WORLD.

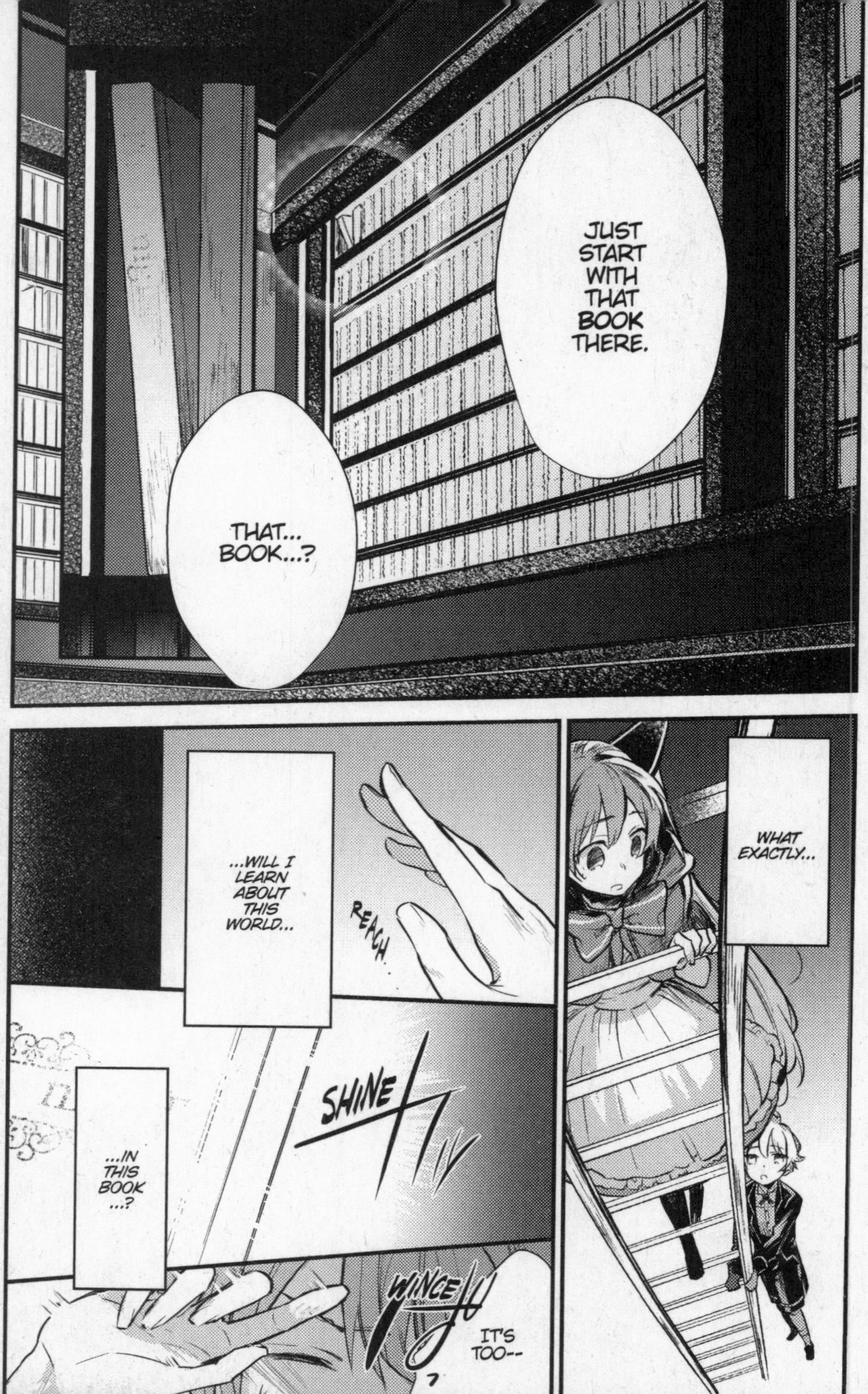
JUST START WITH THAT BOOK THERE.
THAT... BOOK...?
WHAT EXACTLY...
...WILL I LEARN ABOUT THIS WORLD...
REACH.
...IN THIS BOOK...?
SHINE
WINCE
IT'S TOO--

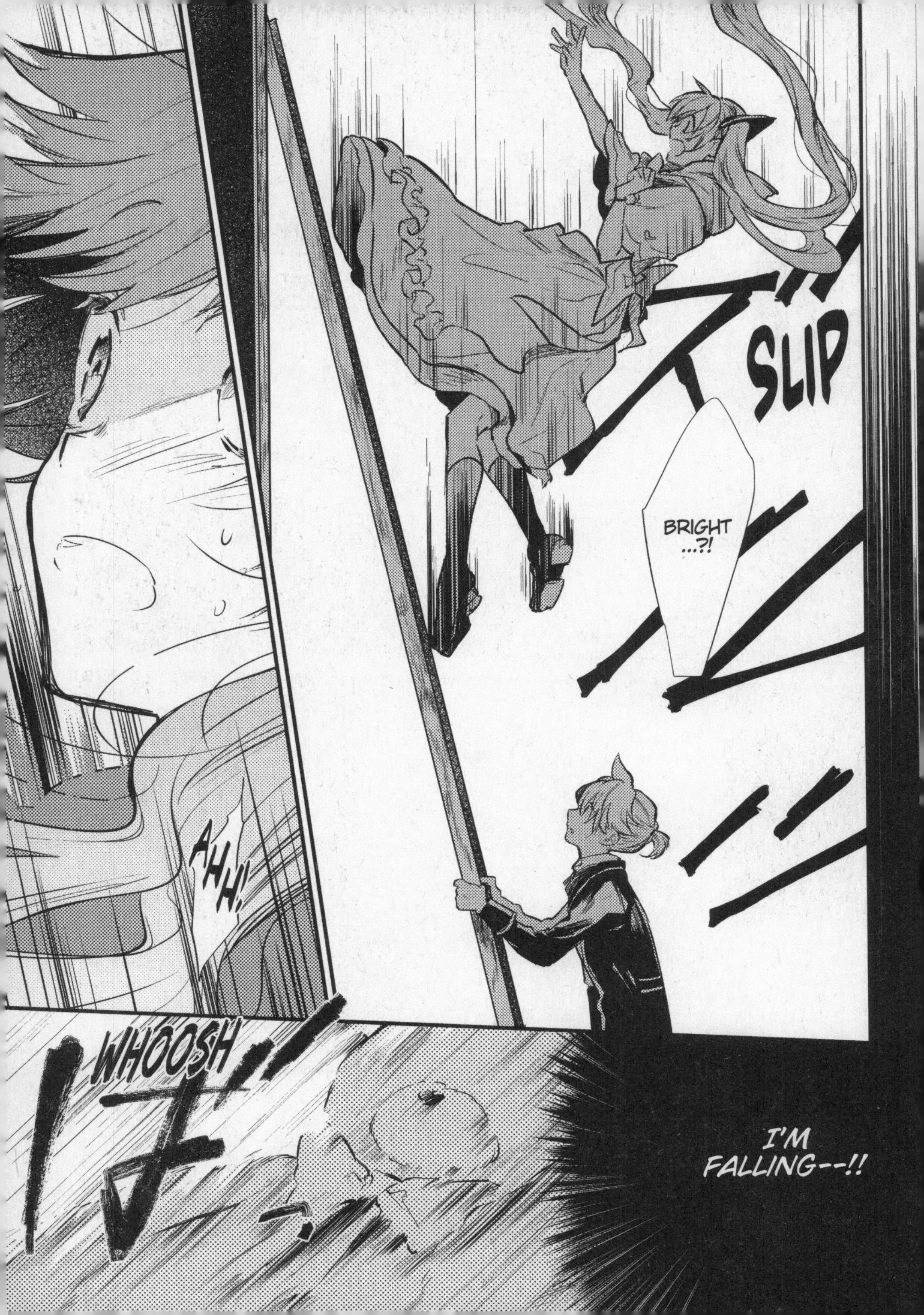
SLIP
BRIGHT ...?!
AHH!
WHOOSH
I'M FALLING--!!

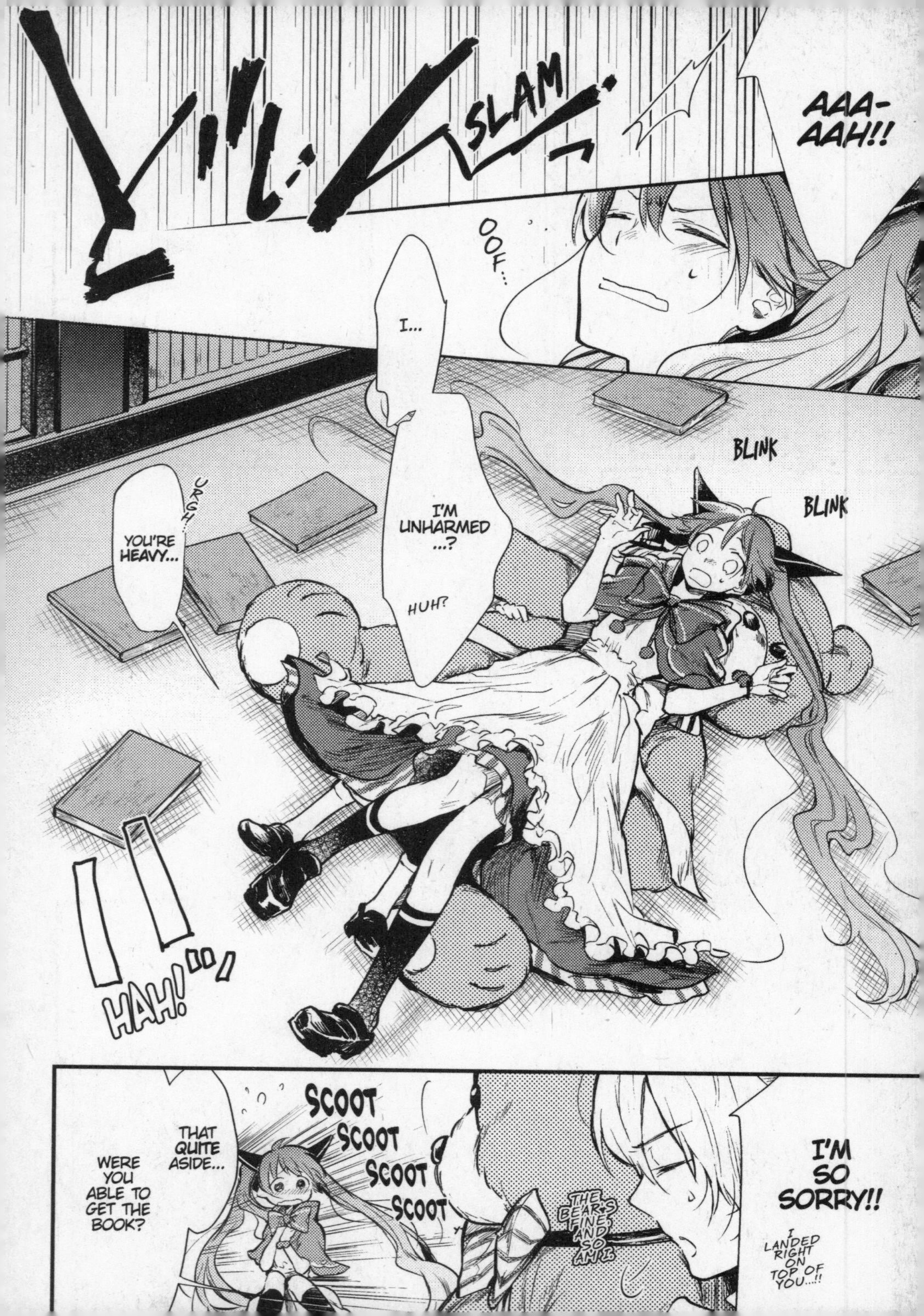
SLAM
AAA-AAH!!
OOF...
I...
I'M UNHARMED...?
HUH?
BLINK
BLINK
URGH...
YOU'RE HEAVY...
HAH!
I'M SO SORRY!!
I LANDED RIGHT ON TOP OF YOU...!!
THE BEAR'S FINE AND SO AM I.
SCOOT SCOOT SCOOT SCOOT
THAT QUITE ASIDE...
WERE YOU ABLE TO GET THE BOOK?

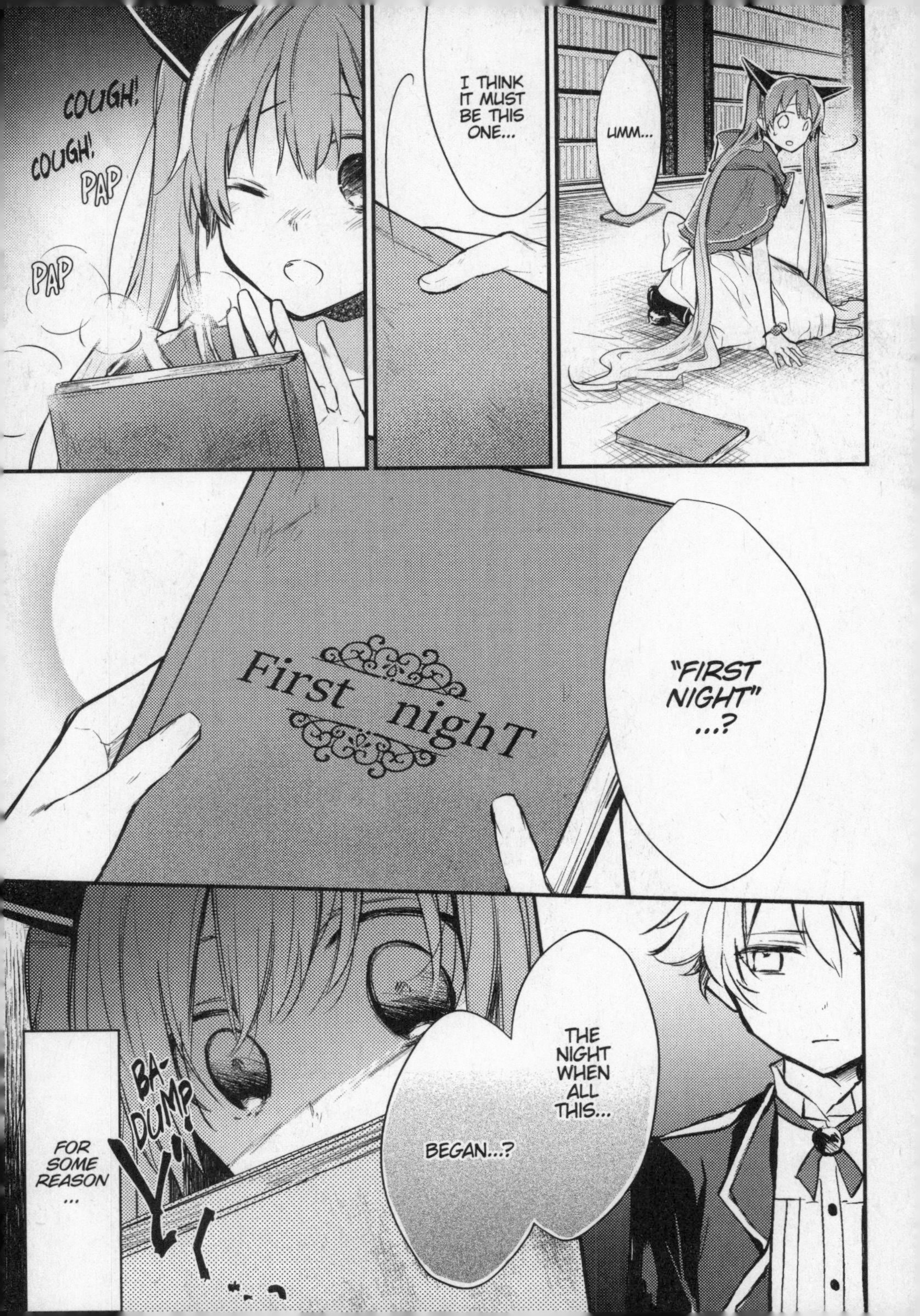
UMM...
I THINK IT MUST BE THIS ONE...
COUGH! COUGH!
PAP
PAP
"FIRST NIGHT" ...?
First nighT
THE NIGHT WHEN ALL THIS...
BEGAN...?
BA-DUMP
FOR SOME REASON ...

I JUST CAN'T OPEN IT.
THERE MUST BE SOMETHING IMPORTANT WRITTEN IN HERE...
AND YET...
I CAN'T BRING MYSELF TO TAKE THAT NEXT STEP.

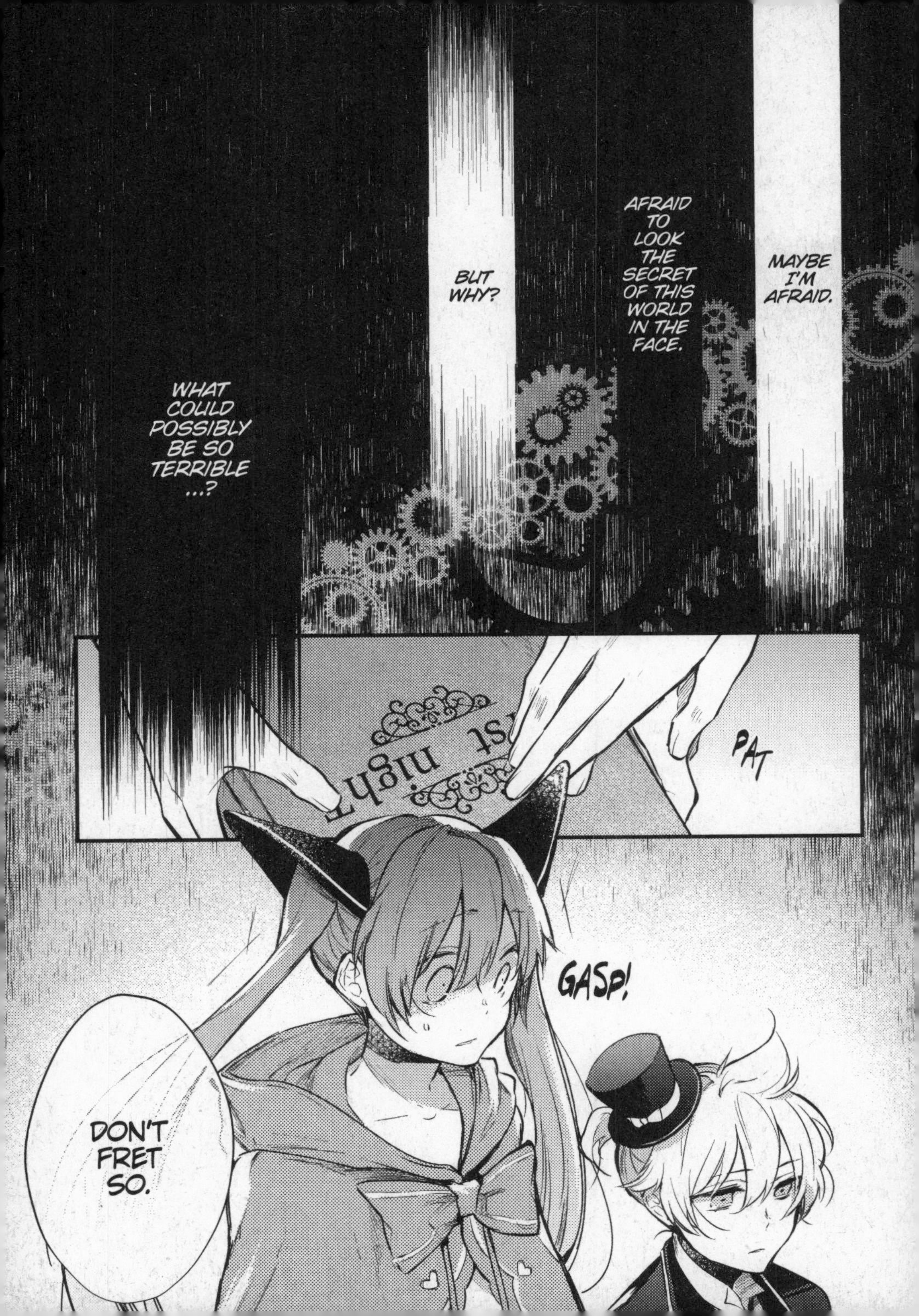
MAYBE I'M AFRAID.
AFRAID TO LOOK THE SECRET OF THIS WORLD IN THE FACE.
BUT WHY?
WHAT COULD POSSIBLY BE SO TERRIBLE ...?
PAT
GASP!
DON'T FRET SO.

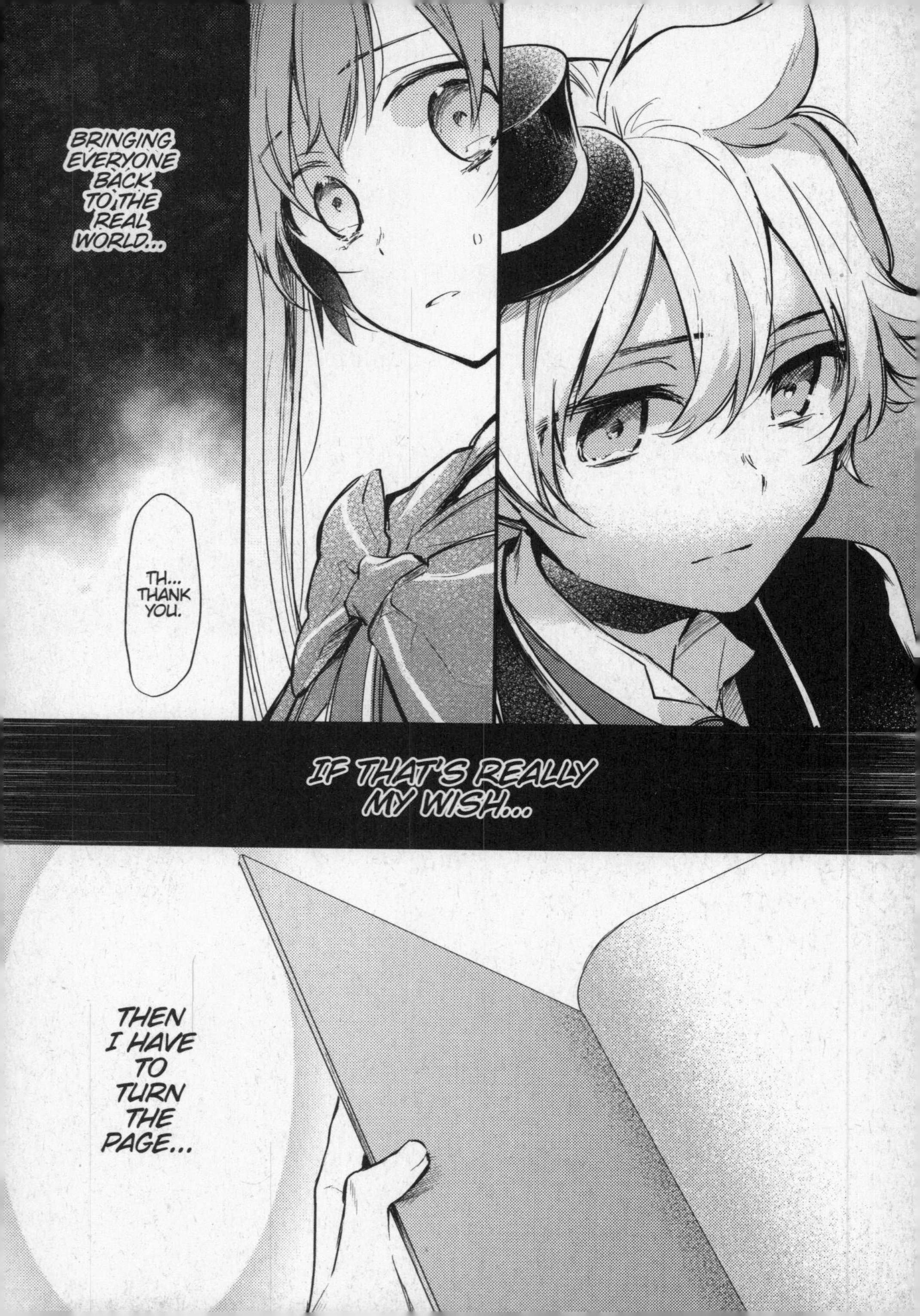
BRINGING EVERYONE BACK TO THE REAL WORLD...
TH... THANK YOU.
IF THAT'S REALLY MY WISH...
THEN I HAVE TO TURN THE PAGE...

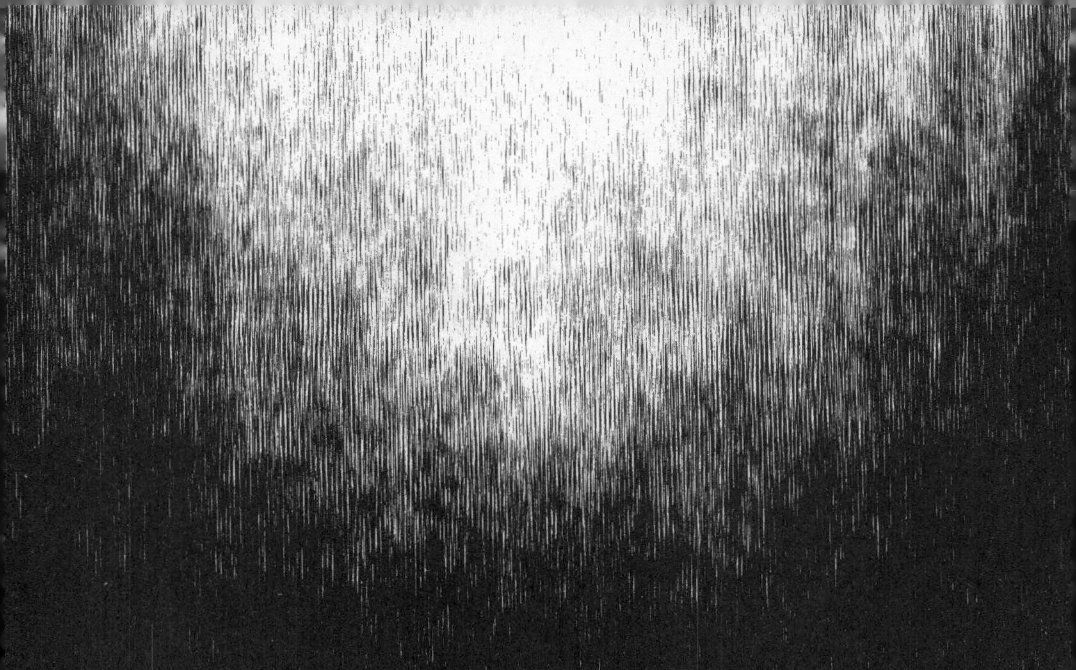

First nighT

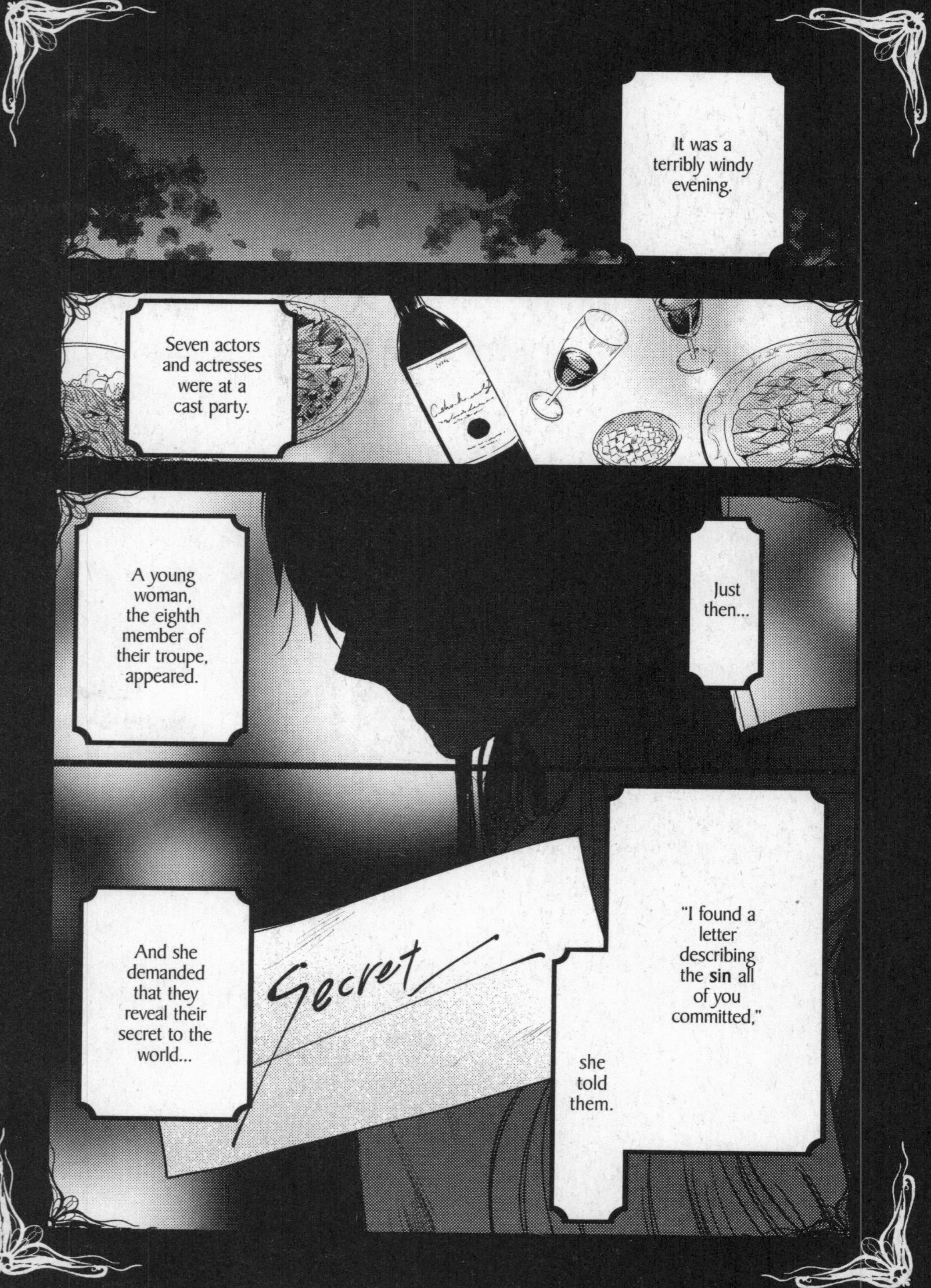
It was a terribly windy evening.
Seven actors and actresses were at a cast party.
Just then...
A young woman, the eighth member of their troupe, appeared.
"I found a letter describing the **sin** all of you committed,"
she told them.
And she demanded that they reveal their secret to the world...
Secret

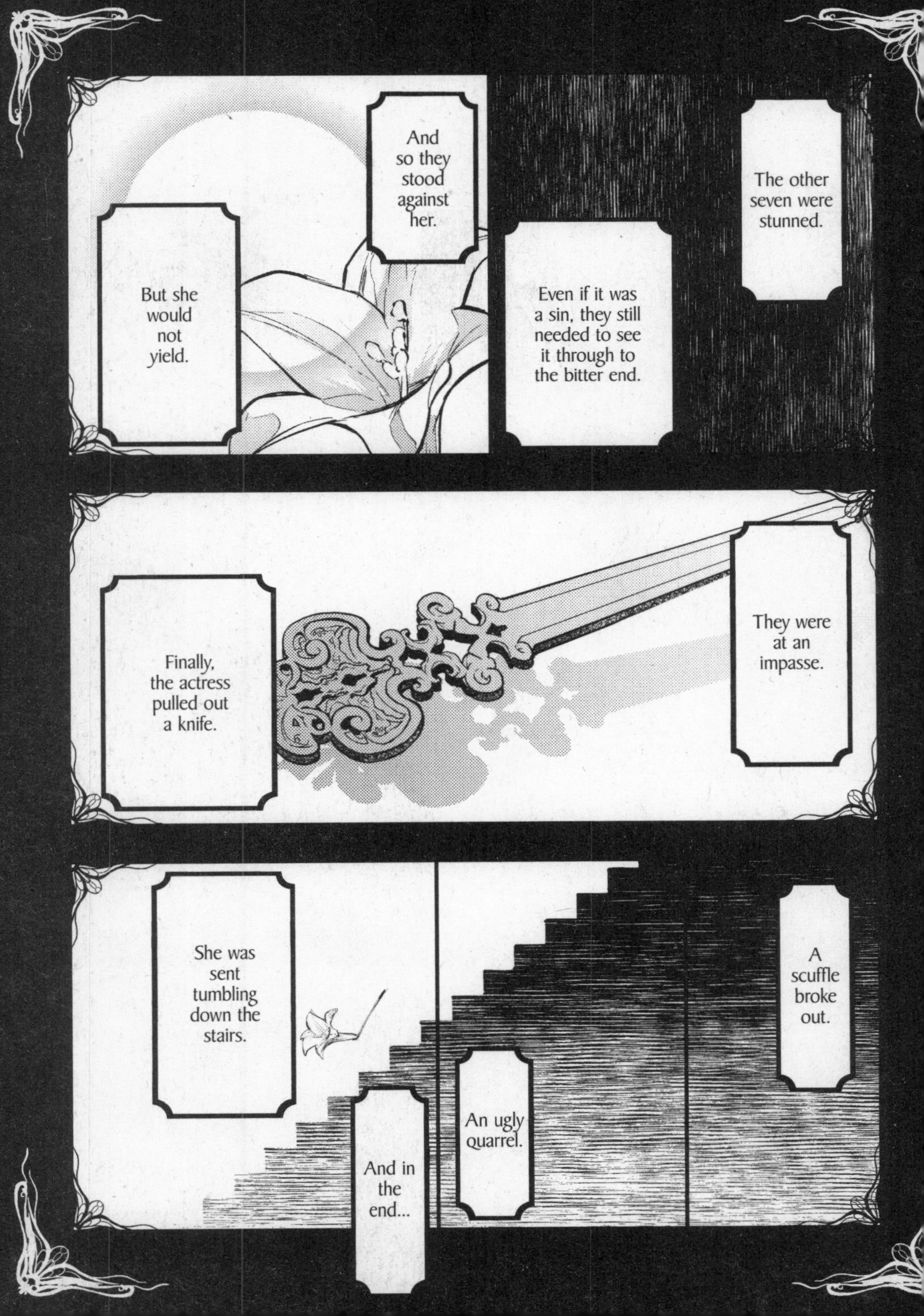

The other seven were stunned.
Even if it was a sin, they still needed to see it through to the bitter end.
And so they stood against her.
But she would not yield.
They were at an impasse.
Finally, the actress pulled out a knife.
A scuffle broke out.
An ugly quarrel.
And in the end...
She was sent tumbling down the stairs.

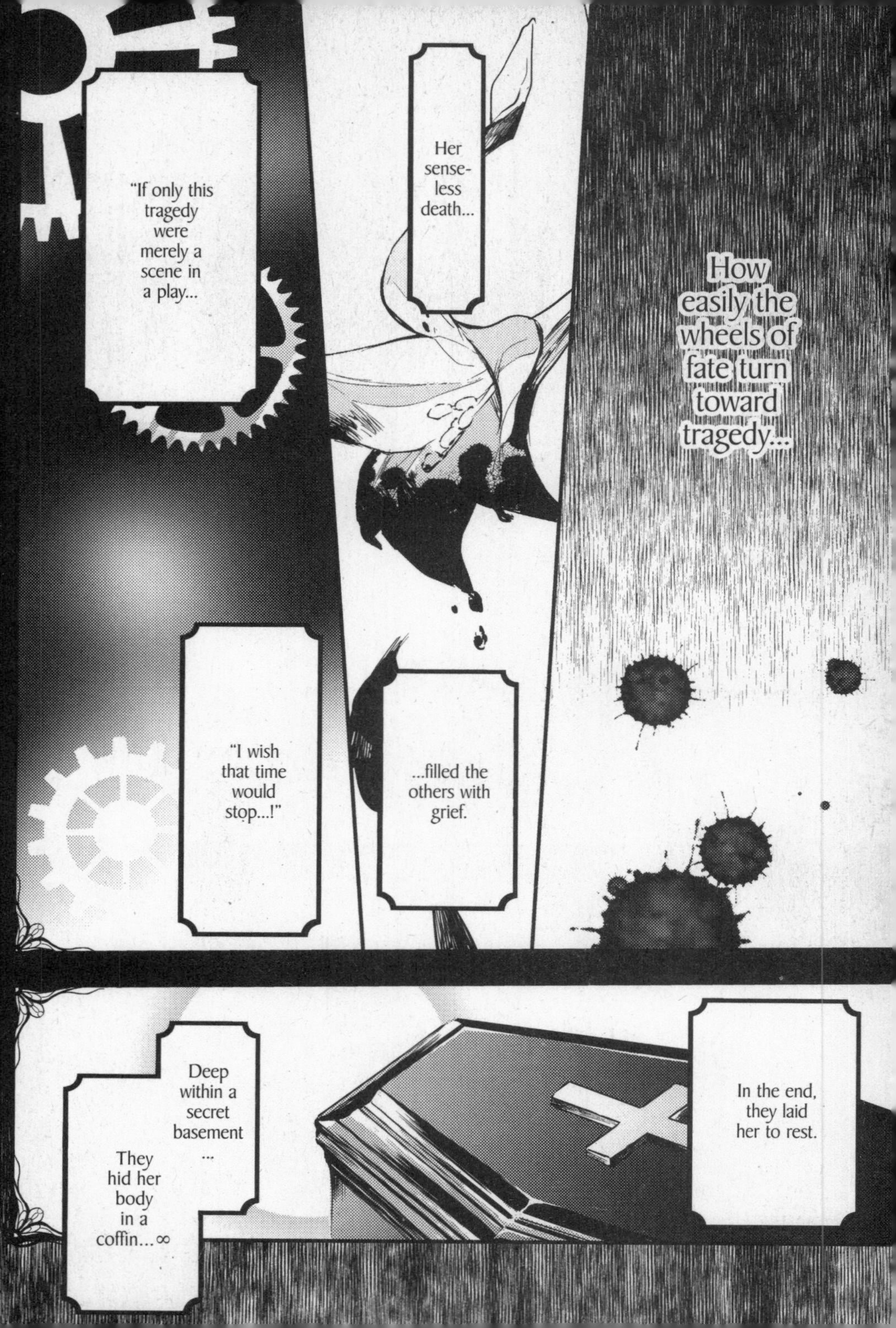
How easily the wheels of fate turn toward tragedy...
Her senseless death...
...filled the others with grief.
"If only this tragedy were merely a scene in a play...
"I wish that time would stop...!"
In the end, they laid her to rest.
Deep within a secret basement...
They hid her body in a coffin...∞

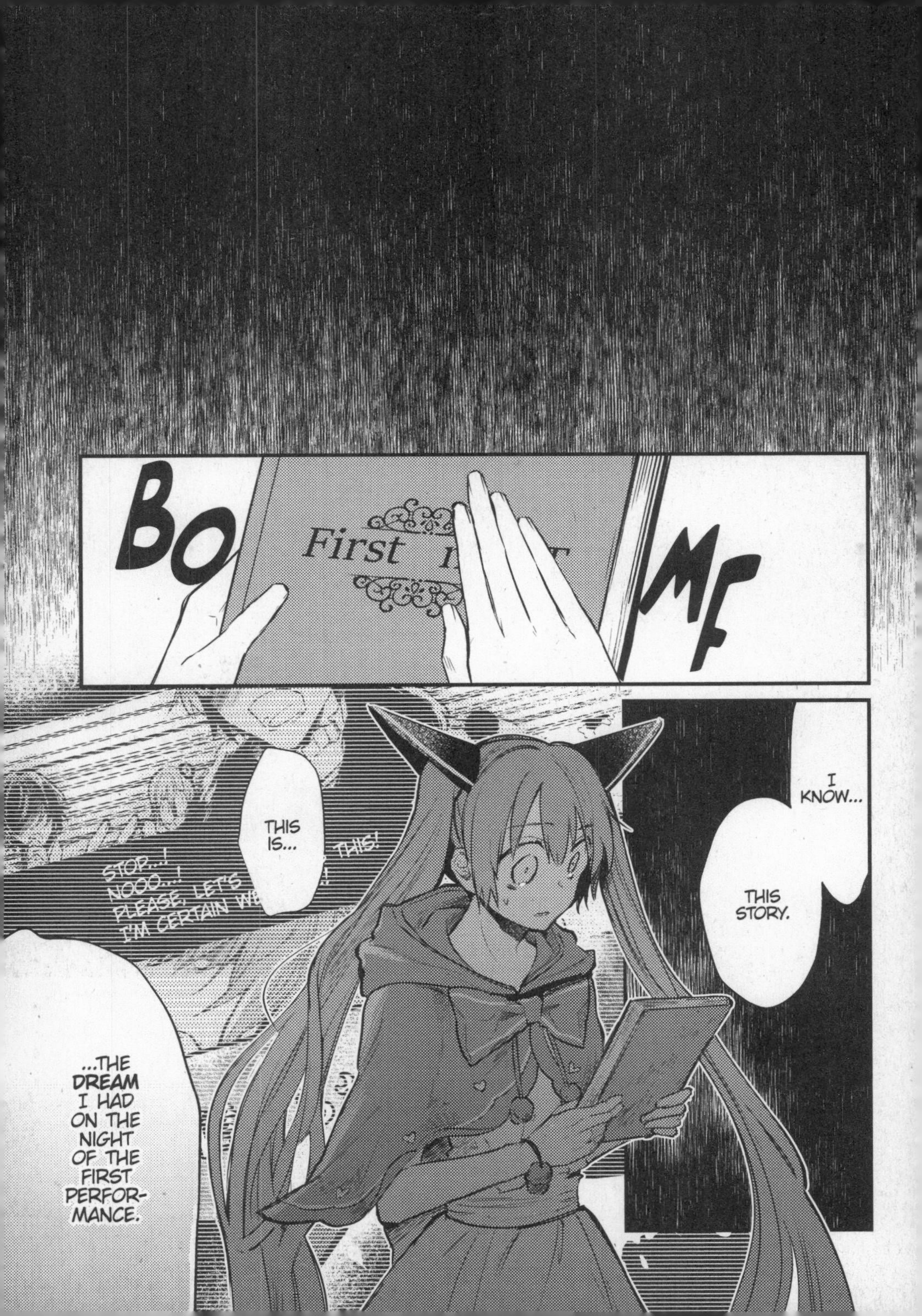

BO
MF
First
I KNOW...
THIS STORY.
THIS IS...
STOP...!
NOOO...!
PLEASE, LET'S
I'M CERTAIN WE
THIS!
...THE DREAM I HAD ON THE NIGHT OF THE FIRST PERFORMANCE.

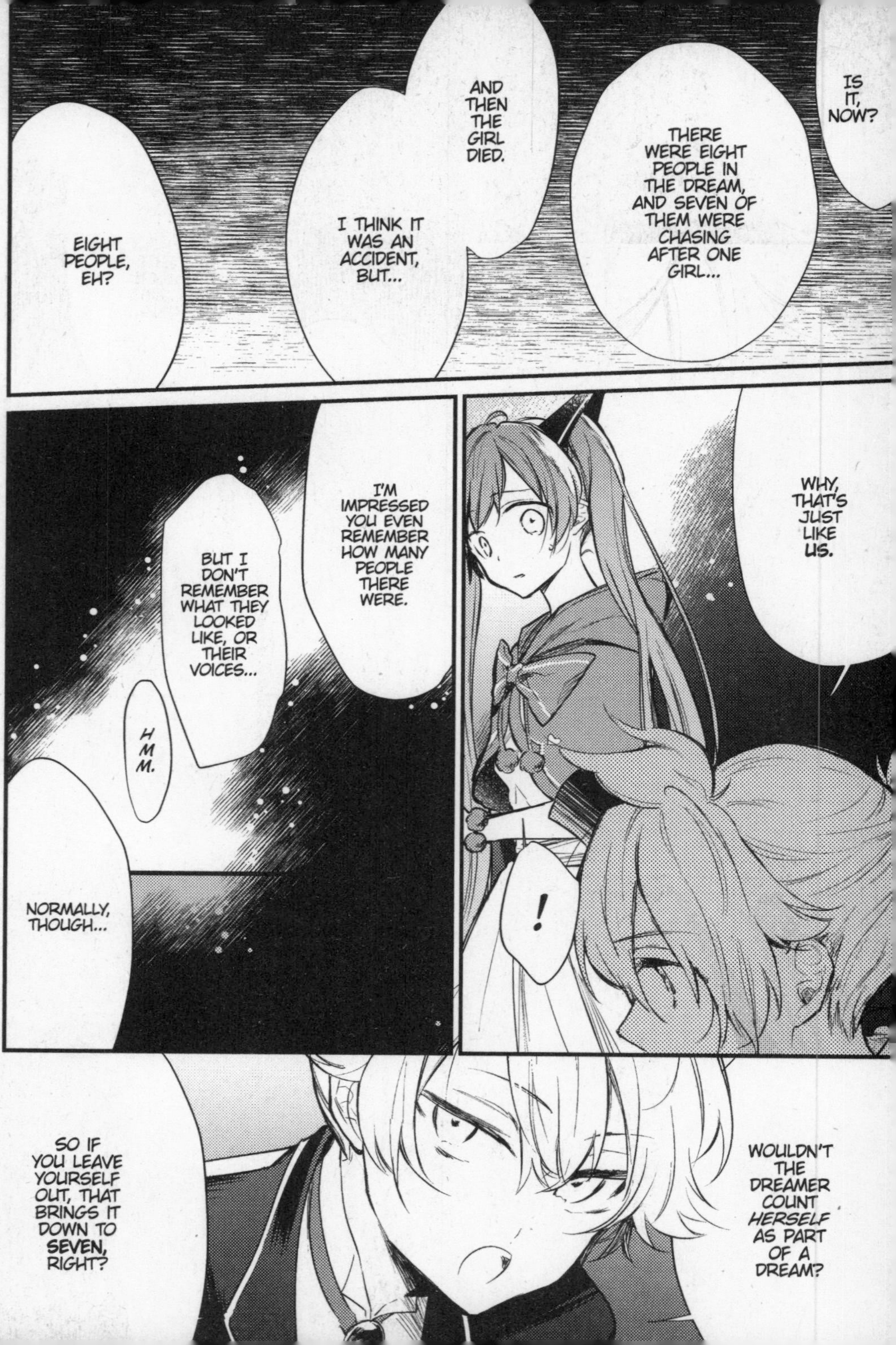
IS IT, NOW?
THERE WERE EIGHT PEOPLE IN THE DREAM, AND SEVEN OF THEM WERE CHASING AFTER ONE GIRL...
AND THEN THE GIRL DIED.
I THINK IT WAS AN ACCIDENT, BUT...
EIGHT PEOPLE, EH?
WHY, THAT'S JUST LIKE **US**.
I'M IMPRESSED YOU EVEN REMEMBER HOW MANY PEOPLE THERE WERE.
BUT I DON'T REMEMBER WHAT THEY LOOKED LIKE, OR THEIR VOICES...
HMM.
!
NORMALLY, THOUGH...
WOULDN'T THE DREAMER COUNT *HERSELF* AS PART OF A DREAM?
SO IF YOU LEAVE YOURSELF OUT, THAT BRINGS IT DOWN TO **SEVEN**, RIGHT?

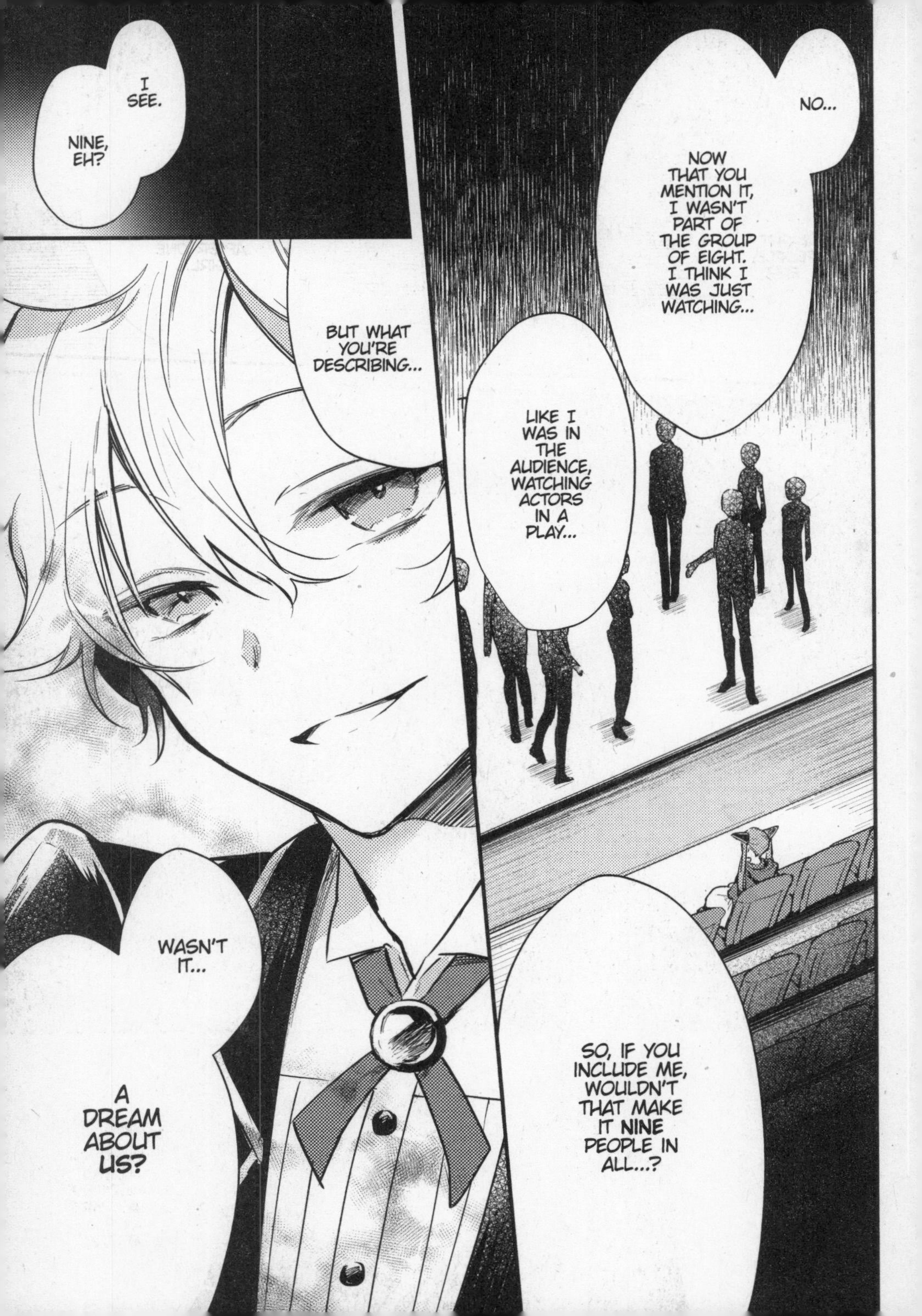
NO...
NOW THAT YOU MENTION IT, I WASN'T PART OF THE GROUP OF EIGHT. I THINK I WAS JUST WATCHING...
I SEE.
NINE, EH?
LIKE I WAS IN THE AUDIENCE, WATCHING ACTORS IN A PLAY...
BUT WHAT YOU'RE DESCRIBING...
SO, IF YOU INCLUDE ME, WOULDN'T THAT MAKE IT NINE PEOPLE IN ALL...?
WASN'T IT...
A DREAM ABOUT US?

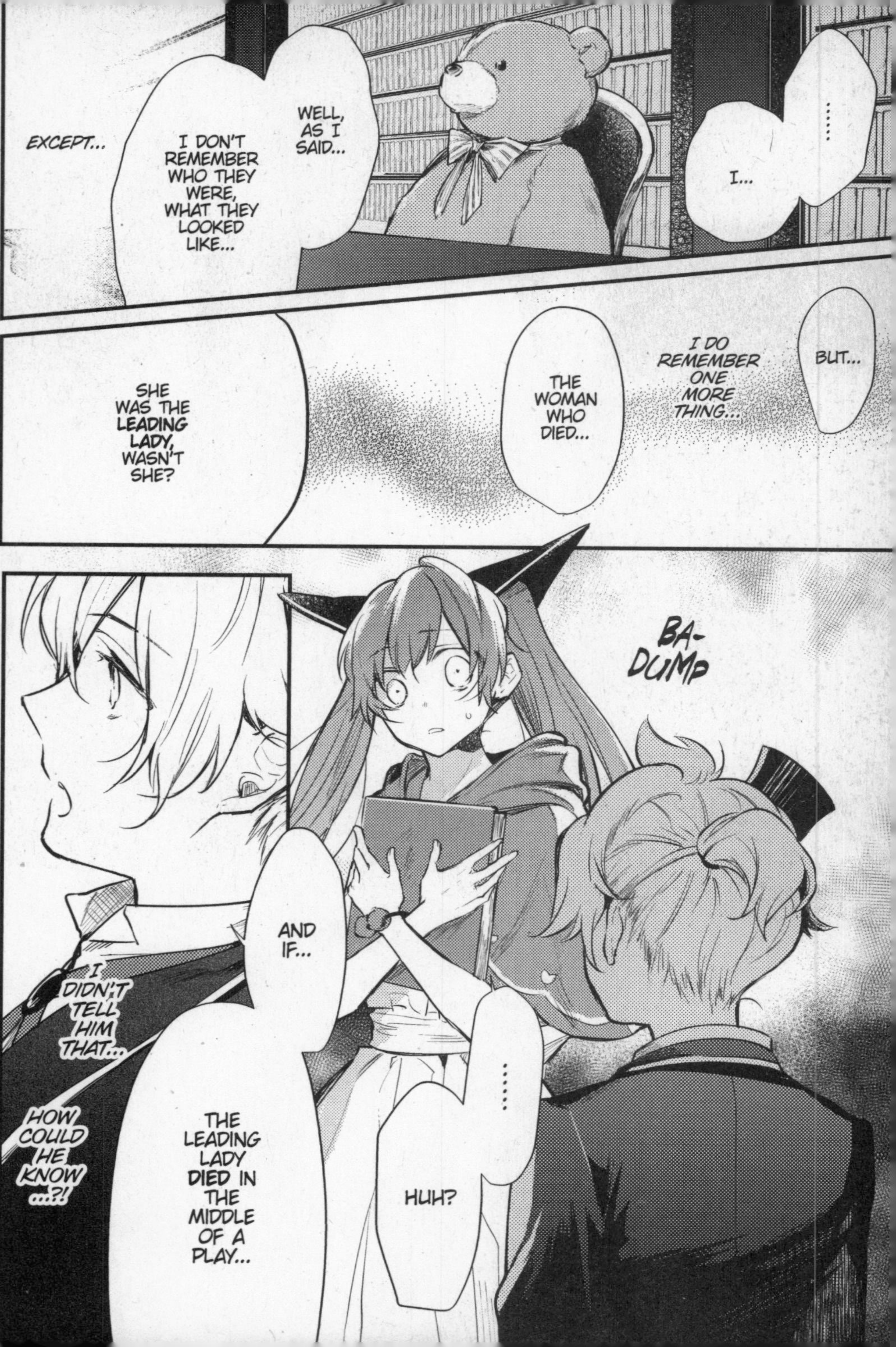
......
I...
WELL, AS I SAID...
I DON'T REMEMBER WHO THEY WERE, WHAT THEY LOOKED LIKE...
EXCEPT...
BUT...
I DO REMEMBER ONE MORE THING...
THE WOMAN WHO DIED...
SHE WAS THE LEADING LADY, WASN'T SHE?
BA-DUMP
......
HUH?
AND IF...
THE LEADING LADY DIED IN THE MIDDLE OF A PLAY...
I DIDN'T TELL HIM THAT...
HOW COULD HE KNOW...?!

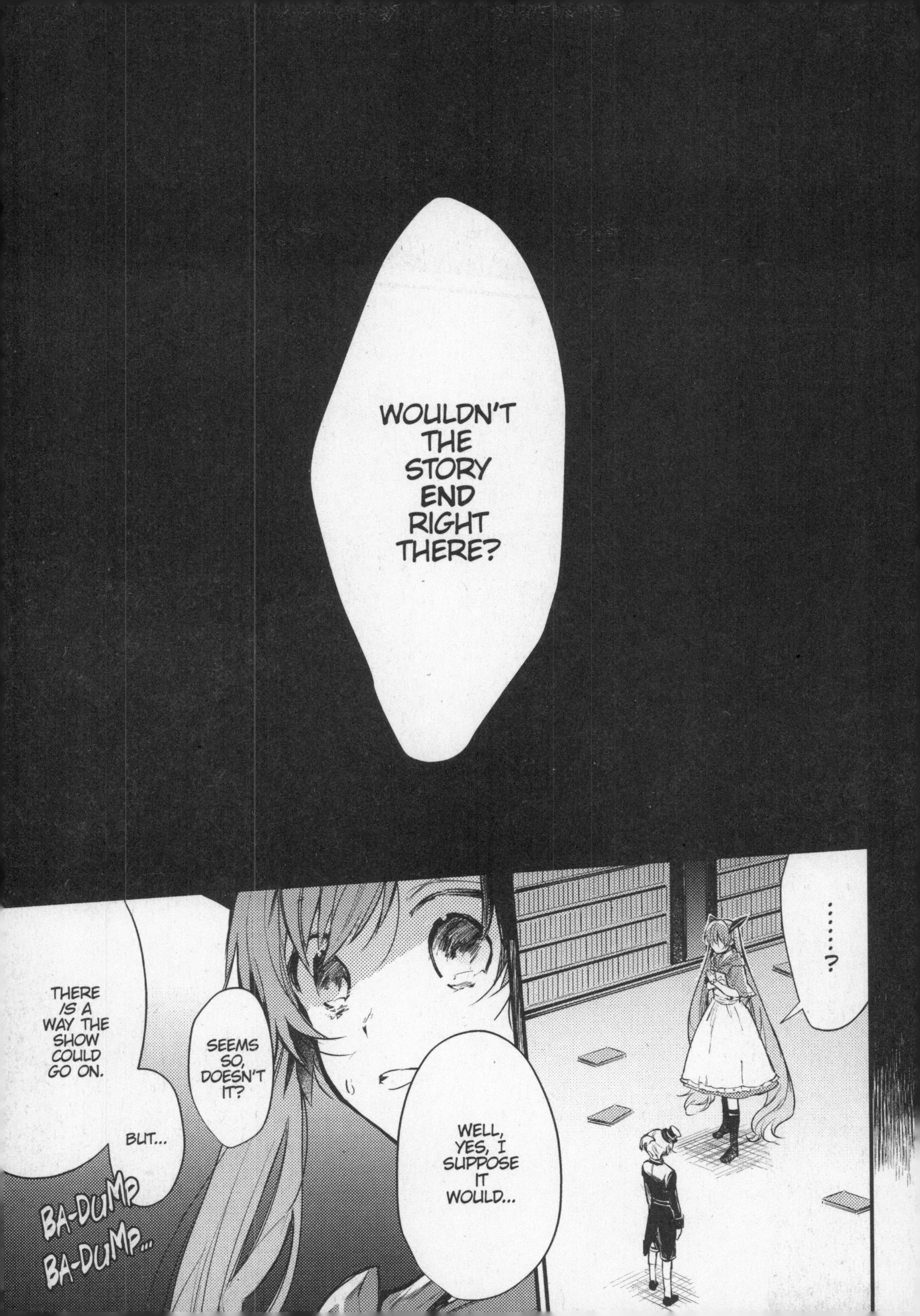
WOULDN'T THE STORY END RIGHT THERE?
......?
WELL, YES, I SUPPOSE IT WOULD...
SEEMS SO, DOESN'T IT?
THERE IS A WAY THE SHOW COULD GO ON.
BUT...
BA-DUMP BA-DUMP...

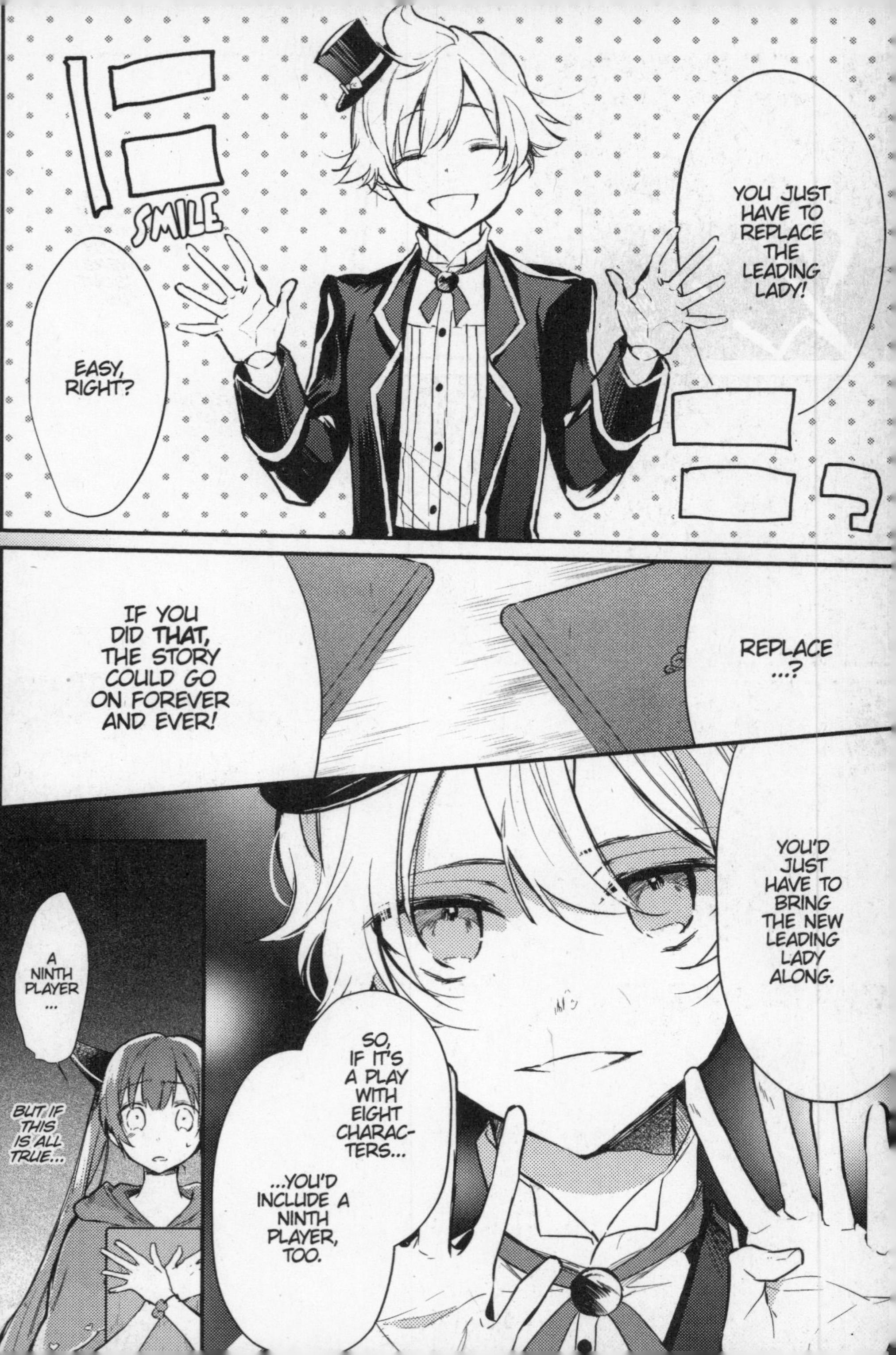
YOU JUST HAVE TO REPLACE THE LEADING LADY!
SMILE
EASY, RIGHT?
REPLACE ...?
IF YOU DID THAT, THE STORY COULD GO ON FOREVER AND EVER!
YOU'D JUST HAVE TO BRING THE NEW LEADING LADY ALONG.
SO, IF IT'S A PLAY WITH EIGHT CHARAC-TERS...
...YOU'D INCLUDE A NINTH PLAYER, TOO.
A NINTH PLAYER ...
BUT IF THIS IS ALL TRUE...

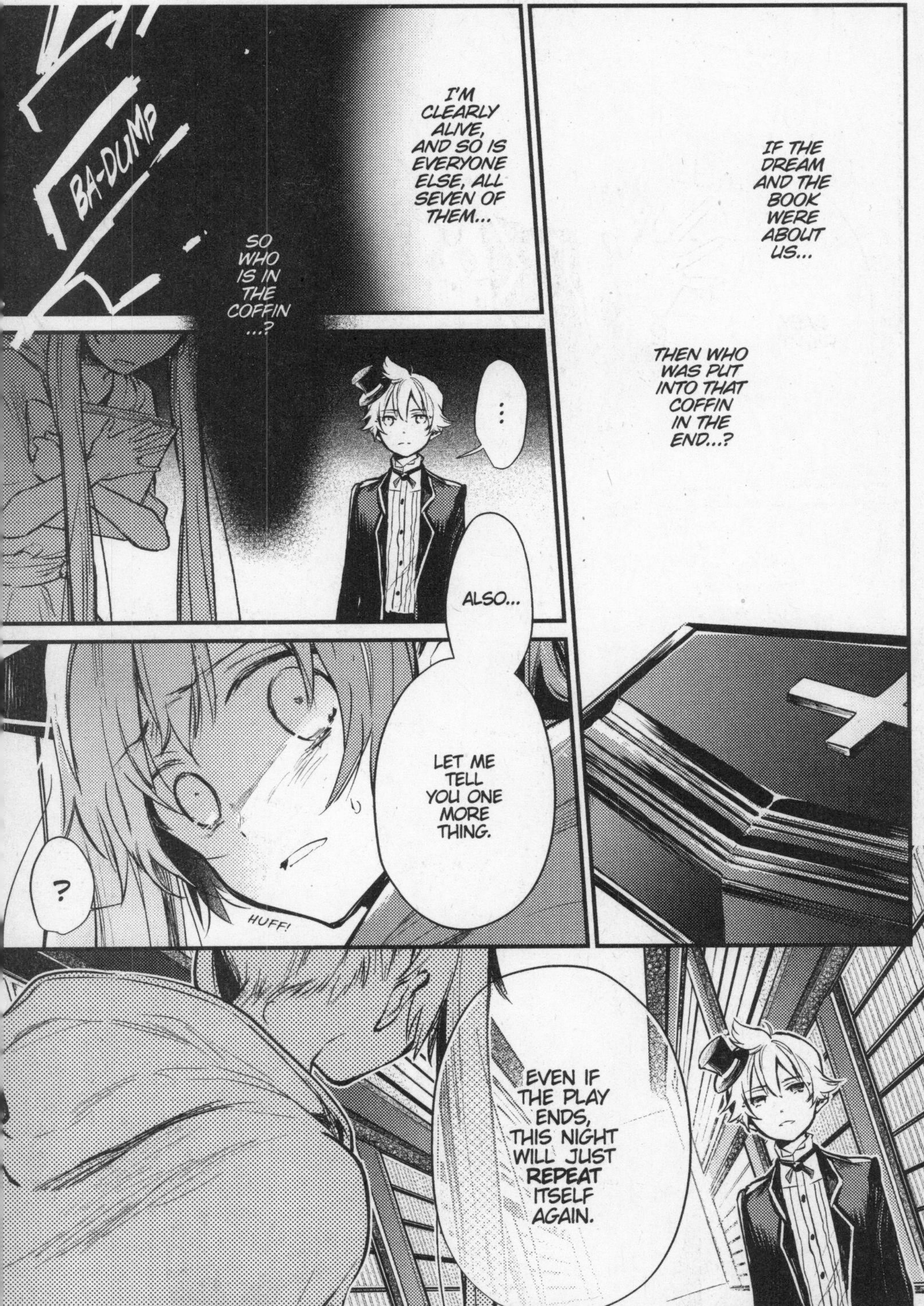
IF THE DREAM AND THE BOOK WERE ABOUT US...
I'M CLEARLY ALIVE, AND SO IS EVERYONE ELSE, ALL SEVEN OF THEM...
BA-DUMP
SO WHO IS IN THE COFFIN ...?
THEN WHO WAS PUT INTO THAT COFFIN IN THE END...?
...
ALSO...
LET ME TELL YOU ONE MORE THING.
?
HUFF!
EVEN IF THE PLAY ENDS, THIS NIGHT WILL JUST REPEAT ITSELF AGAIN.

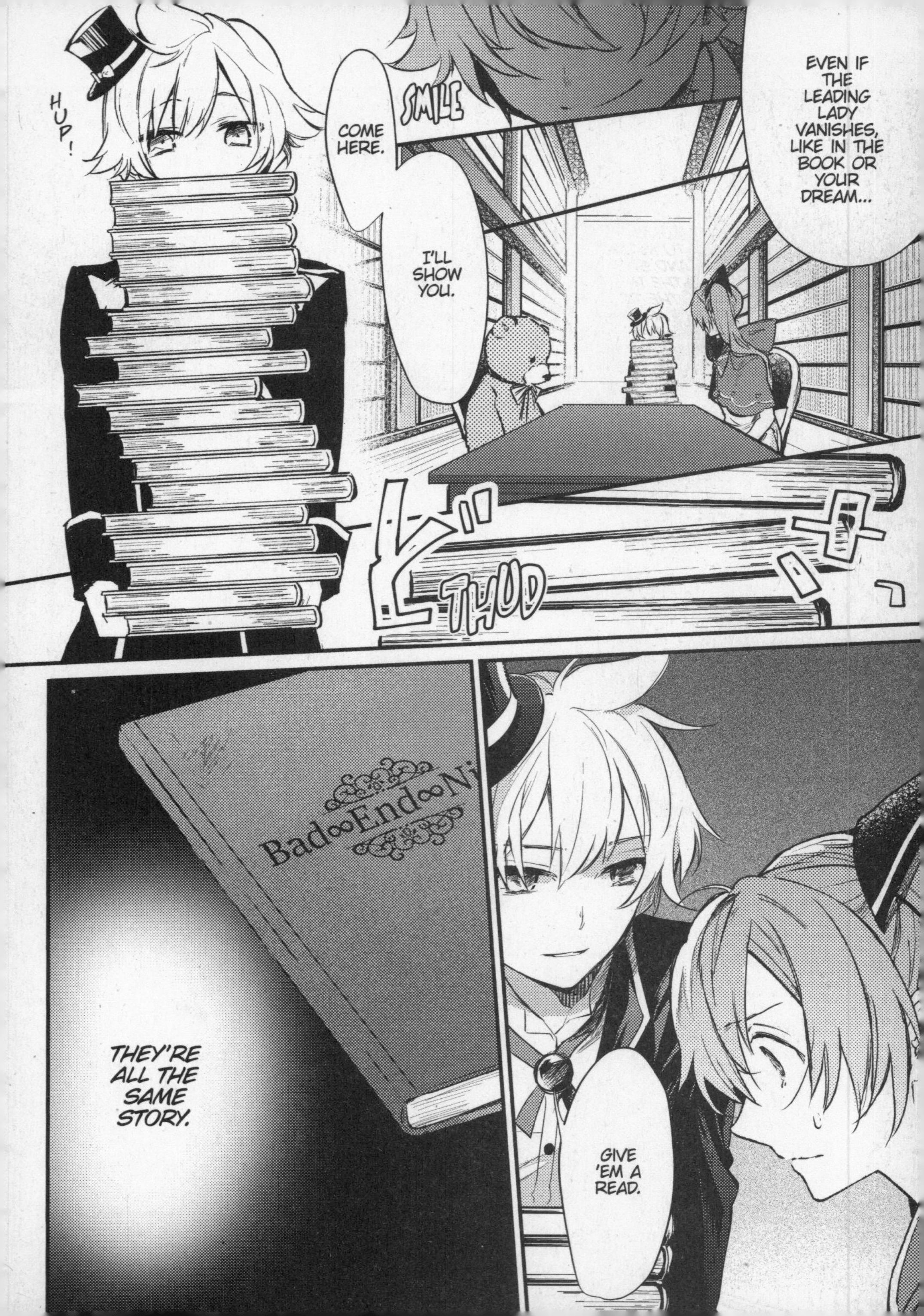
EVEN IF THE LEADING LADY VANISHES, LIKE IN THE BOOK OR YOUR DREAM...
SMILE
COME HERE.
I'LL SHOW YOU.
HUP!
THUD
Bad∞End∞Ni
GIVE 'EM A READ.
THEY'RE ALL THE SAME STORY.

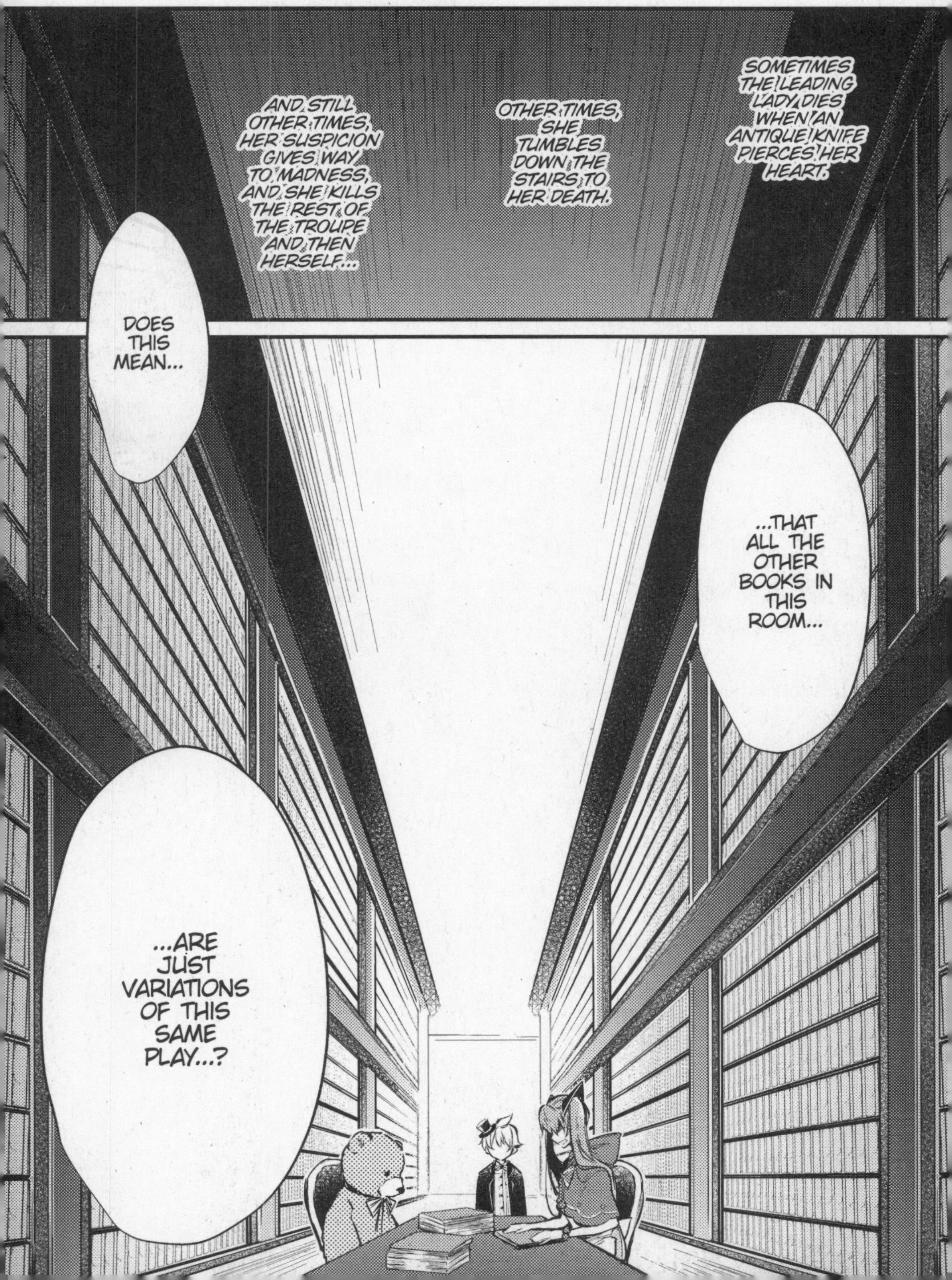
SOMETIMES THE LEADING LADY DIES WHEN AN ANTIQUE KNIFE PIERCES HER HEART.
OTHER TIMES, SHE TUMBLES DOWN THE STAIRS TO HER DEATH.
AND STILL OTHER TIMES, HER SUSPICION GIVES WAY TO MADNESS, AND SHE KILLS THE REST OF THE TROUPE AND THEN HERSELF...
DOES THIS MEAN...
...THAT ALL THE OTHER BOOKS IN THIS ROOM...
...ARE JUST VARIATIONS OF THIS SAME PLAY...?

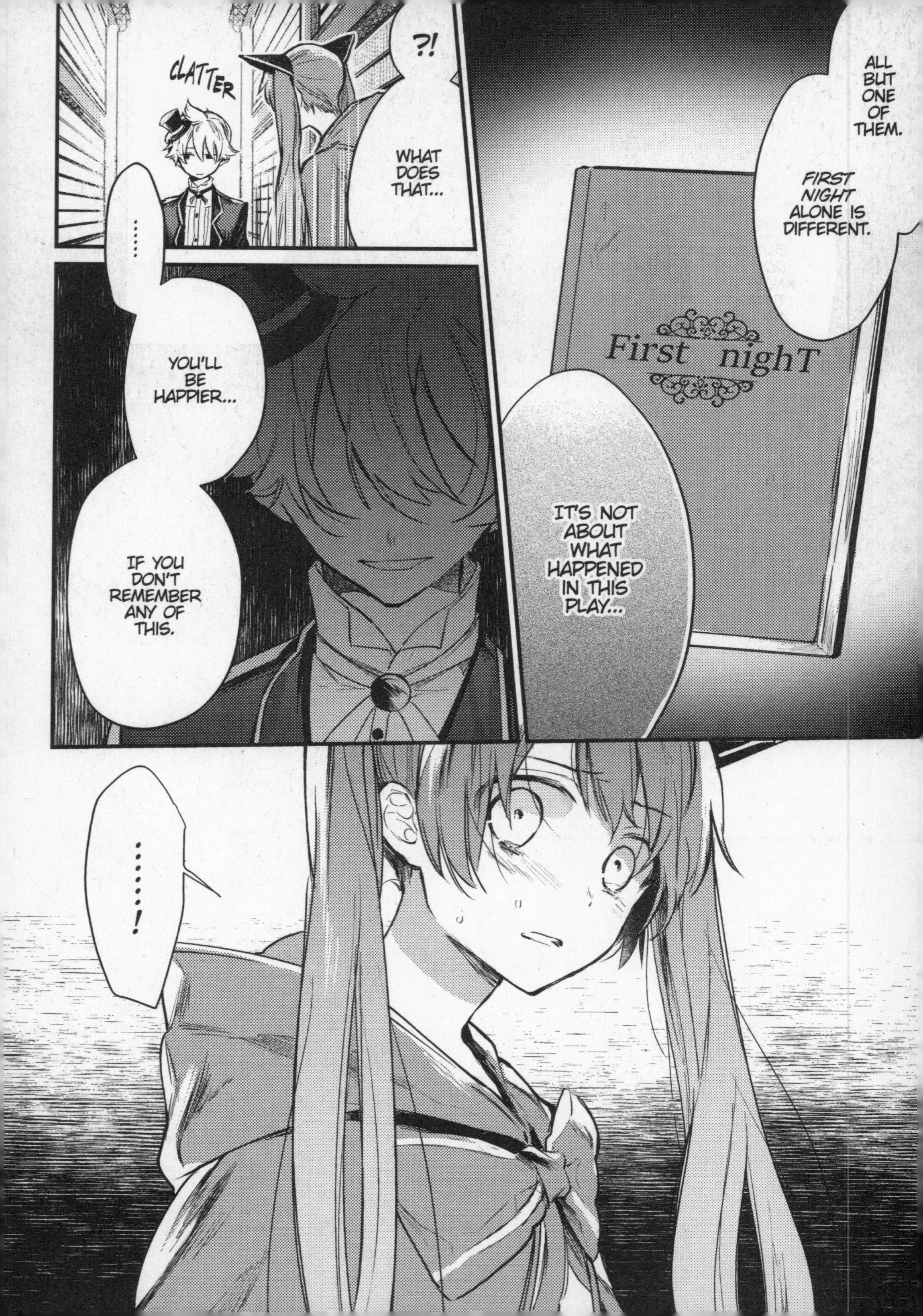
ALL BUT ONE OF THEM.
FIRST NIGHT ALONE IS DIFFERENT.
?!
WHAT DOES THAT...
CLATTER
......
First nighT
IT'S NOT ABOUT WHAT HAPPENED IN THIS PLAY...
YOU'LL BE HAPPIER...
IF YOU DON'T REMEMBER ANY OF THIS.
......!

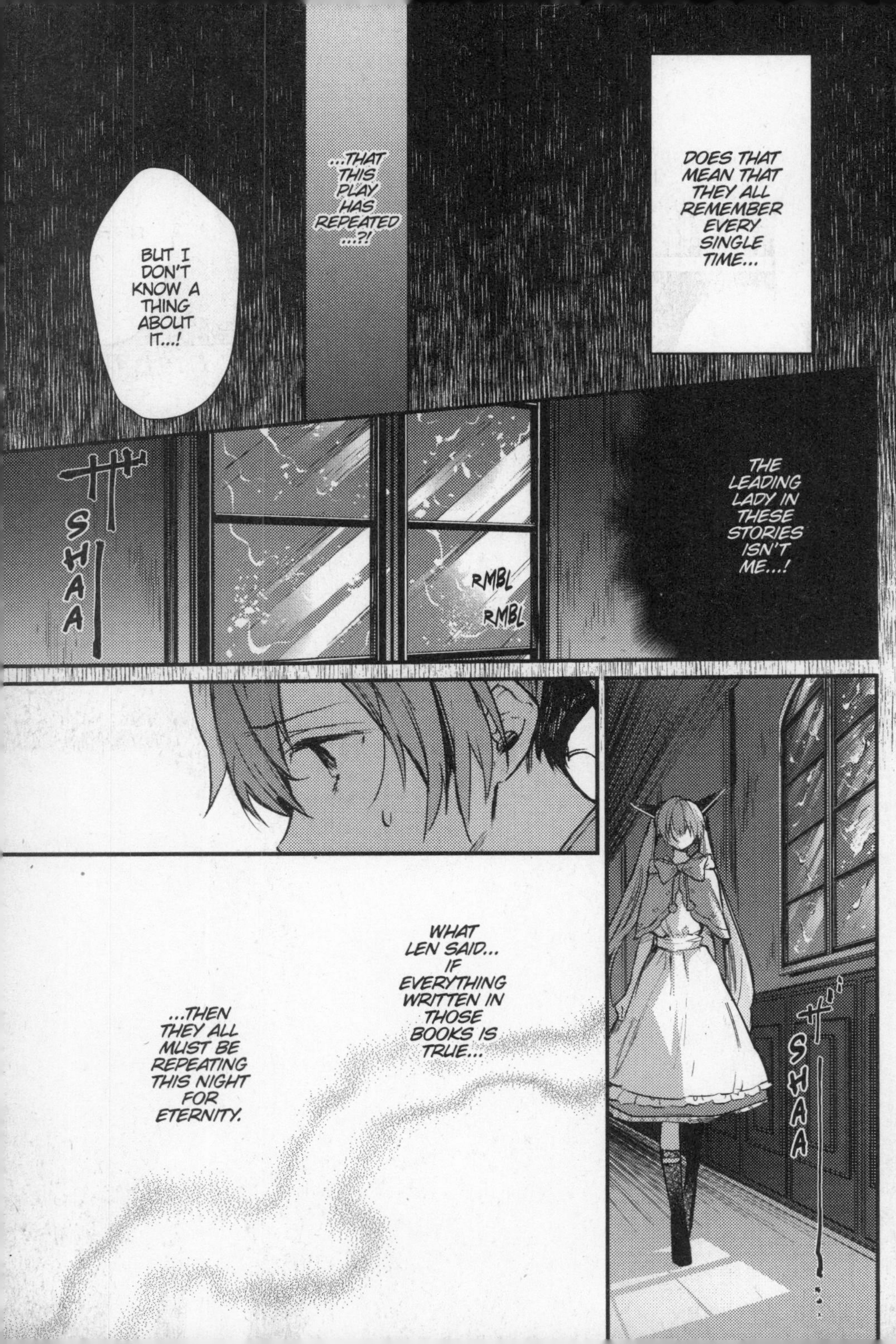
DOES THAT MEAN THAT THEY ALL REMEMBER EVERY SINGLE TIME...
...THAT THIS PLAY HAS REPEATED...?!
BUT I DON'T KNOW A THING ABOUT IT...!
THE LEADING LADY IN THESE STORIES ISN'T ME...!
RMBL
RMBL
SHAA
SHAA...
WHAT LEN SAID... IF EVERYTHING WRITTEN IN THOSE BOOKS IS TRUE...
...THEN THEY ALL MUST BE REPEATING THIS NIGHT FOR ETERNITY.

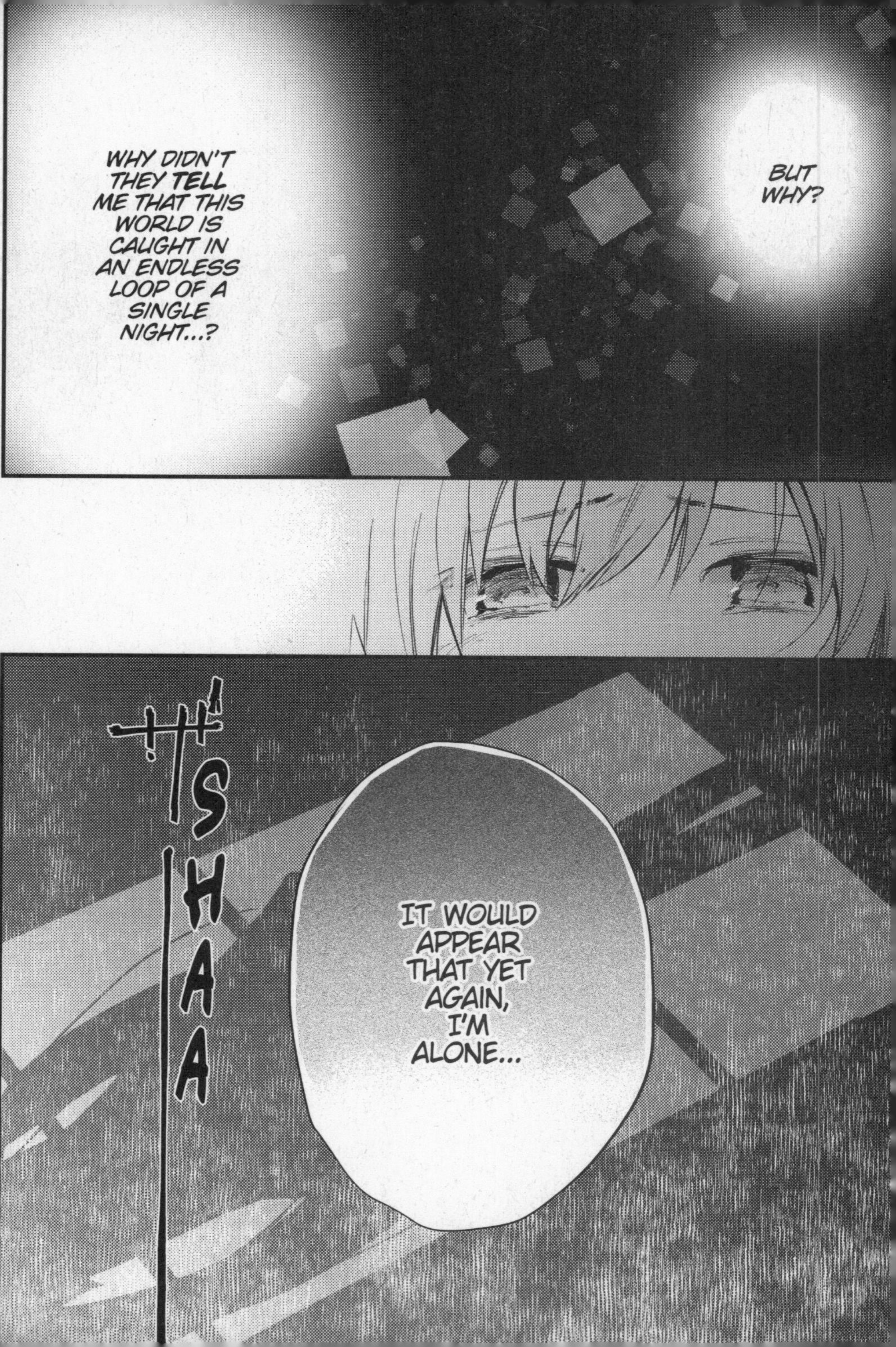
BUT WHY?
WHY DIDN'T THEY TELL ME THAT THIS WORLD IS CAUGHT IN AN ENDLESS LOOP OF A SINGLE NIGHT...?
IT WOULD APPEAR THAT YET AGAIN, I'M ALONE...
SHAA

Bad∞End∞Night
～インセイン・パーティー～

BO
First

Act 8: Behind the Door

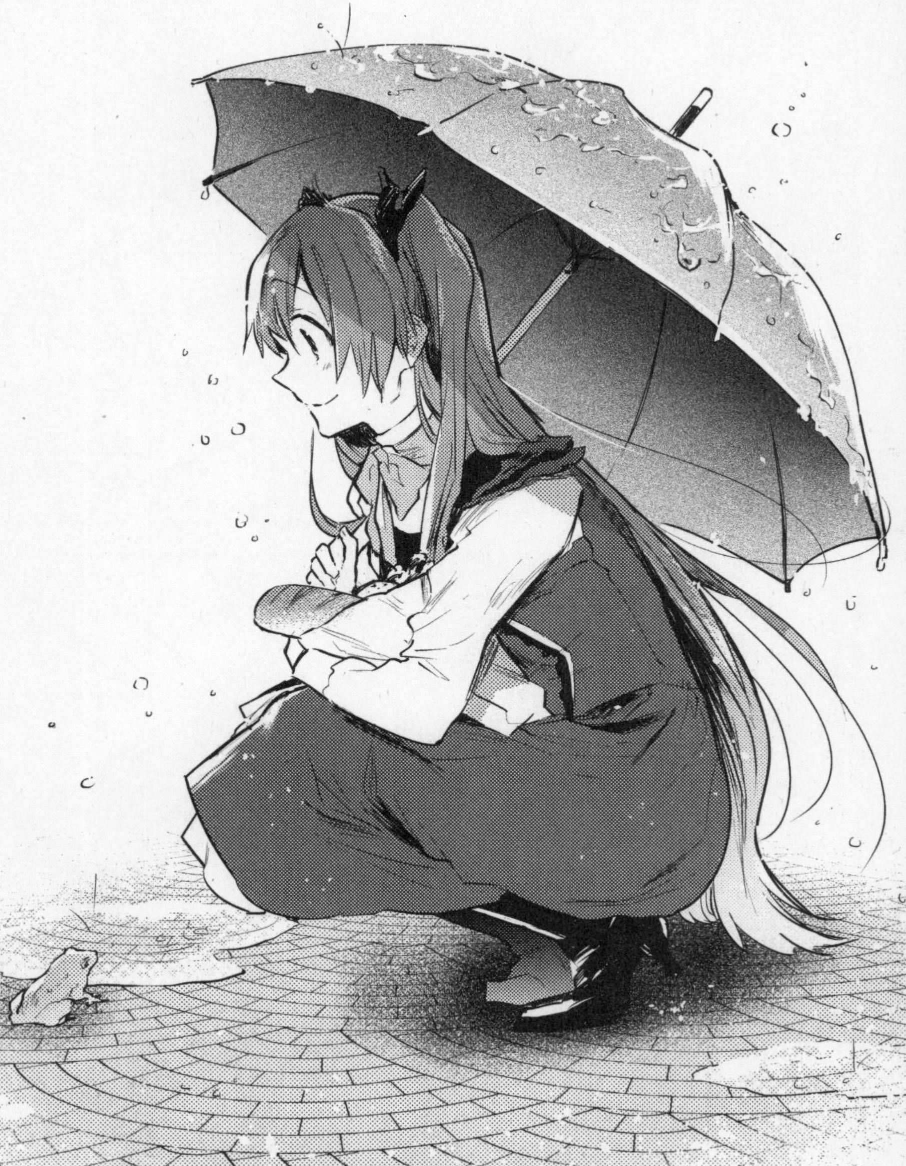

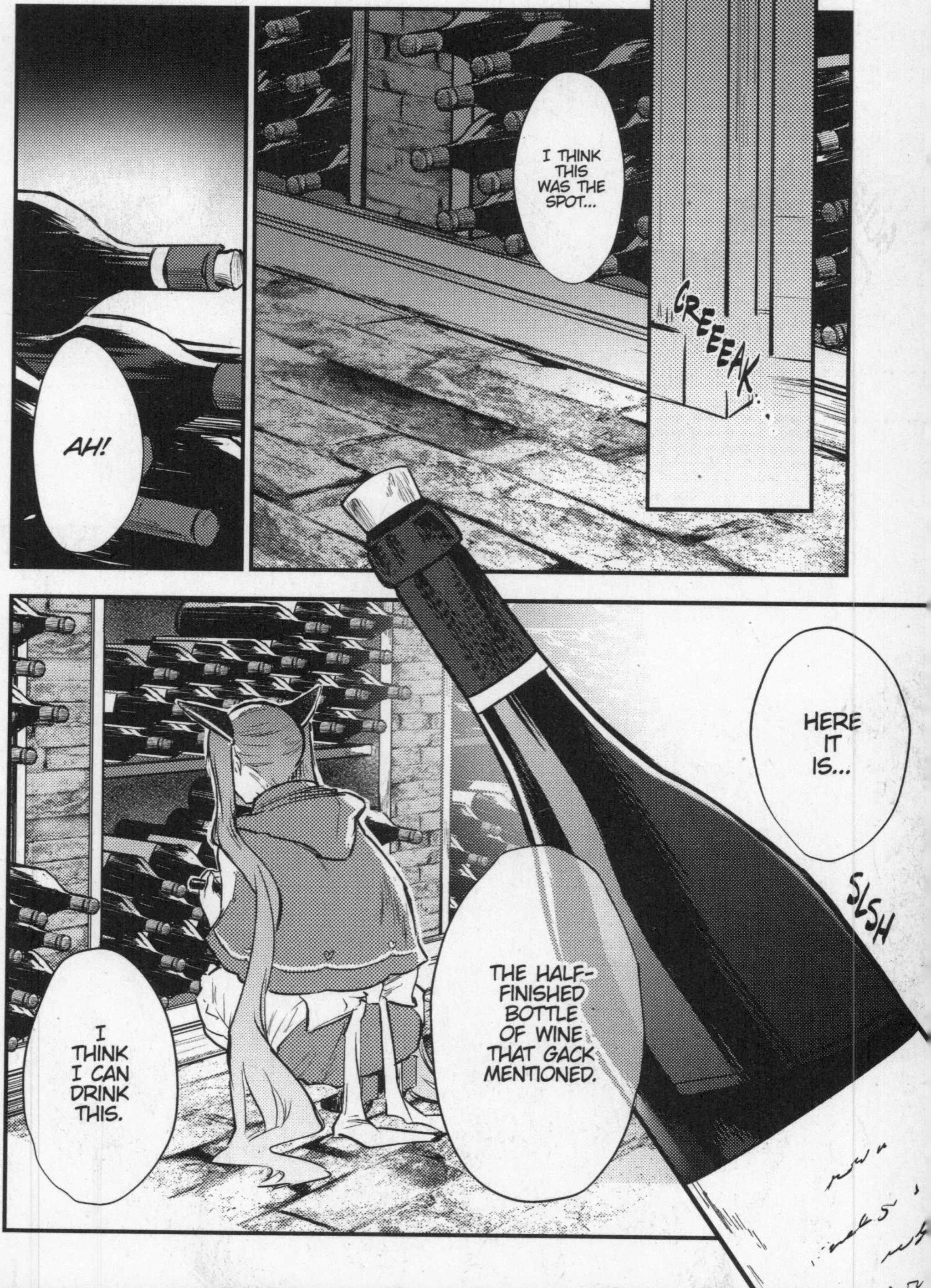
I THINK THIS WAS THE SPOT...
CREEEAK...
AH!
HERE IT IS...
SLSH
THE HALF-FINISHED BOTTLE OF WINE THAT GACK MENTIONED.
I THINK I CAN DRINK THIS.

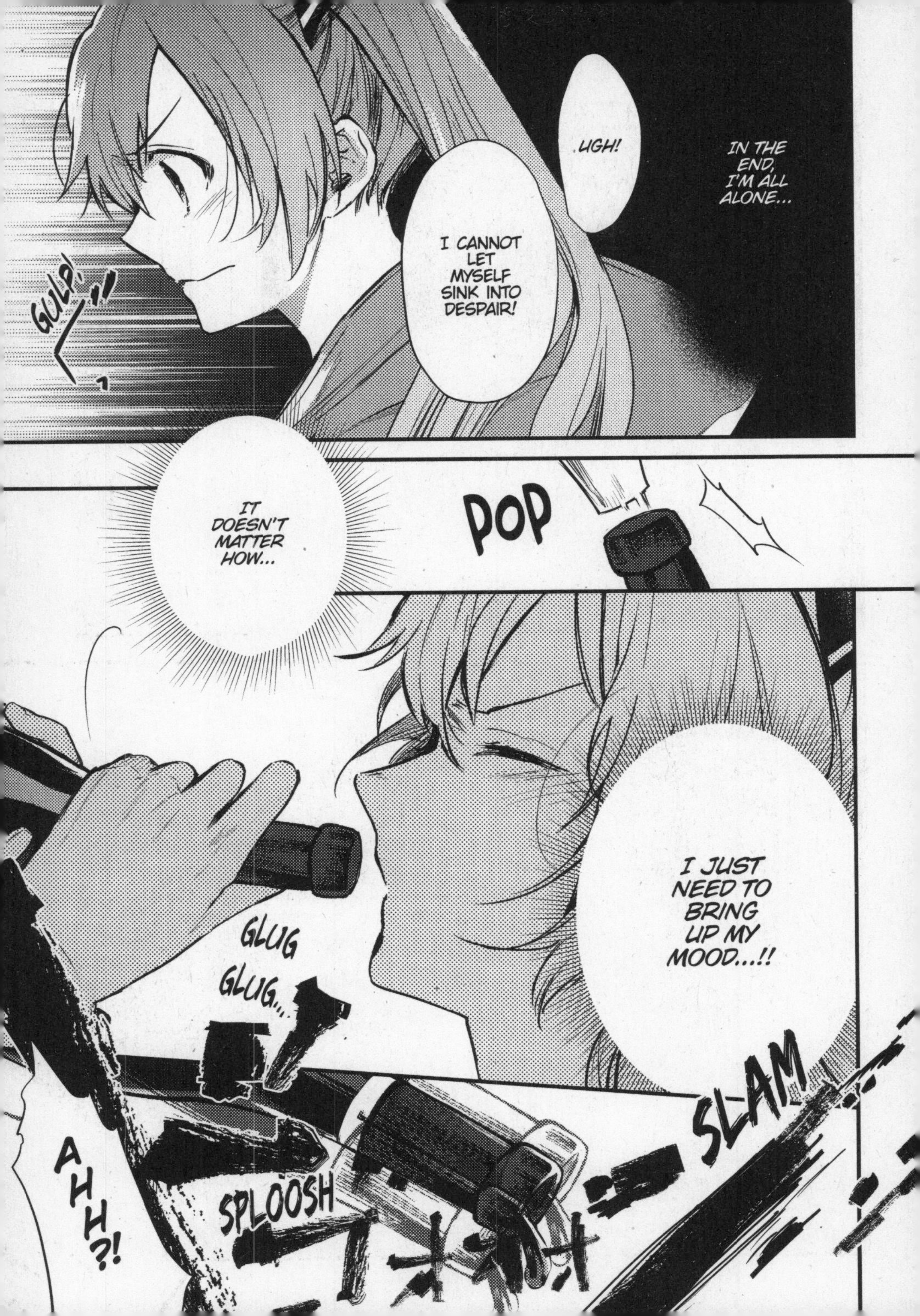
IN THE END, I'M ALL ALONE...
..UGH!
I CANNOT LET MYSELF SINK INTO DESPAIR!
GULP!
POP
IT DOESN'T MATTER HOW...
I JUST NEED TO BRING UP MY MOOD...!!
GLUG GLUG...
SLAM
SPLOOSH
AHH?!

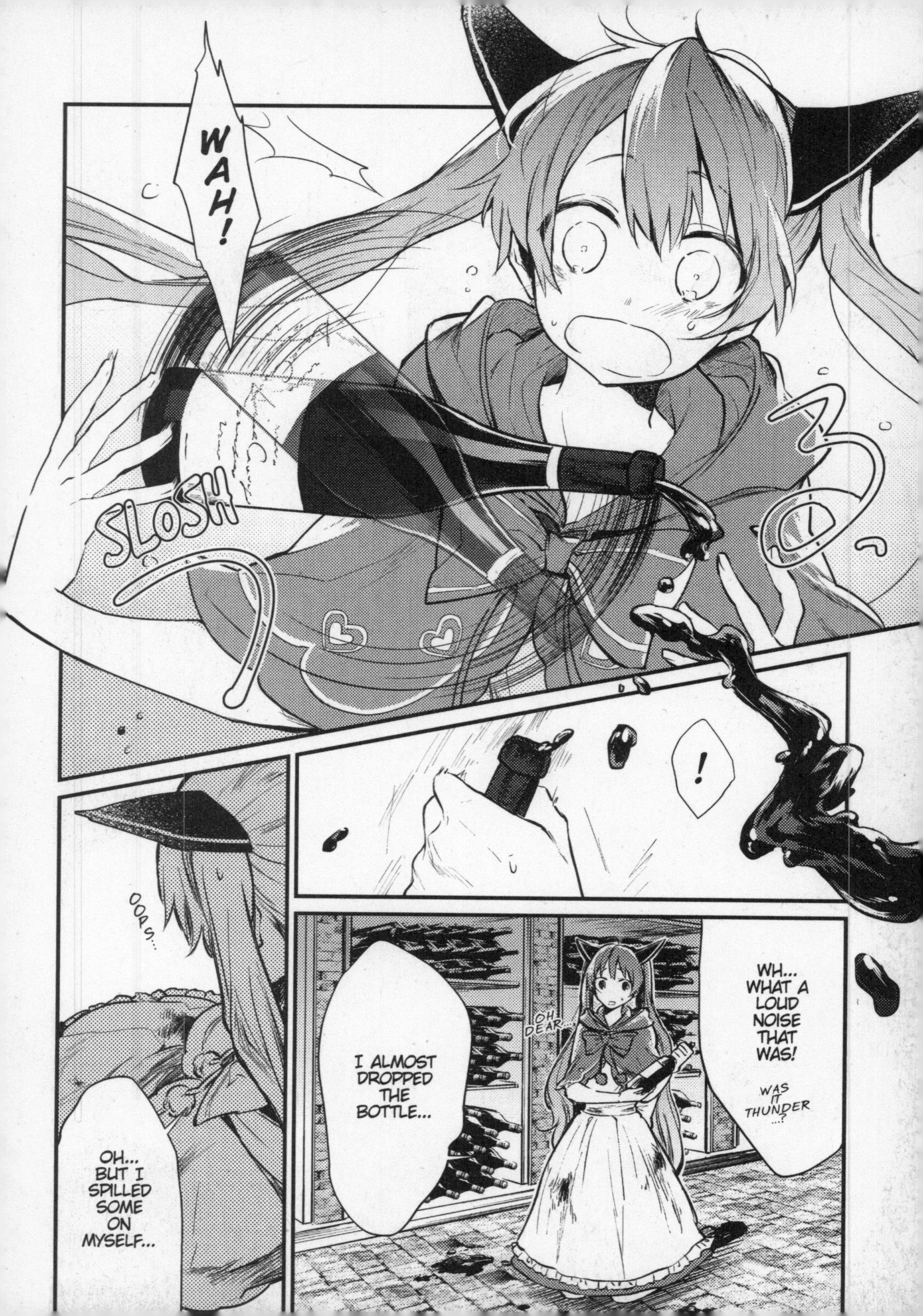
WAH!
SLOSH
!
WH... WHAT A LOUD NOISE THAT WAS!
WAS IT THUNDER...?
I ALMOST DROPPED THE BOTTLE...
OH DEAR...
OOPS...
OH... BUT I SPILLED SOME ON MYSELF...

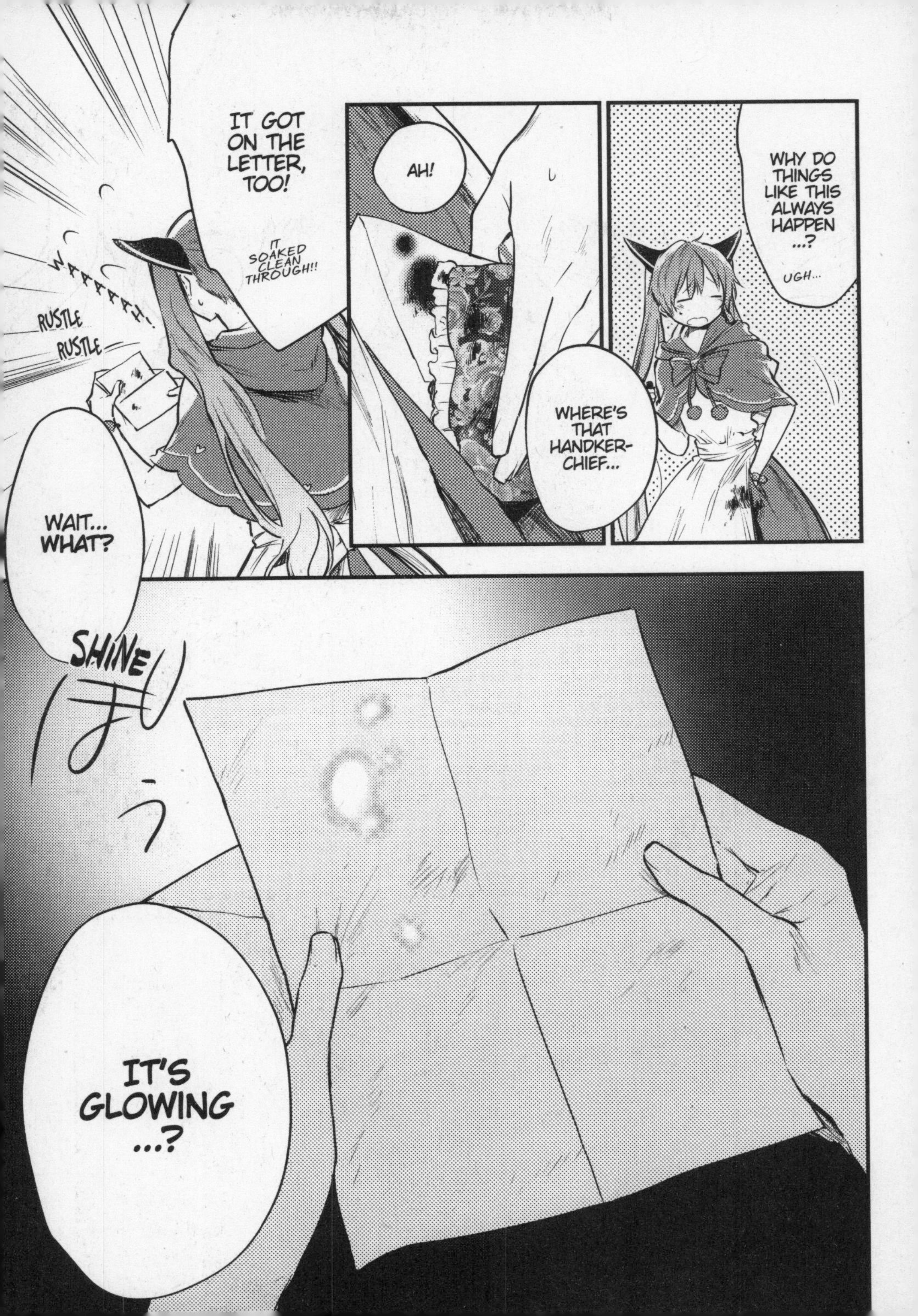
WHY DO THINGS LIKE THIS ALWAYS HAPPEN ...?
UGH...
WHERE'S THAT HANDKER-CHIEF...
AH!
IT GOT ON THE LETTER, TOO!
IT SOAKED CLEAN THROUGH!!
RUSTLE
RUSTLE
WAIT... WHAT?
SHINE
IT'S GLOWING ...?

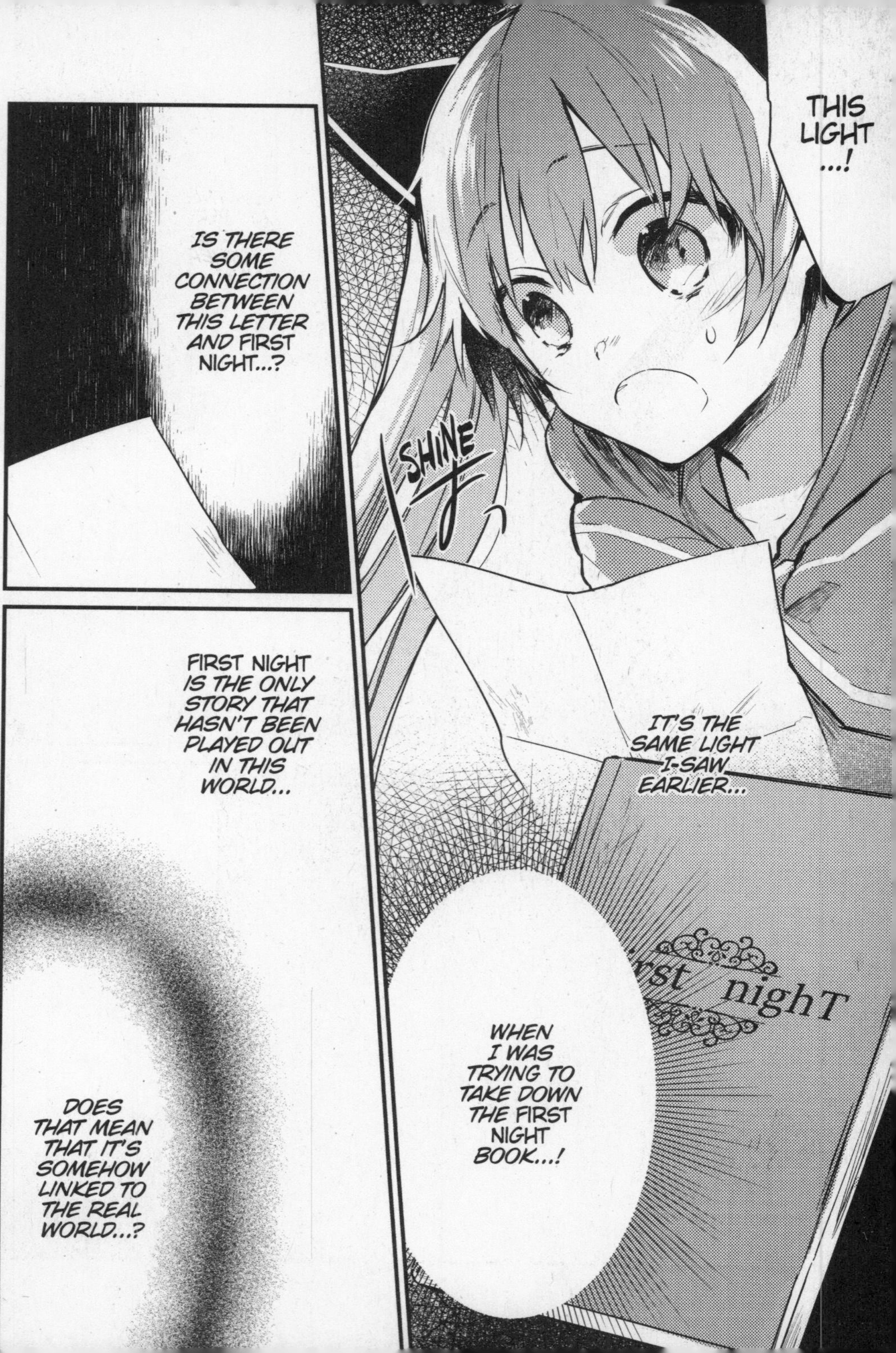
THIS LIGHT ...!
SHINE
IT'S THE SAME LIGHT I SAW EARLIER...
WHEN I WAS TRYING TO TAKE DOWN THE FIRST NIGHT BOOK...!
rst nighT
IS THERE SOME CONNECTION BETWEEN THIS LETTER AND FIRST NIGHT...?
FIRST NIGHT IS THE ONLY STORY THAT HASN'T BEEN PLAYED OUT IN THIS WORLD...
DOES THAT MEAN THAT IT'S SOMEHOW LINKED TO THE REAL WORLD...?

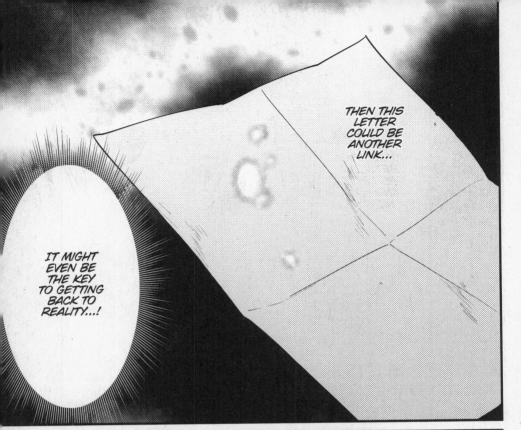

THEN THIS LETTER COULD BE ANOTHER LINK...

IT MIGHT EVEN BE THE KEY TO GETTING BACK TO REALITY...!

SLIDE...

GULP...

MAYBE I CAN USE IT TO WRITE THE "EPILOGUE" THE ENVELOPE MENTIONS ...!!

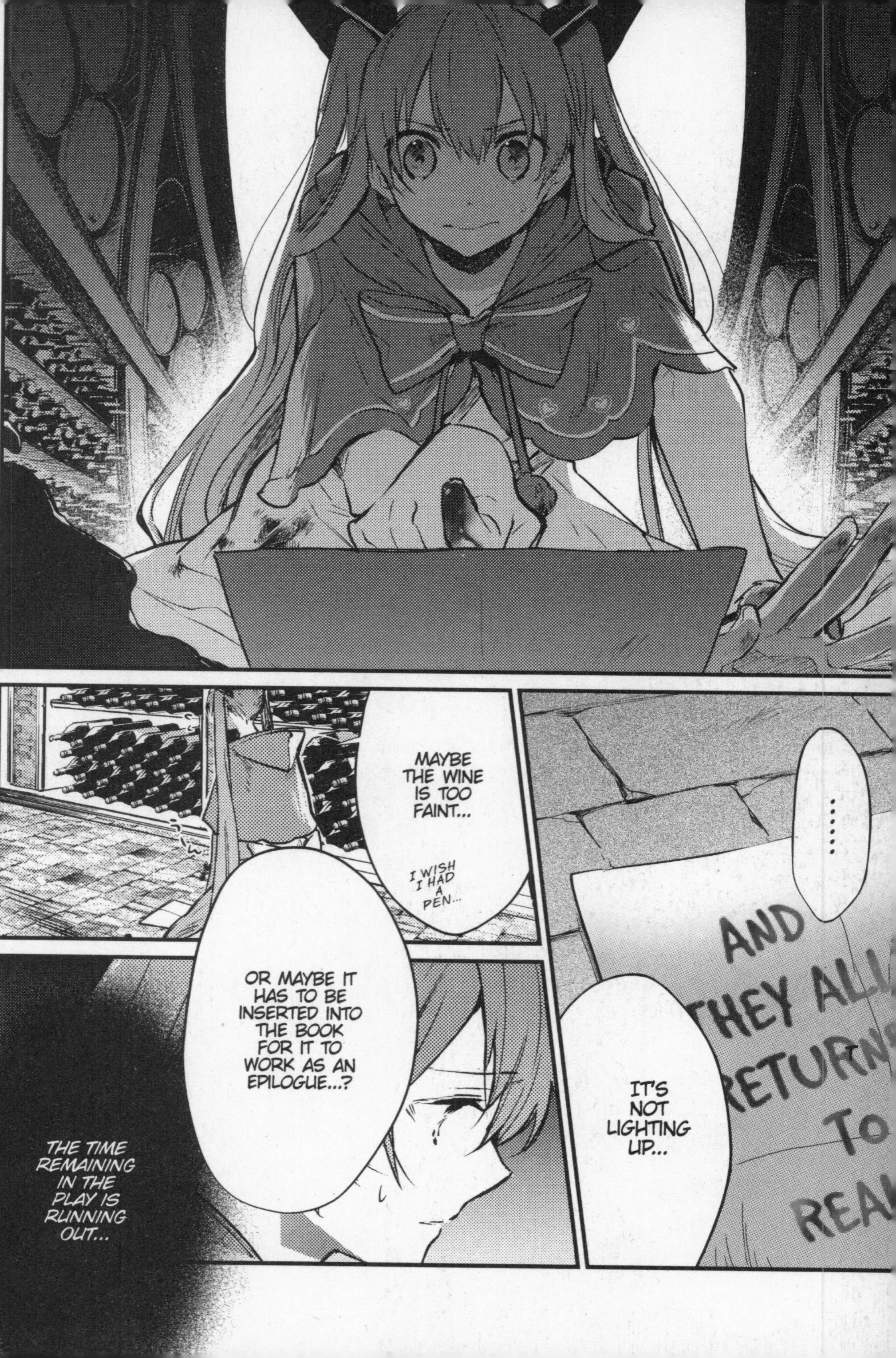
......
MAYBE THE WINE IS TOO FAINT...
I WISH I HAD A PEN...
AND THEY ALL RETURN TO REA
IT'S NOT LIGHTING UP...
OR MAYBE IT HAS TO BE INSERTED INTO THE BOOK FOR IT TO WORK AS AN EPILOGUE...?
THE TIME REMAINING IN THE PLAY IS RUNNING OUT...

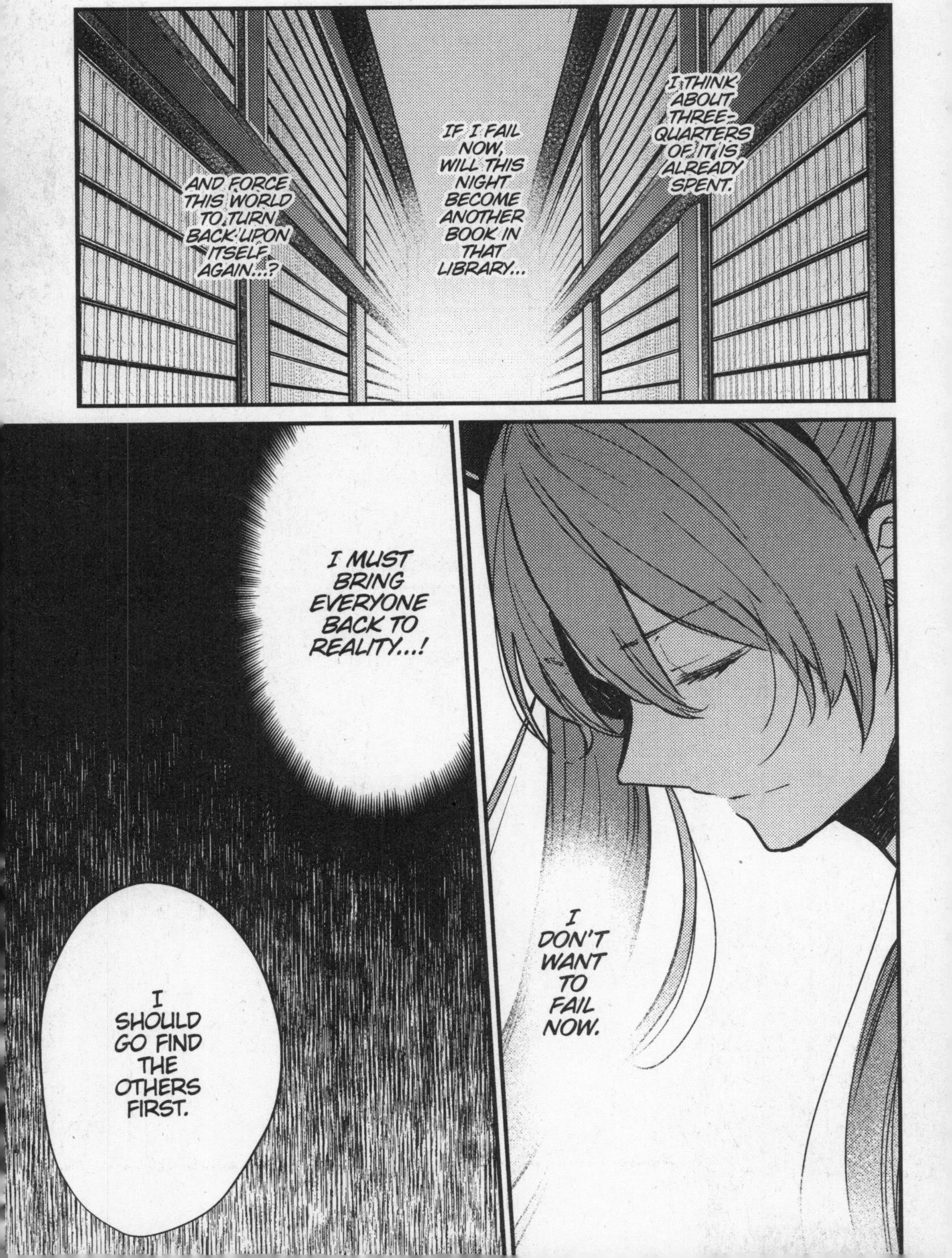
I THINK ABOUT THREE-QUARTERS OF IT IS ALREADY SPENT.
IF I FAIL NOW, WILL THIS NIGHT BECOME ANOTHER BOOK IN THAT LIBRARY...
AND FORCE THIS WORLD TO TURN BACK UPON ITSELF AGAIN...?
I DON'T WANT TO FAIL NOW.
I MUST BRING EVERYONE BACK TO REALITY...!
I SHOULD GO FIND THE OTHERS FIRST.

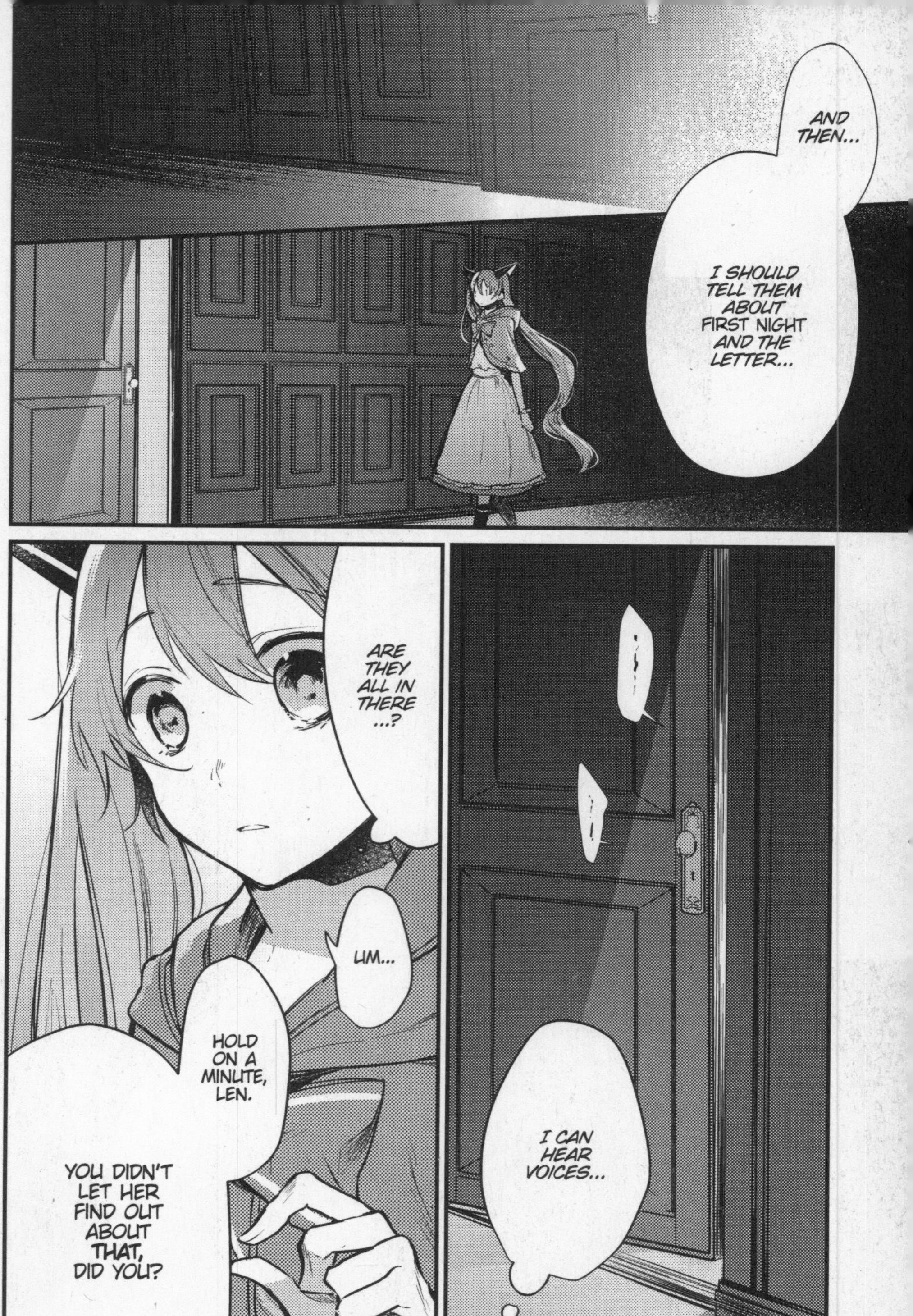
AND THEN...
I SHOULD TELL THEM ABOUT FIRST NIGHT AND THE LETTER...
I CAN HEAR VOICES...
ARE THEY ALL IN THERE ...?
UM...
HOLD ON A MINUTE, LEN.
YOU DIDN'T LET HER FIND OUT ABOUT THAT, DID YOU?

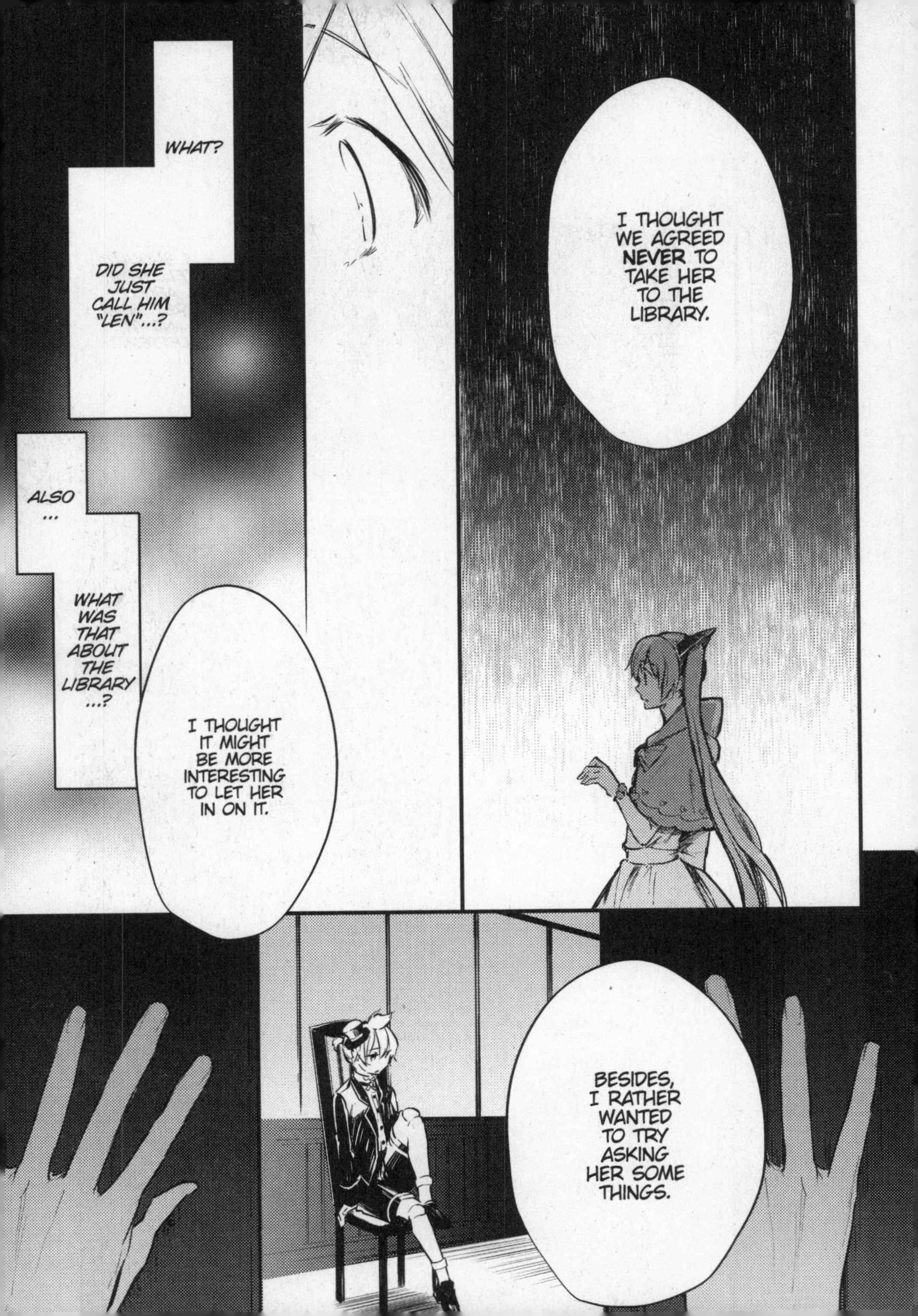
I THOUGHT WE AGREED NEVER TO TAKE HER TO THE LIBRARY.
WHAT?
DID SHE JUST CALL HIM "LEN"...?
ALSO...
WHAT WAS THAT ABOUT THE LIBRARY...?
I THOUGHT IT MIGHT BE MORE INTERESTING TO LET HER IN ON IT.
BESIDES, I RATHER WANTED TO TRY ASKING HER SOME THINGS.

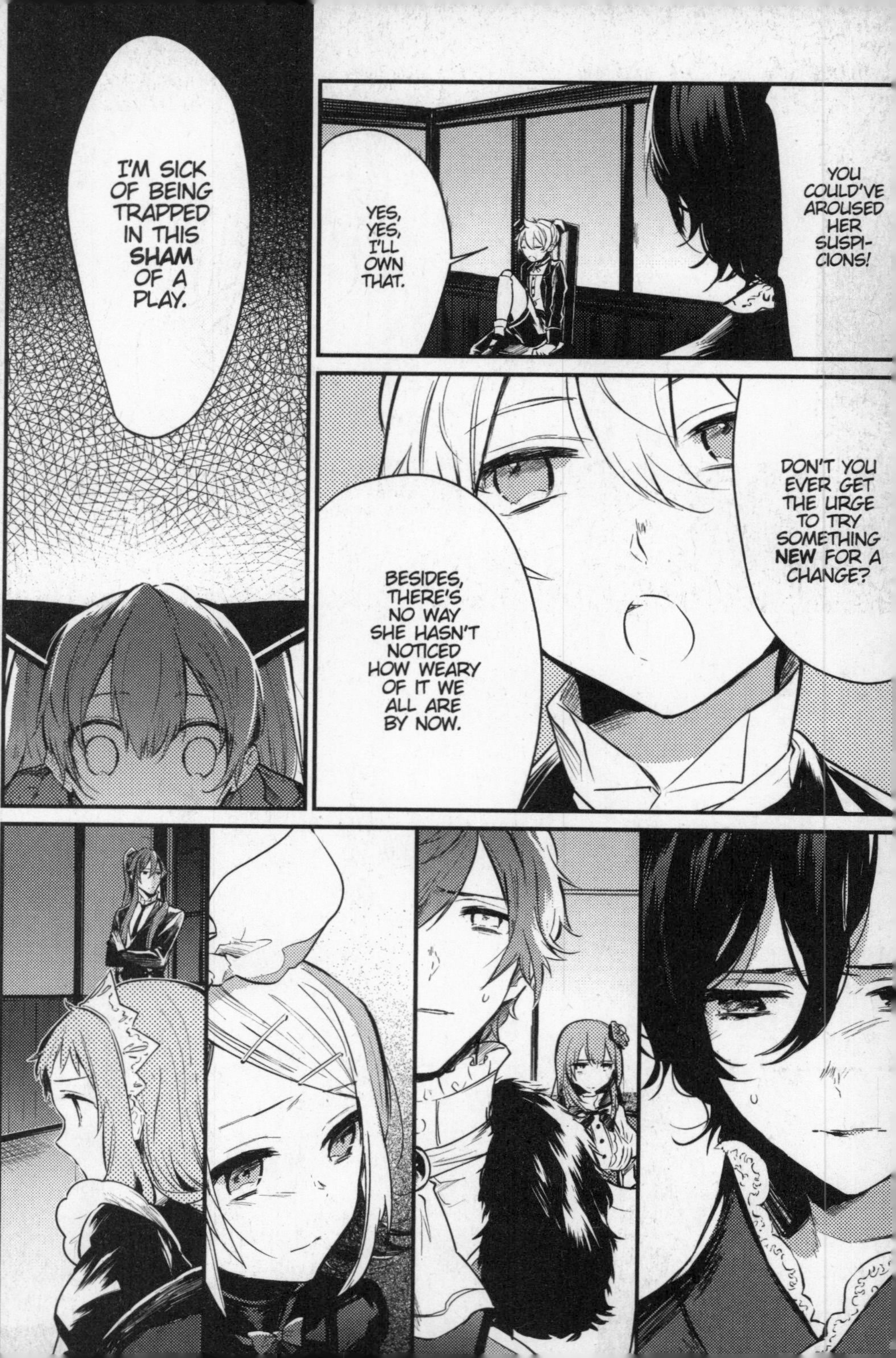
YOU COULD'VE AROUSED HER SUSPICIONS!
YES, YES, I'LL OWN THAT.
DON'T YOU EVER GET THE URGE TO TRY SOMETHING NEW FOR A CHANGE?
BESIDES, THERE'S NO WAY SHE HASN'T NOTICED HOW WEARY OF IT WE ALL ARE BY NOW.
I'M SICK OF BEING TRAPPED IN THIS SHAM OF A PLAY.

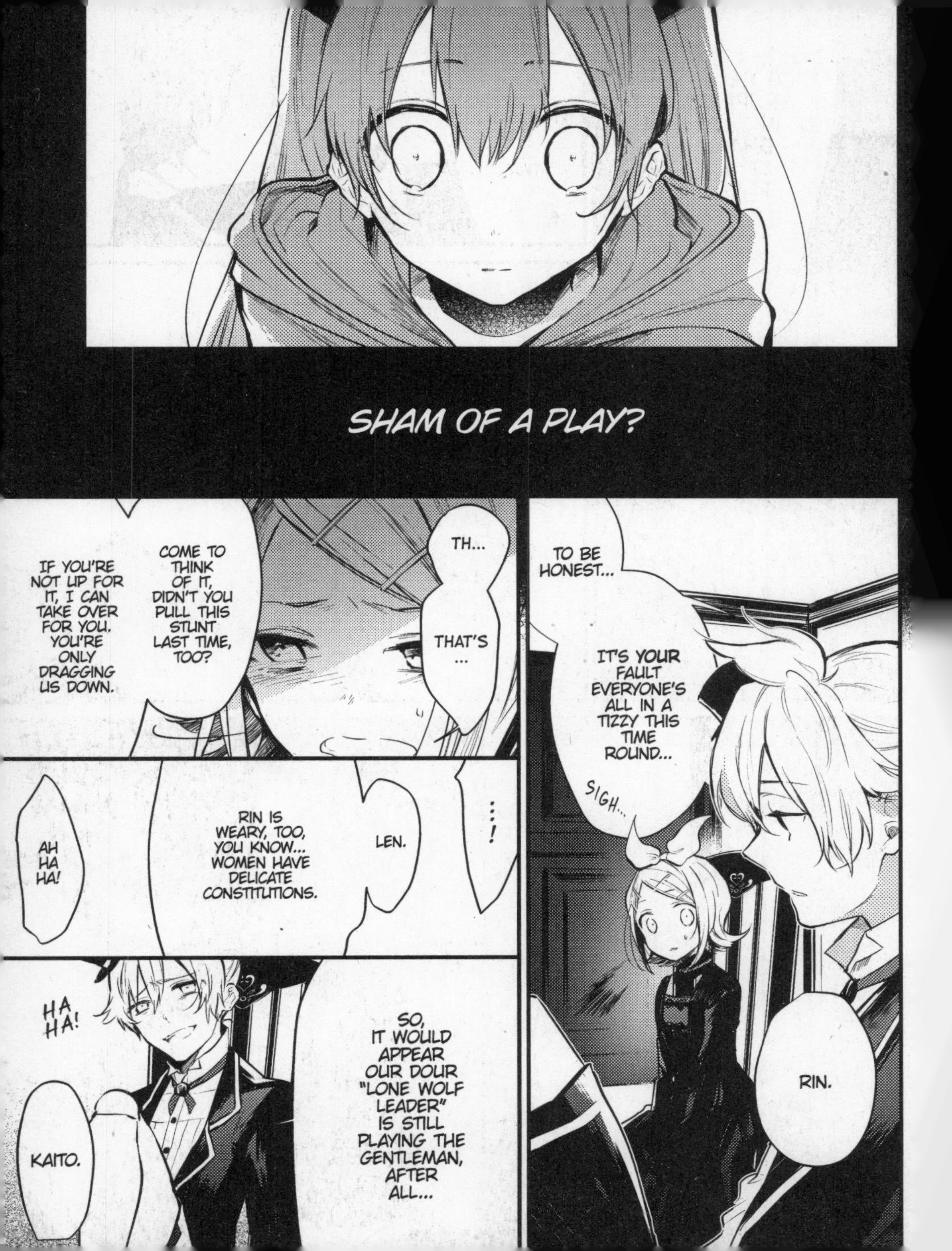
SHAM OF A PLAY?
TO BE HONEST...
IT'S YOUR FAULT EVERYONE'S ALL IN A TIZZY THIS TIME ROUND...
SIGH...
RIN.
TH...
THAT'S ...
COME TO THINK OF IT, DIDN'T YOU PULL THIS STUNT LAST TIME, TOO?
IF YOU'RE NOT UP FOR IT, I CAN TAKE OVER FOR YOU. YOU'RE ONLY DRAGGING US DOWN.
...!
LEN.
RIN IS WEARY, TOO, YOU KNOW... WOMEN HAVE DELICATE CONSTITUTIONS.
AH HA HA!
SO, IT WOULD APPEAR OUR DOUR "LONE WOLF LEADER" IS STILL PLAYING THE GENTLEMAN, AFTER ALL...
HA HA!
KAITO.

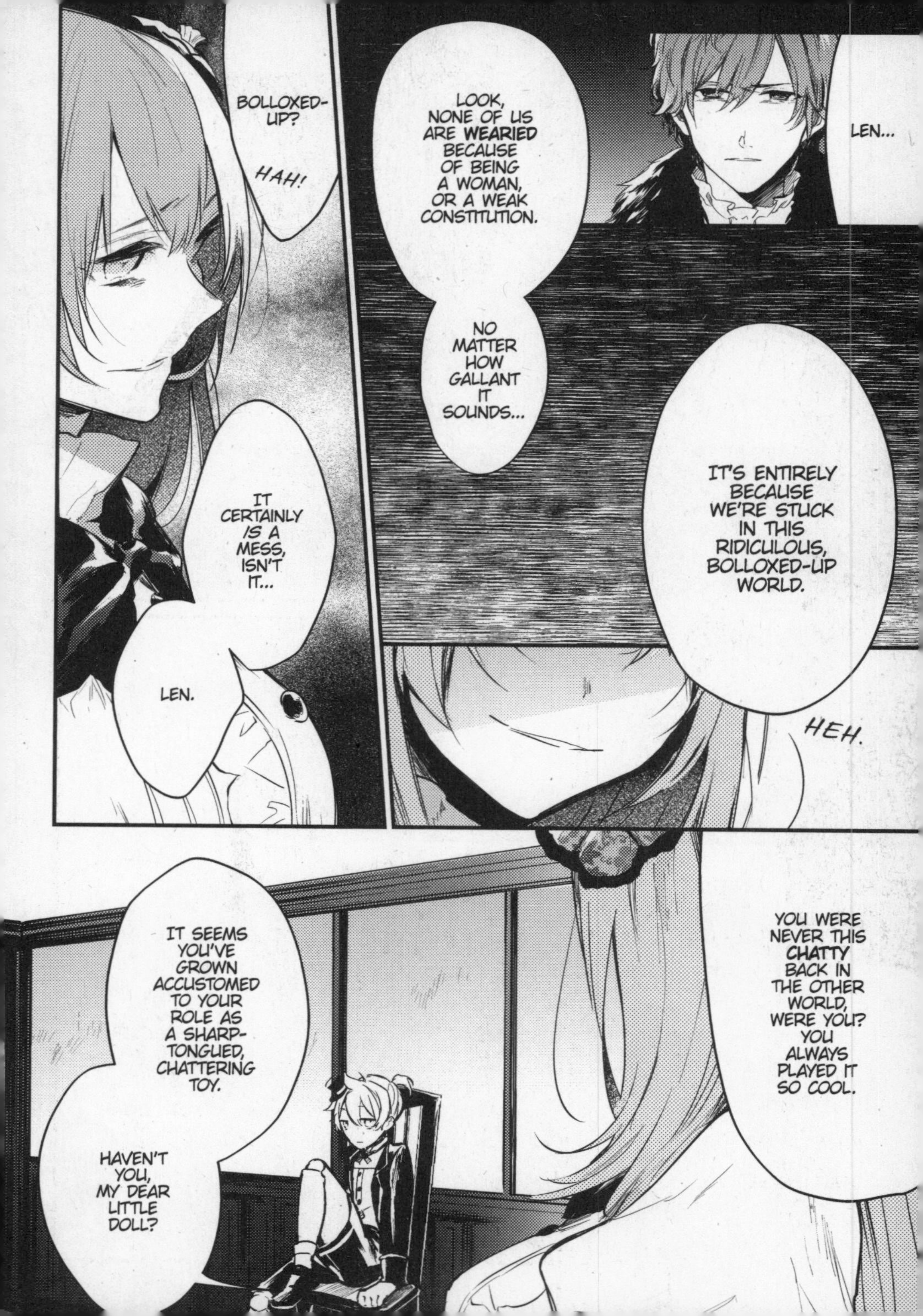
LEN...
LOOK, NONE OF US ARE WEARIED BECAUSE OF BEING A WOMAN, OR A WEAK CONSTITUTION.
NO MATTER HOW GALLANT IT SOUNDS...
IT'S ENTIRELY BECAUSE WE'RE STUCK IN THIS RIDICULOUS, BOLLOXED-UP WORLD.
HEH.
BOLLOXED-UP?
HAH!
IT CERTAINLY IS A MESS, ISN'T IT...
LEN.
YOU WERE NEVER THIS CHATTY BACK IN THE OTHER WORLD, WERE YOU? YOU ALWAYS PLAYED IT SO COOL.
IT SEEMS YOU'VE GROWN ACCUSTOMED TO YOUR ROLE AS A SHARP-TONGUED, CHATTERING TOY.
HAVEN'T YOU, MY DEAR LITTLE DOLL?

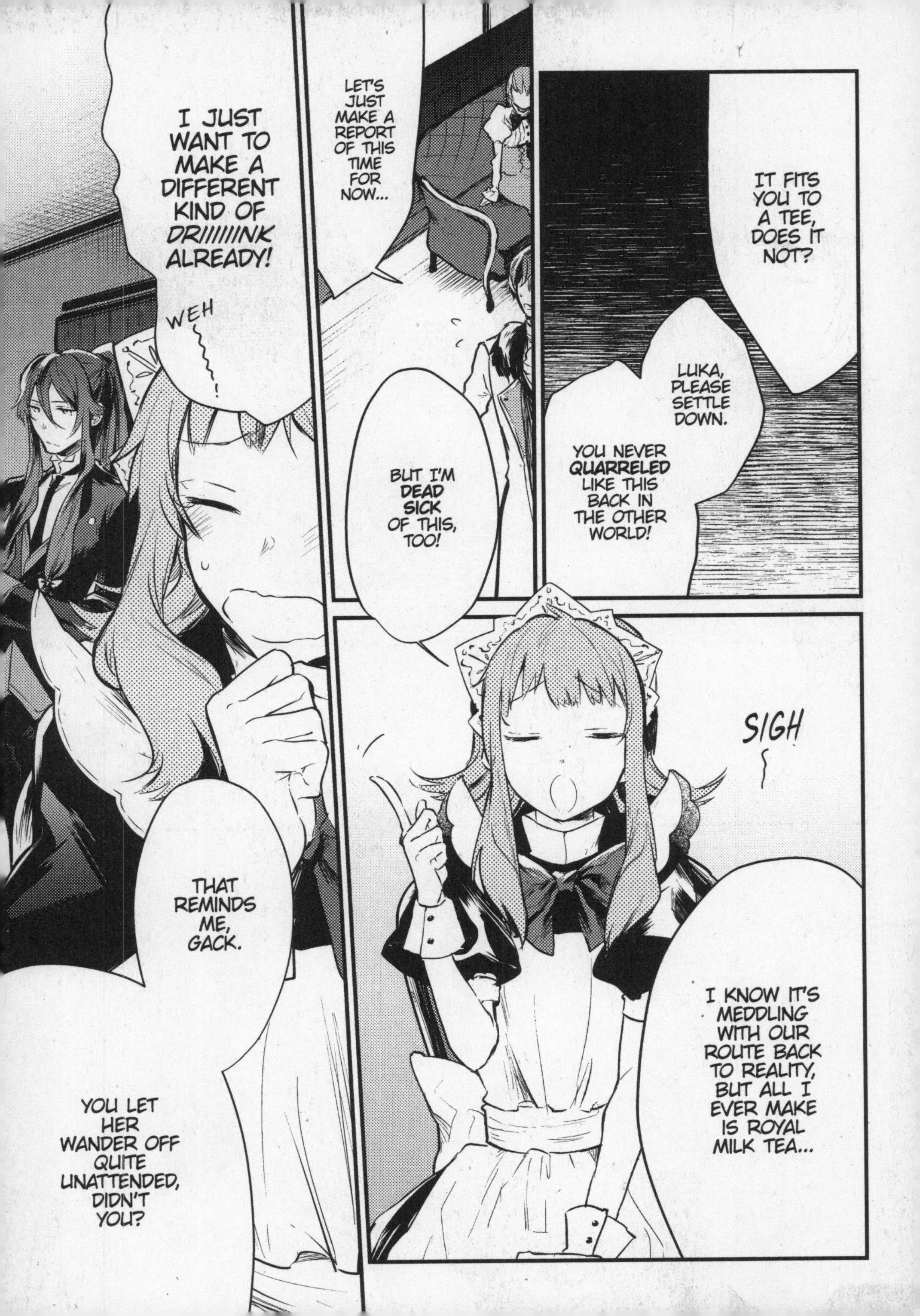
IT FITS YOU TO A TEE, DOES IT NOT?
LUKA, PLEASE SETTLE DOWN.
YOU NEVER QUARRELED LIKE THIS BACK IN THE OTHER WORLD!
LET'S JUST MAKE A REPORT OF THIS TIME FOR NOW...
BUT I'M DEAD SICK OF THIS, TOO!
SIGH
I KNOW IT'S MEDDLING WITH OUR ROUTE BACK TO REALITY, BUT ALL I EVER MAKE IS ROYAL MILK TEA...
I JUST WANT TO MAKE A DIFFERENT KIND OF DRIIIIIIINK ALREADY!
WEH
THAT REMINDS ME, GACK.
YOU LET HER WANDER OFF QUITE UNATTENDED, DIDN'T YOU?

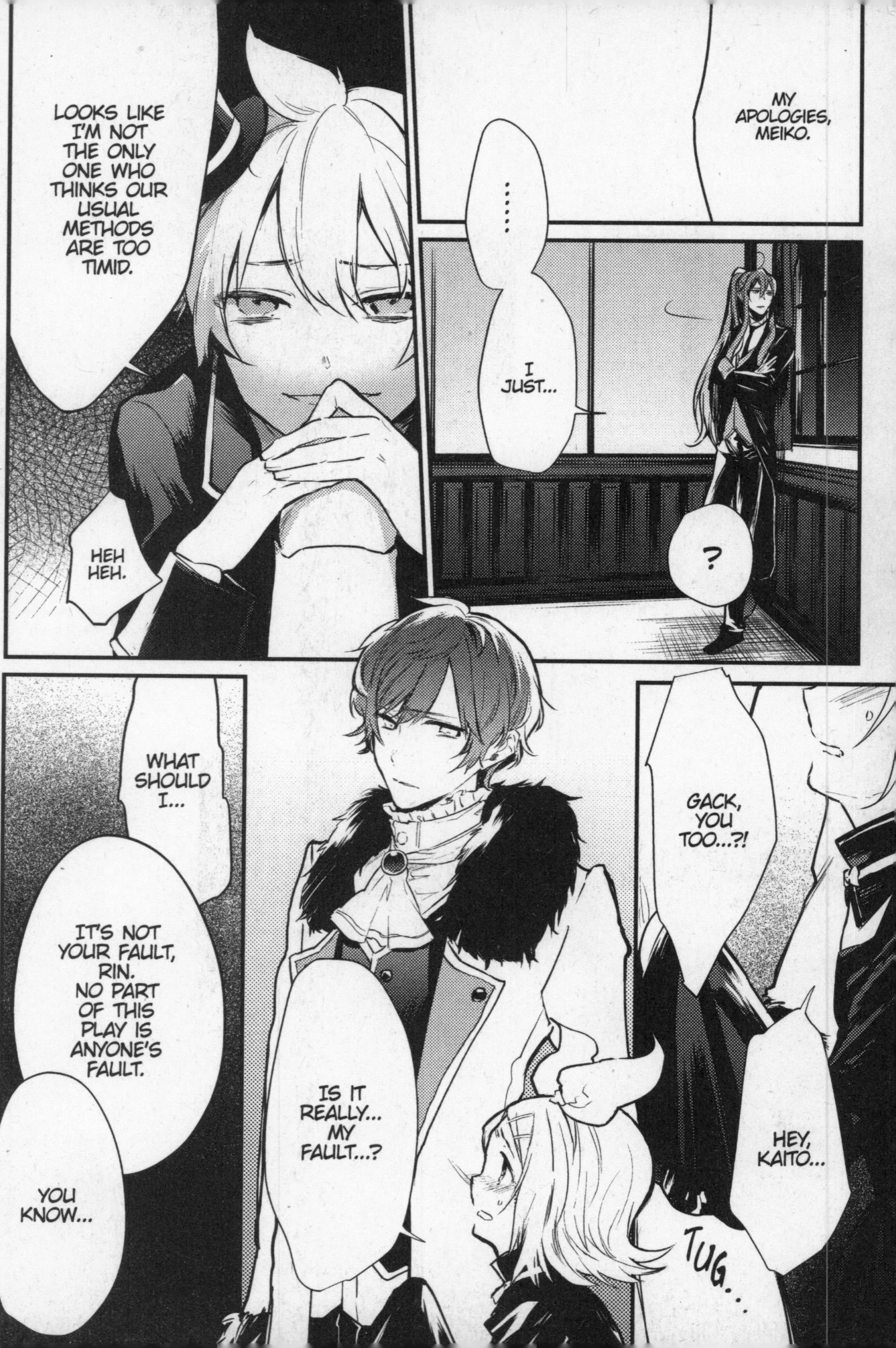

MY APOLOGIES, MEIKO.
......
I JUST...
?
LOOKS LIKE I'M NOT THE ONLY ONE WHO THINKS OUR USUAL METHODS ARE TOO TIMID.
HEH HEH.
GACK, YOU TOO...?!
HEY, KAITO...
TUG...
IS IT REALLY... MY FAULT...?
WHAT SHOULD I...
IT'S NOT YOUR FAULT, RIN. NO PART OF THIS PLAY IS ANYONE'S FAULT.
YOU KNOW...

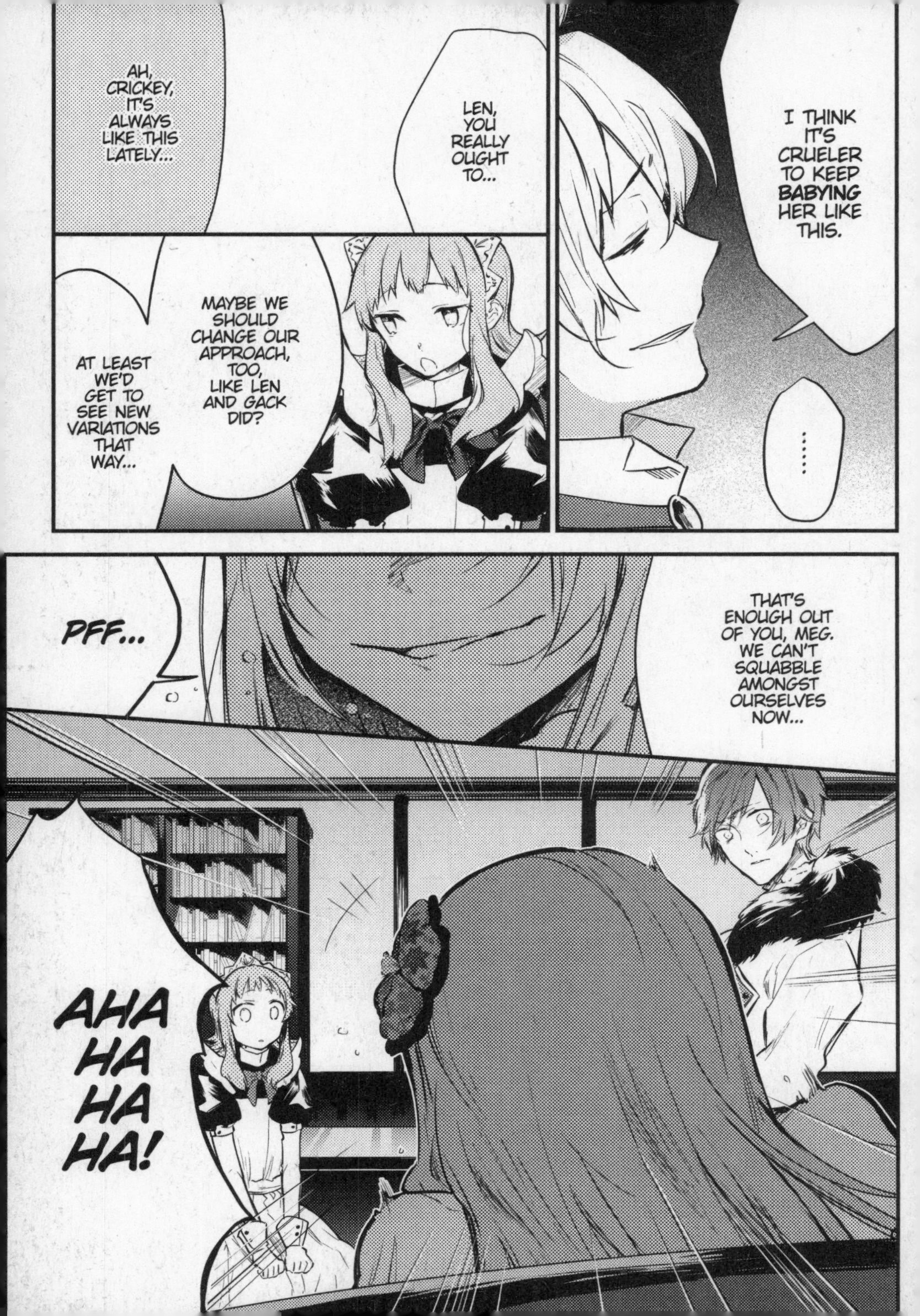
I THINK IT'S CRUELER TO KEEP BABYING HER LIKE THIS.
......
LEN, YOU REALLY OUGHT TO...
AH, CRICKEY, IT'S ALWAYS LIKE THIS LATELY...
MAYBE WE SHOULD CHANGE OUR APPROACH, TOO, LIKE LEN AND GACK DID?
AT LEAST WE'D GET TO SEE NEW VARIATIONS THAT WAY...
THAT'S ENOUGH OUT OF YOU, MEG. WE CAN'T SQUABBLE AMONGST OURSELVES NOW...
PFF...
AHA HA HA HA HA!

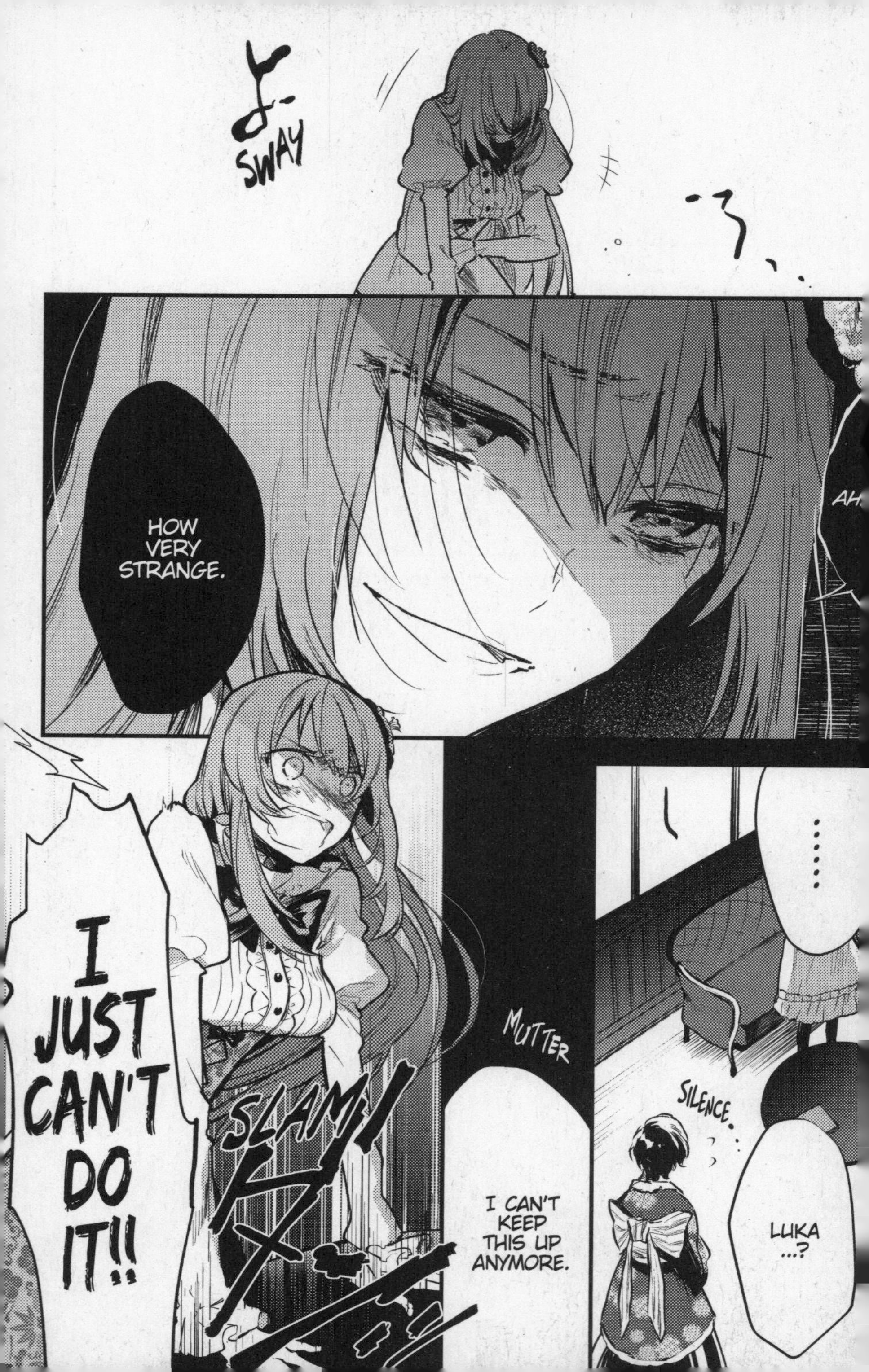
SWAY
AH
HOW VERY STRANGE.
......
SILENCE.
LUKA ...?
MUTTER
I CAN'T KEEP THIS UP ANYMORE.
I JUST CAN'T DO IT!!
SLAM!

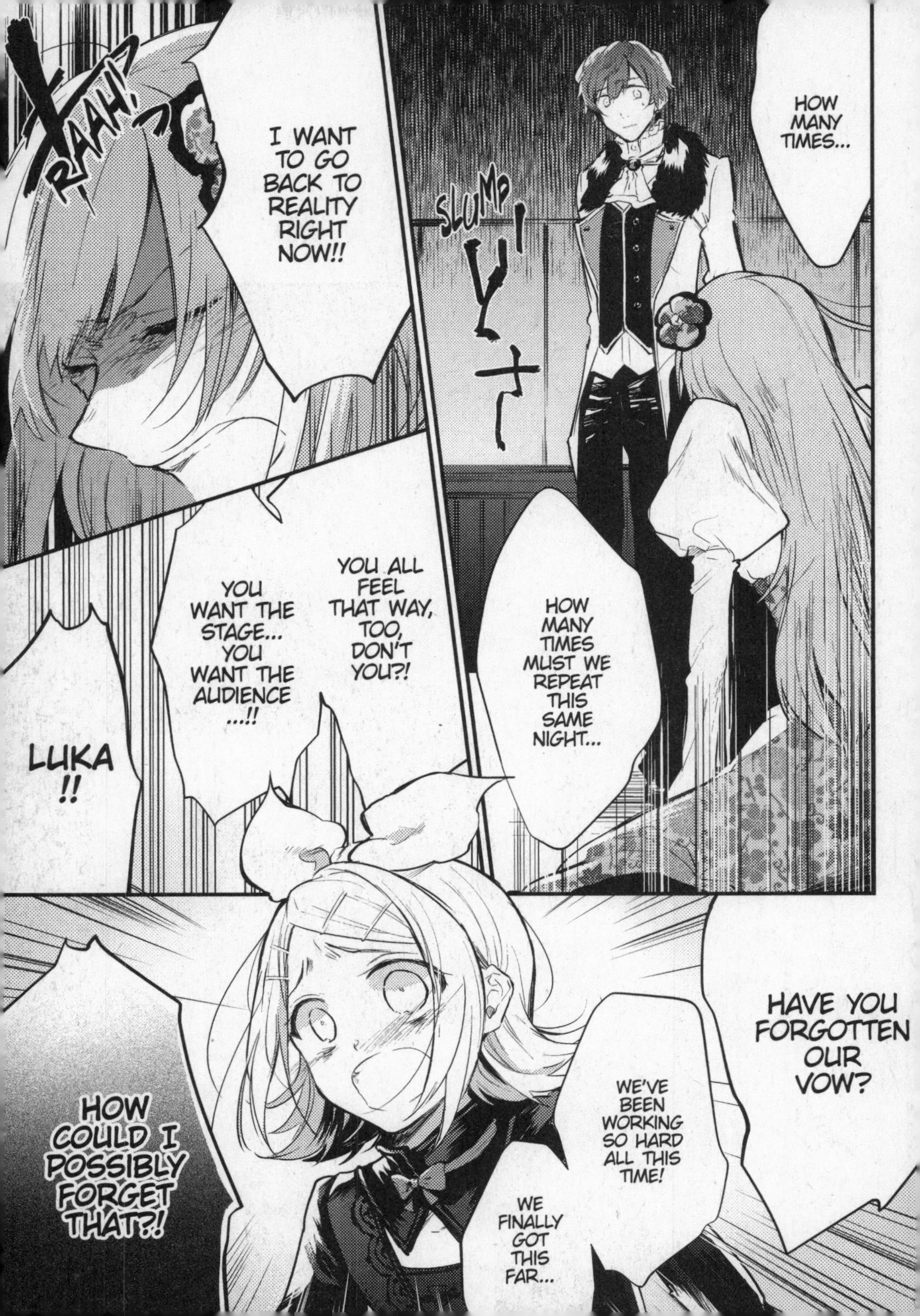
HOW MANY TIMES...
SLUMP
HOW MANY TIMES MUST WE REPEAT THIS SAME NIGHT...
I WANT TO GO BACK TO REALITY RIGHT NOW!!
YOU ALL FEEL THAT WAY, TOO, DON'T YOU?!
YOU WANT THE STAGE... YOU WANT THE AUDIENCE ...!!
LUKA !!
HAVE YOU FORGOTTEN OUR VOW?
WE'VE BEEN WORKING SO HARD ALL THIS TIME!
WE FINALLY GOT THIS FAR...
HOW COULD I POSSIBLY FORGET THAT?!

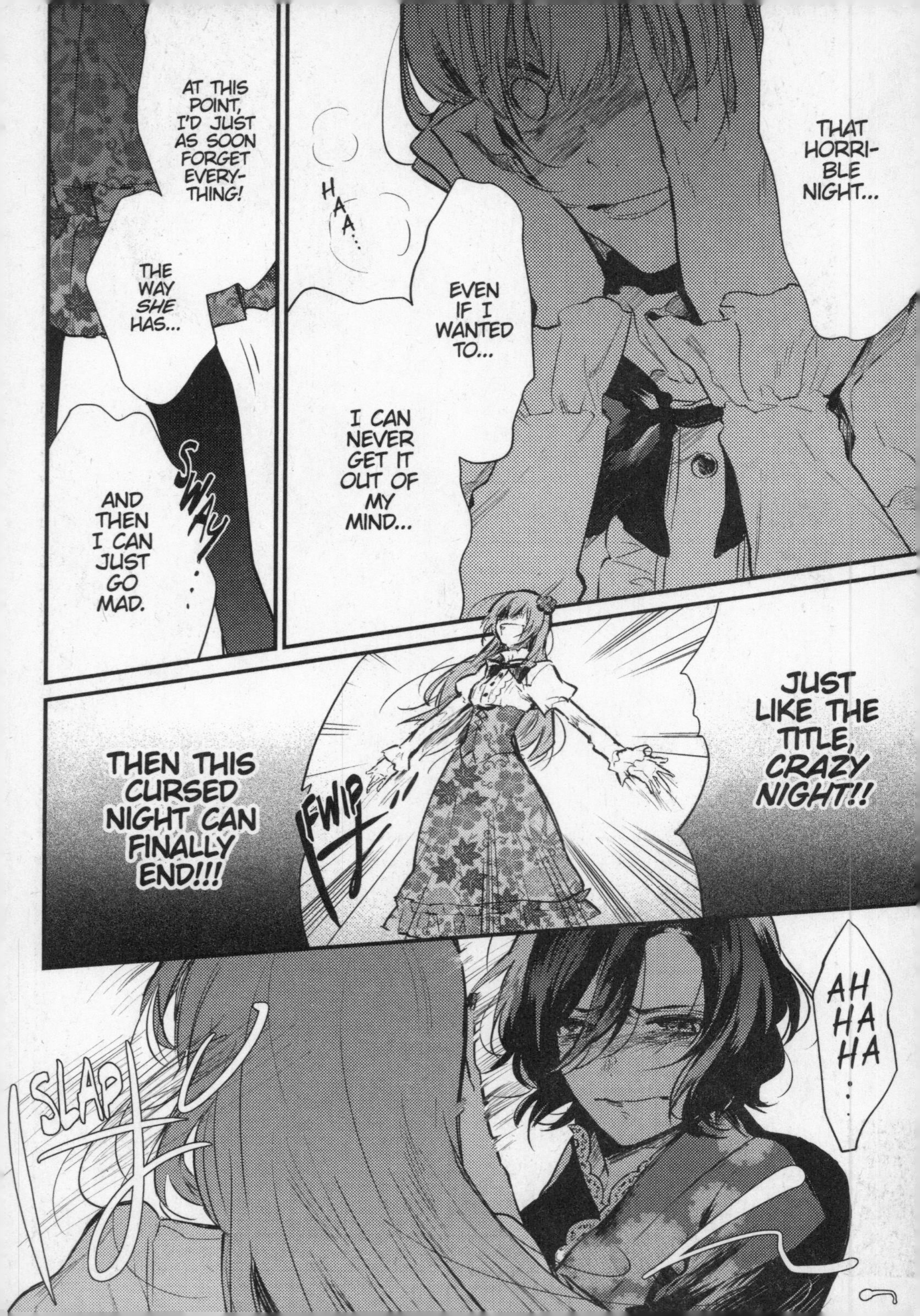
THAT HORRIBLE NIGHT...
HAA...
EVEN IF I WANTED TO...
I CAN NEVER GET IT OUT OF MY MIND...
AT THIS POINT, I'D JUST AS SOON FORGET EVERYTHING!
THE WAY SHE HAS...
SWAY...
AND THEN I CAN JUST GO MAD.
JUST LIKE THE TITLE, CRAZY NIGHT!!
FWIP
THEN THIS CURSED NIGHT CAN FINALLY END!!!
AH HA HA HA...
SLAP

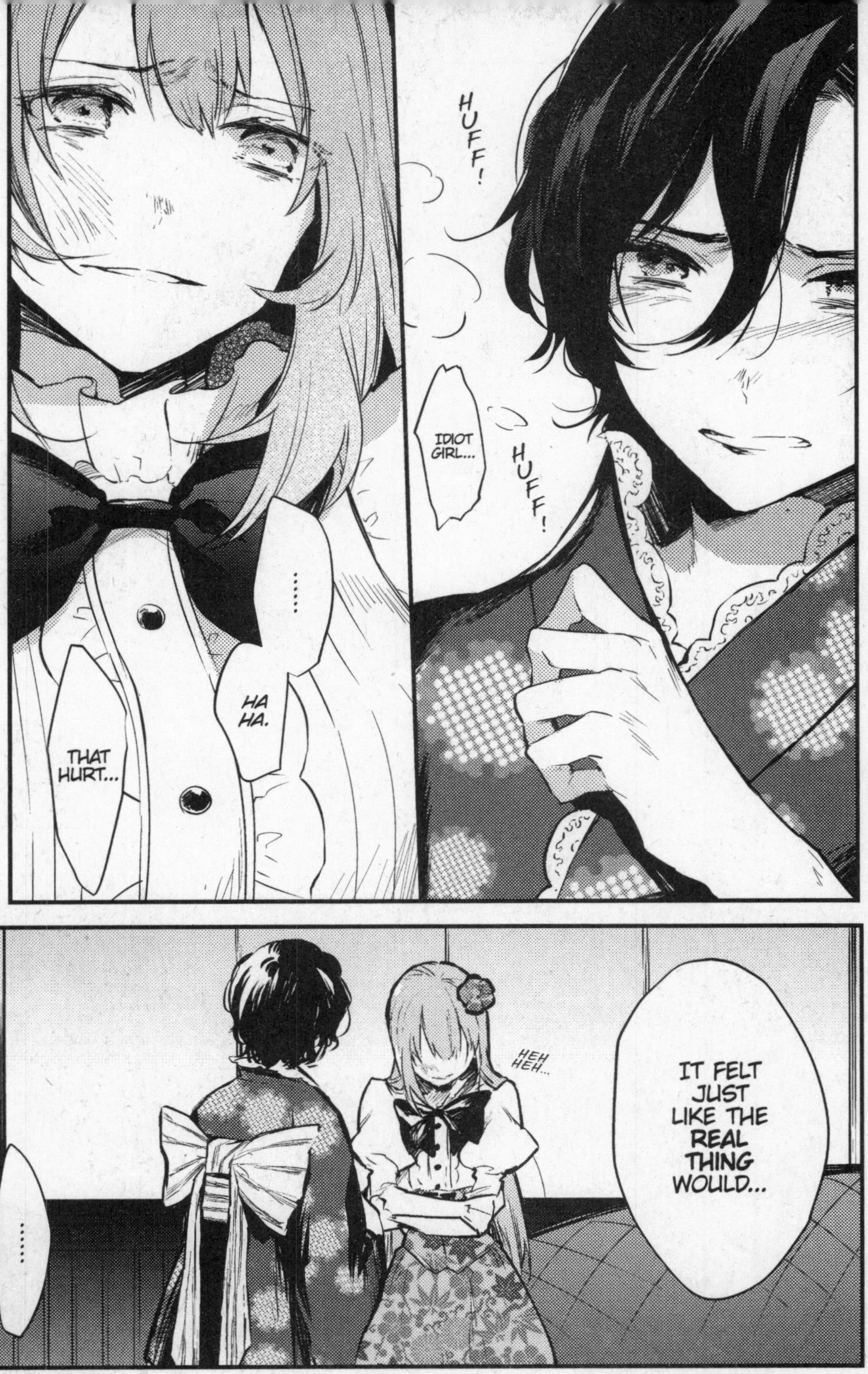
HUFF!
HUFF!
IDIOT GIRL...
......
HA HA.
THAT HURT...
IT FELT JUST LIKE THE REAL THING WOULD...
HEH HEH...
......

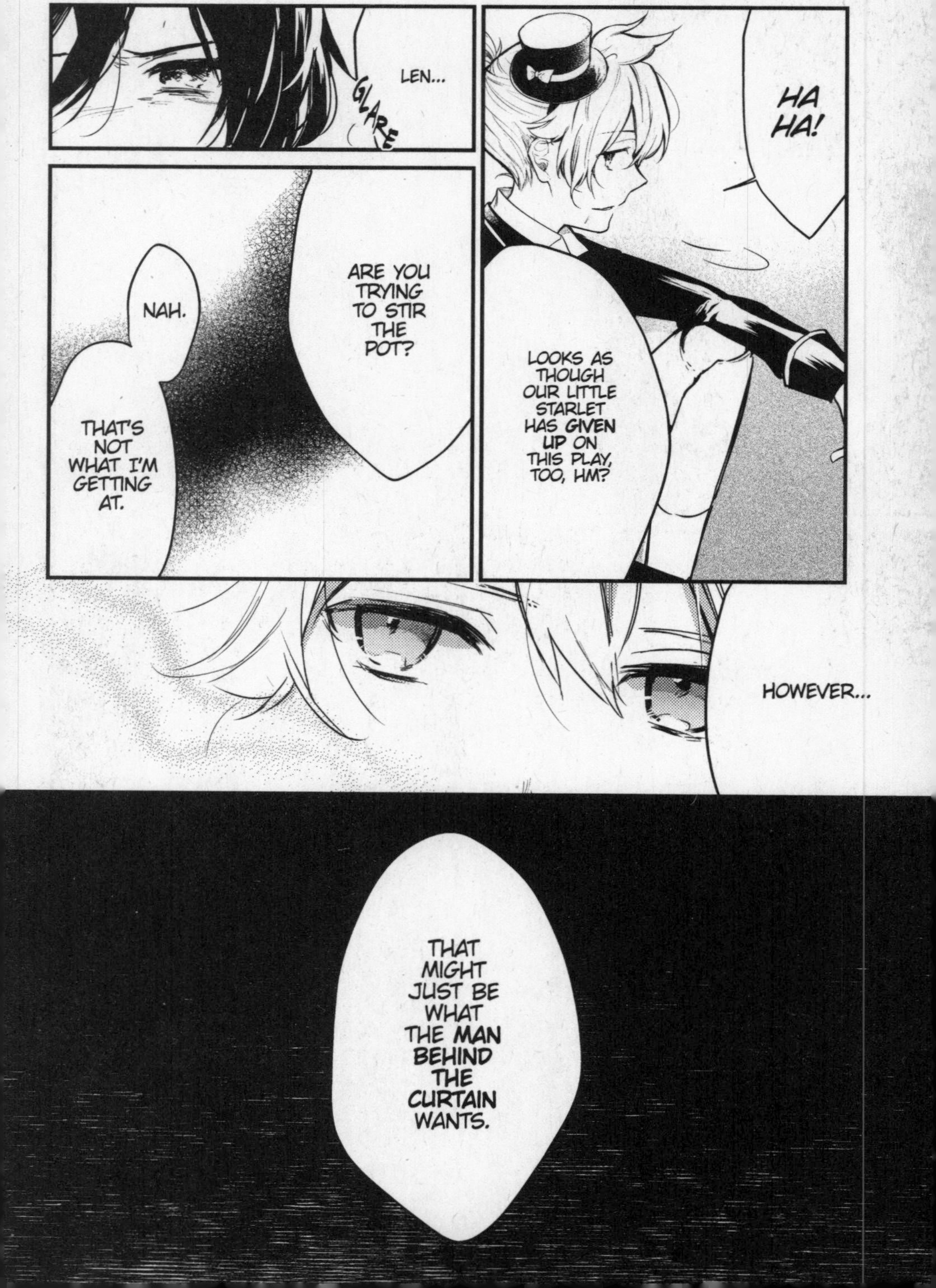
HA HA!
LOOKS AS THOUGH OUR LITTLE STARLET HAS GIVEN UP ON THIS PLAY, TOO, HM?
LEN...
GLARE
ARE YOU TRYING TO STIR THE POT?
NAH.
THAT'S NOT WHAT I'M GETTING AT.
HOWEVER...
THAT MIGHT JUST BE WHAT THE MAN BEHIND THE CURTAIN WANTS.

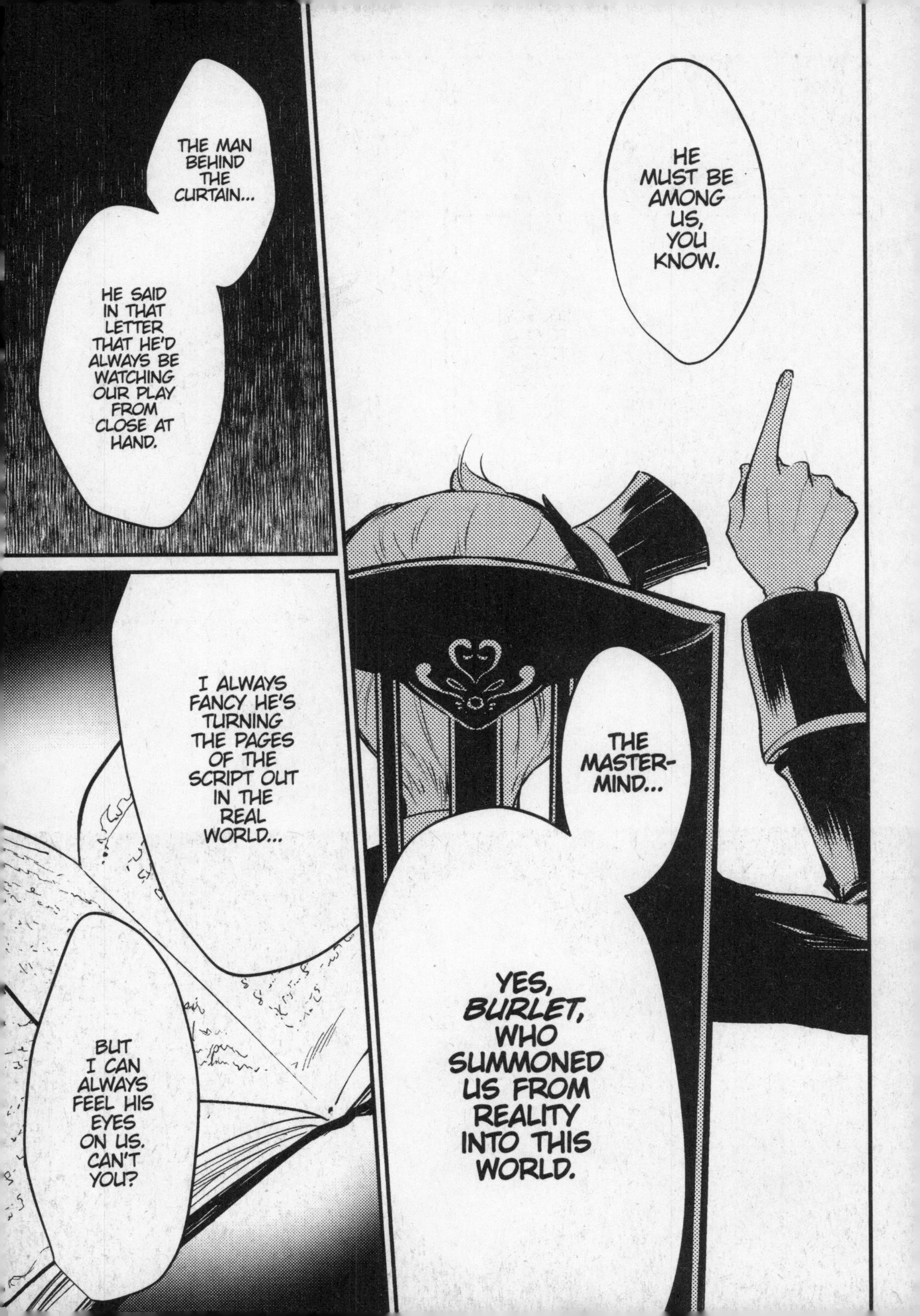
HE MUST BE AMONG US, YOU KNOW.
THE MASTER-MIND...
YES, *BURLET*, WHO SUMMONED US FROM REALITY INTO THIS WORLD.
THE MAN BEHIND THE CURTAIN...
HE SAID IN THAT LETTER THAT HE'D ALWAYS BE WATCHING OUR PLAY FROM CLOSE AT HAND.
I ALWAYS FANCY HE'S TURNING THE PAGES OF THE SCRIPT OUT IN THE REAL WORLD...
BUT I CAN ALWAYS FEEL HIS EYES ON US. CAN'T YOU?

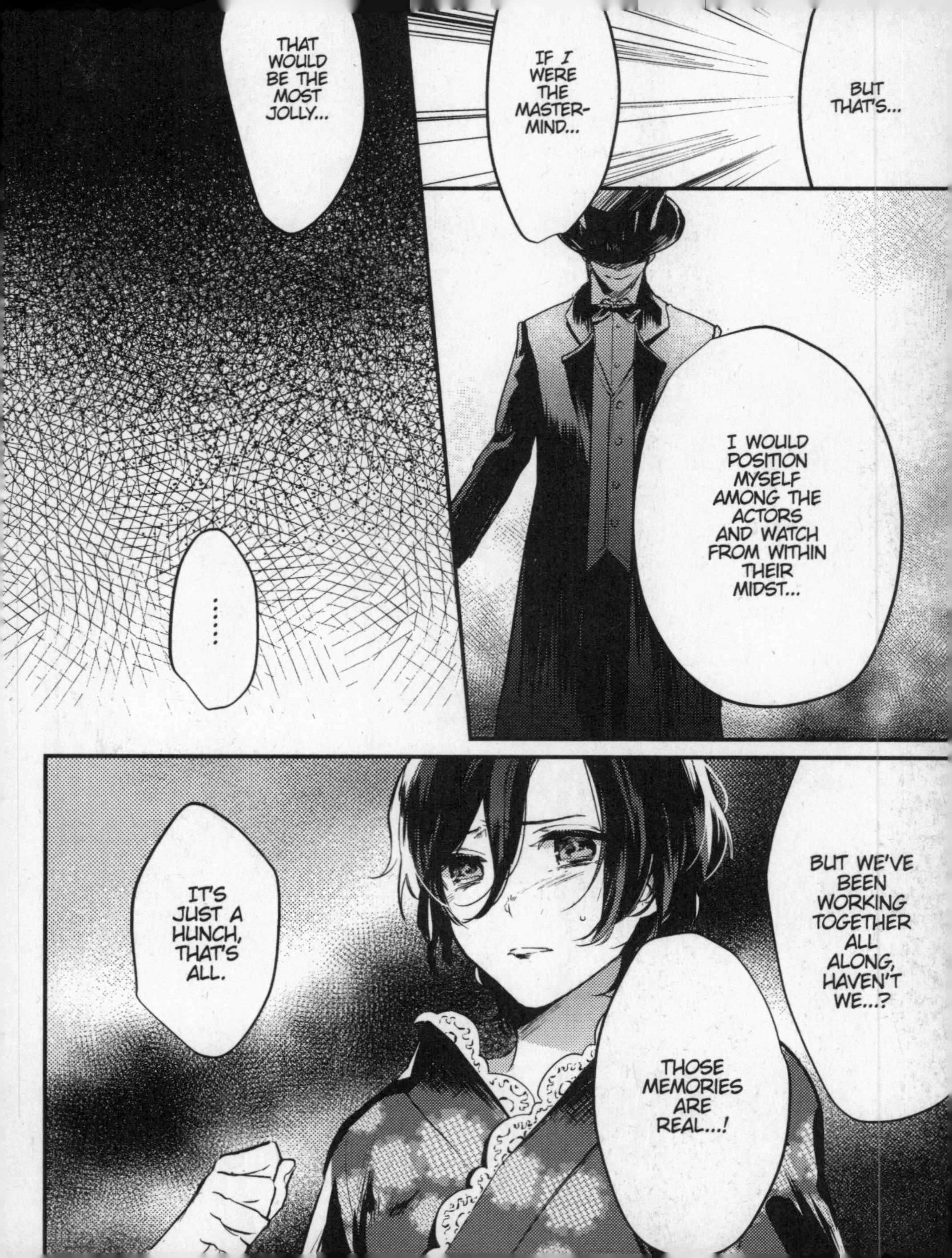
BUT THAT'S...
IF I WERE THE MASTER-MIND...
I WOULD POSITION MYSELF AMONG THE ACTORS AND WATCH FROM WITHIN THEIR MIDST...
THAT WOULD BE THE MOST JOLLY...
......
BUT WE'VE BEEN WORKING TOGETHER ALL ALONG, HAVEN'T WE...?
THOSE MEMORIES ARE REAL...!
IT'S JUST A HUNCH, THAT'S ALL.

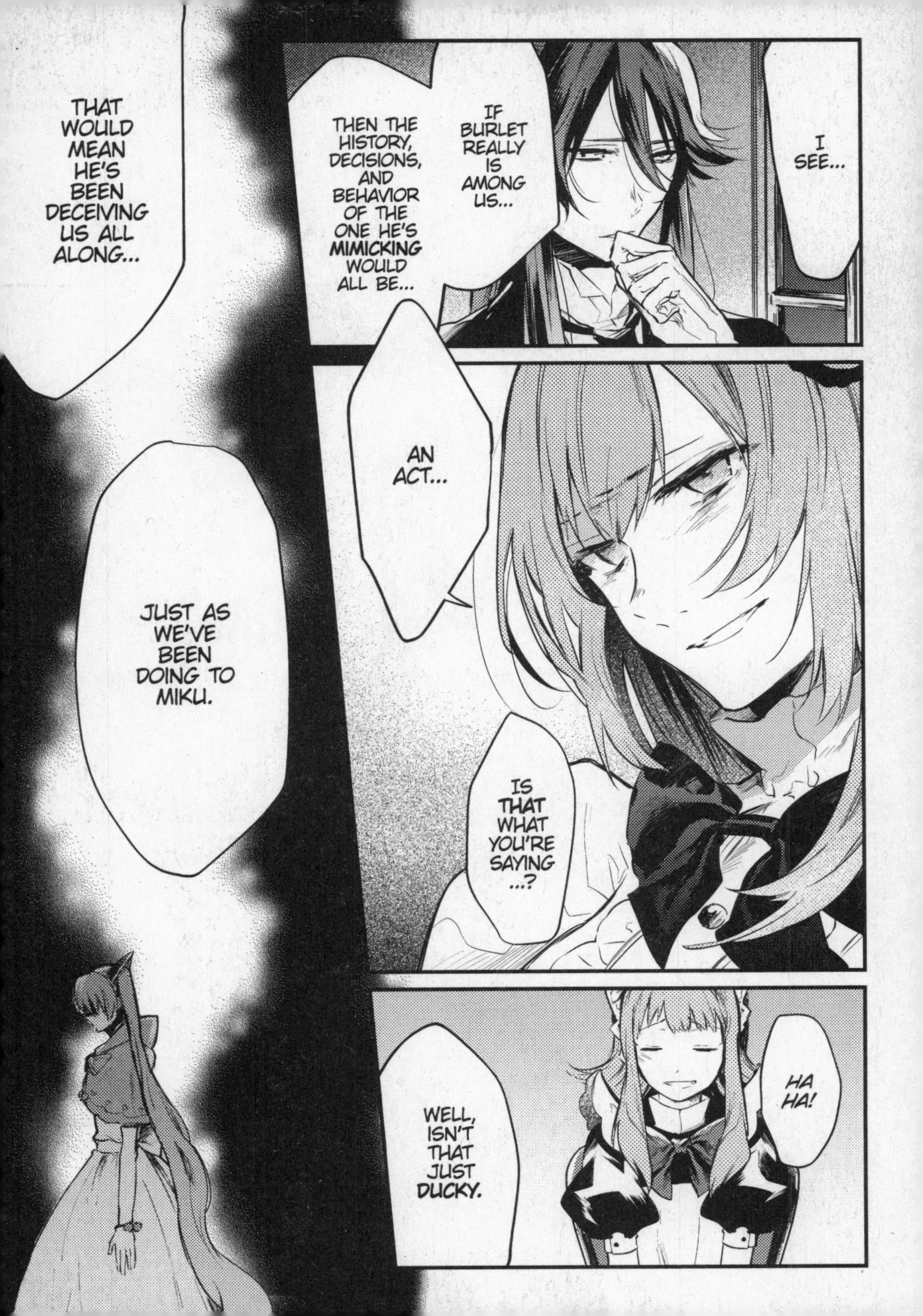
I SEE...
IF BURLET REALLY IS AMONG US...
THEN THE HISTORY, DECISIONS, AND BEHAVIOR OF THE ONE HE'S MIMICKING WOULD ALL BE...
AN ACT...
IS THAT WHAT YOU'RE SAYING ...?
HA HA!
WELL, ISN'T THAT JUST DUCKY.
THAT WOULD MEAN HE'S BEEN DECEIVING US ALL ALONG...
JUST AS WE'VE BEEN DOING TO MIKU.

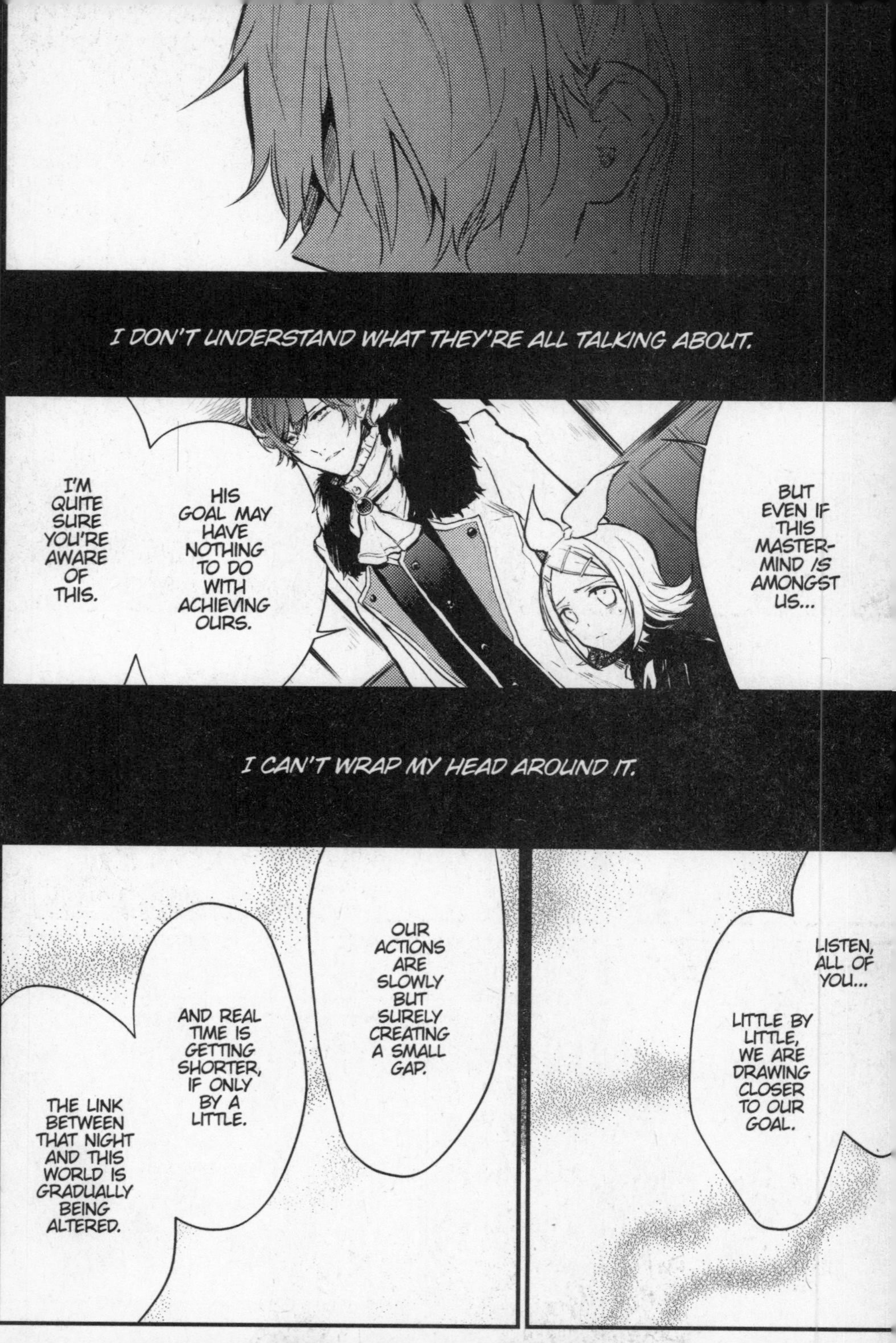
I DON'T UNDERSTAND WHAT THEY'RE ALL TALKING ABOUT.
BUT EVEN IF THIS MASTERMIND IS AMONGST US...
HIS GOAL MAY HAVE NOTHING TO DO WITH ACHIEVING OURS.
I'M QUITE SURE YOU'RE AWARE OF THIS.
I CAN'T WRAP MY HEAD AROUND IT.
LISTEN, ALL OF YOU...
LITTLE BY LITTLE, WE ARE DRAWING CLOSER TO OUR GOAL.
OUR ACTIONS ARE SLOWLY BUT SURELY CREATING A SMALL GAP.
AND REAL TIME IS GETTING SHORTER, IF ONLY BY A LITTLE.
THE LINK BETWEEN THAT NIGHT AND THIS WORLD IS GRADUALLY BEING ALTERED.

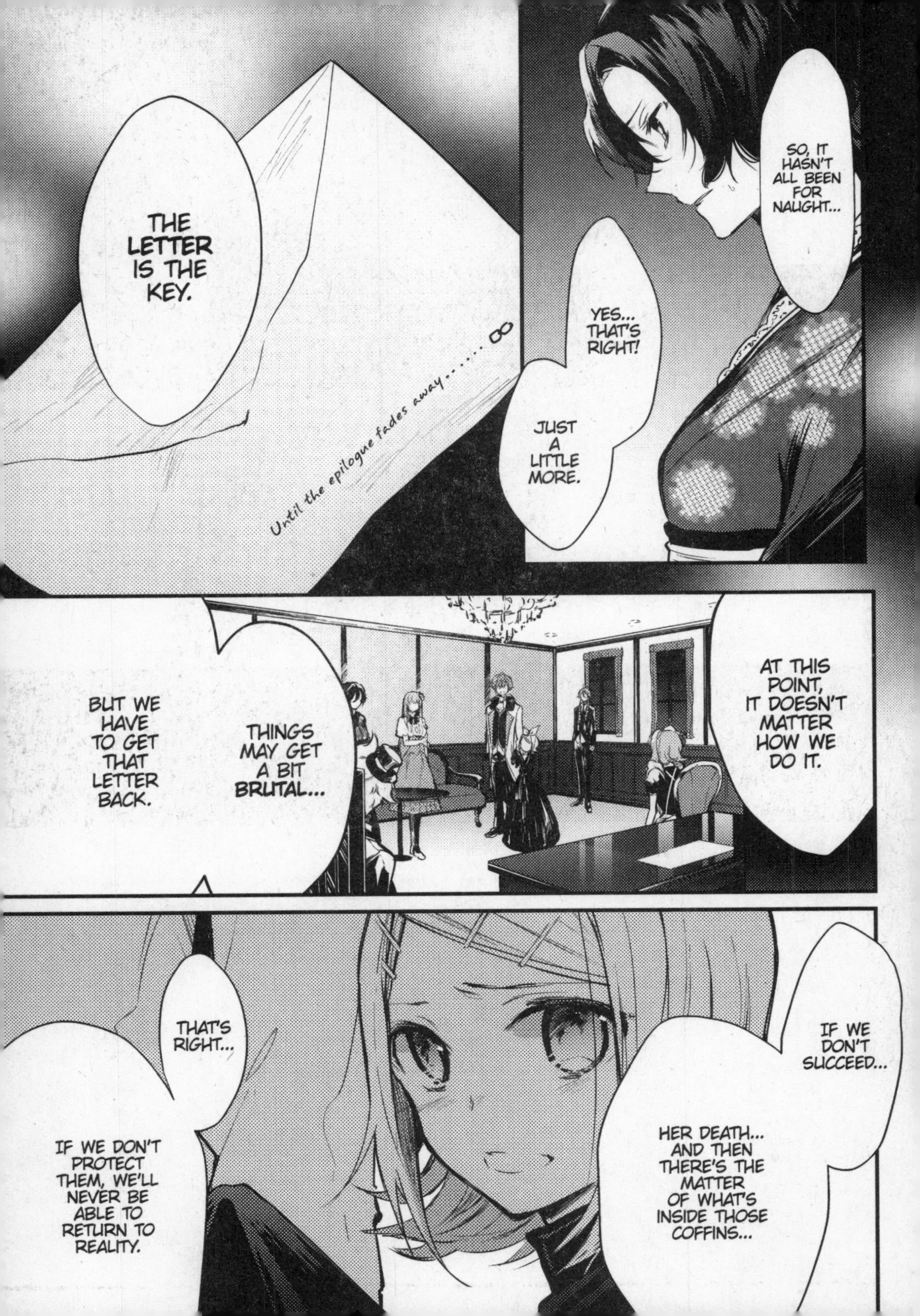
SO, IT HASN'T ALL BEEN FOR NAUGHT...
YES... THAT'S RIGHT!
JUST A LITTLE MORE.
THE LETTER IS THE KEY.
Until the epilogue fades away......∞
AT THIS POINT, IT DOESN'T MATTER HOW WE DO IT.
THINGS MAY GET A BIT BRUTAL...
BUT WE HAVE TO GET THAT LETTER BACK.
IF WE DON'T SUCCEED...
HER DEATH... AND THEN THERE'S THE MATTER OF WHAT'S INSIDE THOSE COFFINS...
THAT'S RIGHT...
IF WE DON'T PROTECT THEM, WE'LL NEVER BE ABLE TO RETURN TO REALITY.

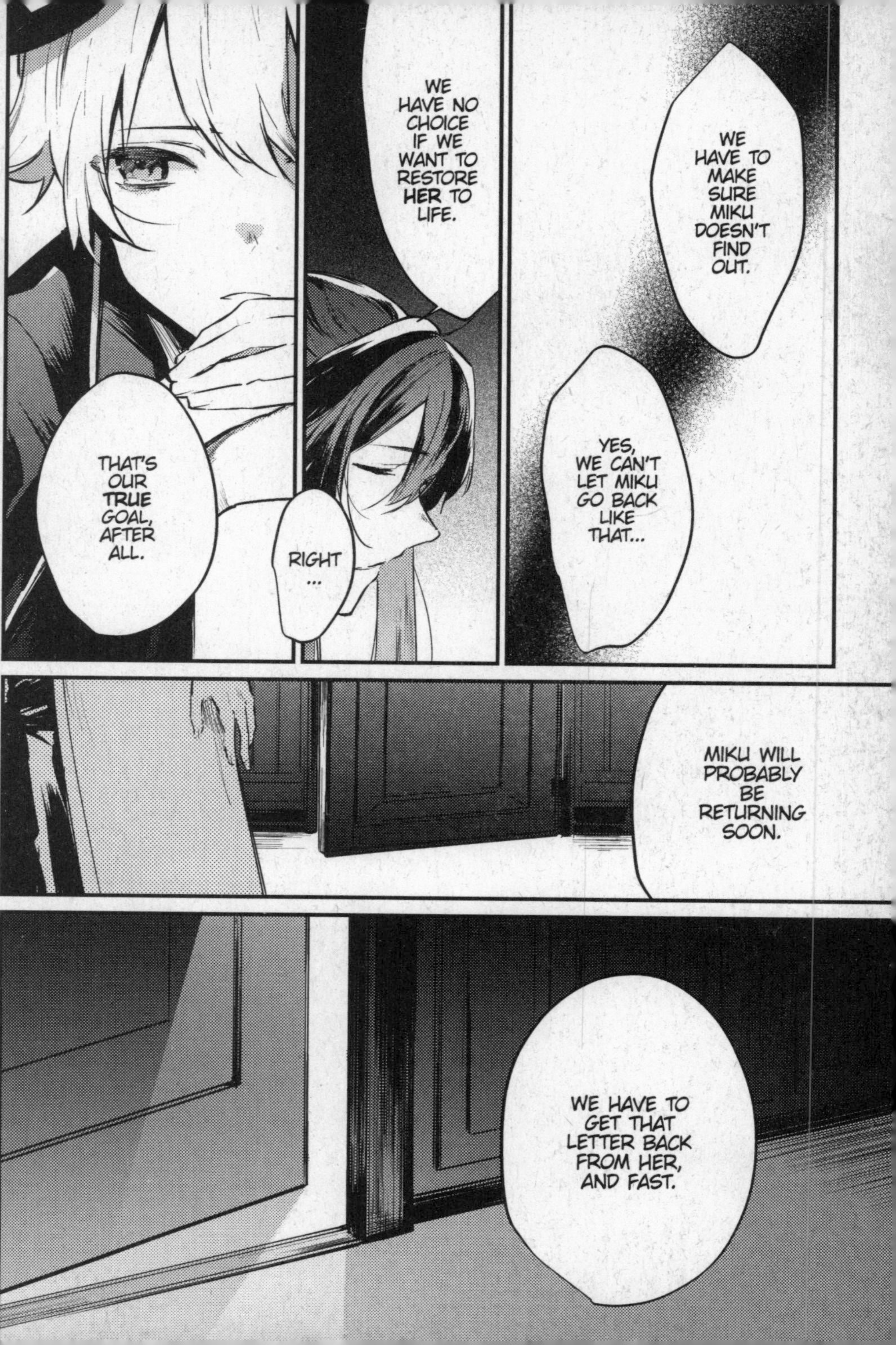
WE HAVE TO MAKE SURE MIKU DOESN'T FIND OUT.
YES, WE CAN'T LET MIKU GO BACK LIKE THAT...
WE HAVE NO CHOICE IF WE WANT TO RESTORE **HER** TO LIFE.
RIGHT...
THAT'S OUR **TRUE** GOAL, AFTER ALL.
MIKU WILL PROBABLY BE RETURNING SOON.
WE HAVE TO GET THAT LETTER BACK FROM HER, AND FAST.

Bad∞End∞Night
～インセイン・パーティー～

Act 9: Determined Eyes

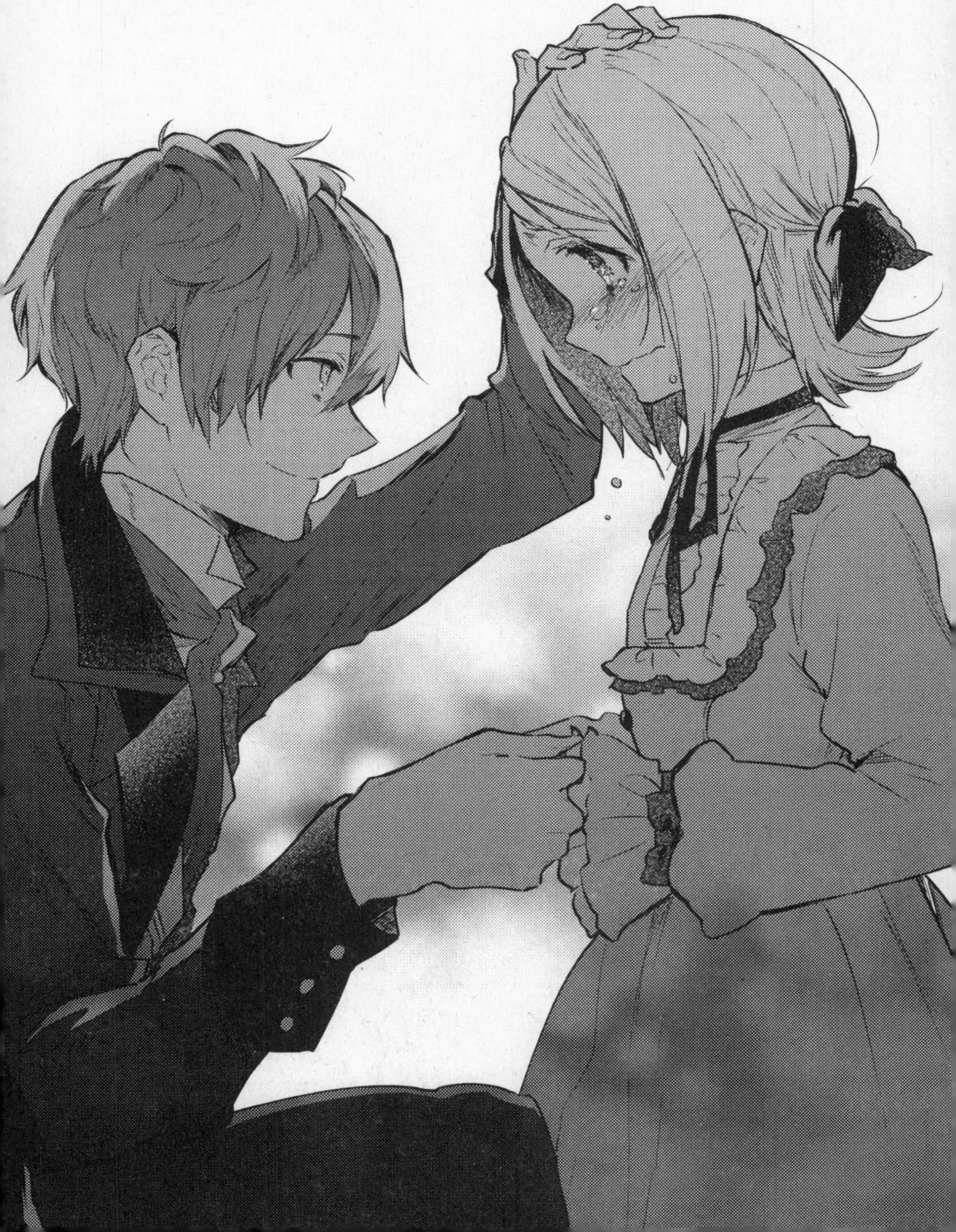

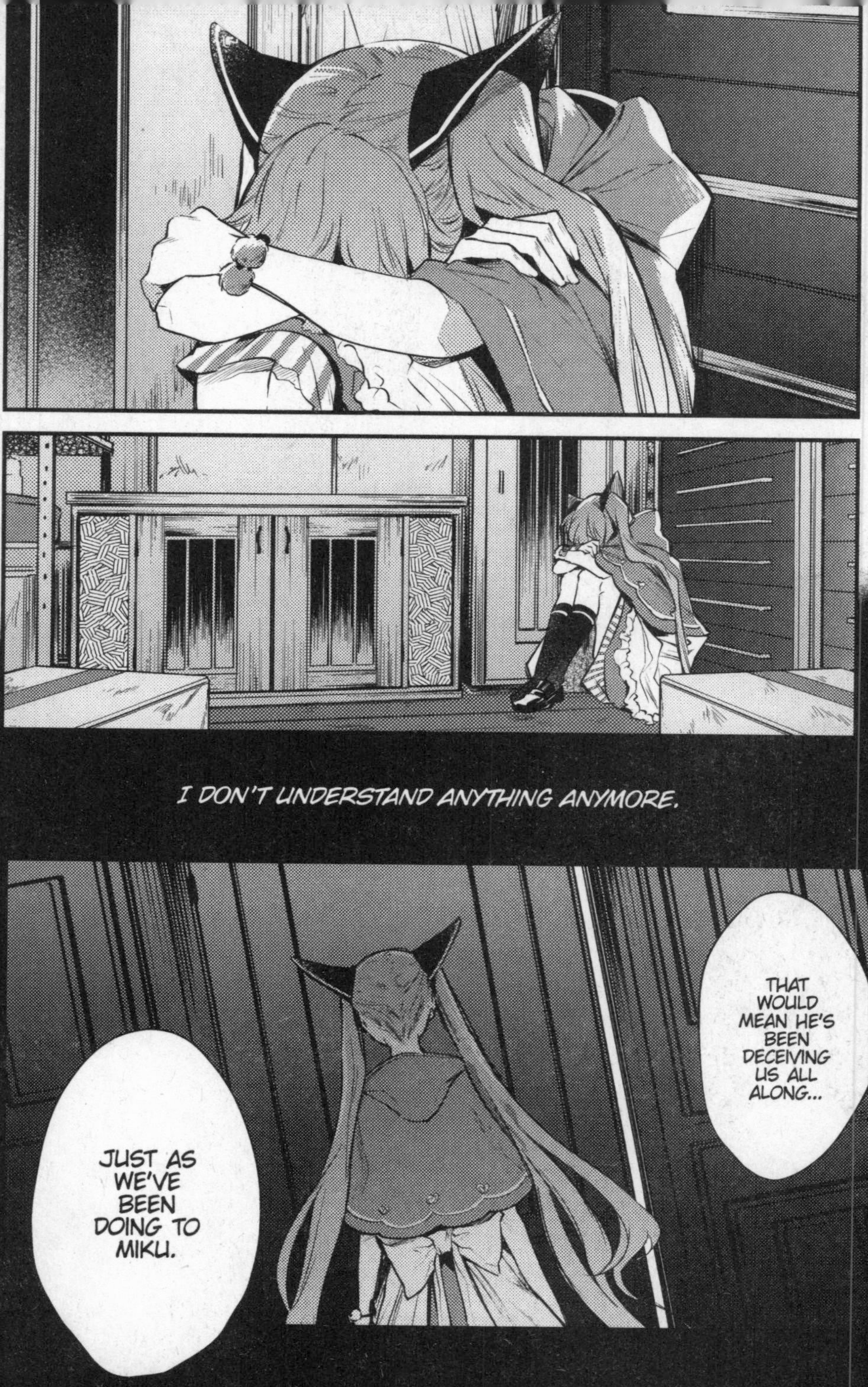
I DON'T UNDERSTAND ANYTHING ANYMORE.
THAT WOULD MEAN HE'S BEEN DECEIVING US ALL ALONG...
JUST AS WE'VE BEEN DOING TO MIKU.

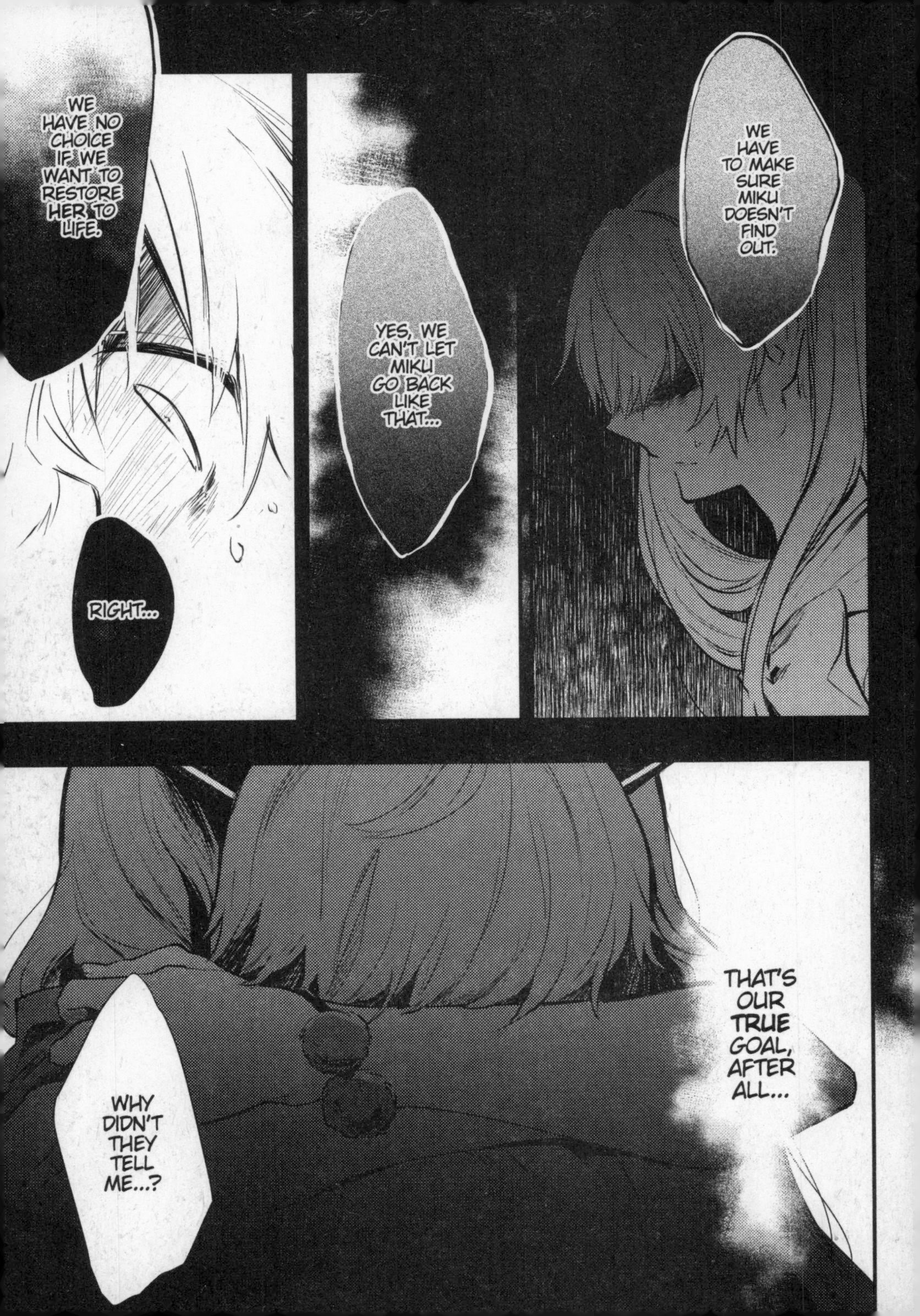
WE HAVE TO MAKE SURE MIKU DOESN'T FIND OUT.
YES, WE CAN'T LET MIKU GO BACK LIKE THAT...
WE HAVE NO CHOICE IF WE WANT TO RESTORE HER TO LIFE.
RIGHT...
THAT'S OUR TRUE GOAL, AFTER ALL...
WHY DIDN'T THEY TELL ME...?

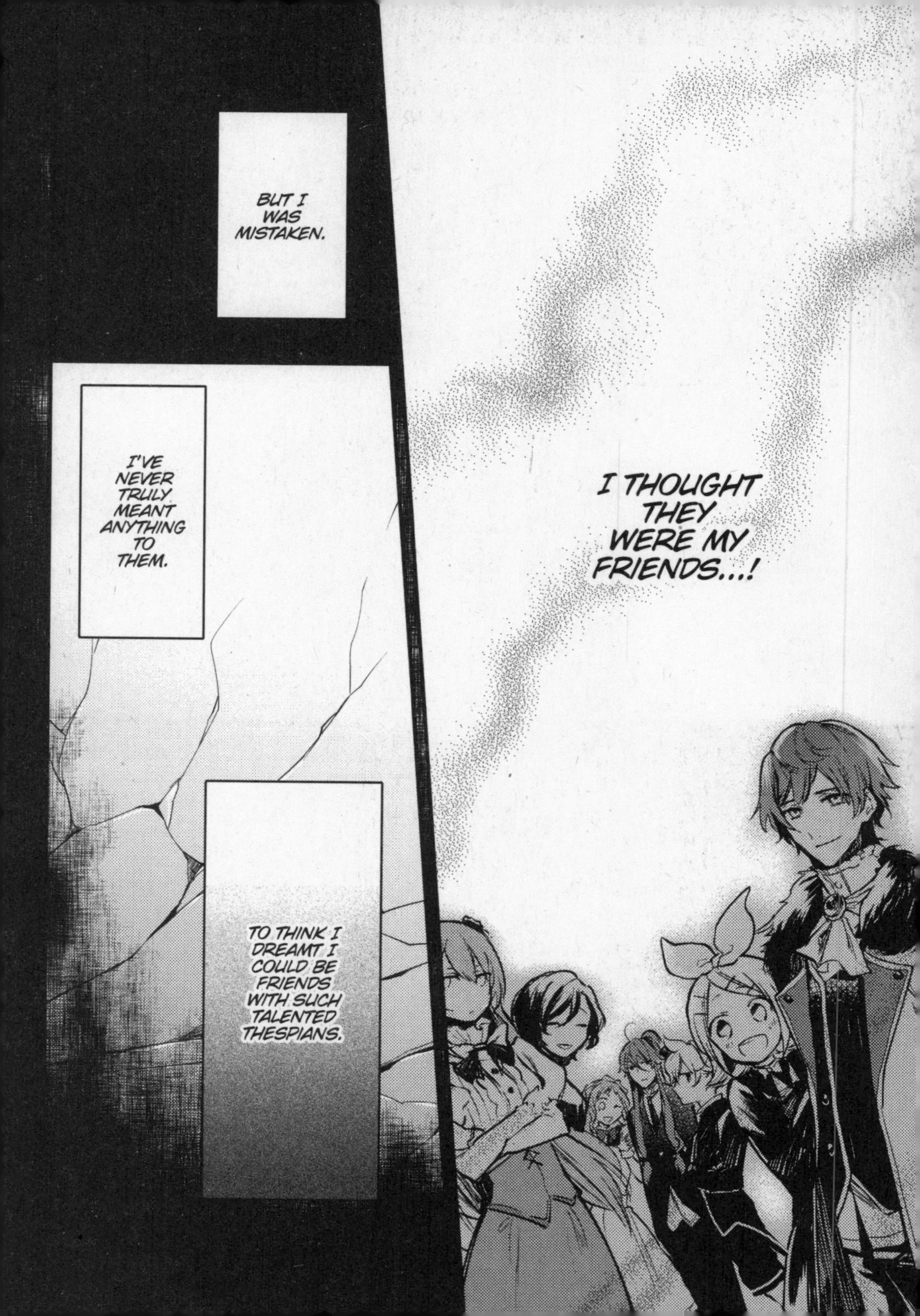
I THOUGHT THEY WERE MY FRIENDS...!
BUT I WAS MISTAKEN.
I'VE NEVER TRULY MEANT ANYTHING TO THEM.
TO THINK I DREAMT I COULD BE FRIENDS WITH SUCH TALENTED THESPIANS.

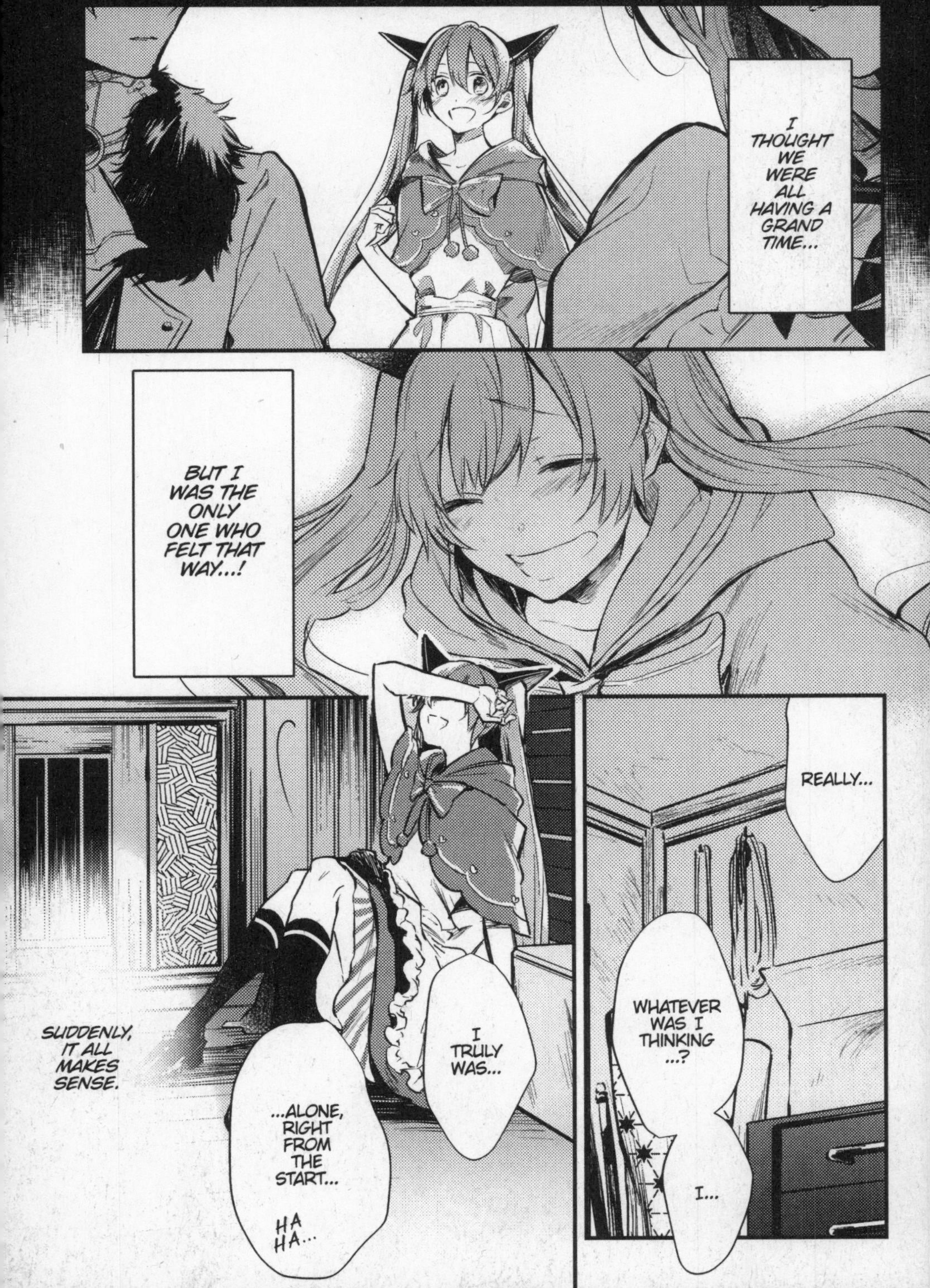
I THOUGHT WE WERE ALL HAVING A GRAND TIME...
BUT I WAS THE ONLY ONE WHO FELT THAT WAY...!
REALLY...
WHATEVER WAS I THINKING ...?
I...
I TRULY WAS...
...ALONE, RIGHT FROM THE START...
HA HA...
SUDDENLY, IT ALL MAKES SENSE.

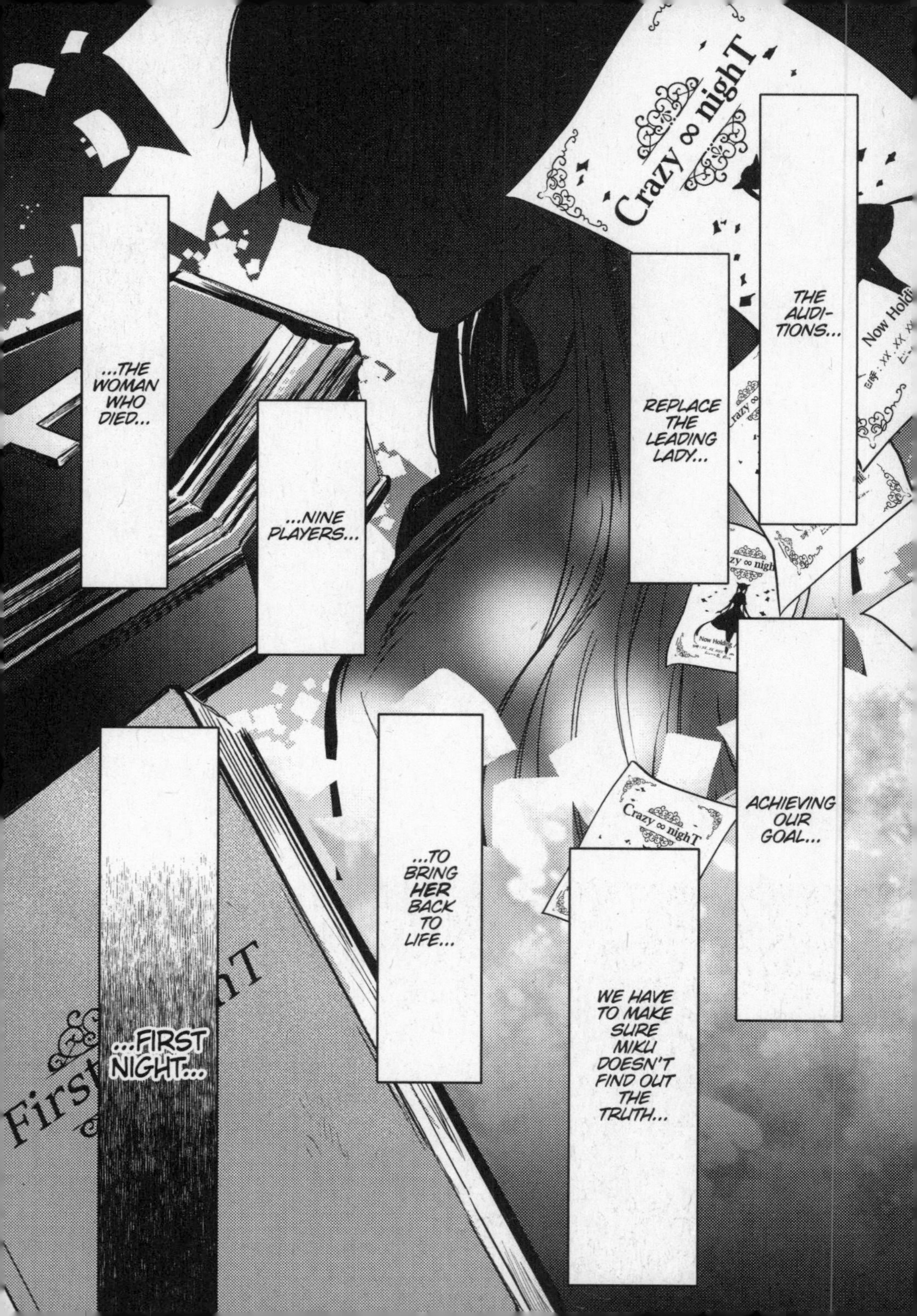
Crazy ∞ nighT
THE AUDITIONS...
REPLACE THE LEADING LADY...
...NINE PLAYERS...
...THE WOMAN WHO DIED...
ACHIEVING OUR GOAL...
Crazy ∞ nighT
WE HAVE TO MAKE SURE MIKU DOESN'T FIND OUT THE TRUTH...
...TO BRING HER BACK TO LIFE...
...FIRST NIGHT...

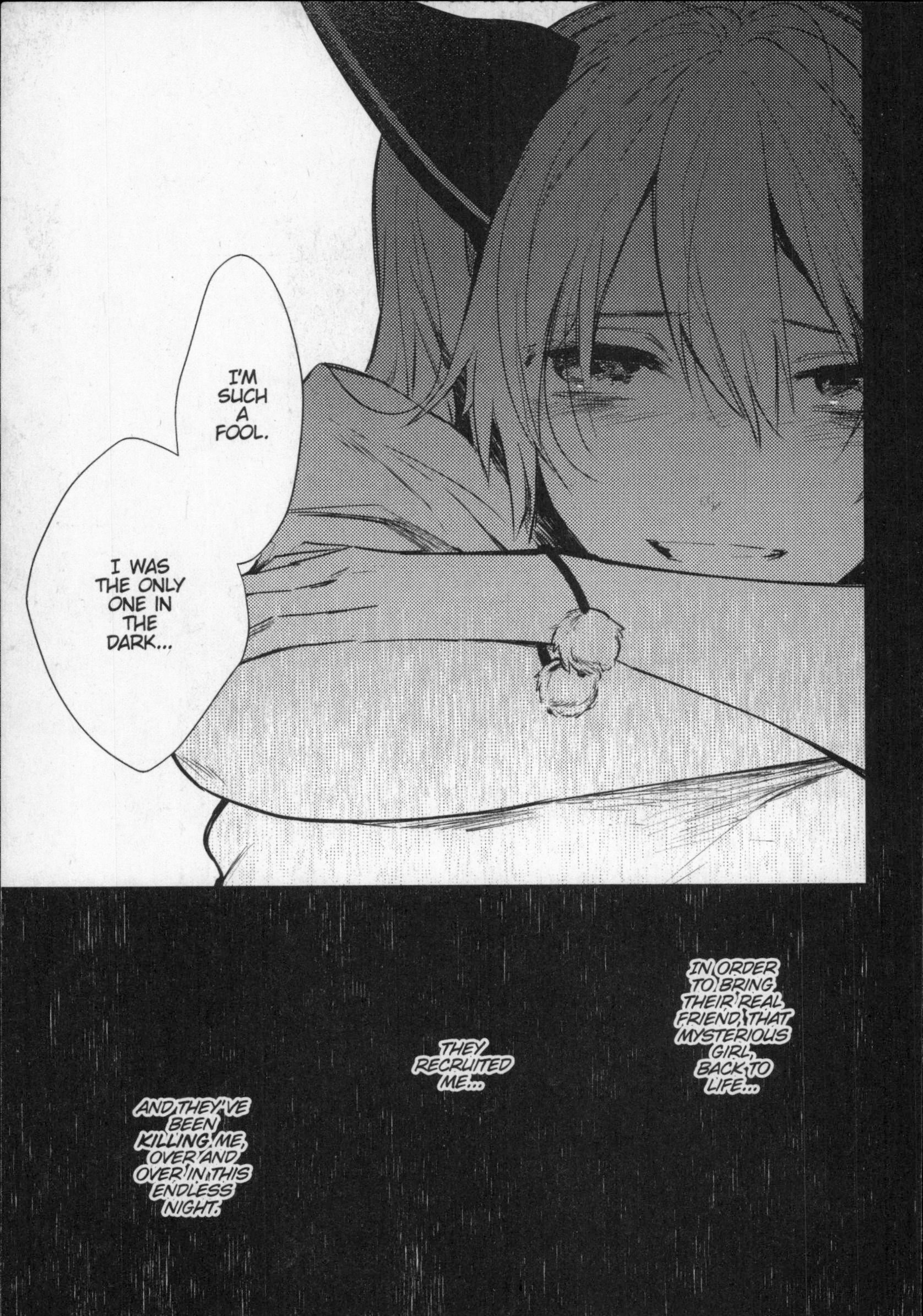
I'M SUCH A FOOL.
I WAS THE ONLY ONE IN THE DARK...
IN ORDER TO BRING THEIR REAL FRIEND, THAT MYSTERIOUS GIRL, BACK TO LIFE...
THEY RECRUITED ME...
AND THEY'VE BEEN KILLING ME, OVER AND OVER IN THIS ENDLESS NIGHT.

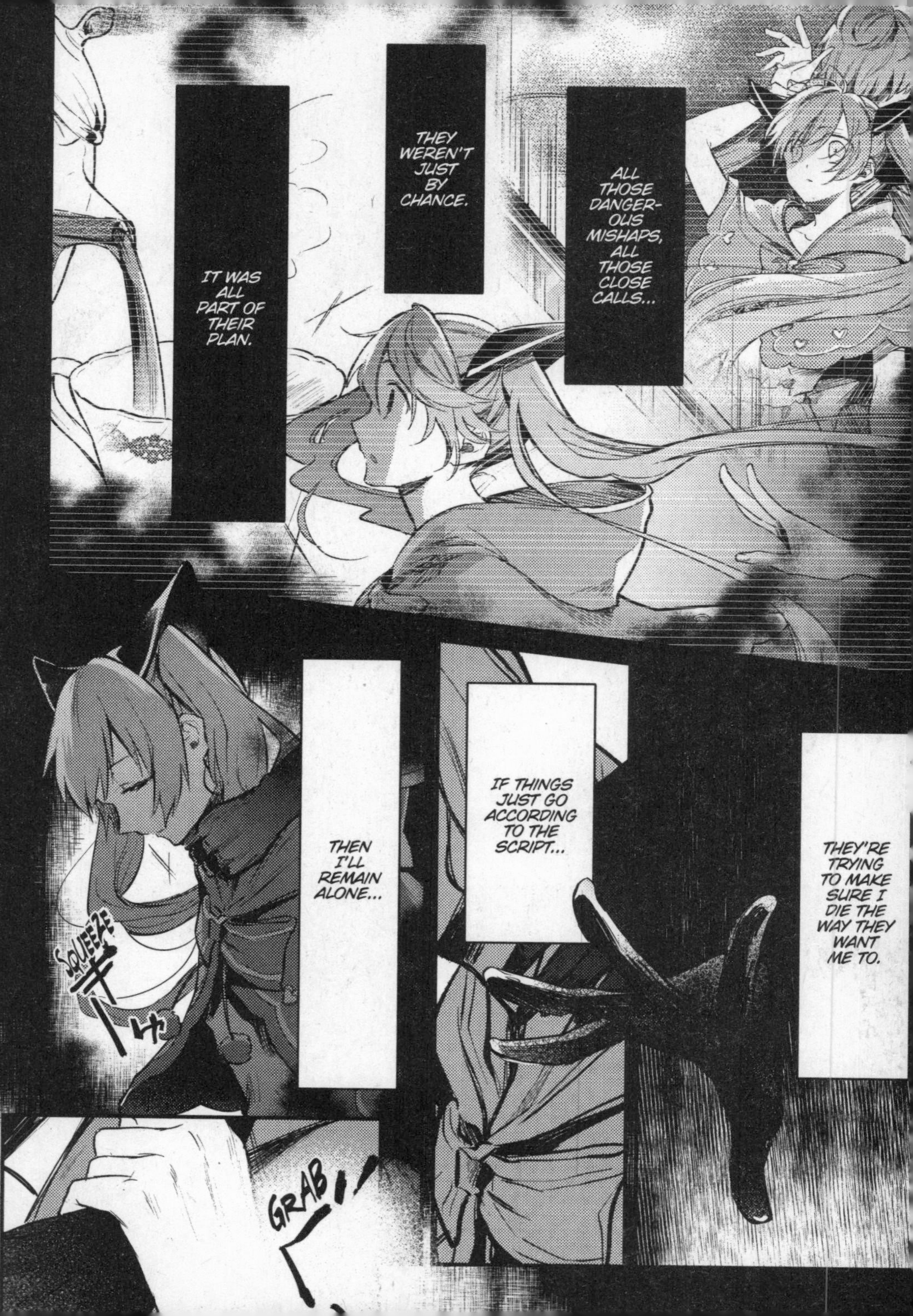
ALL THOSE DANGER-OUS MISHAPS, ALL THOSE CLOSE CALLS...
THEY WEREN'T JUST BY CHANCE.
IT WAS ALL PART OF THEIR PLAN.
THEY'RE TRYING TO MAKE SURE I DIE THE WAY THEY WANT ME TO.
IF THINGS JUST GO ACCORDING TO THE SCRIPT...
THEN I'LL REMAIN ALONE...
SQUEEZE
GRAB

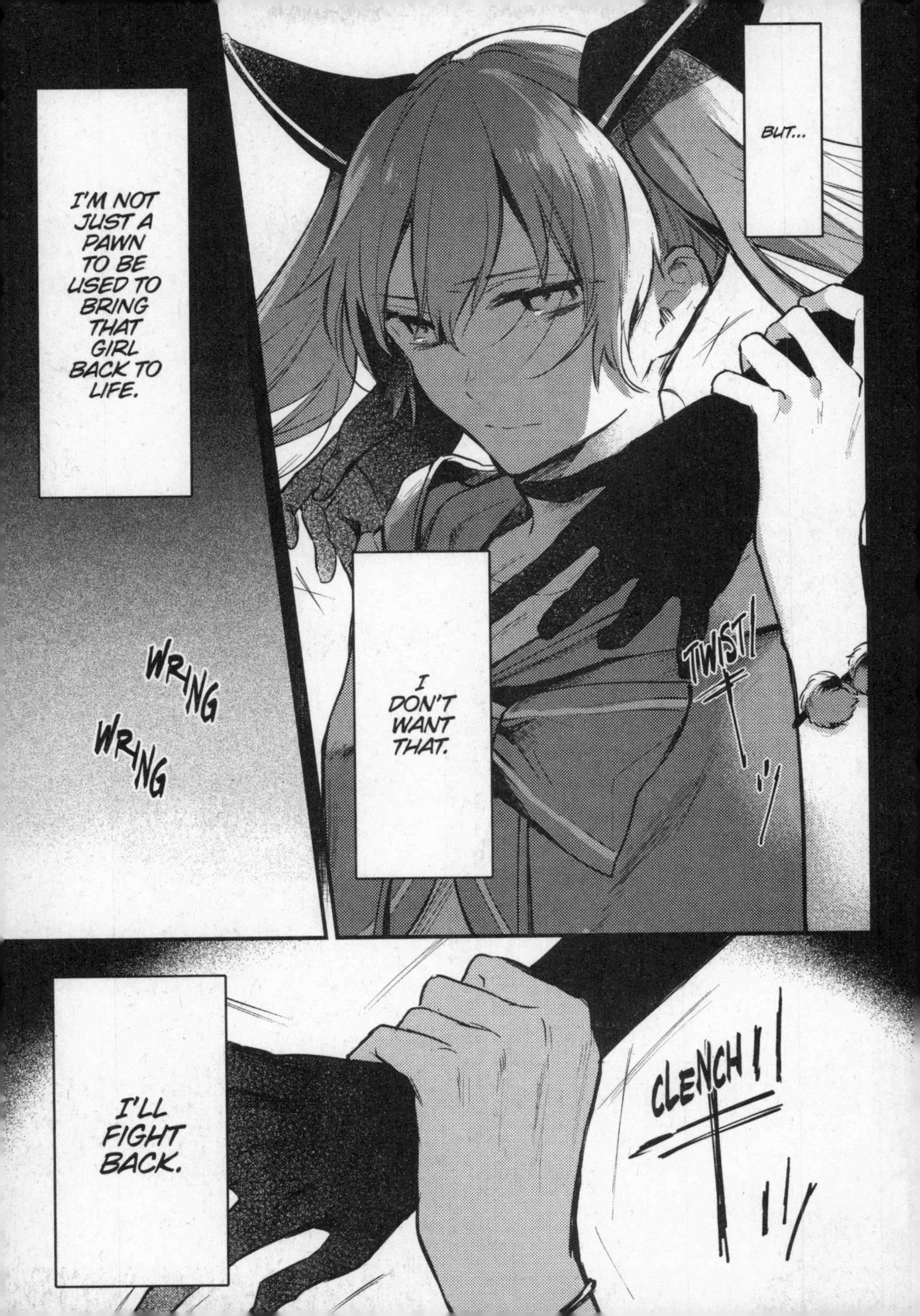
BUT...
I'M NOT JUST A PAWN TO BE USED TO BRING THAT GIRL BACK TO LIFE.
TWIST!!
I DON'T WANT THAT.
WRING
WRING
CLENCH!!
I'LL FIGHT BACK.

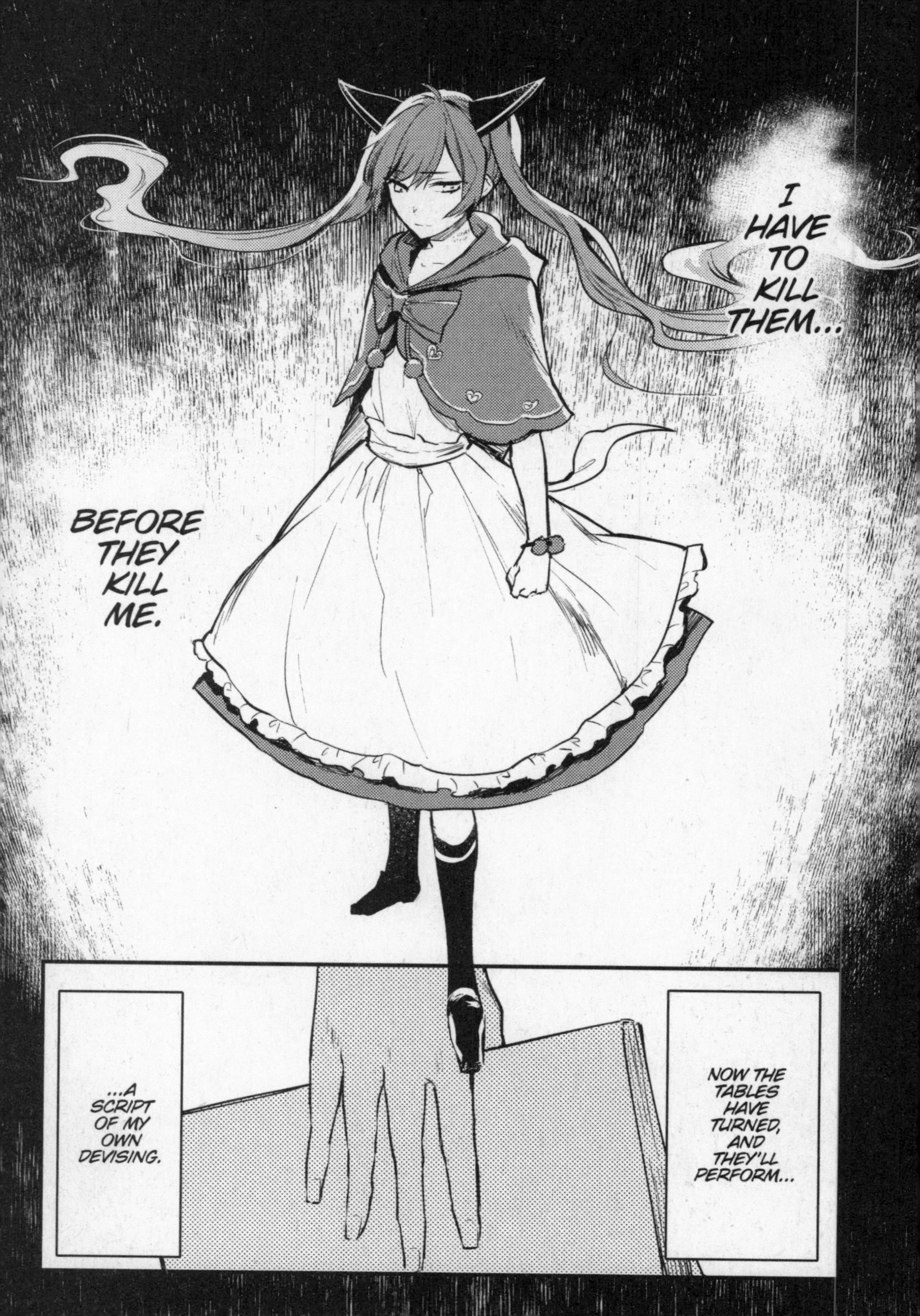
I HAVE TO KILL THEM...
BEFORE THEY KILL ME.
NOW THE TABLES HAVE TURNED, AND THEY'LL PERFORM...
...A SCRIPT OF MY OWN DEVISING.

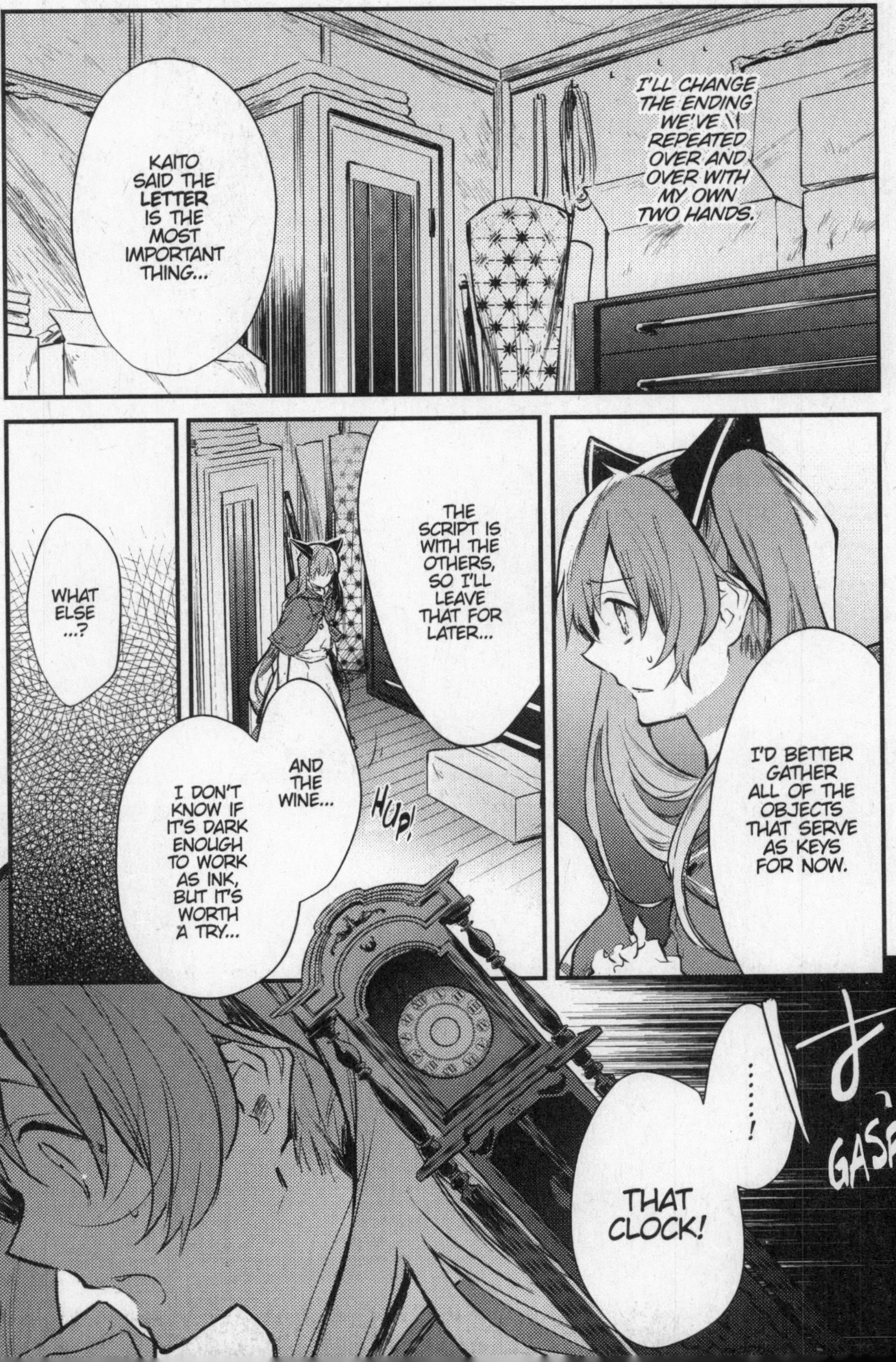
I'LL CHANGE THE ENDING WE'VE REPEATED OVER AND OVER WITH MY OWN TWO HANDS.
KAITO SAID THE LETTER IS THE MOST IMPORTANT THING...
I'D BETTER GATHER ALL OF THE OBJECTS THAT SERVE AS KEYS FOR NOW.
THE SCRIPT IS WITH THE OTHERS, SO I'LL LEAVE THAT FOR LATER...
AND THE WINE...
I DON'T KNOW IF IT'S DARK ENOUGH TO WORK AS INK, BUT IT'S WORTH A TRY...
HUP!
WHAT ELSE ...?
GASP!
......!
THAT CLOCK!

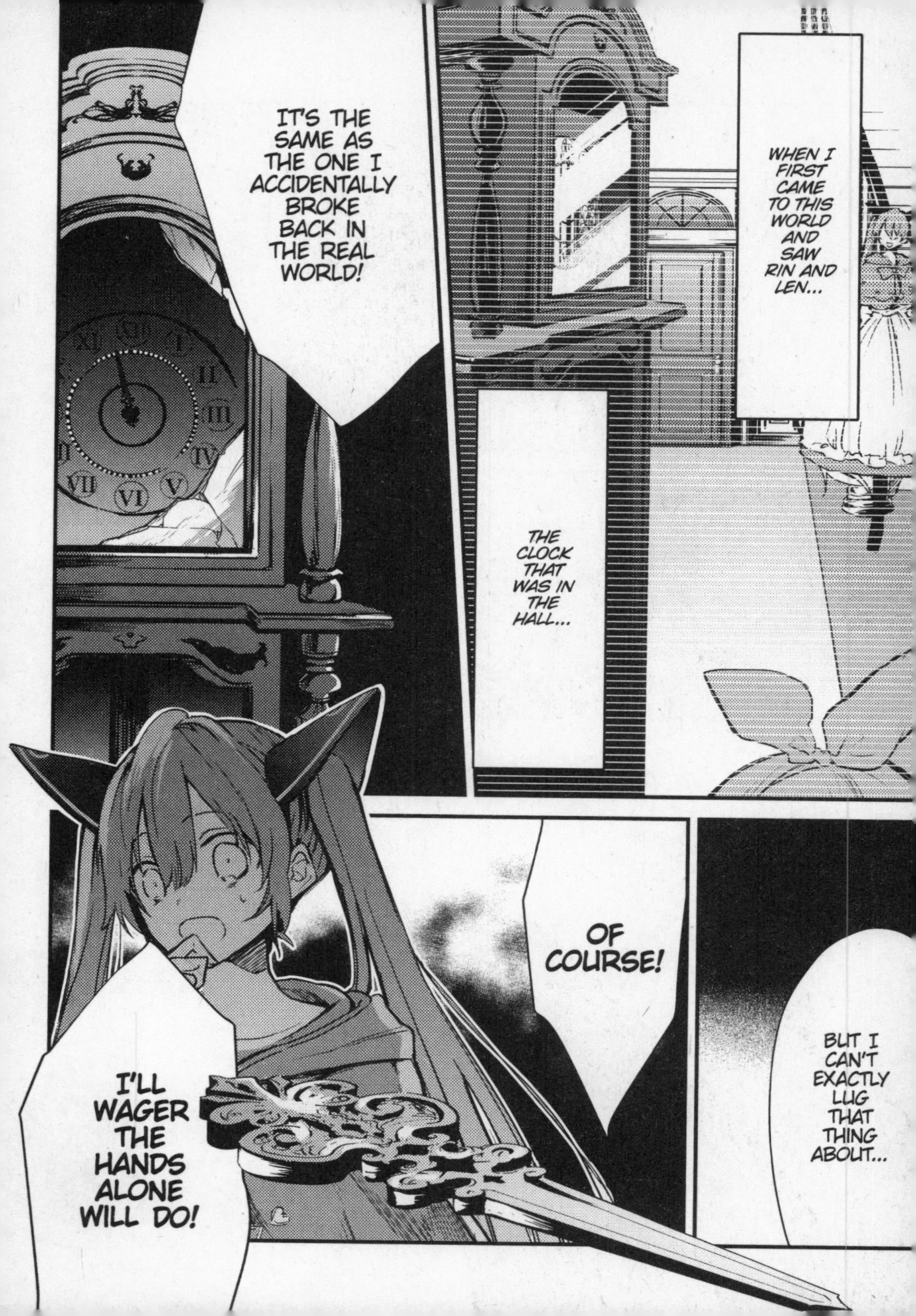
WHEN I FIRST CAME TO THIS WORLD AND SAW RIN AND LEN...
THE CLOCK THAT WAS IN THE HALL...
IT'S THE SAME AS THE ONE I ACCIDENTALLY BROKE BACK IN THE REAL WORLD!
BUT I CAN'T EXACTLY LUG THAT THING ABOUT...
OF COURSE!
I'LL WAGER THE HANDS ALONE WILL DO!

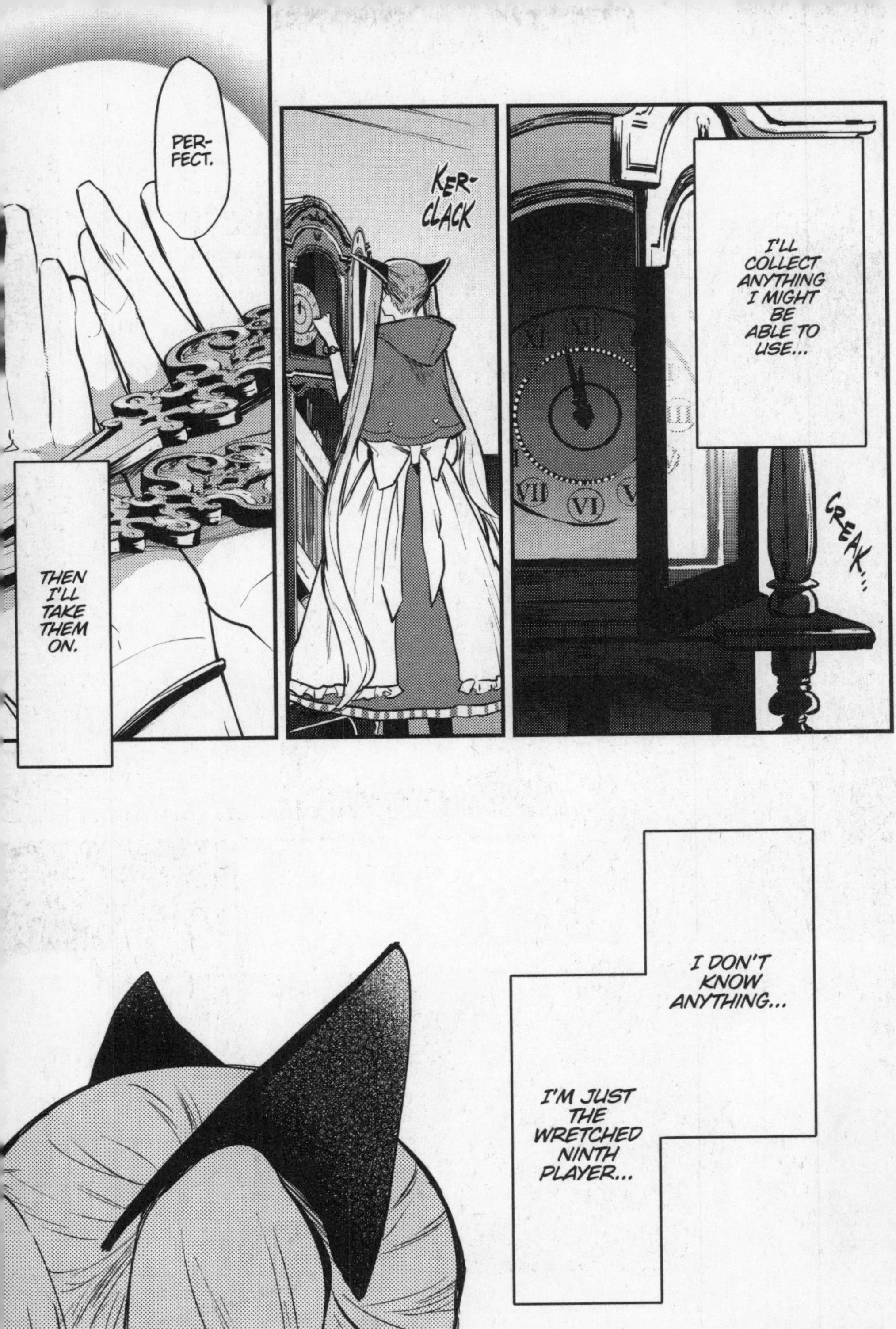
I'LL COLLECT ANYTHING I MIGHT BE ABLE TO USE...
CREAK...
KER-CLACK
PER-FECT.
THEN I'LL TAKE THEM ON.
I DON'T KNOW ANYTHING...
I'M JUST THE WRETCHED NINTH PLAYER...

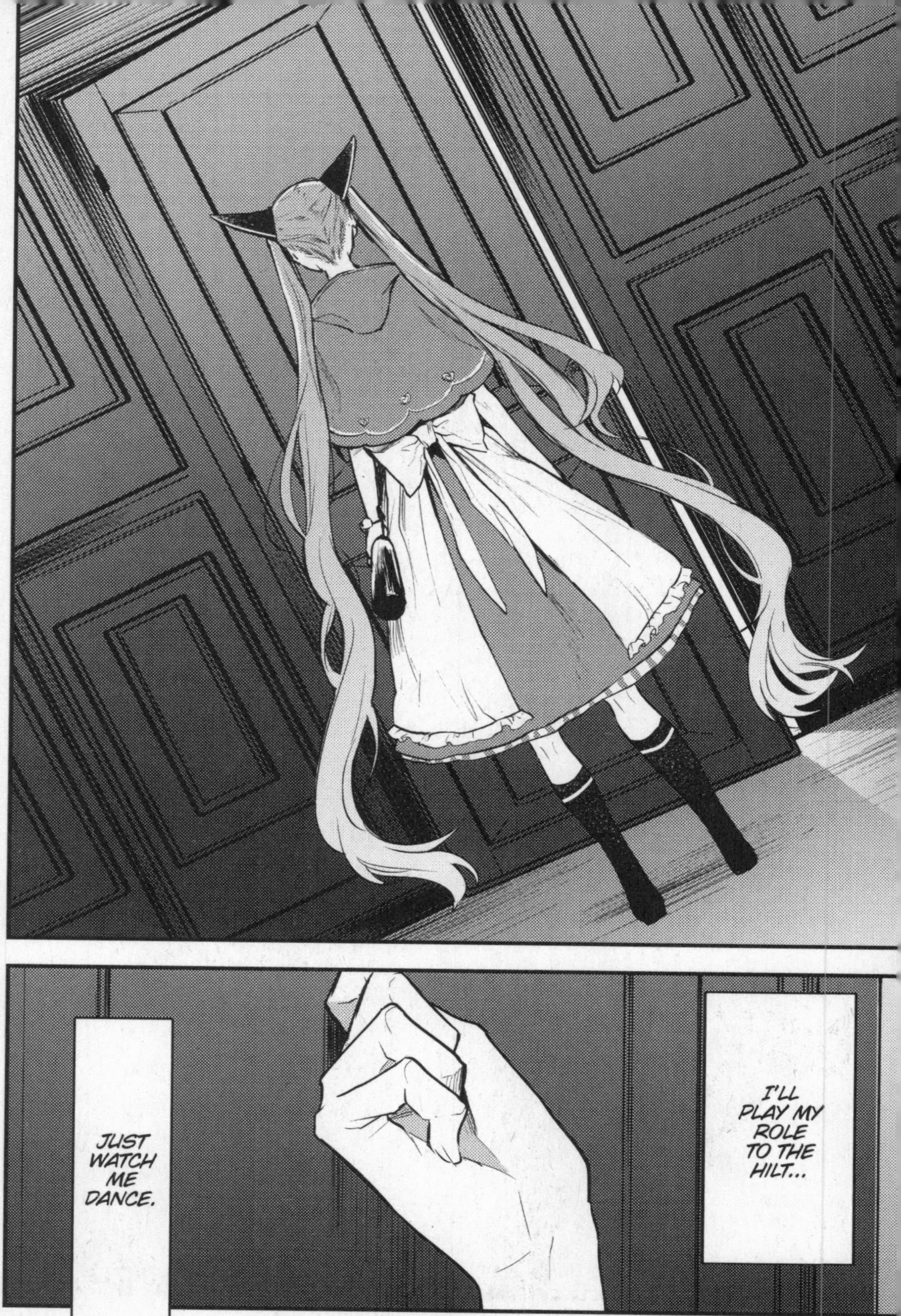
I'LL PLAY MY ROLE TO THE HILT...
JUST WATCH ME DANCE.

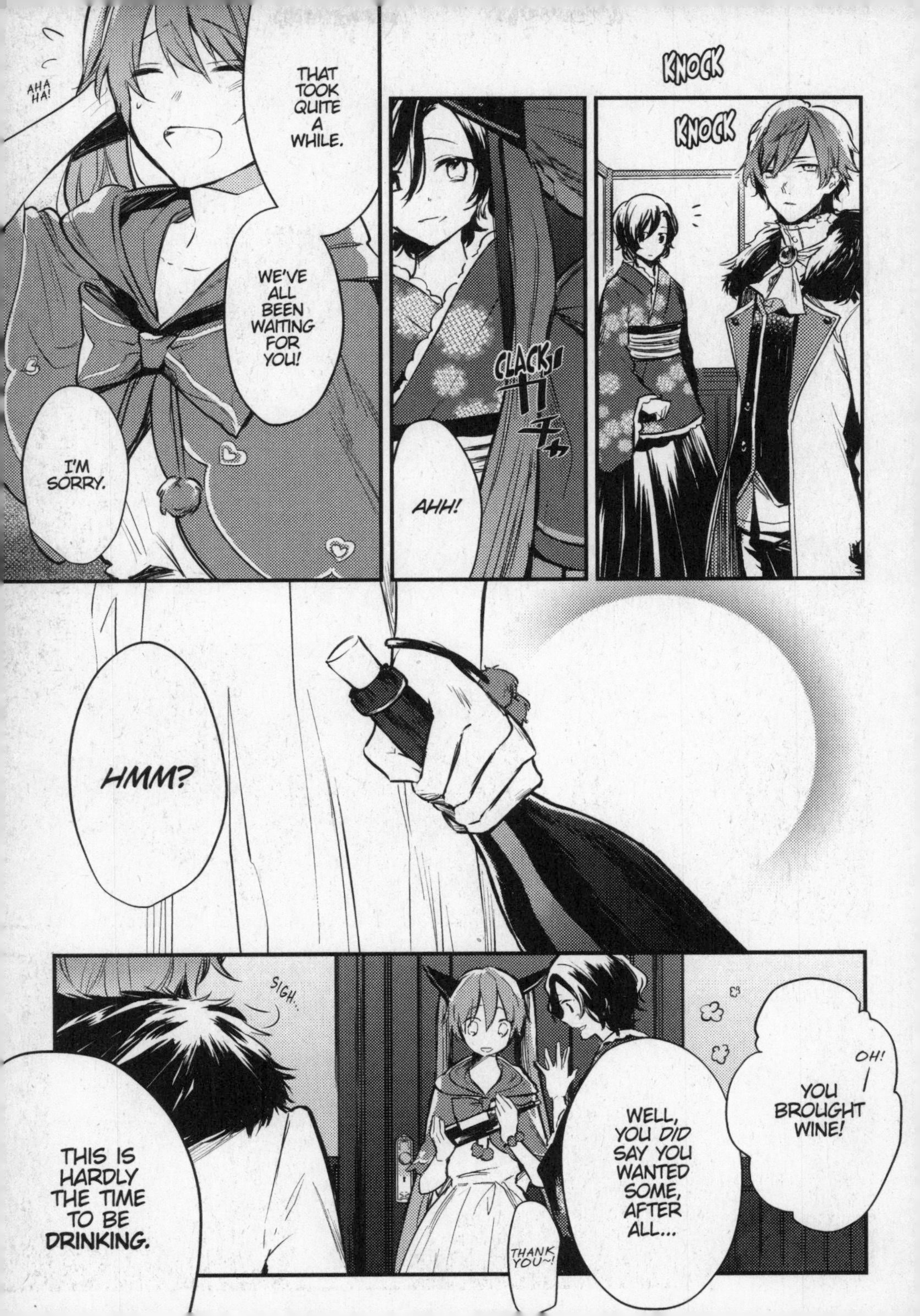
KNOCK
KNOCK
CLACK
AHH!
THAT TOOK QUITE A WHILE.
AHA HA!
WE'VE ALL BEEN WAITING FOR YOU!
I'M SORRY.
HMM?
OH!
YOU BROUGHT WINE!
WELL, YOU DID SAY YOU WANTED SOME, AFTER ALL...
THANK YOU~!
SIGH...
THIS IS HARDLY THE TIME TO BE DRINKING.

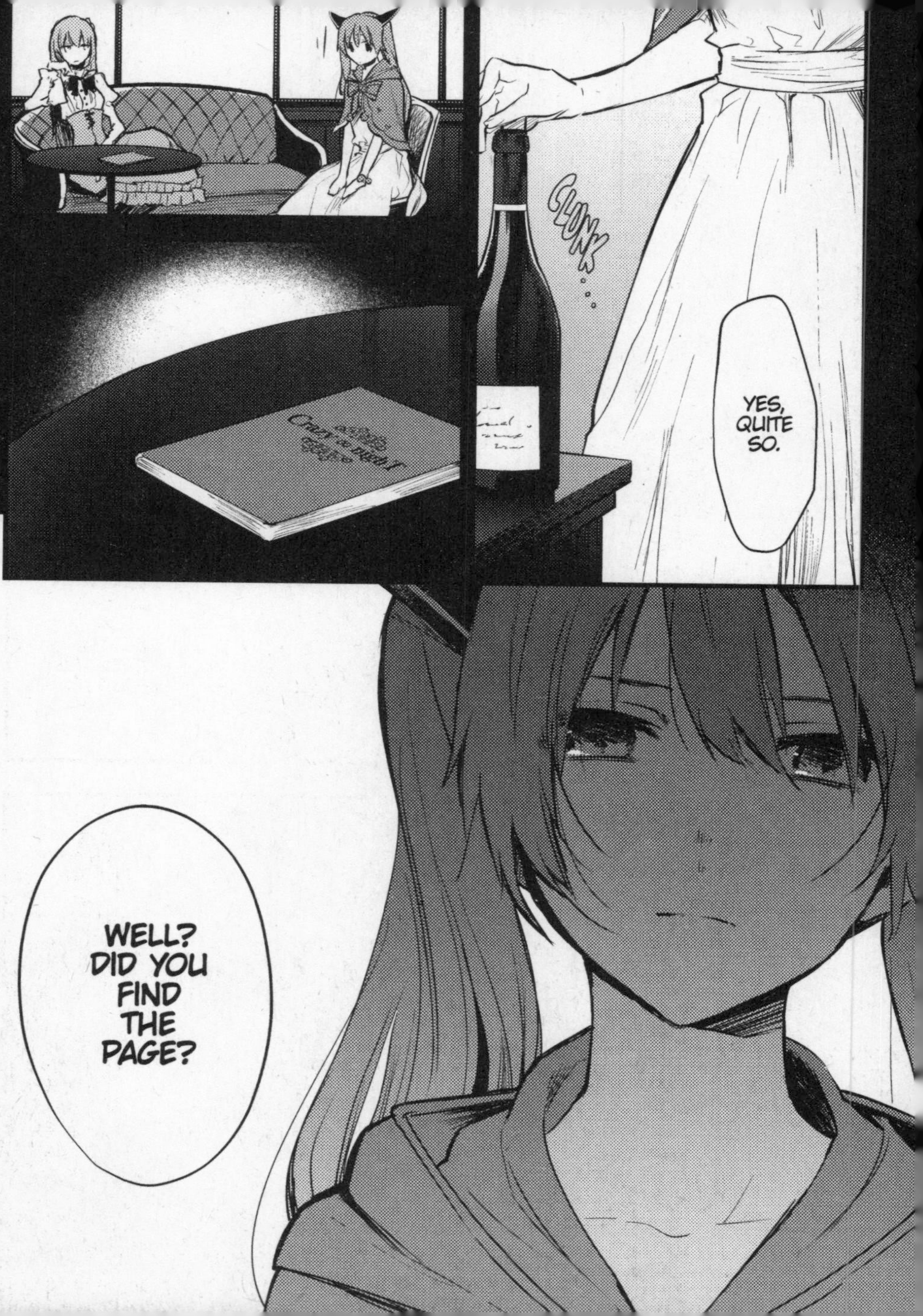
CLUNK
YES, QUITE SO.
WELL? DID YOU FIND THE PAGE?

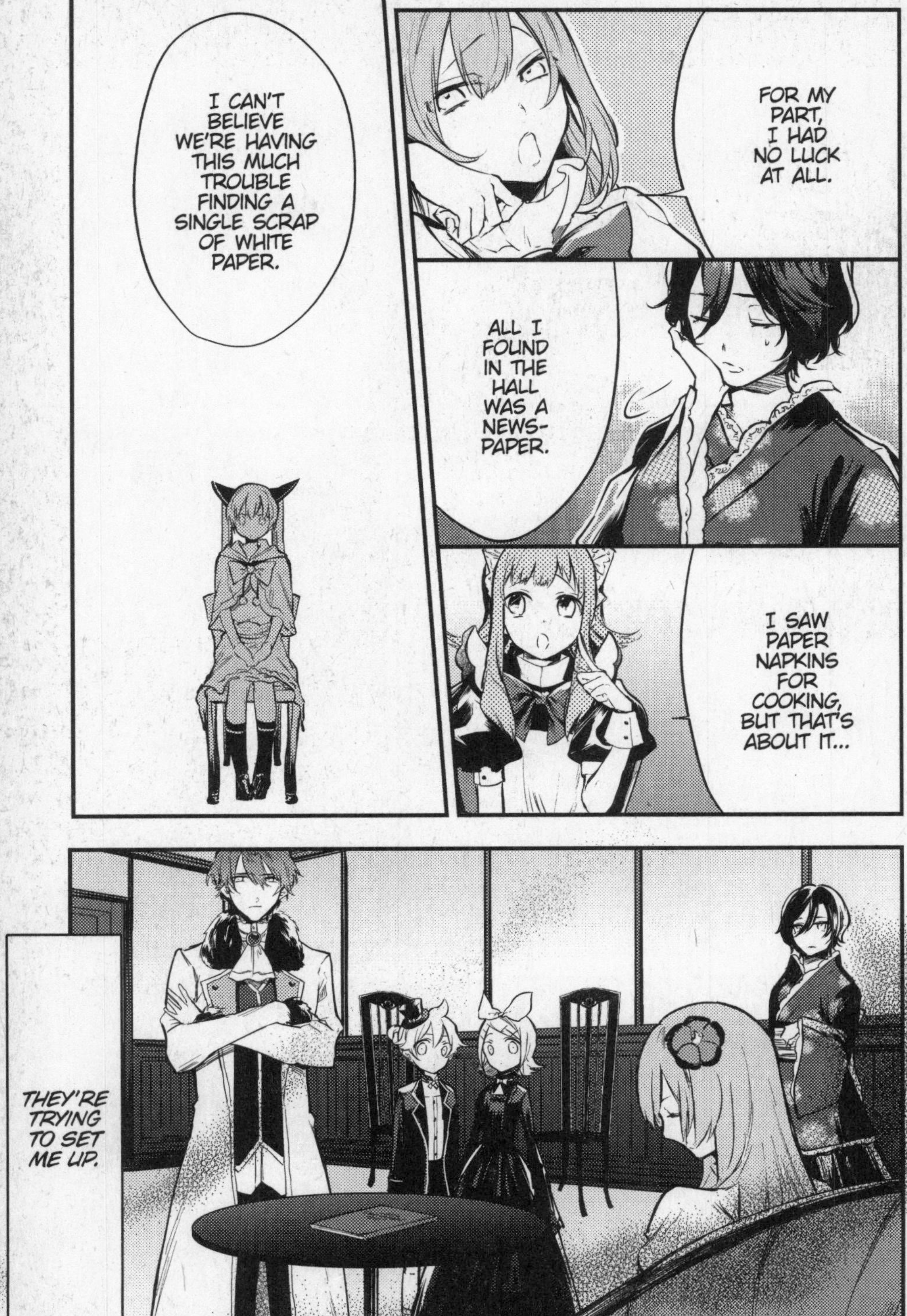
FOR MY PART, I HAD NO LUCK AT ALL.
ALL I FOUND IN THE HALL WAS A NEWS-PAPER.
I SAW PAPER NAPKINS FOR COOKING, BUT THAT'S ABOUT IT...
I CAN'T BELIEVE WE'RE HAVING THIS MUCH TROUBLE FINDING A SINGLE SCRAP OF WHITE PAPER.
THEY'RE TRYING TO SET ME UP.

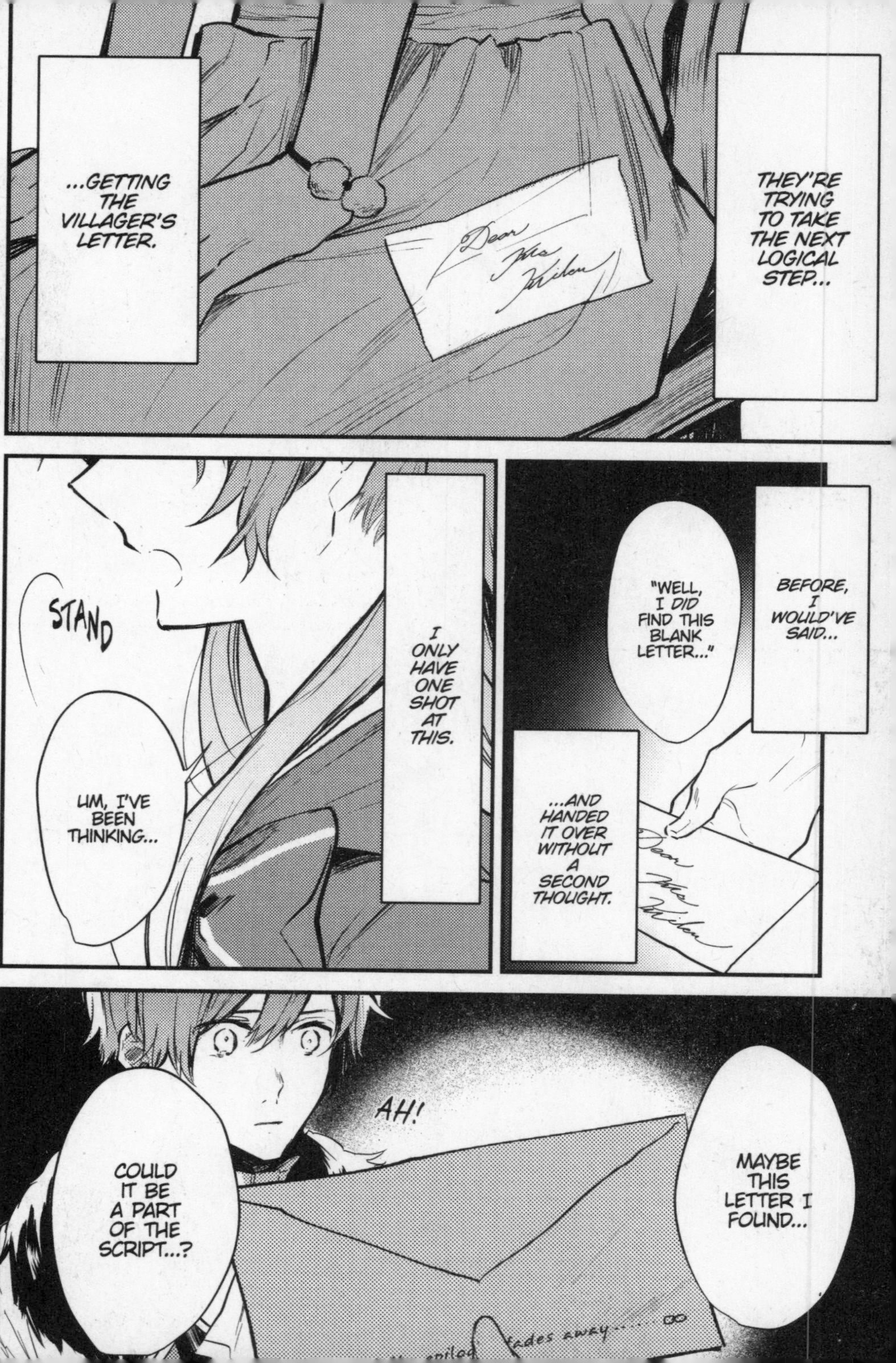
THEY'RE TRYING TO TAKE THE NEXT LOGICAL STEP...
...GETTING THE VILLAGER'S LETTER.
BEFORE, I WOULD'VE SAID...
"WELL, I *DID* FIND THIS BLANK LETTER..."
...AND HANDED IT OVER WITHOUT A SECOND THOUGHT.
I ONLY HAVE ONE SHOT AT THIS.
STAND
UM, I'VE BEEN THINKING...
MAYBE THIS LETTER I FOUND...
AH!
COULD IT BE A PART OF THE SCRIPT...?
fades away......

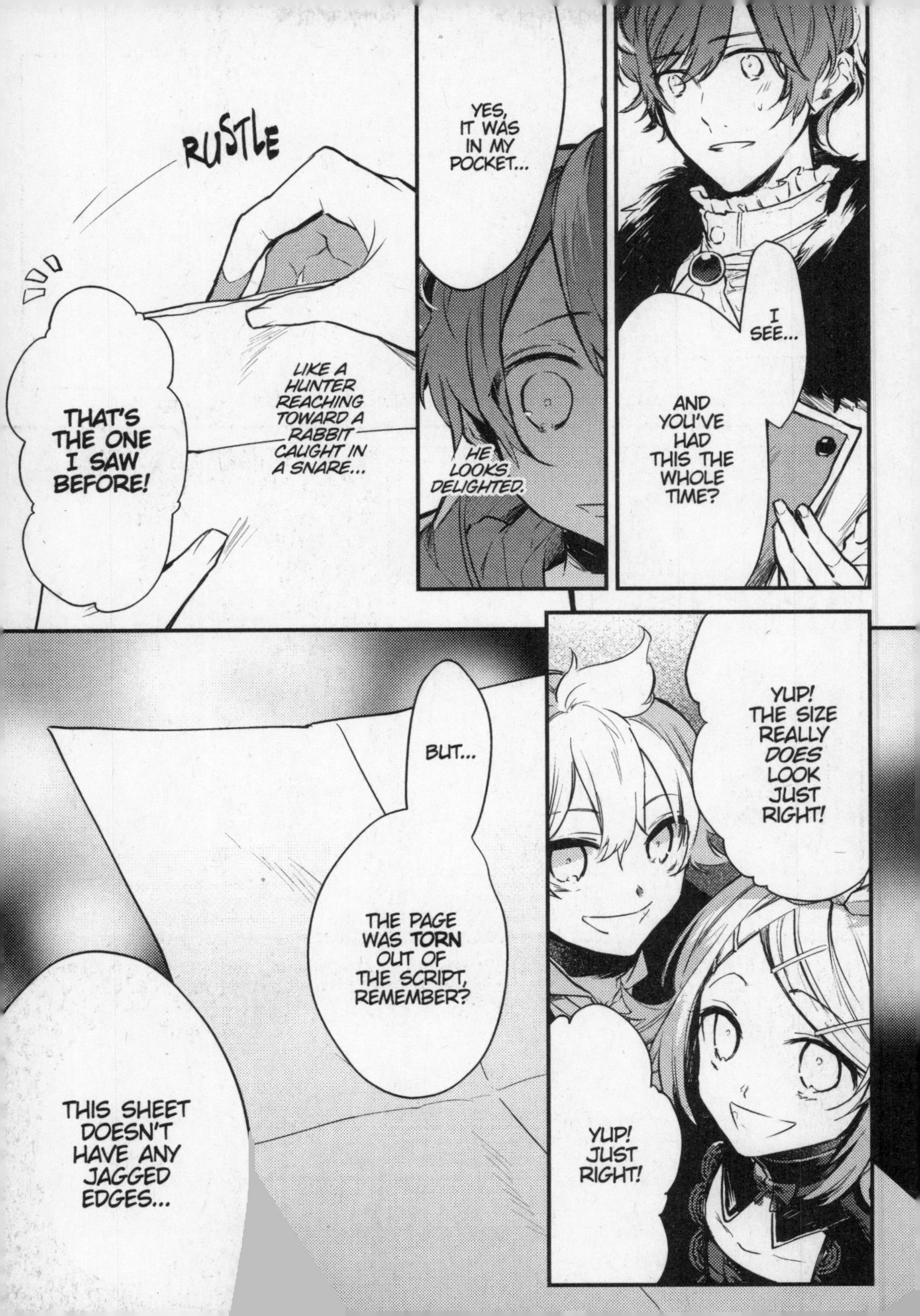
I SEE...
AND YOU'VE HAD THIS THE WHOLE TIME?
YES, IT WAS IN MY POCKET...
HE LOOKS DELIGHTED.
RUSTLE
LIKE A HUNTER REACHING TOWARD A RABBIT CAUGHT IN A SNARE...
THAT'S THE ONE I SAW BEFORE!
YUP! THE SIZE REALLY *DOES* LOOK JUST RIGHT!
YUP! JUST RIGHT!
BUT...
THE PAGE WAS **TORN** OUT OF THE SCRIPT, REMEMBER?
THIS SHEET DOESN'T HAVE ANY JAGGED EDGES...

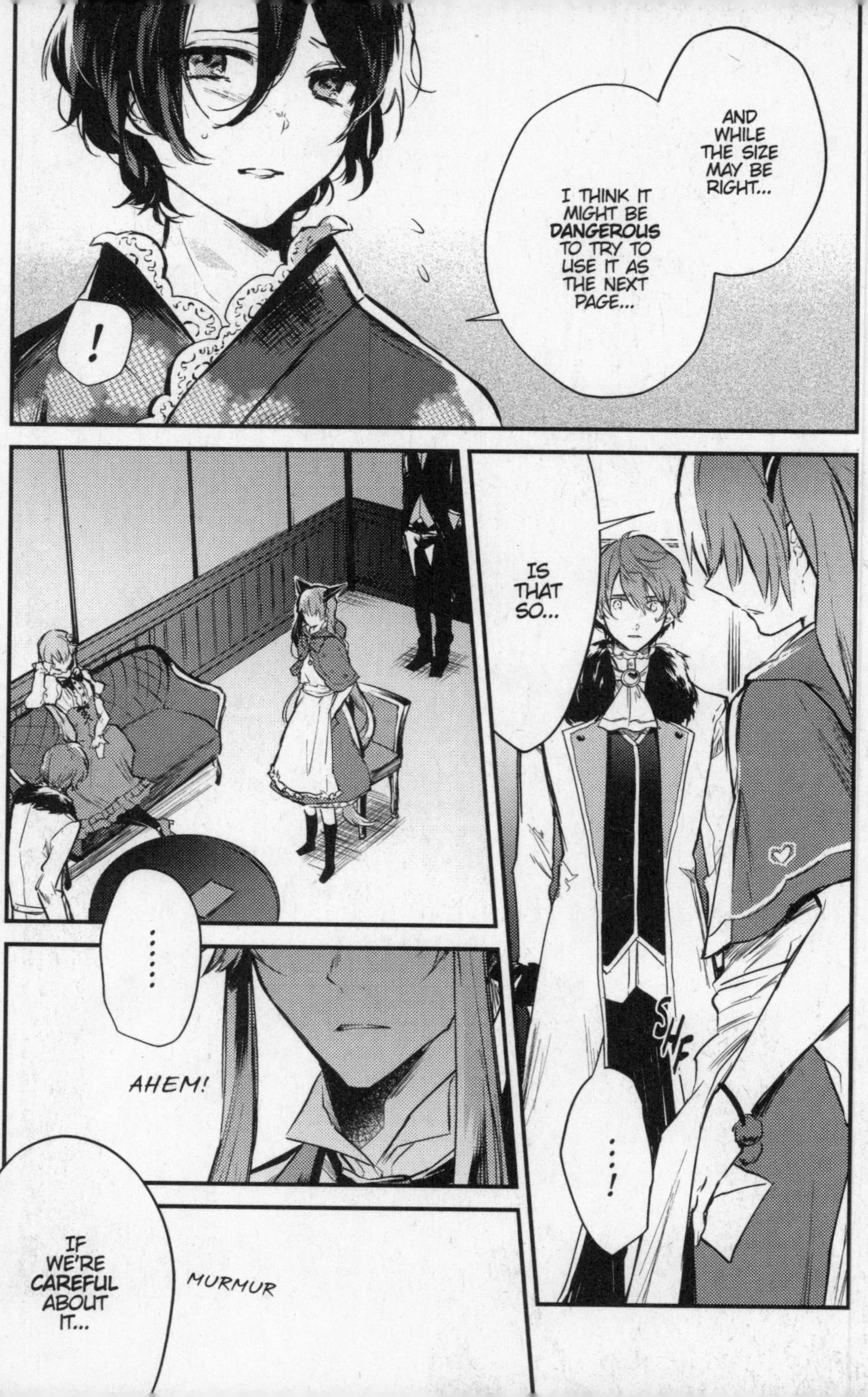
AND WHILE THE SIZE MAY BE RIGHT...
I THINK IT MIGHT BE **DANGEROUS** TO TRY TO USE IT AS THE NEXT PAGE...
!
IS THAT SO...
SHF
...!
......
AHEM!
MURMUR
IF WE'RE **CAREFUL** ABOUT IT...

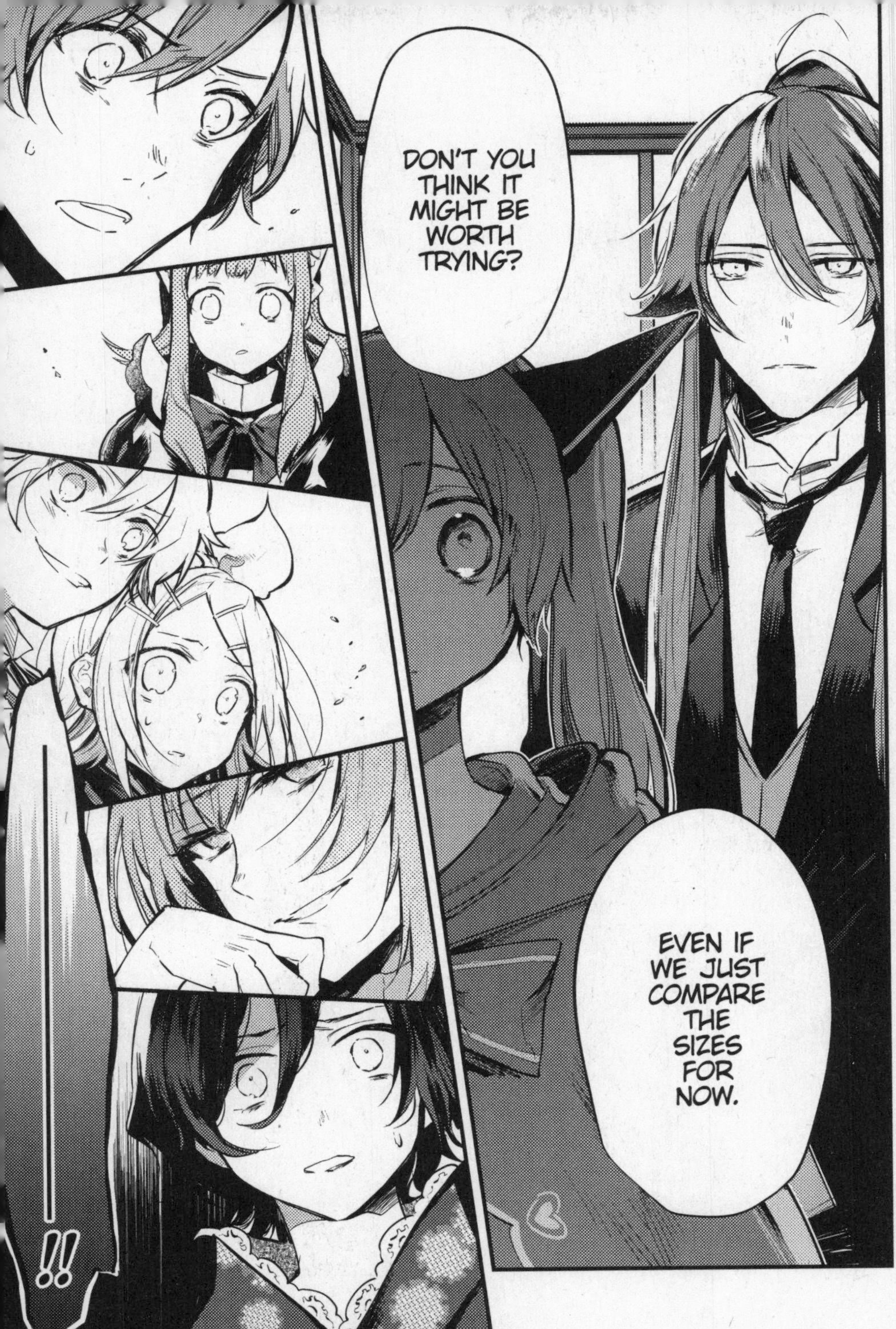
DON'T YOU THINK IT MIGHT BE WORTH TRYING?
EVEN IF WE JUST COMPARE THE SIZES FOR NOW.
——!!

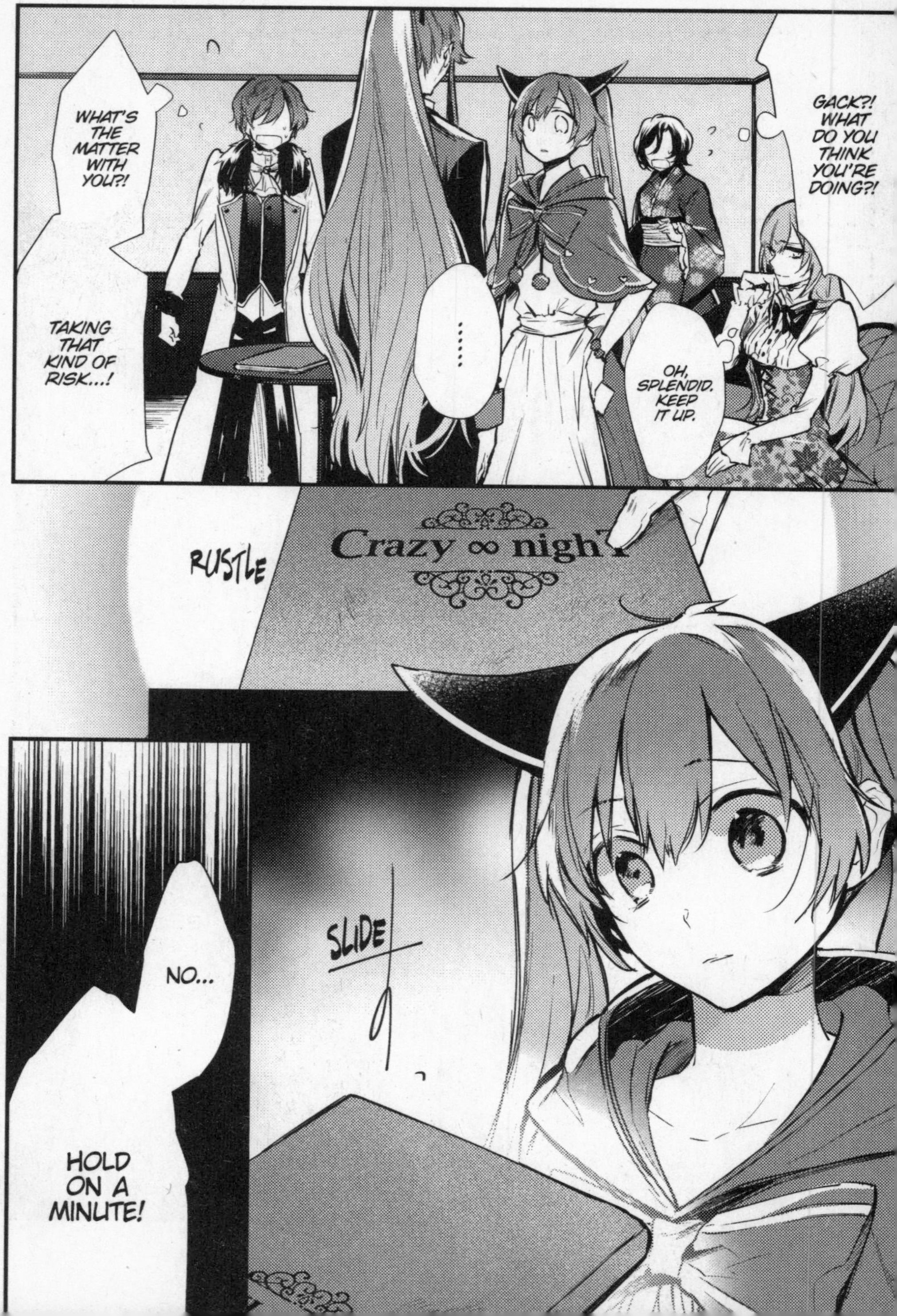
GACK?! WHAT DO YOU THINK YOU'RE DOING?!
OH, SPLENDID. KEEP IT UP.
......
WHAT'S THE MATTER WITH YOU?!
TAKING THAT KIND OF RISK...!
Crazy ∞ nighT
RUSTLE
SLIDE
NO...
HOLD ON A MINUTE!

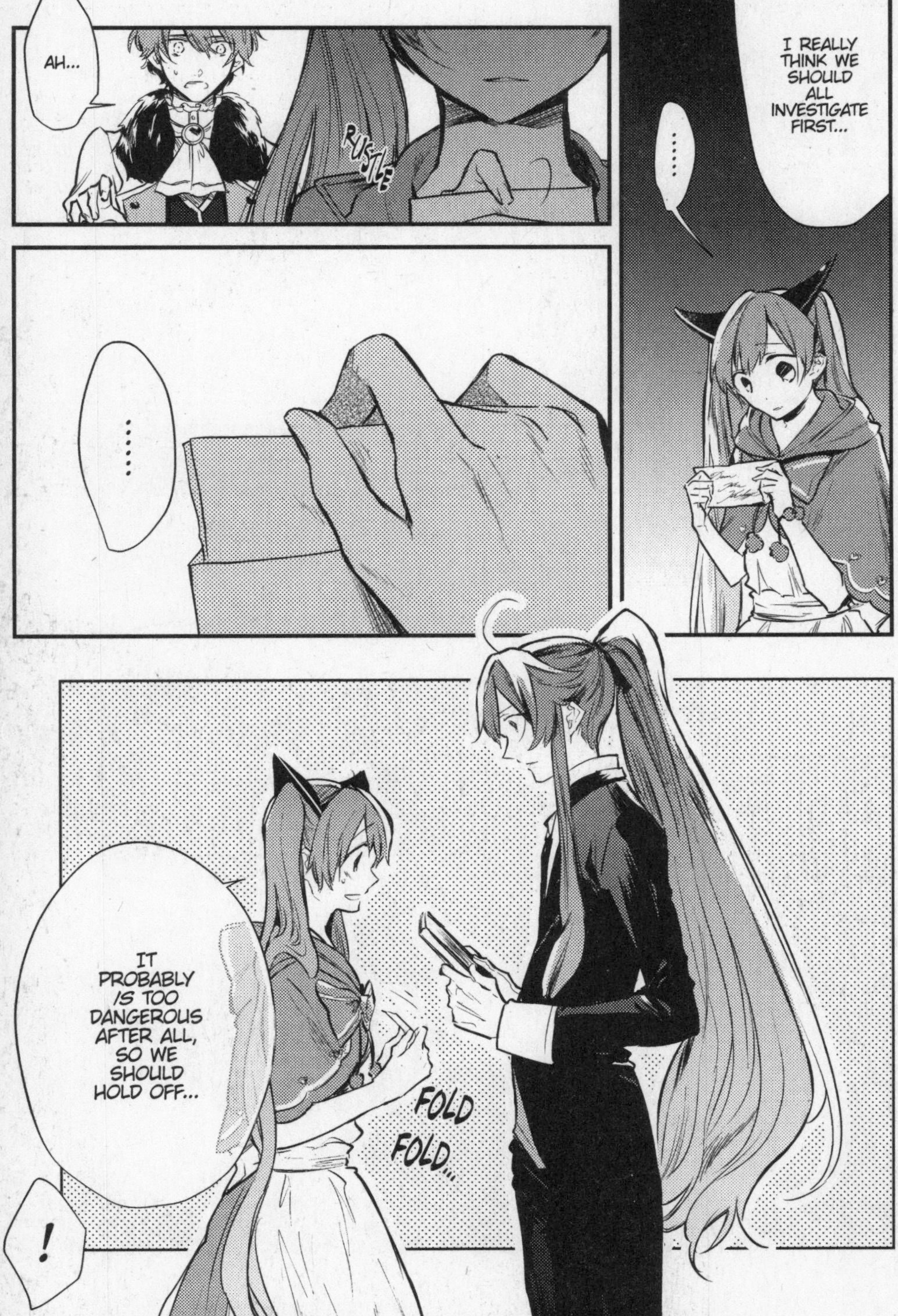
I REALLY THINK WE SHOULD ALL INVESTIGATE FIRST...
......
AH...
RUSTLE
......
FOLD
FOLD...
IT PROBABLY IS TOO DANGEROUS AFTER ALL, SO WE SHOULD HOLD OFF...
!

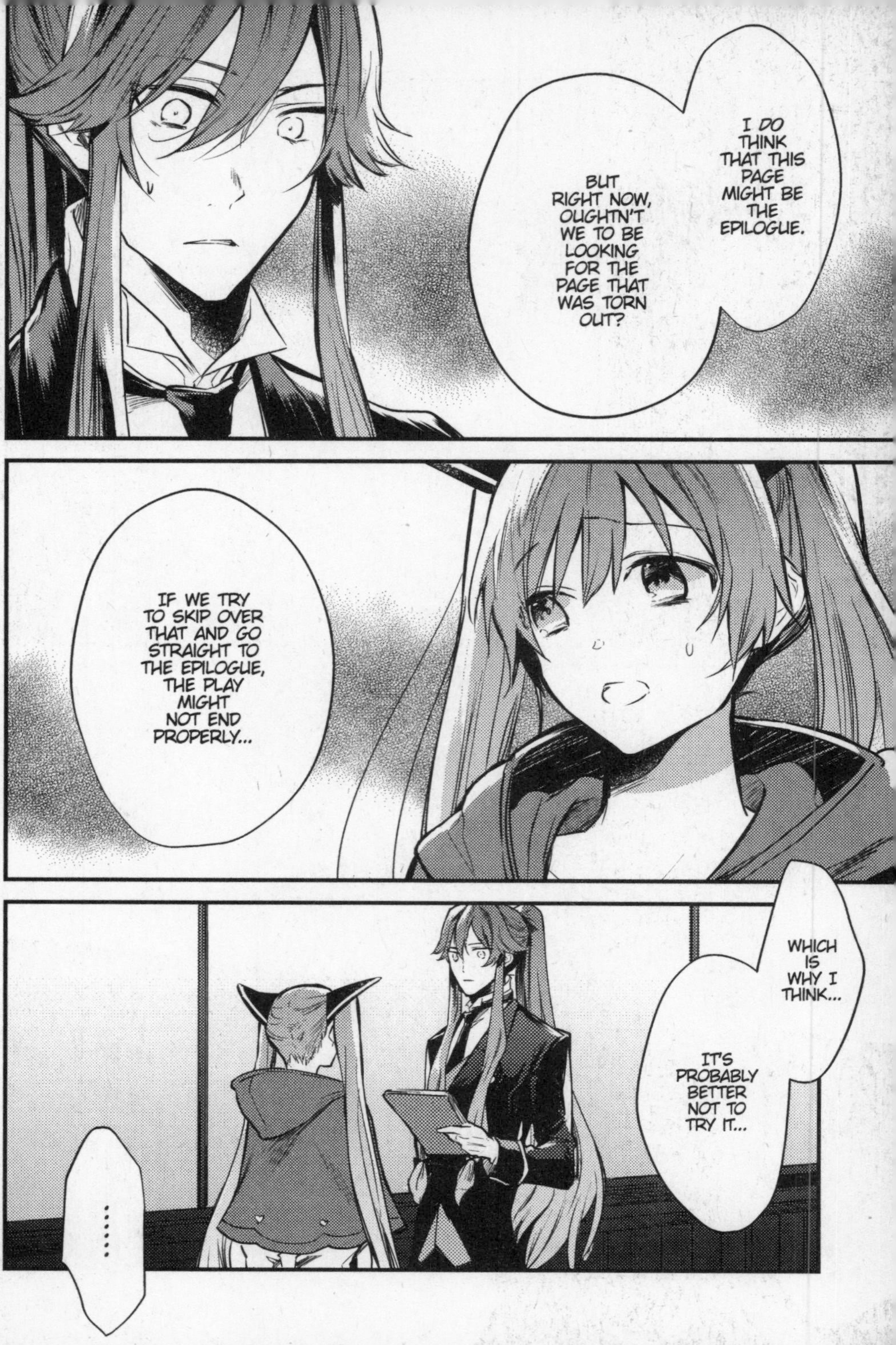
I DO THINK THAT THIS PAGE MIGHT BE THE EPILOGUE.
BUT RIGHT NOW, OUGHTN'T WE TO BE LOOKING FOR THE PAGE THAT WAS TORN OUT?
IF WE TRY TO SKIP OVER THAT AND GO STRAIGHT TO THE EPILOGUE, THE PLAY MIGHT NOT END PROPERLY...
WHICH IS WHY I THINK...
IT'S PROBABLY BETTER NOT TO TRY IT...
......

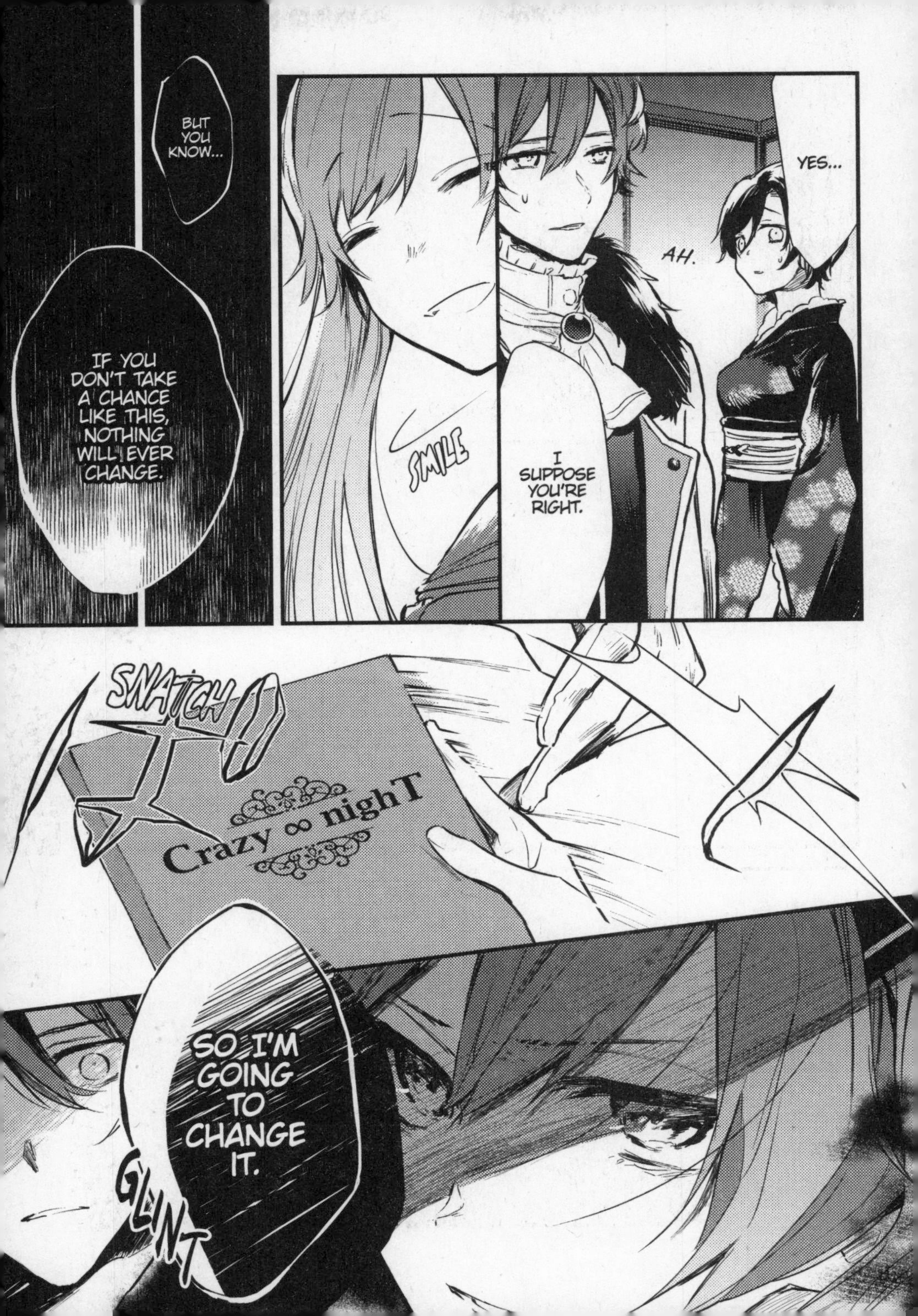
YES...
AH.
I SUPPOSE YOU'RE RIGHT.
SMILE
BUT YOU KNOW...
IF YOU DON'T TAKE A CHANCE LIKE THIS, NOTHING WILL EVER CHANGE.
SNATCH
Crazy ∞ nighT
SO I'M GOING TO CHANGE IT.
GLINT

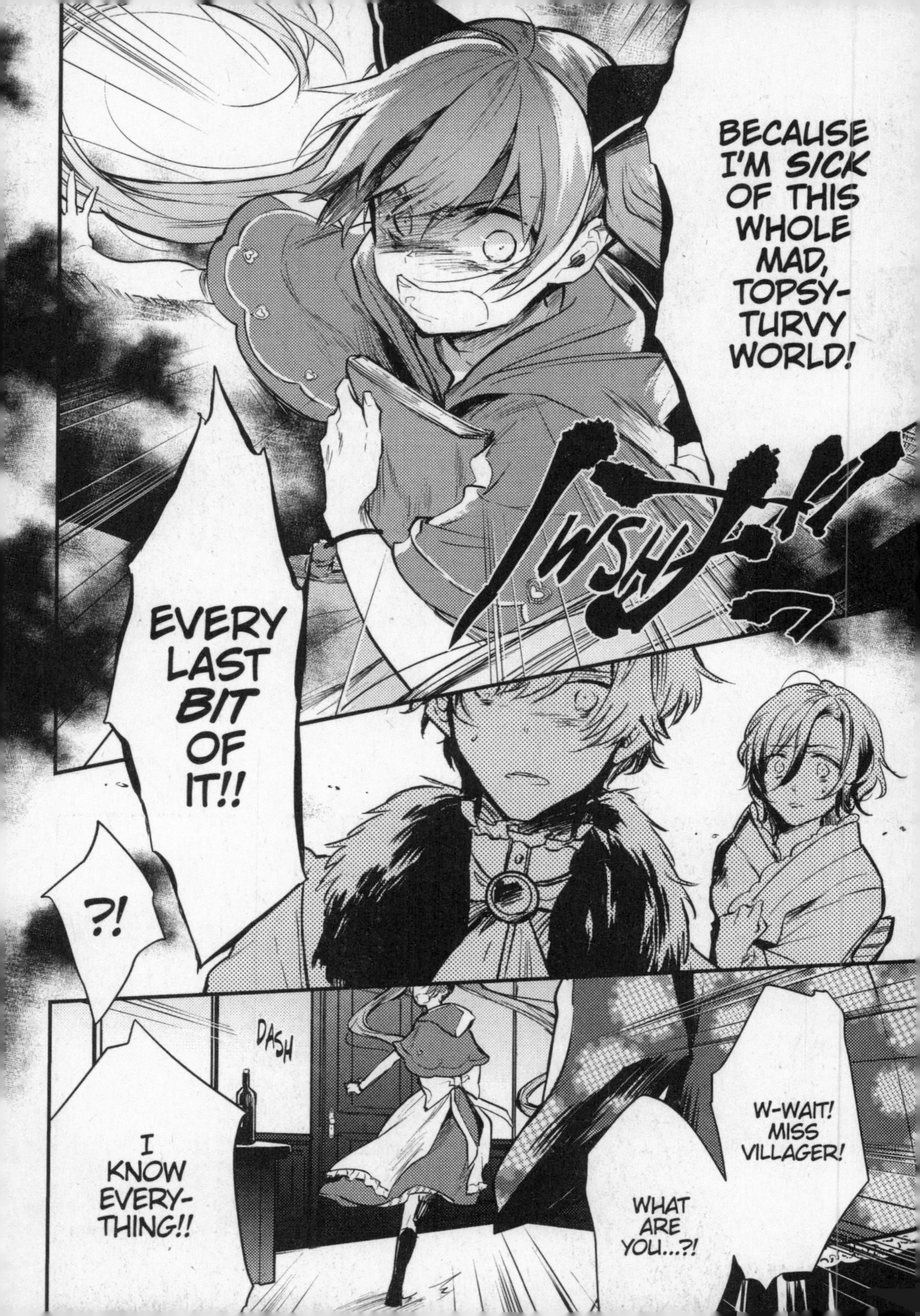
BECAUSE I'M SICK OF THIS WHOLE MAD, TOPSY-TURVY WORLD!
WSH
EVERY LAST BIT OF IT!!
?!
W-WAIT! MISS VILLAGER!
WHAT ARE YOU...?!
DASH
I KNOW EVERY-THING!!

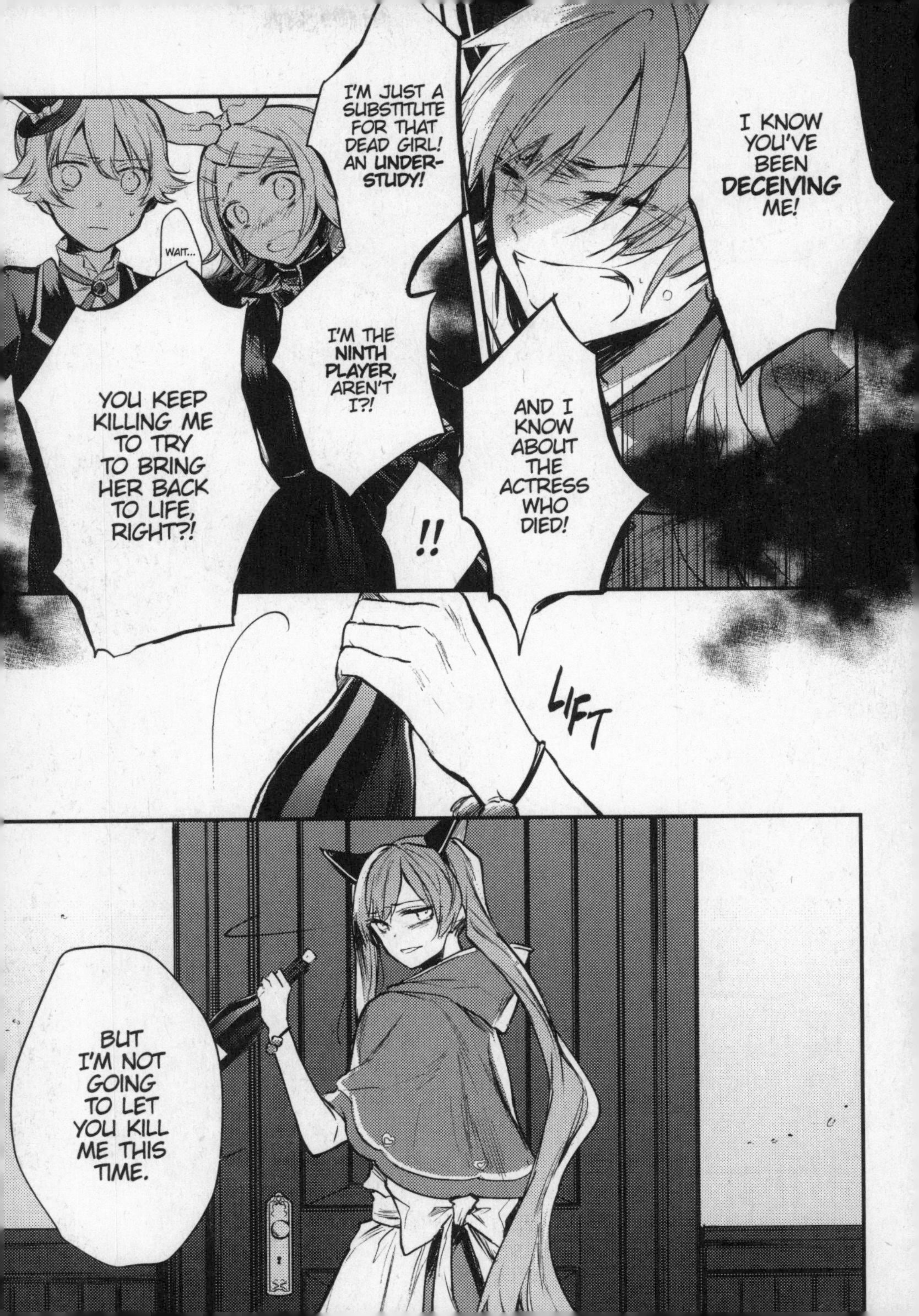
I KNOW YOU'VE BEEN DECEIVING ME!
I'M JUST A SUBSTITUTE FOR THAT DEAD GIRL! AN UNDERSTUDY!
WAIT...
AND I KNOW ABOUT THE ACTRESS WHO DIED!
I'M THE NINTH PLAYER, AREN'T I?!
!!
YOU KEEP KILLING ME TO TRY TO BRING HER BACK TO LIFE, RIGHT?!
LIFT
BUT I'M NOT GOING TO LET YOU KILL ME THIS TIME.

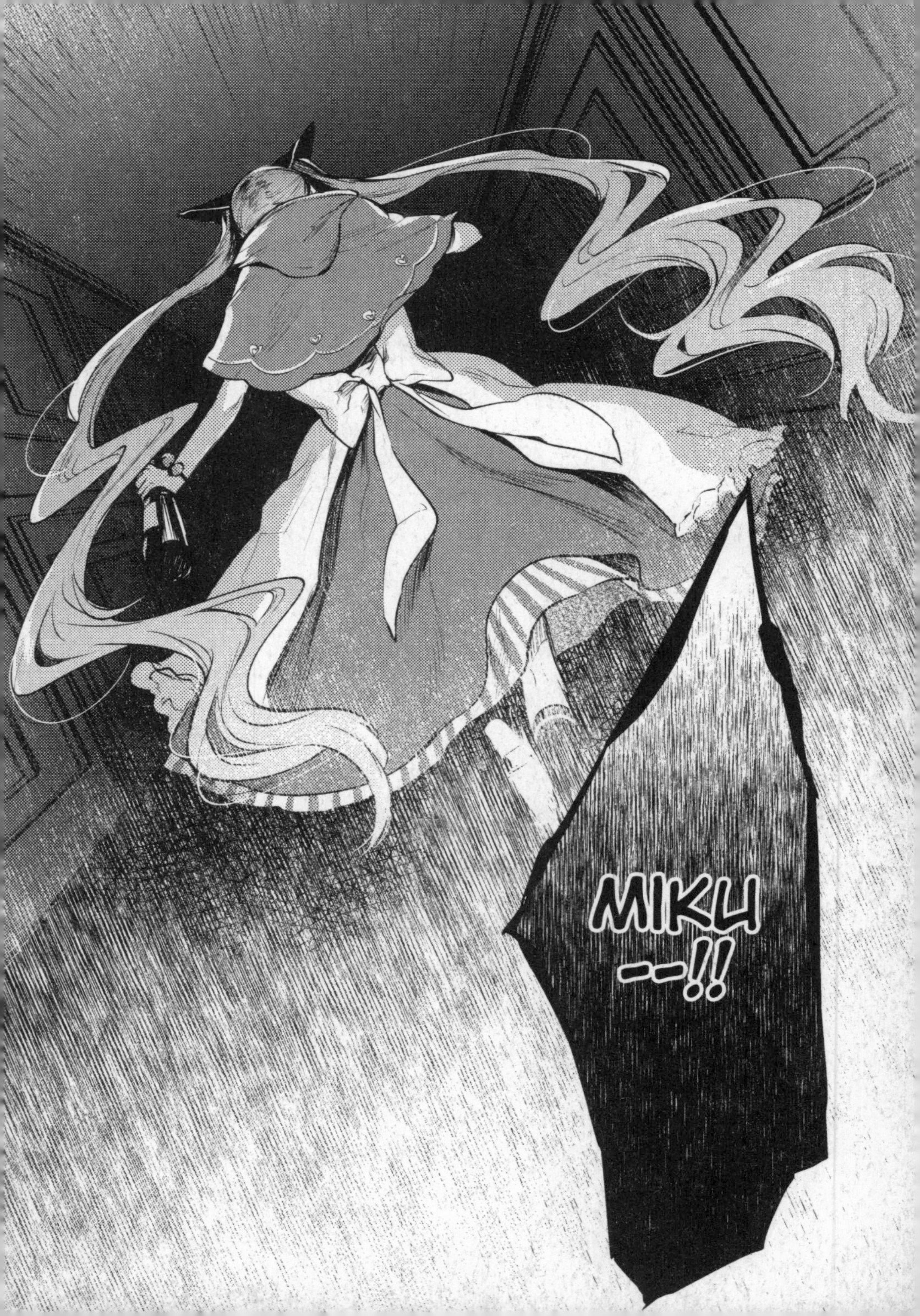
MIKU --!!

Bad∞End∞Night
～インセイン・パーティー～

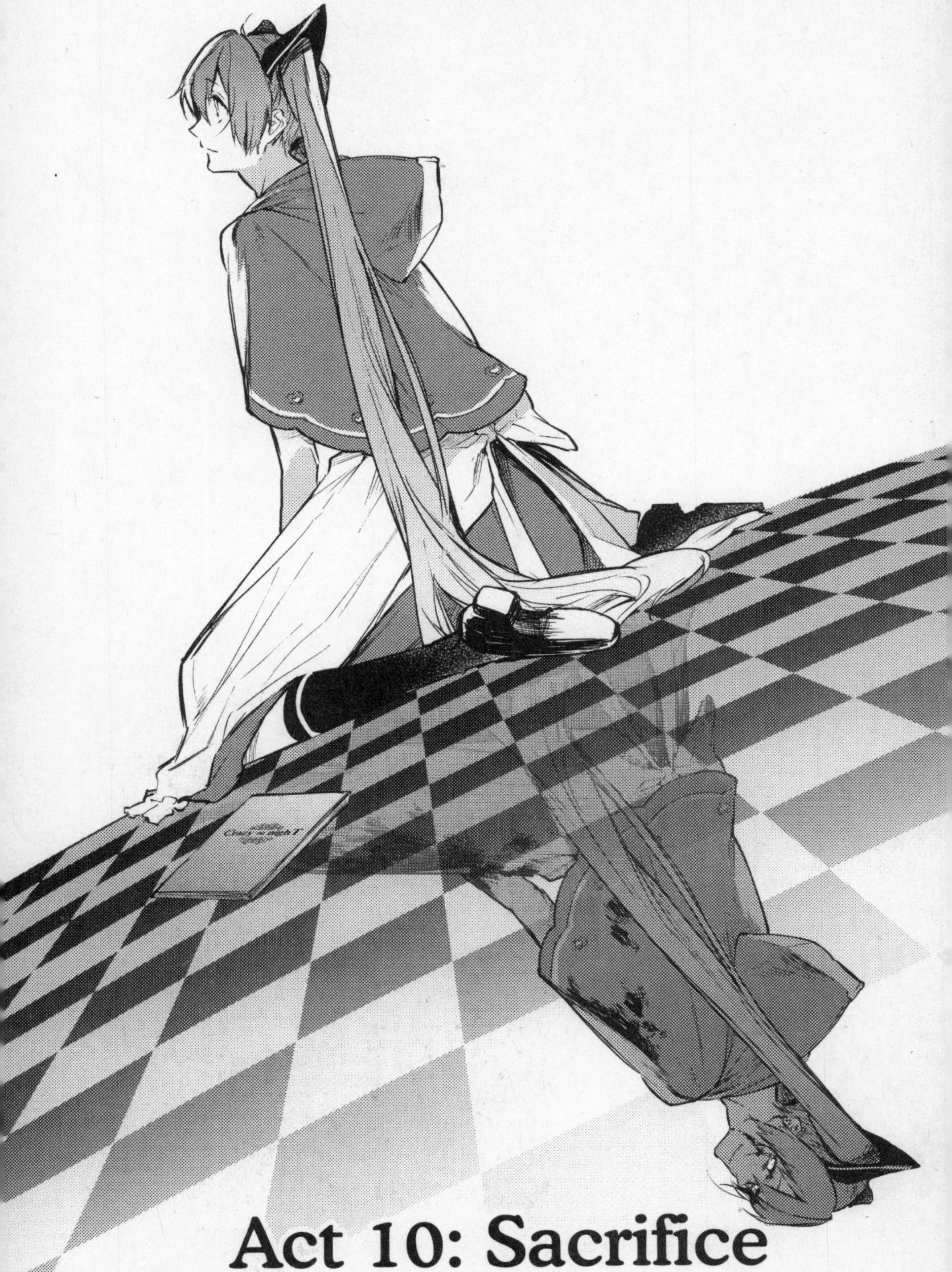

Act 10: Sacrifice

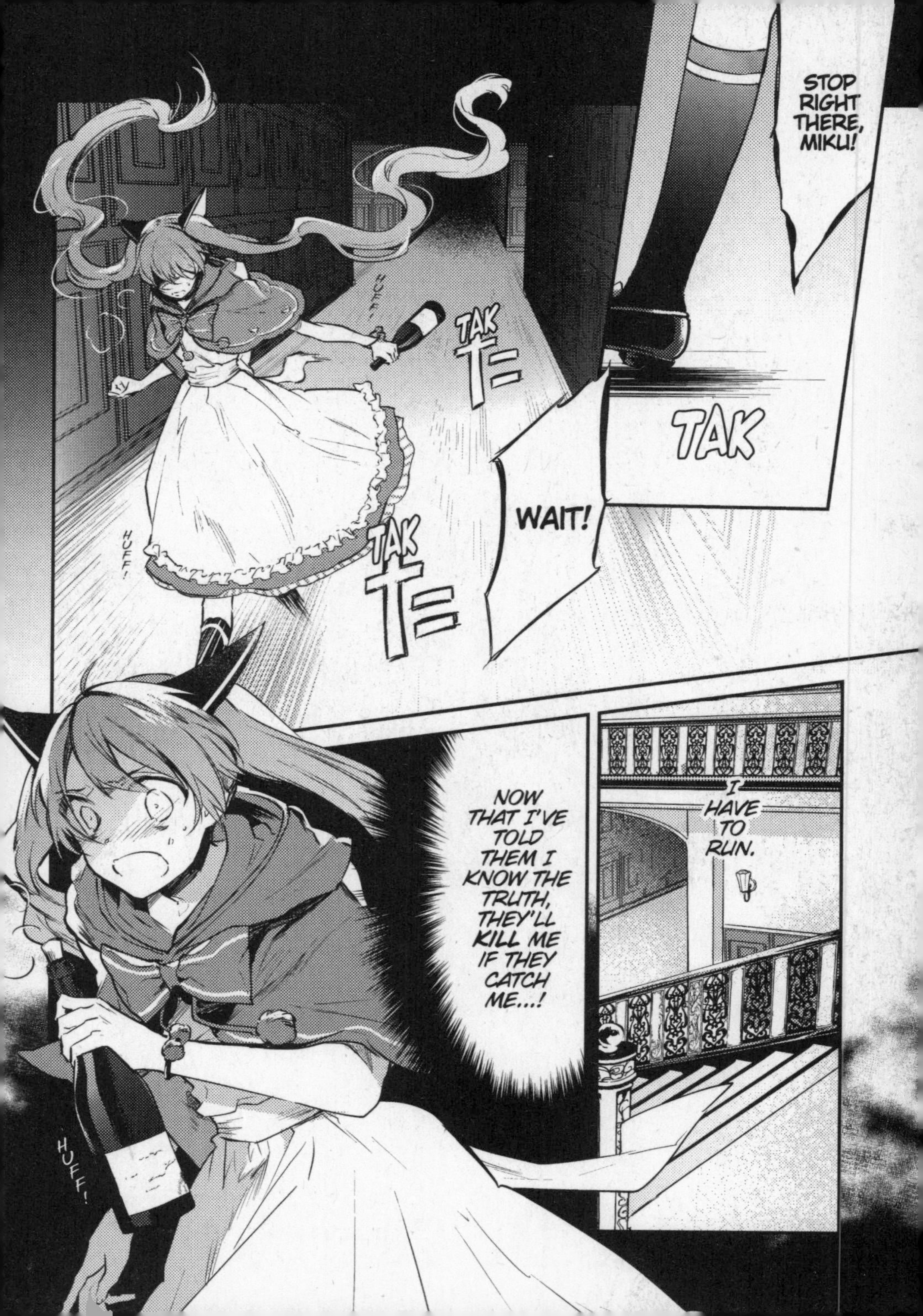
STOP RIGHT THERE, MIKU!
TAK
WAIT!
TAK
HUFF!
TAK
HUFF!
I HAVE TO RUN.
NOW THAT I'VE TOLD THEM I KNOW THE TRUTH, THEY'LL KILL ME IF THEY CATCH ME...!
HUFF!

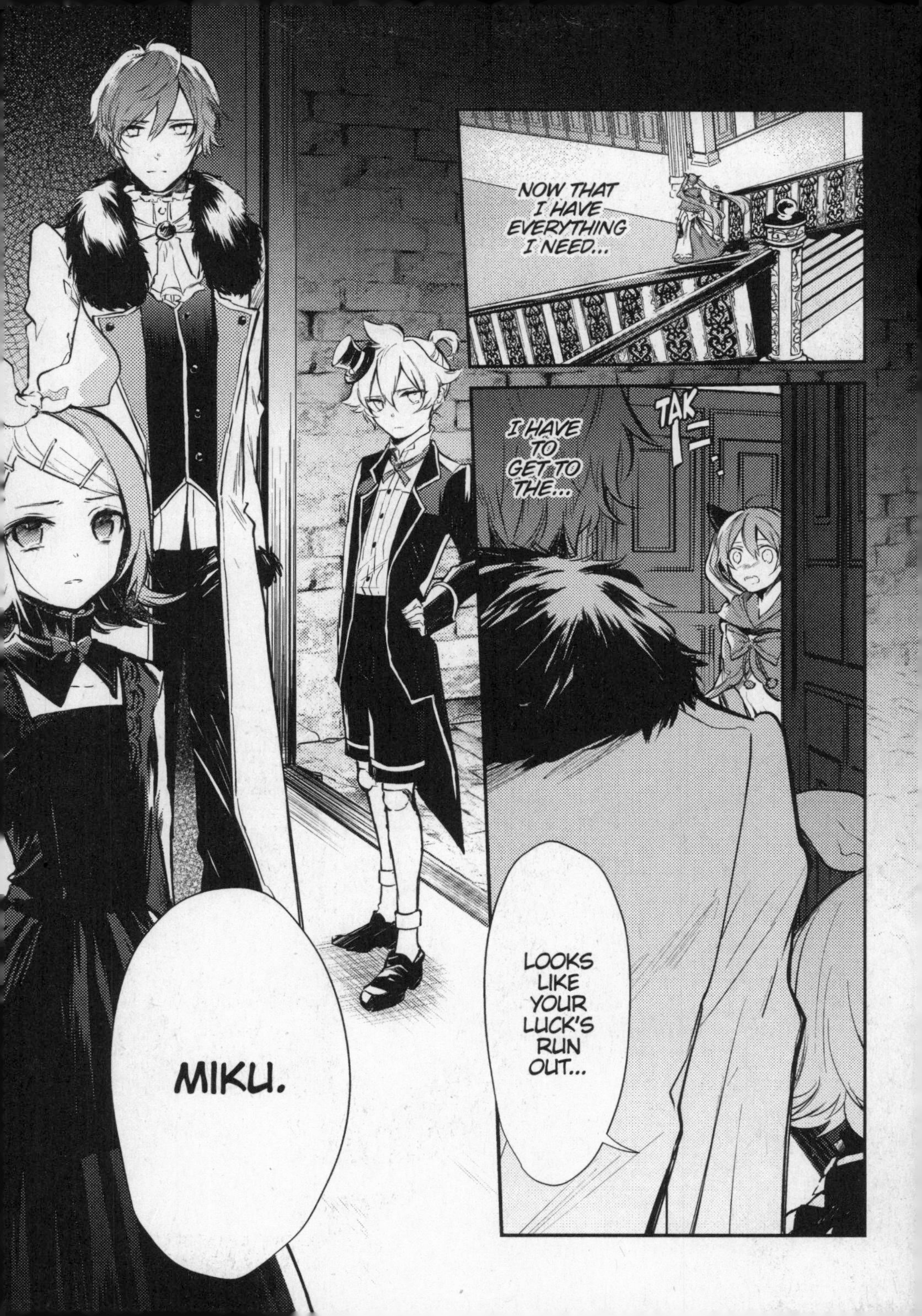
NOW THAT I HAVE EVERYTHING I NEED...
I HAVE TO GET TO THE...
TAK
LOOKS LIKE YOUR LUCK'S RUN OUT...
MIKU.

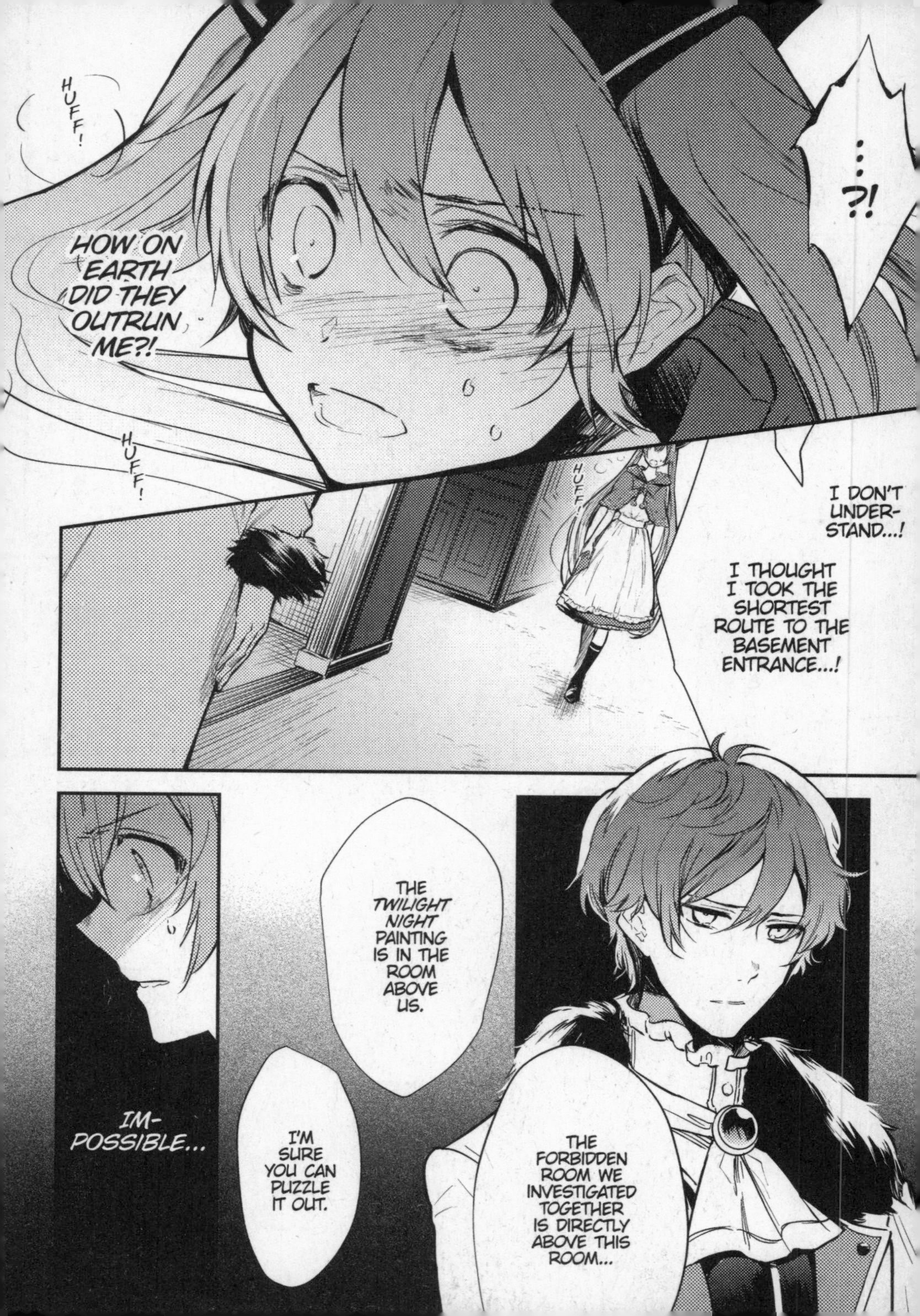
...?!
HUFF!
HOW ON EARTH DID THEY OUTRUN ME?!
HUFF!
HUFF!
I DON'T UNDER-STAND...!
I THOUGHT I TOOK THE SHORTEST ROUTE TO THE BASEMENT ENTRANCE...!
THE FORBIDDEN ROOM WE INVESTIGATED TOGETHER IS DIRECTLY ABOVE THIS ROOM...
THE *TWILIGHT NIGHT* PAINTING IS IN THE ROOM ABOVE US.
I'M SURE YOU CAN PUZZLE IT OUT.
IM-POSSIBLE...

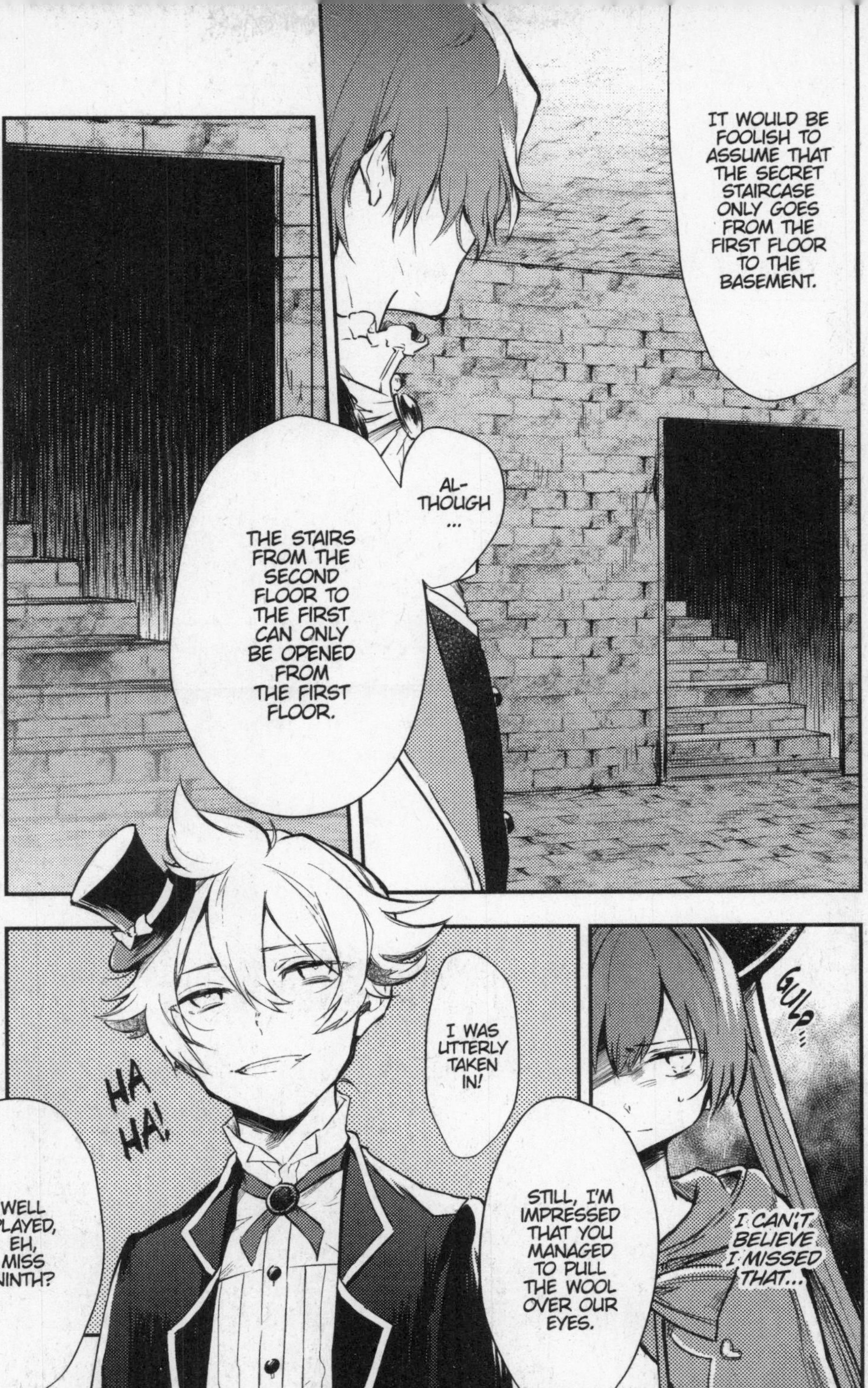
IT WOULD BE FOOLISH TO ASSUME THAT THE SECRET STAIRCASE ONLY GOES FROM THE FIRST FLOOR TO THE BASEMENT.
AL-THOUGH...
THE STAIRS FROM THE SECOND FLOOR TO THE FIRST CAN ONLY BE OPENED FROM THE FIRST FLOOR.
GULP...
I CAN'T BELIEVE I MISSED THAT...
I WAS UTTERLY TAKEN IN!
HA HA!
STILL, I'M IMPRESSED THAT YOU MANAGED TO PULL THE WOOL OVER OUR EYES.
WELL PLAYED, EH, MISS NINTH?

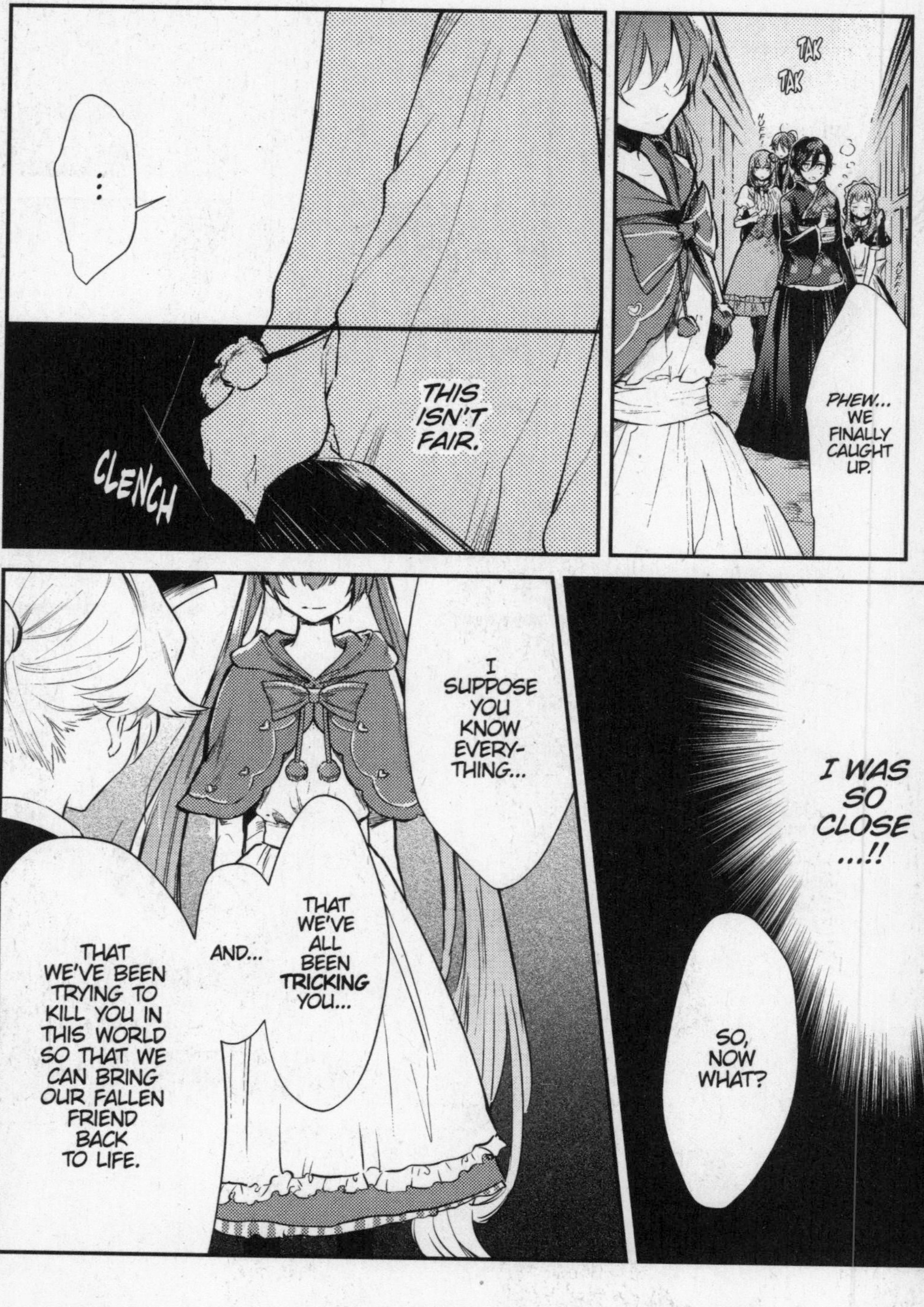
TAK
TAK
HUFF
HUFF
PHEW... WE FINALLY CAUGHT UP.
...
THIS ISN'T FAIR.
CLENCH
I WAS SO CLOSE ...!!
SO, NOW WHAT?
I SUPPOSE YOU KNOW EVERY-THING...
THAT WE'VE ALL BEEN TRICKING YOU...
AND...
THAT WE'VE BEEN TRYING TO KILL YOU IN THIS WORLD SO THAT WE CAN BRING OUR FALLEN FRIEND BACK TO LIFE.

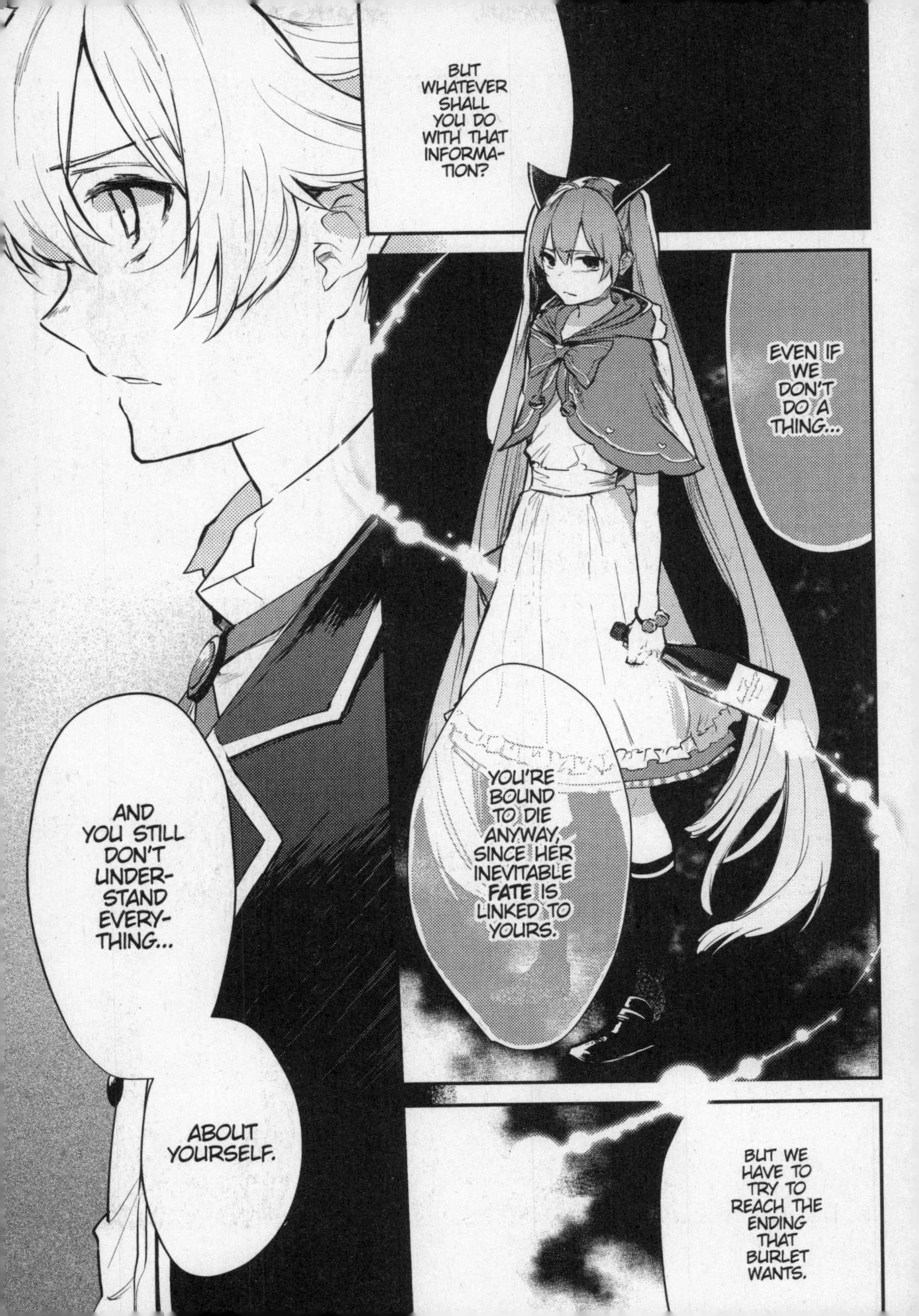
BUT WHATEVER SHALL YOU DO WITH THAT INFORMATION?
EVEN IF WE DON'T DO A THING...
YOU'RE BOUND TO DIE ANYWAY, SINCE HER INEVITABLE FATE IS LINKED TO YOURS.
BUT WE HAVE TO TRY TO REACH THE ENDING THAT BURLET WANTS.
AND YOU STILL DON'T UNDER-STAND EVERY-THING...
ABOUT YOURSELF.

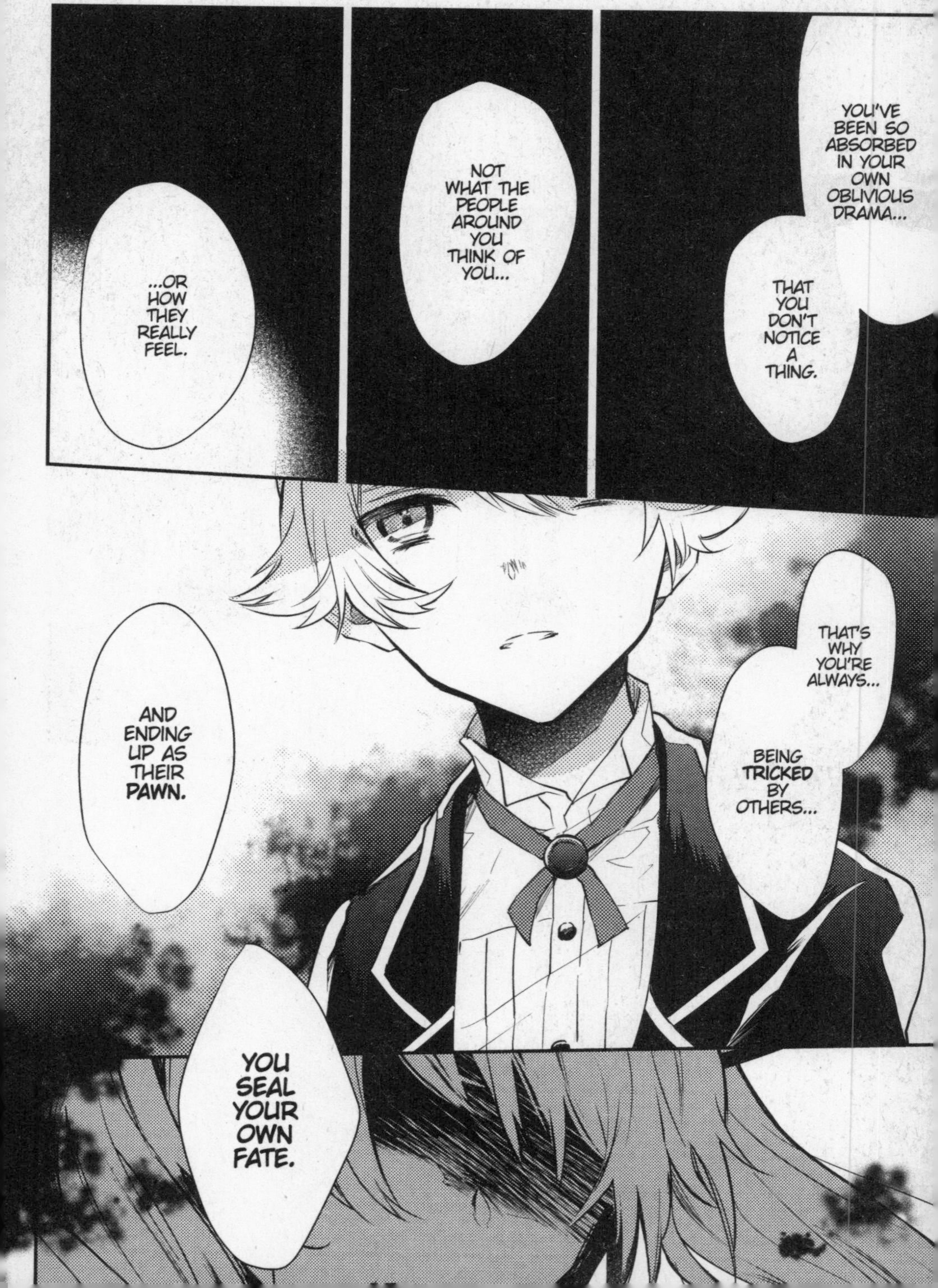
YOU'VE BEEN SO ABSORBED IN YOUR OWN OBLIVIOUS DRAMA...
THAT YOU DON'T NOTICE A THING.
NOT WHAT THE PEOPLE AROUND YOU THINK OF YOU...
...OR HOW THEY REALLY FEEL.
THAT'S WHY YOU'RE ALWAYS...
BEING TRICKED BY OTHERS...
AND ENDING UP AS THEIR PAWN.
YOU SEAL YOUR OWN FATE.

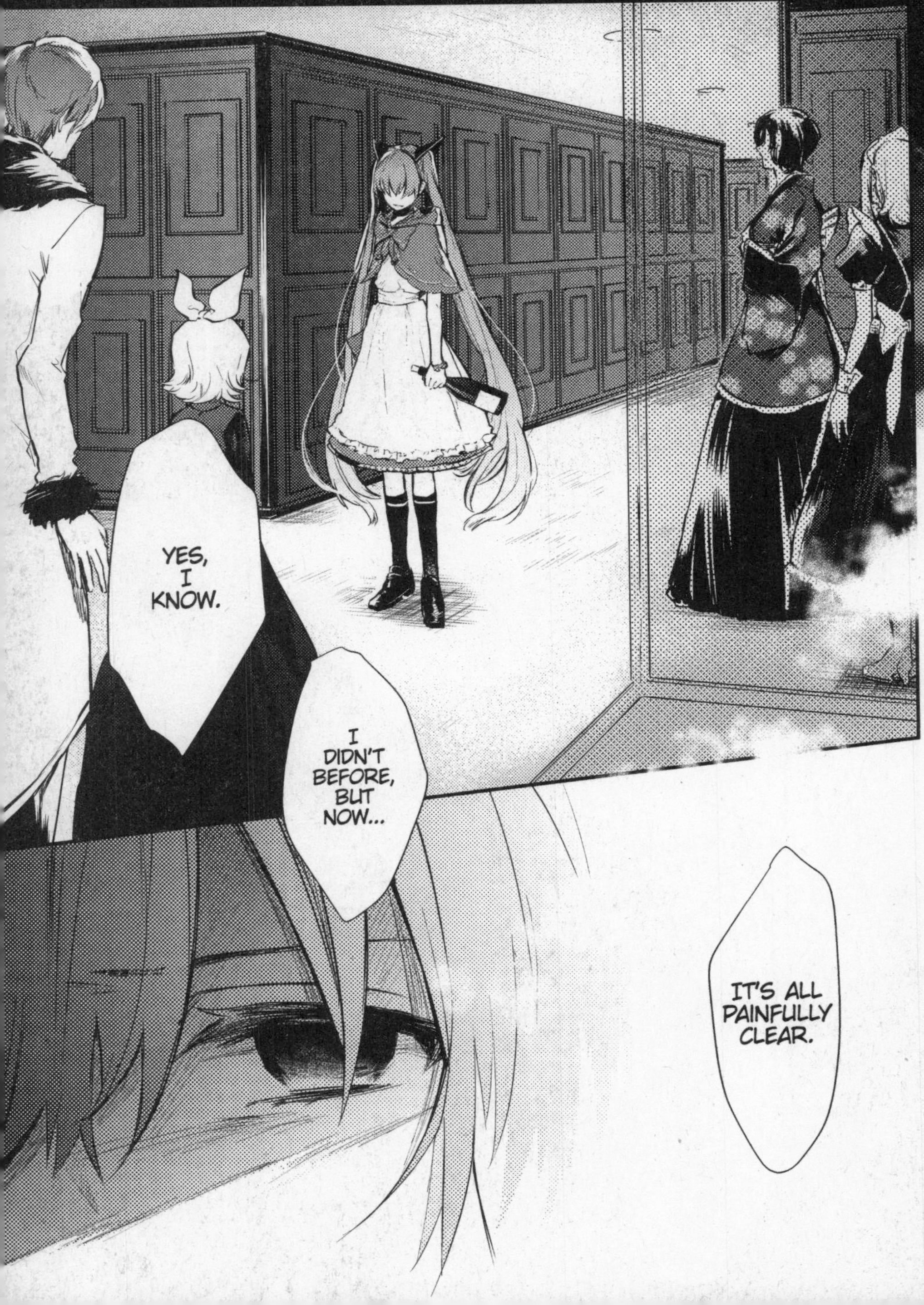
YES, I KNOW.
I DIDN'T BEFORE, BUT NOW...
IT'S ALL PAINFULLY CLEAR.

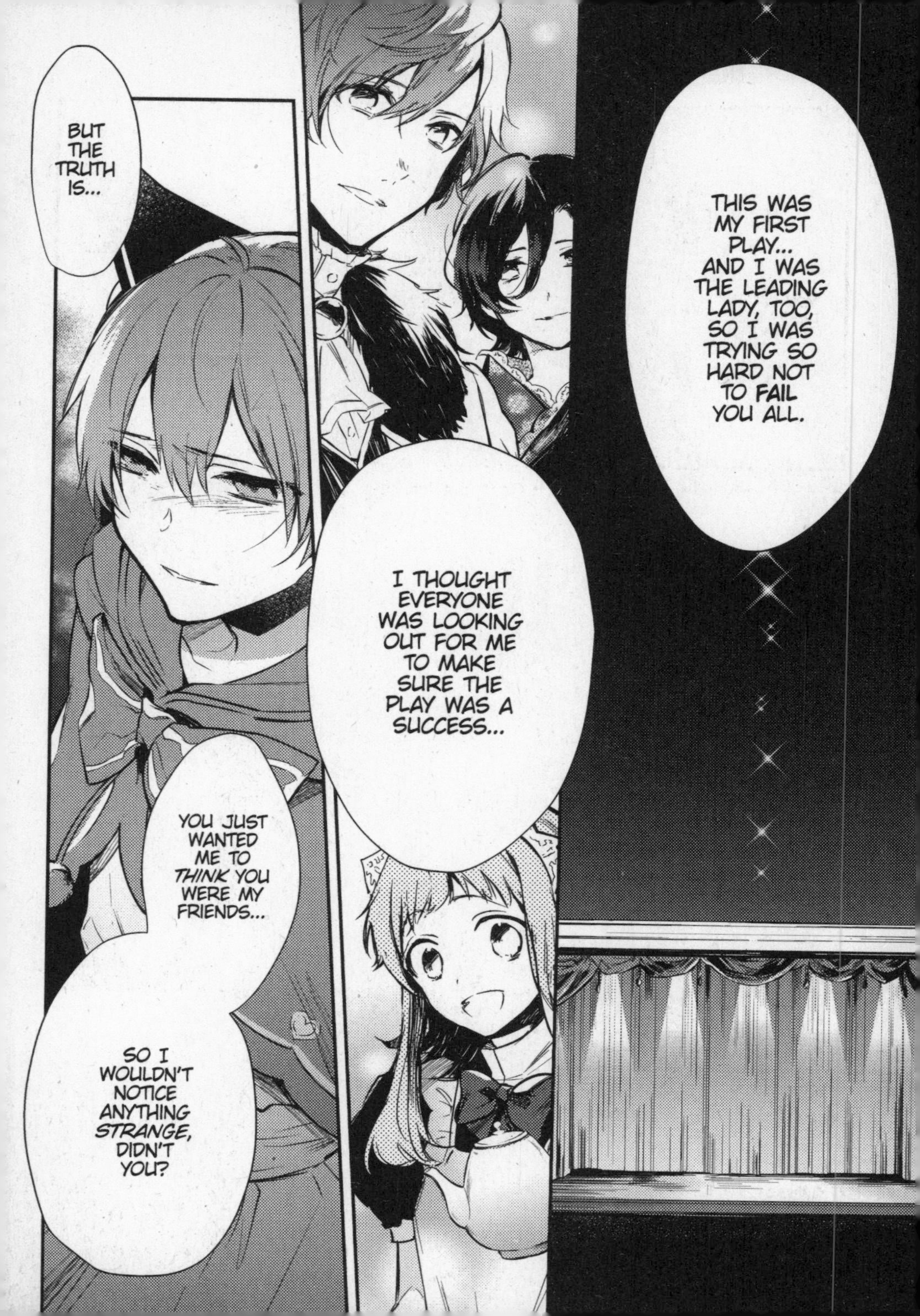

THIS WAS MY FIRST PLAY... AND I WAS THE LEADING LADY, TOO, SO I WAS TRYING SO HARD NOT TO **FAIL** YOU ALL.
I THOUGHT EVERYONE WAS LOOKING OUT FOR ME TO MAKE SURE THE PLAY WAS A SUCCESS...
BUT THE TRUTH IS...
YOU JUST WANTED ME TO *THINK* YOU WERE MY FRIENDS...
SO I WOULDN'T NOTICE ANYTHING *STRANGE*, DIDN'T YOU?

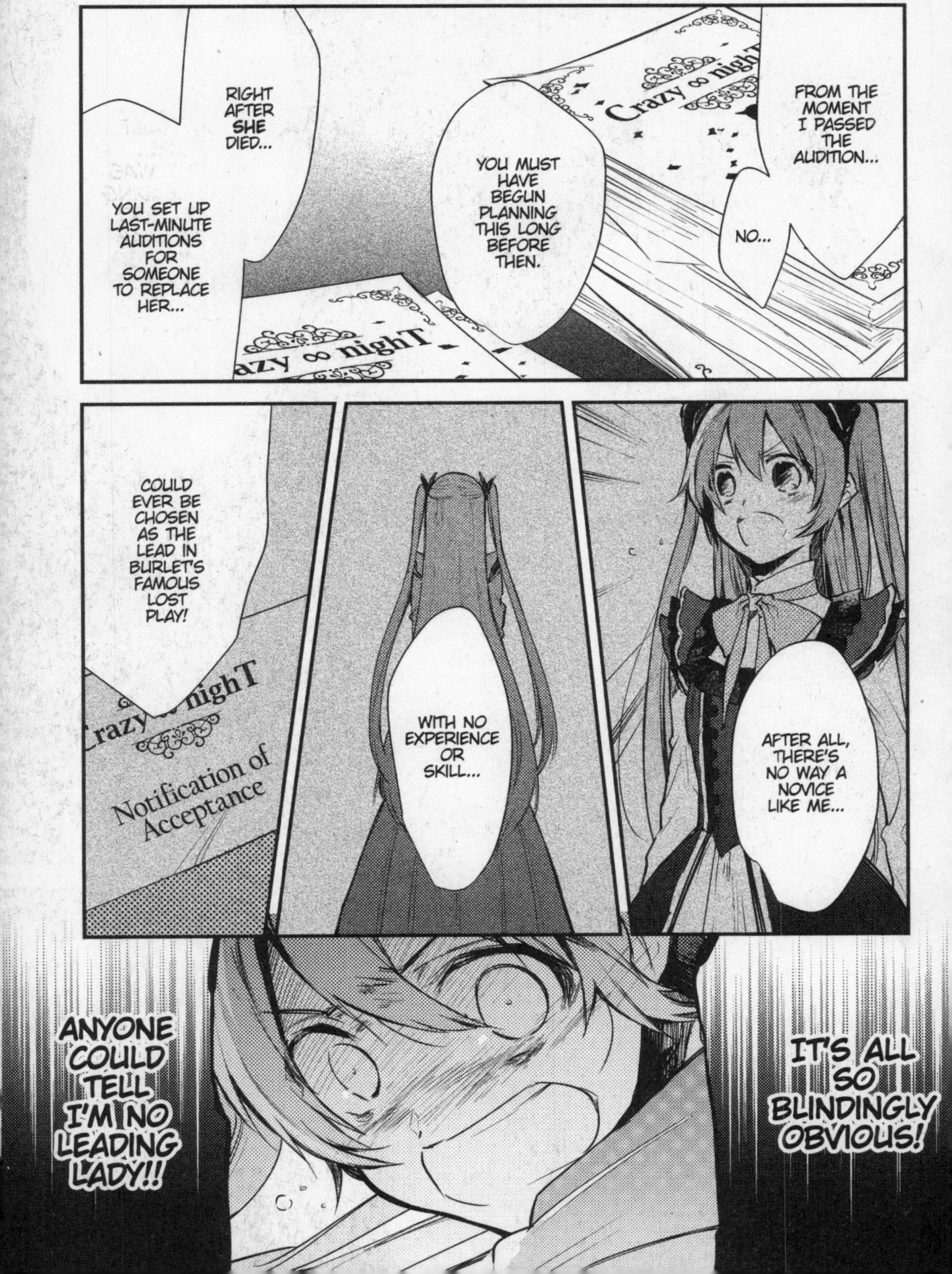
Crazy ∞ nighT
FROM THE MOMENT I PASSED THE AUDITION...
NO...
YOU MUST HAVE BEGUN PLANNING THIS LONG BEFORE THEN.
RIGHT AFTER SHE DIED...
YOU SET UP LAST-MINUTE AUDITIONS FOR SOMEONE TO REPLACE HER...
Crazy ∞ nighT
AFTER ALL, THERE'S NO WAY A NOVICE LIKE ME...
WITH NO EXPERIENCE OR SKILL...
COULD EVER BE CHOSEN AS THE LEAD IN BURLET'S FAMOUS LOST PLAY!
Crazy ∞ nighT
Notification of Acceptance
IT'S ALL SO BLINDINGLY OBVIOUS!
ANYONE COULD TELL I'M NO LEADING LADY!!

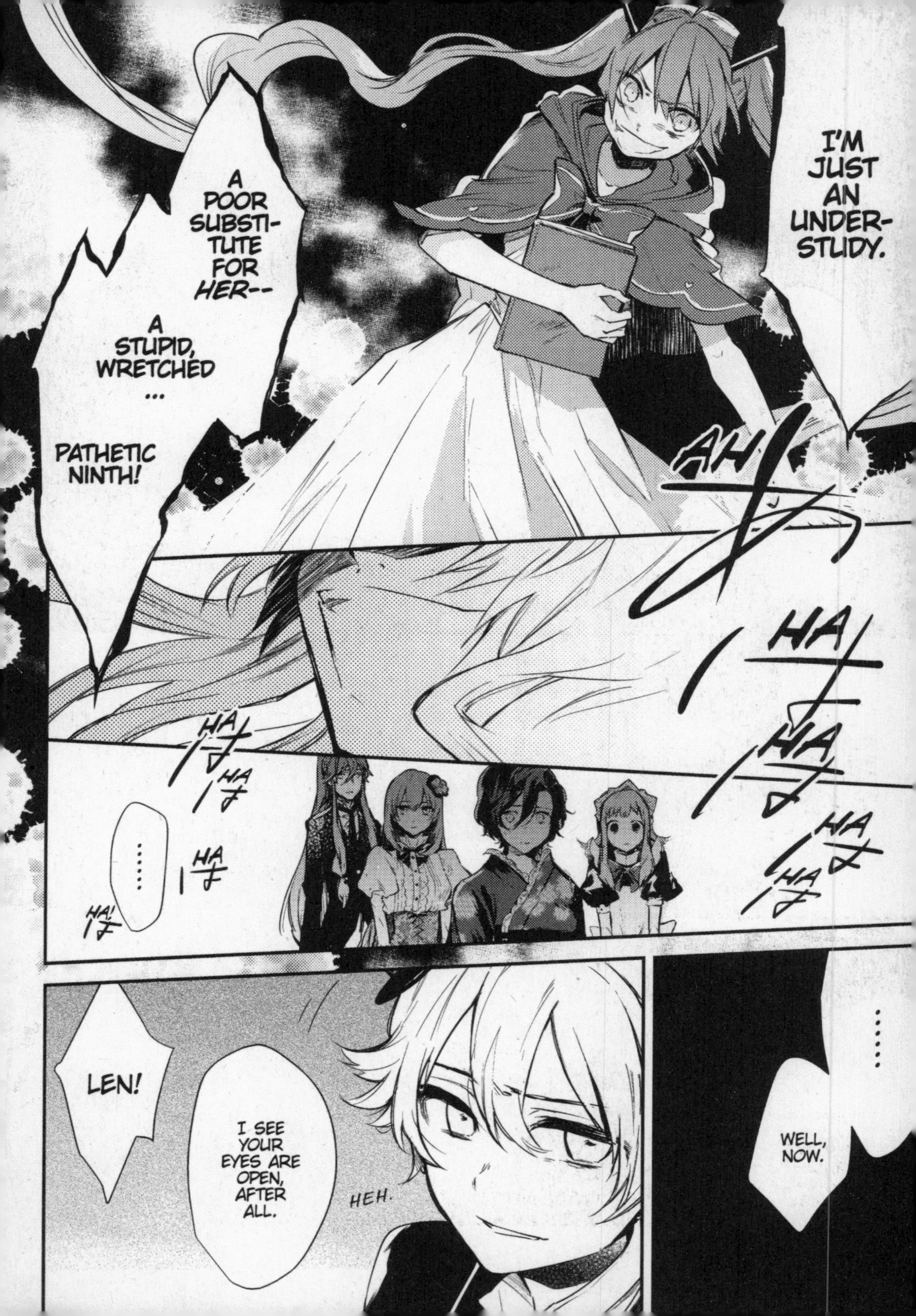
I'M JUST AN UNDER-STUDY.
A POOR SUBSTITUTE FOR HER--
A STUPID, WRETCHED ...
PATHETIC NINTH!
AH
HA
HA
HA
HA
HA
HA
HA
HA
......
......
WELL, NOW.
HEH.
I SEE YOUR EYES ARE OPEN, AFTER ALL.
LEN!

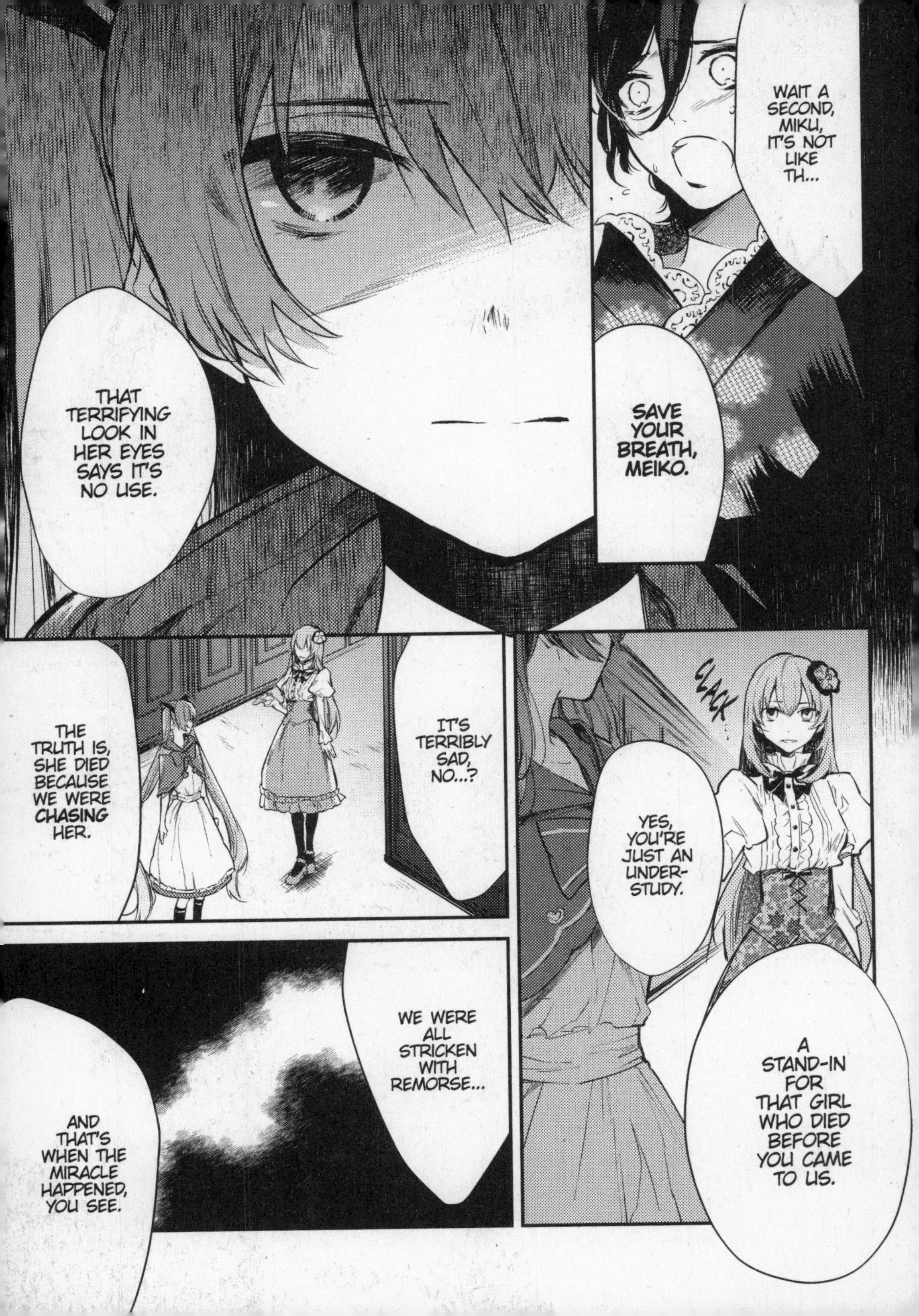
WAIT A SECOND, MIKU, IT'S NOT LIKE TH...
SAVE YOUR BREATH, MEIKO.
THAT TERRIFYING LOOK IN HER EYES SAYS IT'S NO USE.
CLACK
YES, YOU'RE JUST AN UNDER-STUDY.
A STAND-IN FOR THAT GIRL WHO DIED BEFORE YOU CAME TO US.
IT'S TERRIBLY SAD, NO...?
THE TRUTH IS, SHE DIED BECAUSE WE WERE CHASING HER.
WE WERE ALL STRICKEN WITH REMORSE...
AND THAT'S WHEN THE MIRACLE HAPPENED, YOU SEE.

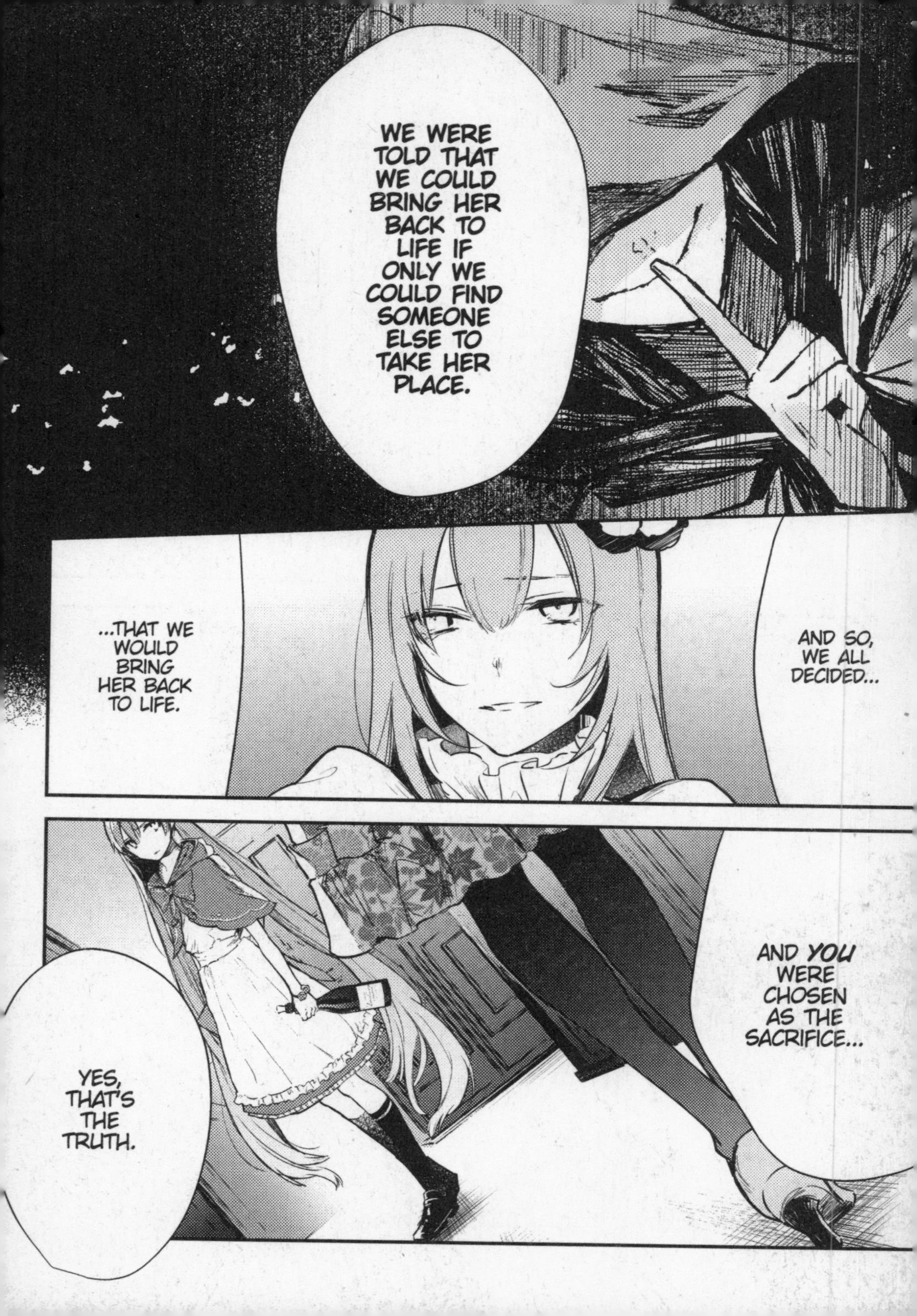
WE WERE TOLD THAT WE COULD BRING HER BACK TO LIFE IF ONLY WE COULD FIND SOMEONE ELSE TO TAKE HER PLACE.
AND SO, WE ALL DECIDED...
...THAT WE WOULD BRING HER BACK TO LIFE.
AND *YOU* WERE CHOSEN AS THE SACRIFICE...
YES, THAT'S THE TRUTH.

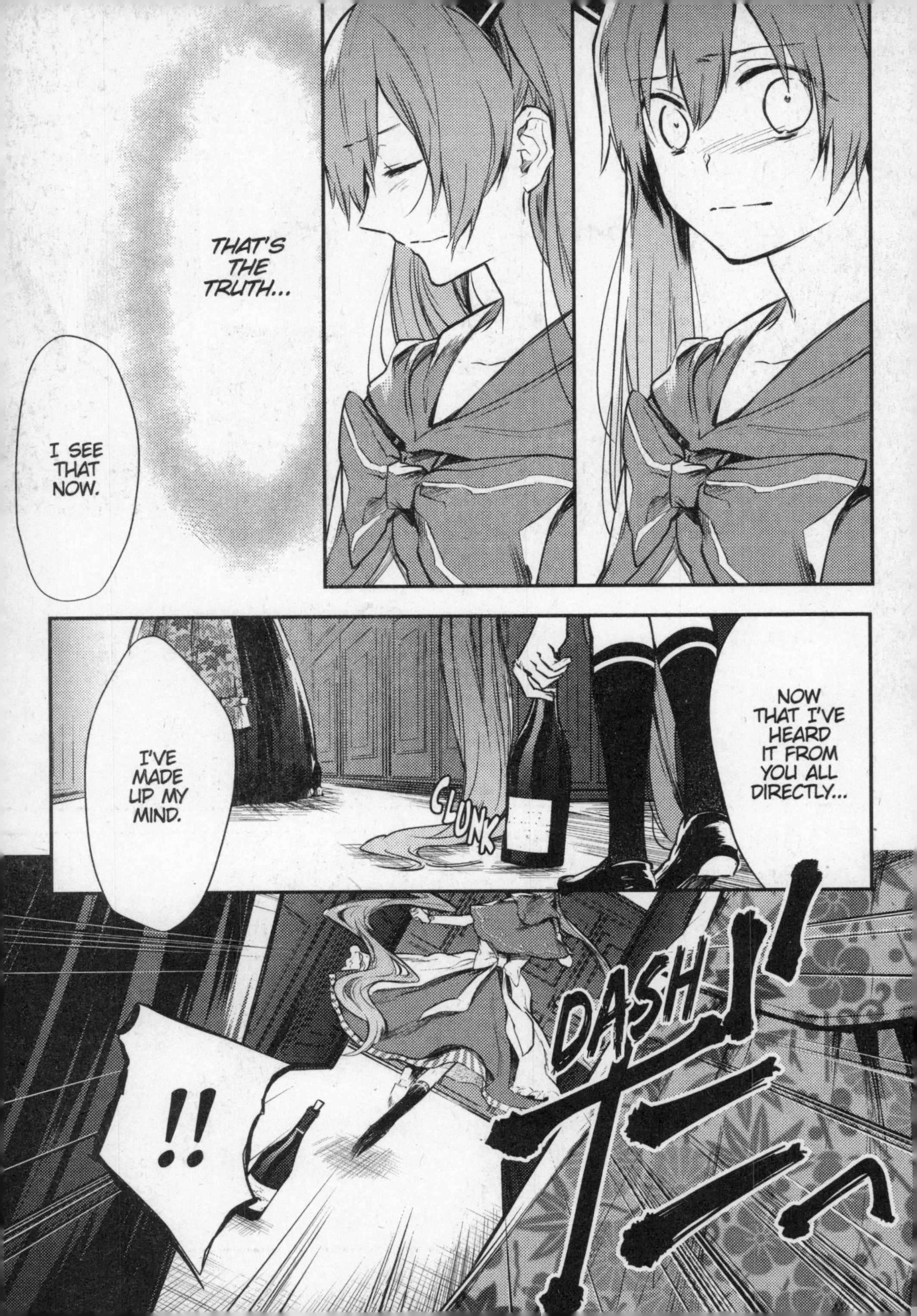
THAT'S THE TRUTH...
I SEE THAT NOW.
NOW THAT I'VE HEARD IT FROM YOU ALL DIRECTLY...
CLUNK
I'VE MADE UP MY MIND.
DASH
!!

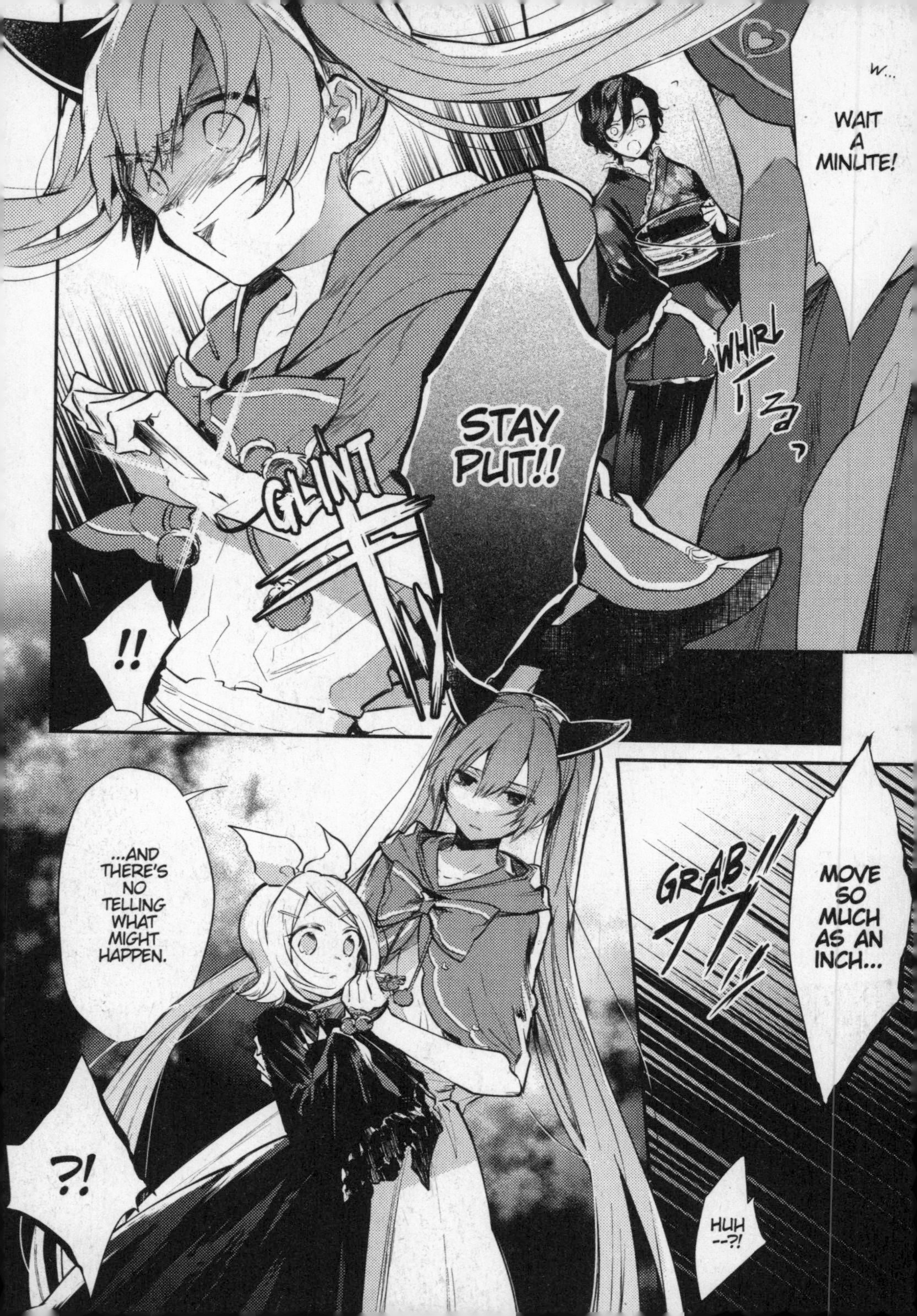
W...
WAIT A MINUTE!
WHIRL
STAY PUT!!
GLINT
!!
MOVE SO MUCH AS AN INCH...
GRAB
...AND THERE'S NO TELLING WHAT MIGHT HAPPEN.
HUH--?!
?!

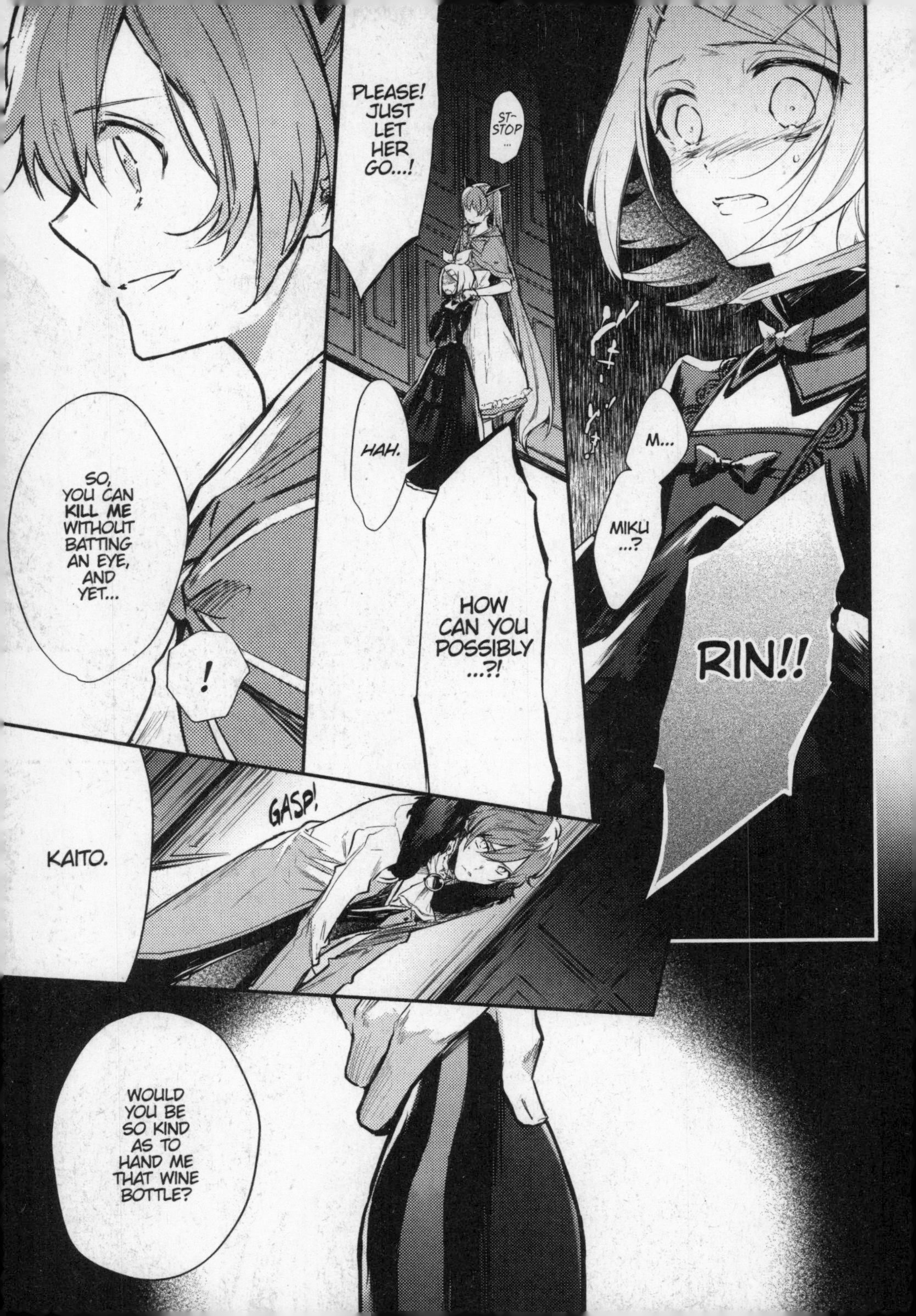
M...
MIKU...?
RIN!!
ST-STOP...
PLEASE! JUST LET HER GO...!
HAH.
HOW CAN YOU POSSIBLY...?!
SO, YOU CAN KILL ME WITHOUT BATTING AN EYE, AND YET...
!
GASP!
KAITO.
WOULD YOU BE SO KIND AS TO HAND ME THAT WINE BOTTLE?

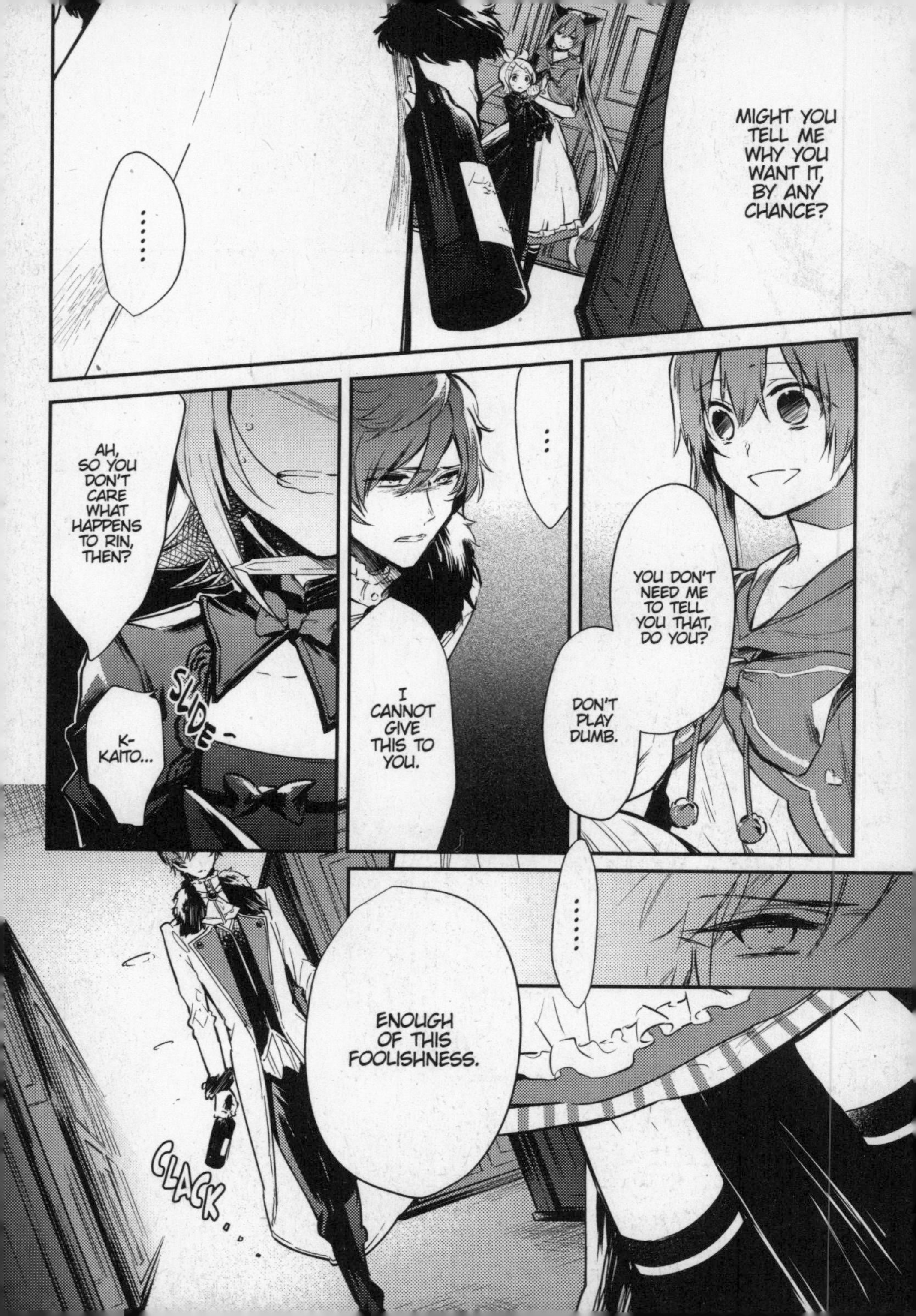
MIGHT YOU TELL ME WHY YOU WANT IT, BY ANY CHANCE?
......
YOU DON'T NEED ME TO TELL YOU THAT, DO YOU?
DON'T PLAY DUMB.
...
I CANNOT GIVE THIS TO YOU.
AH, SO YOU DON'T CARE WHAT HAPPENS TO RIN, THEN?
SLIDE
K-KAITO...
......
ENOUGH OF THIS FOOLISHNESS.
CLACK

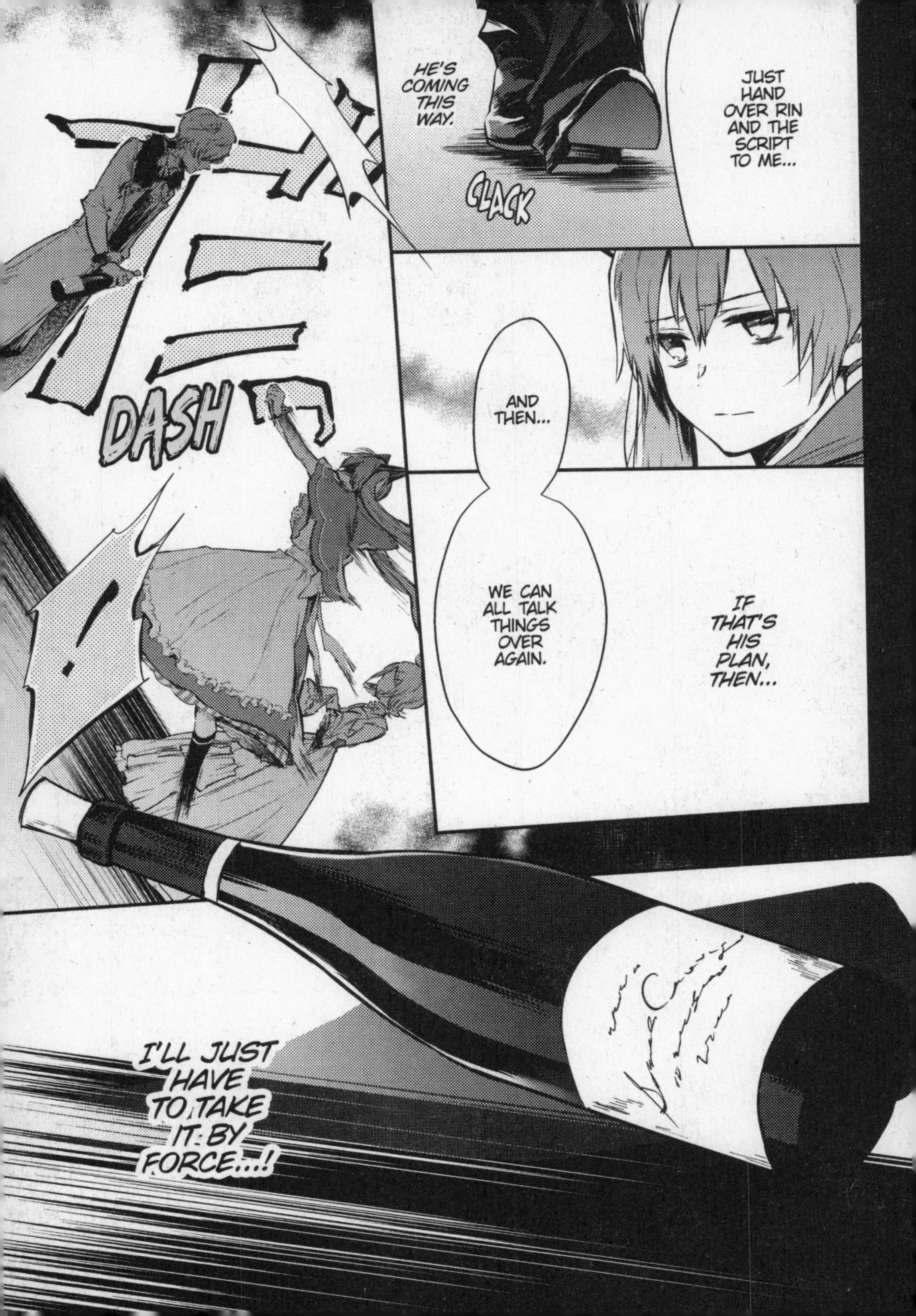
JUST HAND OVER RIN AND THE SCRIPT TO ME...
HE'S COMING THIS WAY.
CLACK
AND THEN...
WE CAN ALL TALK THINGS OVER AGAIN.
IF THAT'S HIS PLAN, THEN...
DASH
I'LL JUST HAVE TO TAKE IT BY FORCE...!

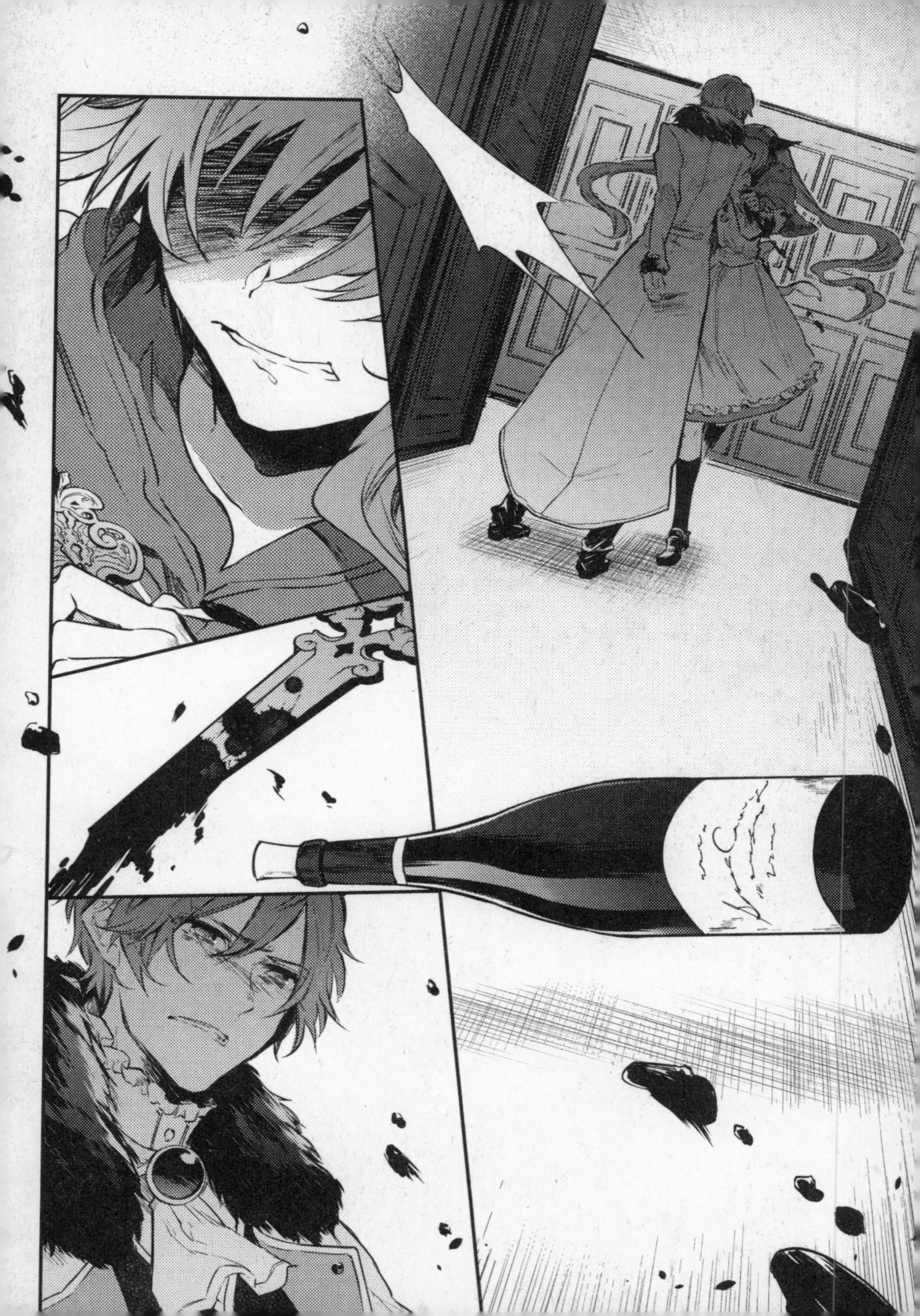

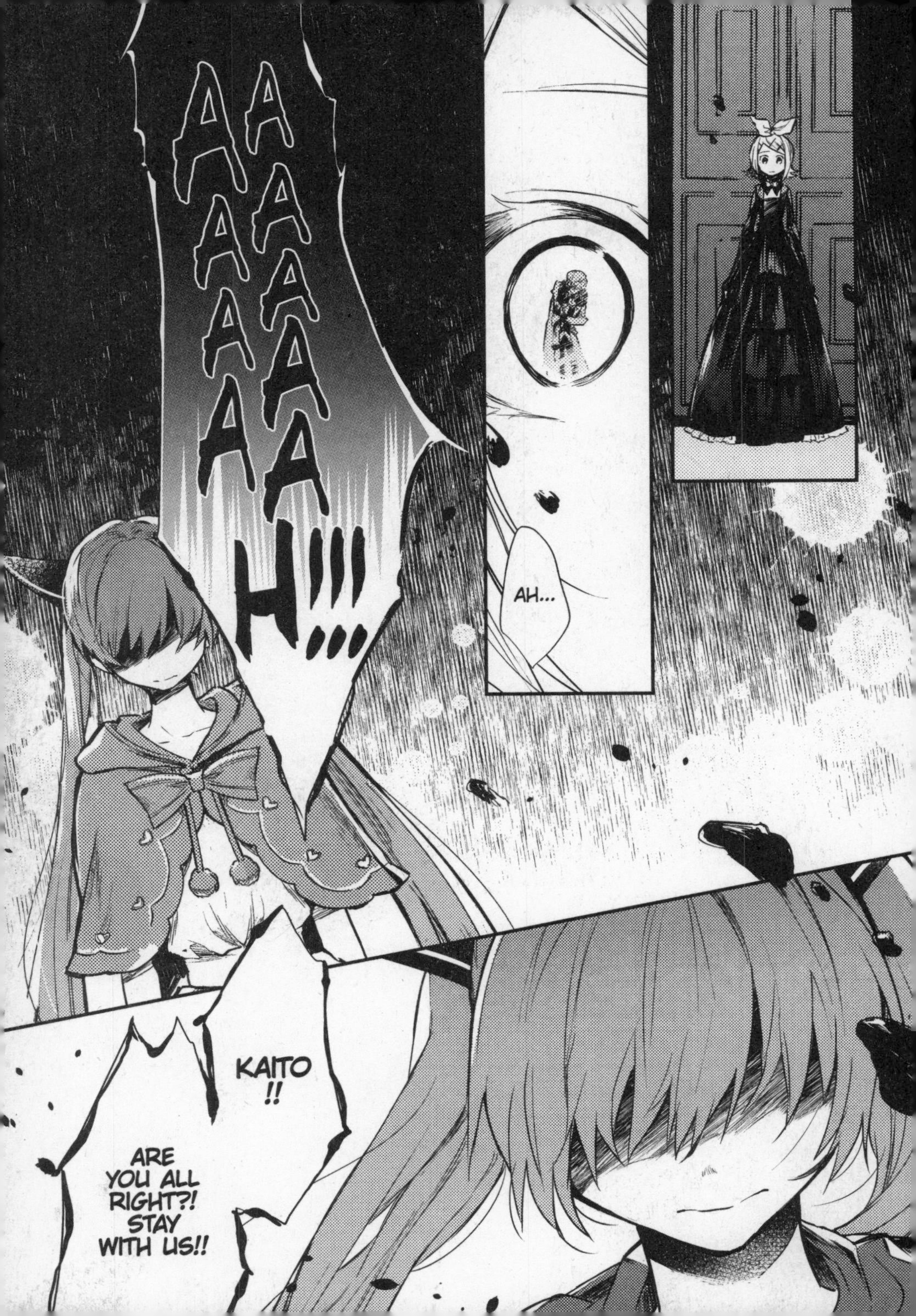
AH...
AAAAAAAAAAAH!!!
KAITO!!
ARE YOU ALL RIGHT?! STAY WITH US!!

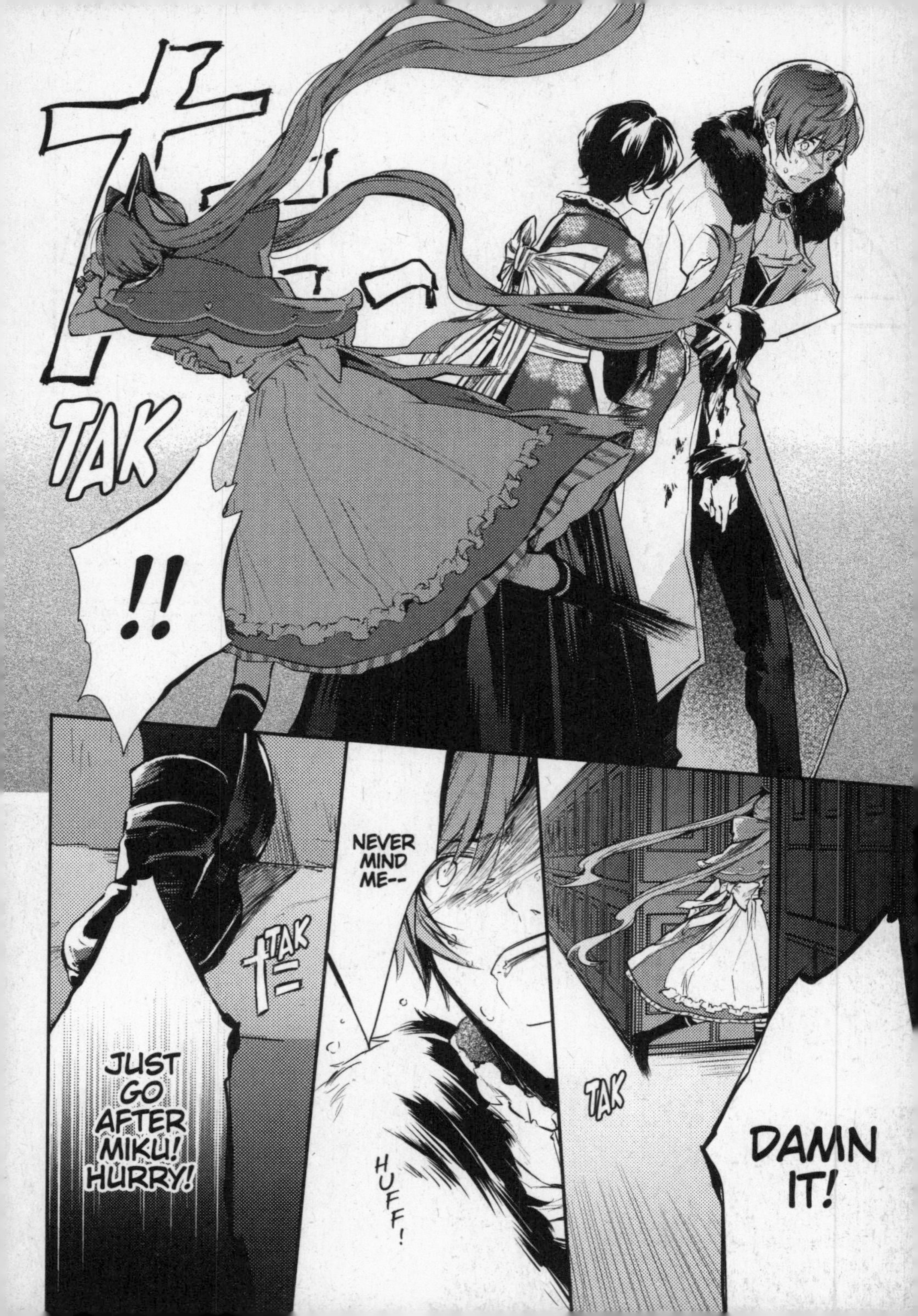
TAK
!!
TAK
DAMN IT!
NEVER MIND ME--
HUFF!
TAK
JUST GO AFTER MIKU! HURRY!

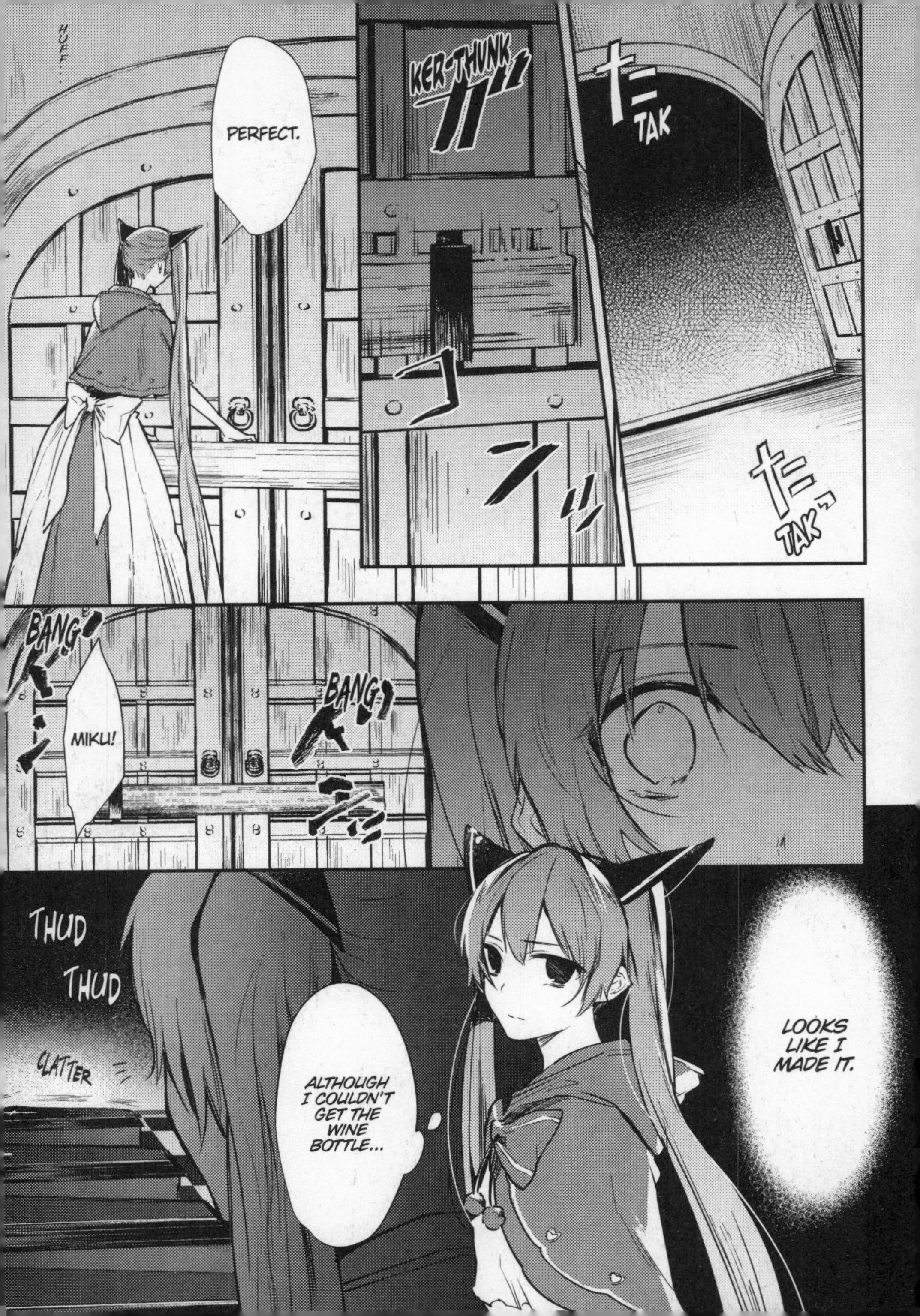

TAK
TAK
KER-THUNK
HUFF...
PERFECT.
BANG!
BANG!
MIKU!
LOOKS LIKE I MADE IT.
ALTHOUGH I COULDN'T GET THE WINE BOTTLE...
THUD
THUD
CLATTER

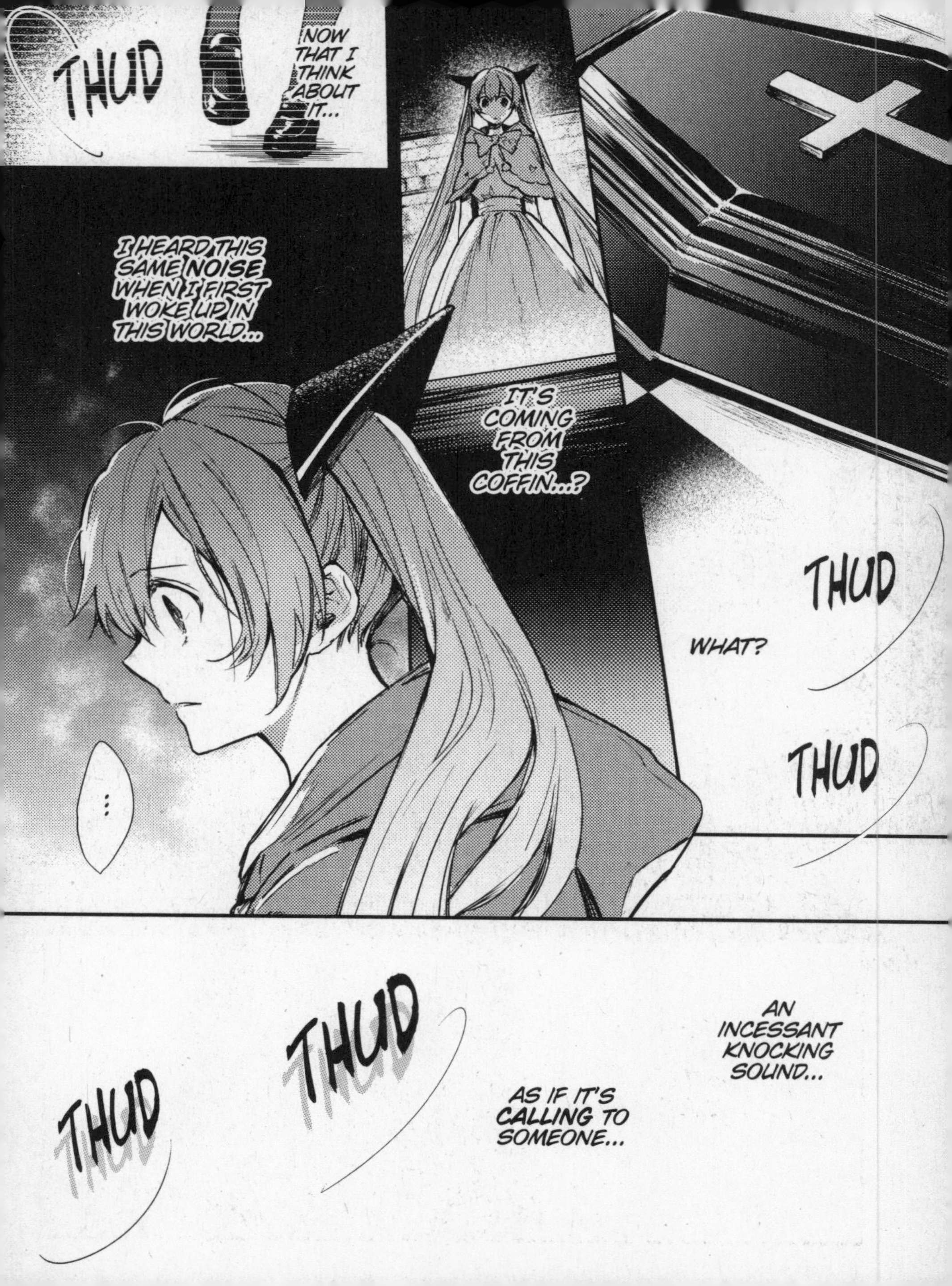
THUD
NOW THAT I THINK ABOUT IT...
I HEARD THIS SAME NOISE WHEN I FIRST WOKE UP IN THIS WORLD...
IT'S COMING FROM THIS COFFIN...?
THUD
WHAT?
THUD
...
AN INCESSANT KNOCKING SOUND...
AS IF IT'S CALLING TO SOMEONE...
THUD
THUD

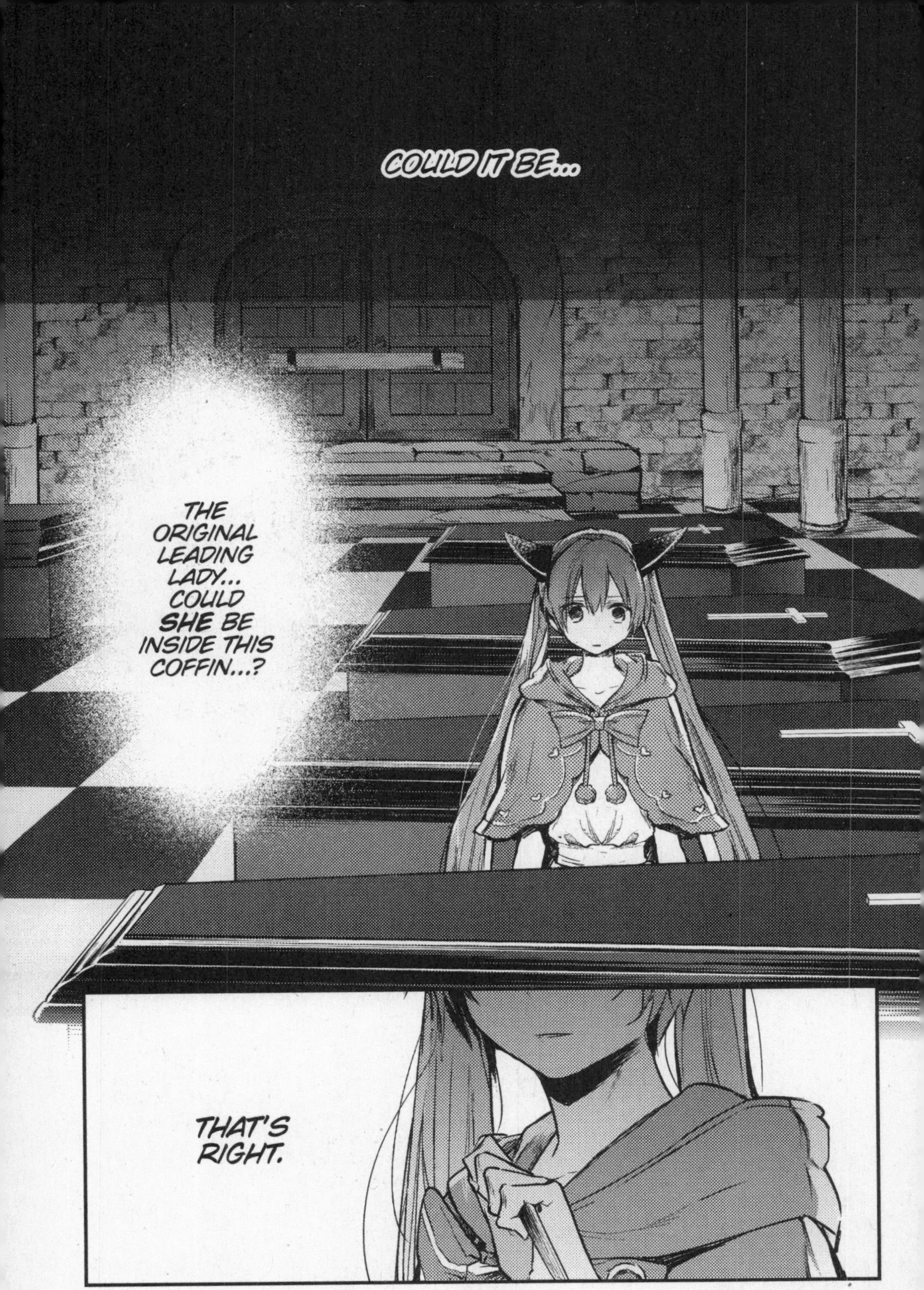
COULD IT BE...
THE ORIGINAL LEADING LADY... COULD SHE BE INSIDE THIS COFFIN...?
THAT'S RIGHT.

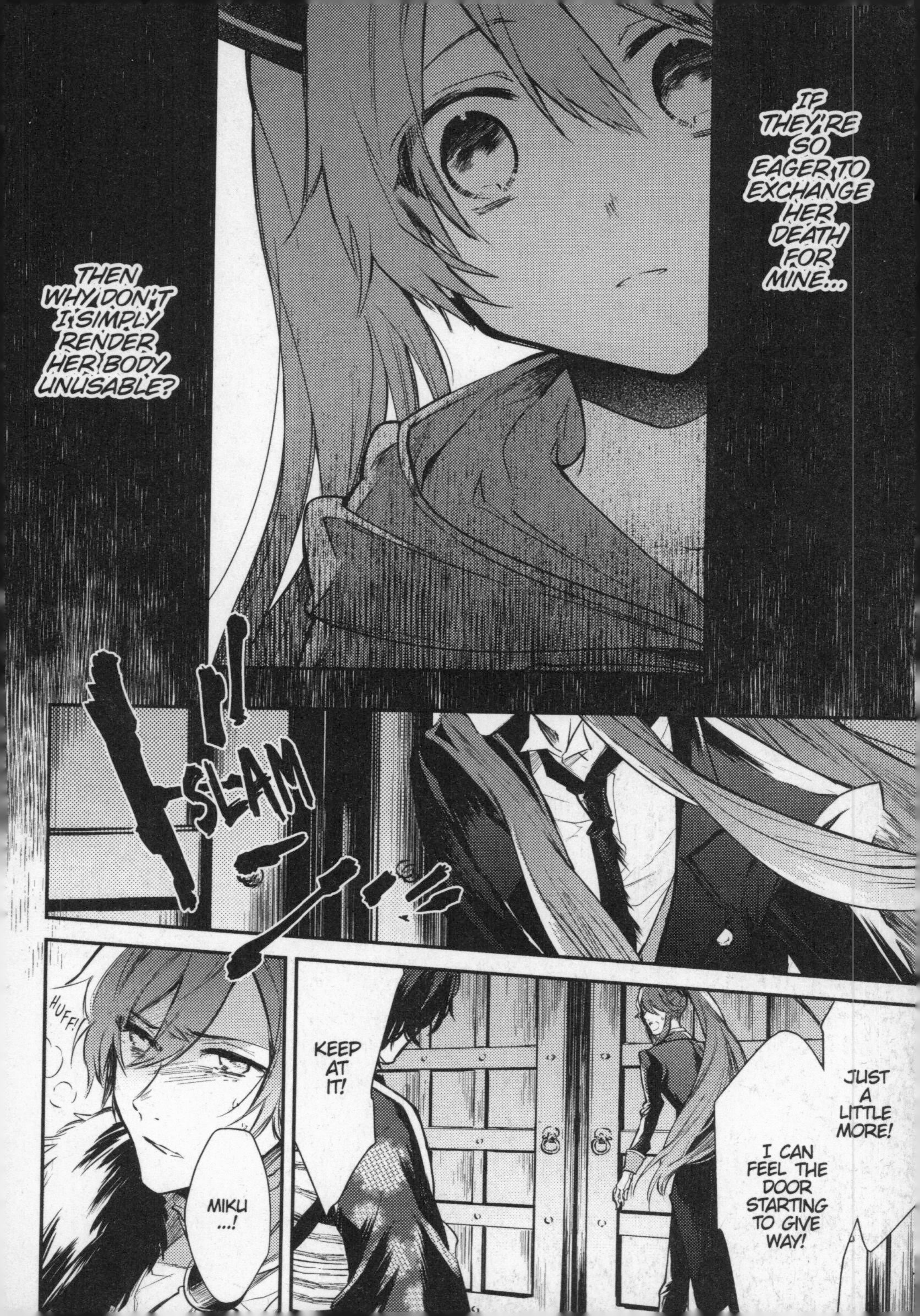
IF THEY'RE SO EAGER TO EXCHANGE HER DEATH FOR MINE...
THEN WHY DON'T I SIMPLY RENDER HER BODY UNUSABLE?
SLAM
JUST A LITTLE MORE!
I CAN FEEL THE DOOR STARTING TO GIVE WAY!
KEEP AT IT!
MIKU ...!
HUFF!

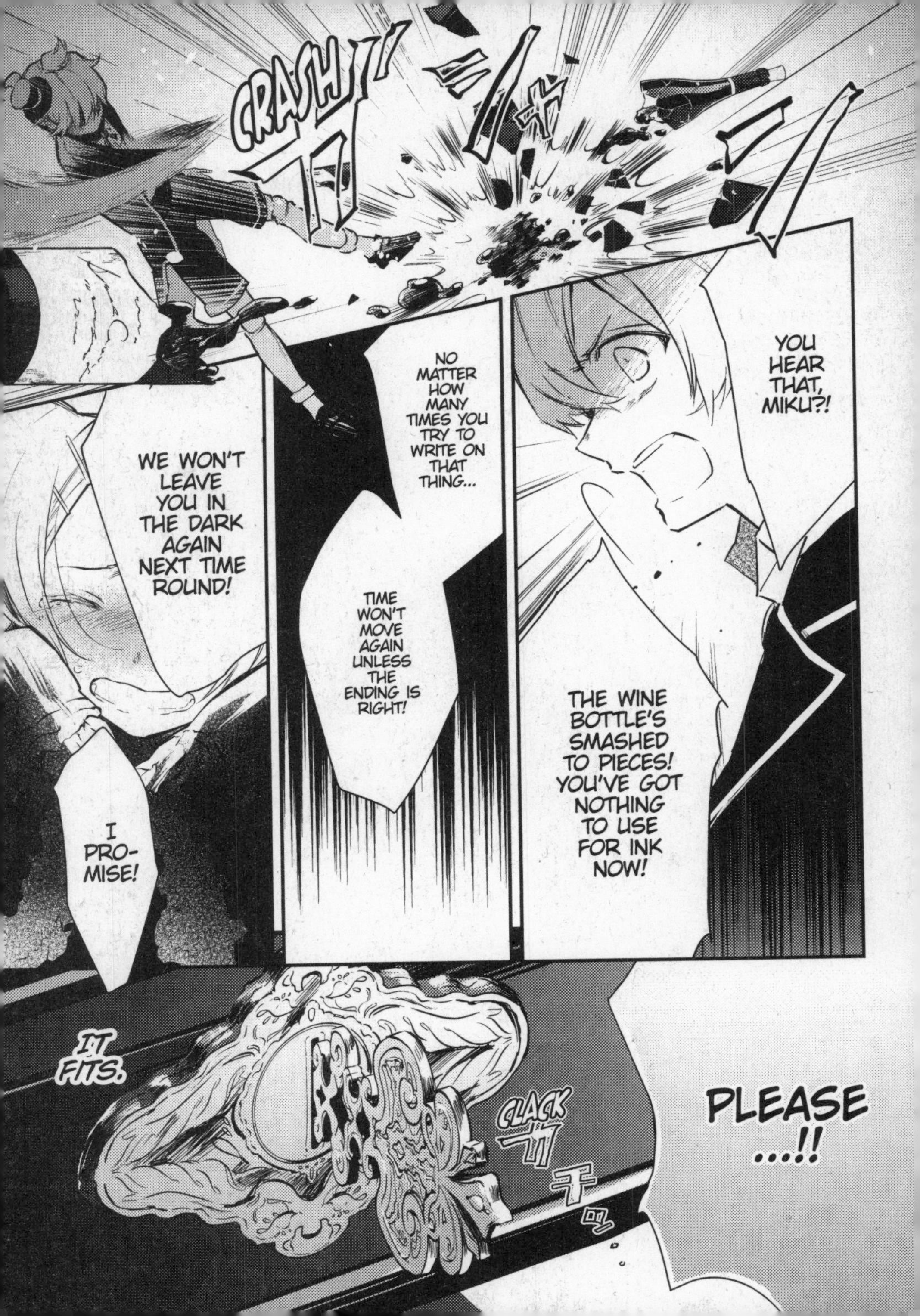
CRASH
YOU HEAR THAT, MIKU?!
THE WINE BOTTLE'S SMASHED TO PIECES! YOU'VE GOT NOTHING TO USE FOR INK NOW!
NO MATTER HOW MANY TIMES YOU TRY TO WRITE ON THAT THING...
TIME WON'T MOVE AGAIN UNLESS THE ENDING IS RIGHT!
WE WON'T LEAVE YOU IN THE DARK AGAIN NEXT TIME ROUND!
I PRO-MISE!
PLEASE ...!!
CLACK
IT FITS.

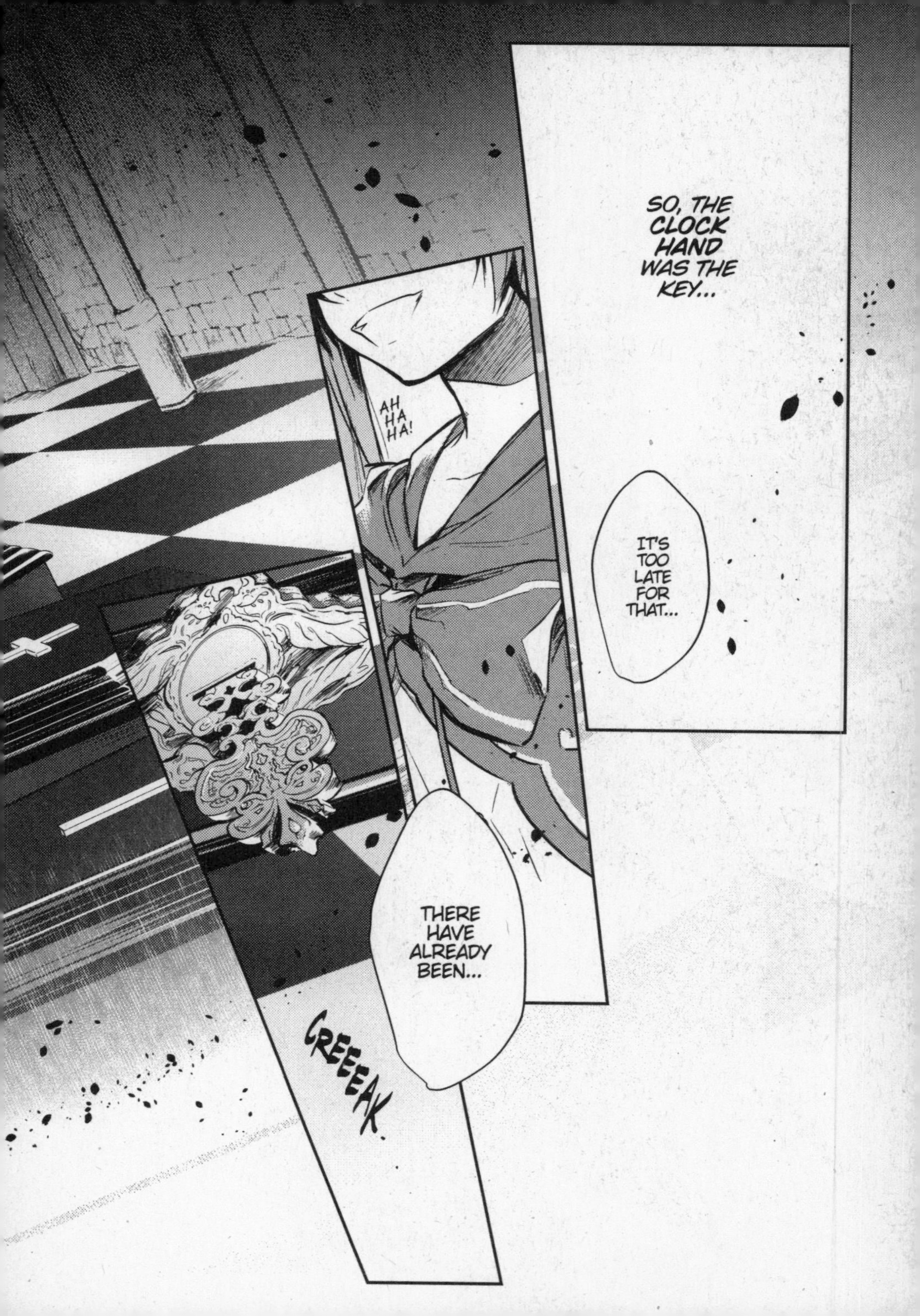
SO, THE CLOCK HAND WAS THE KEY...
AH HA HA!
IT'S TOO LATE FOR THAT...
THERE HAVE ALREADY BEEN...
CREEEAK

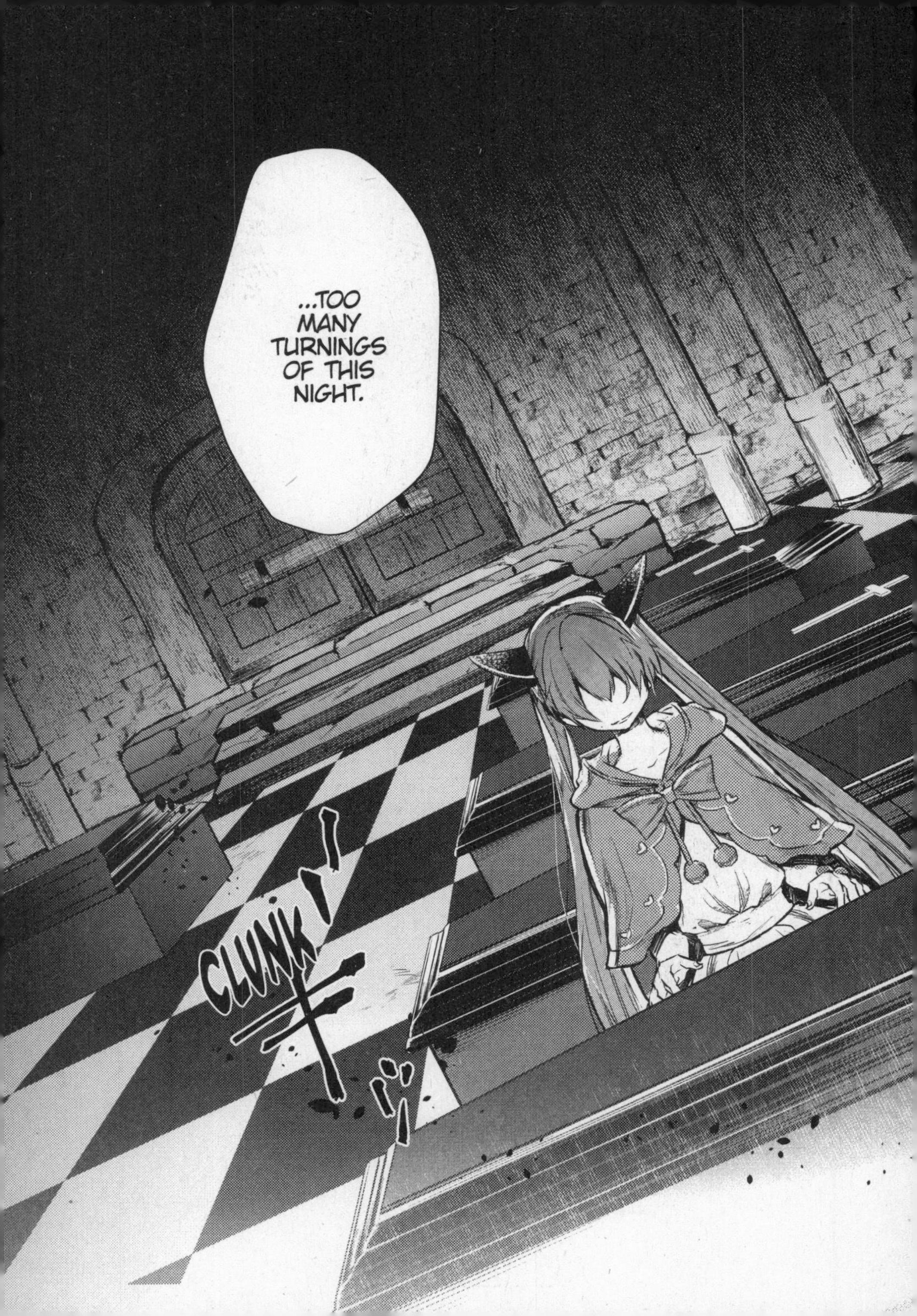
...TOO MANY TURNINGS OF THIS NIGHT.
CLUNK

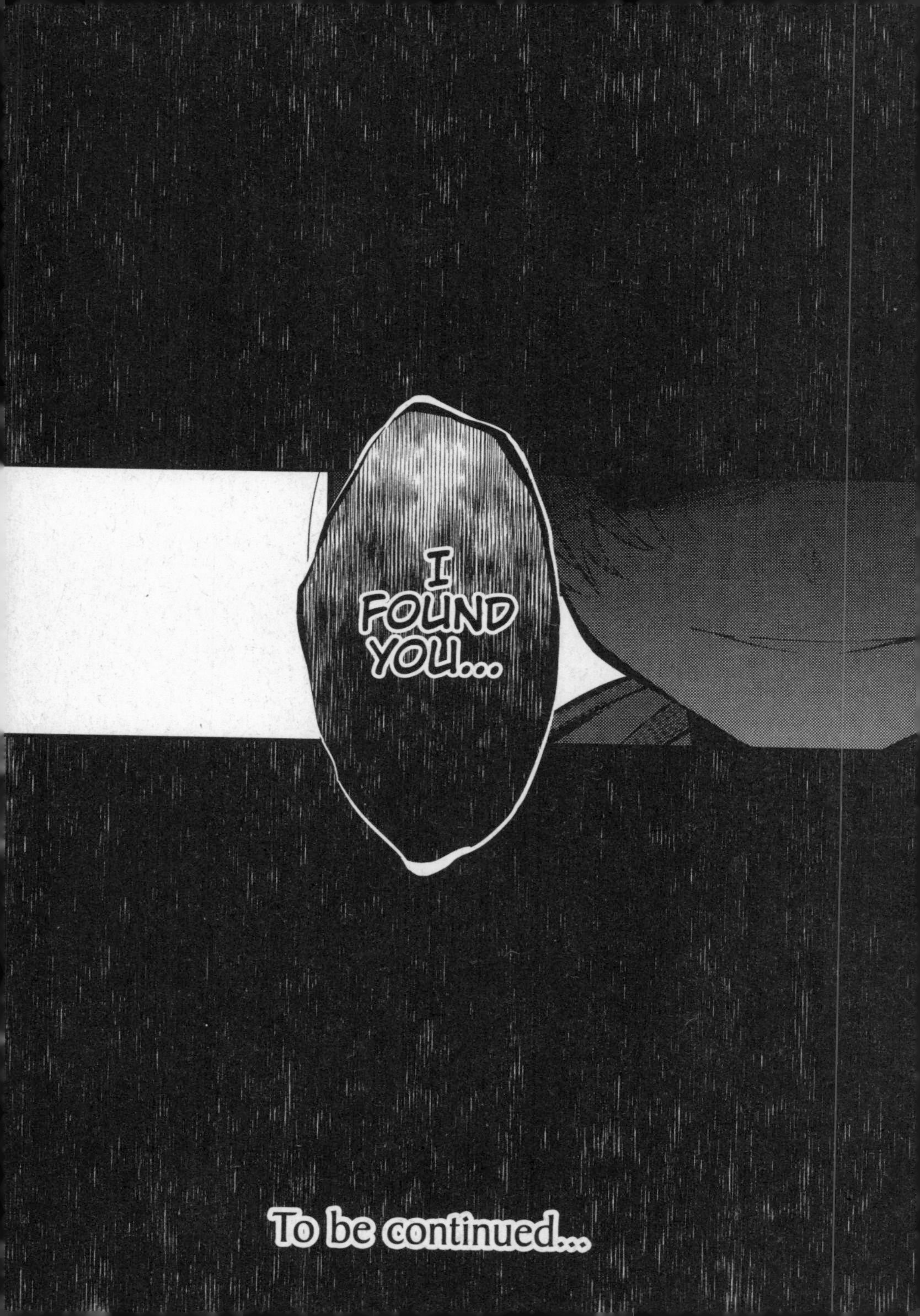
I FOUND YOU...
To be continued...

Bad∞End∞Night

～インセイン・パーティー～

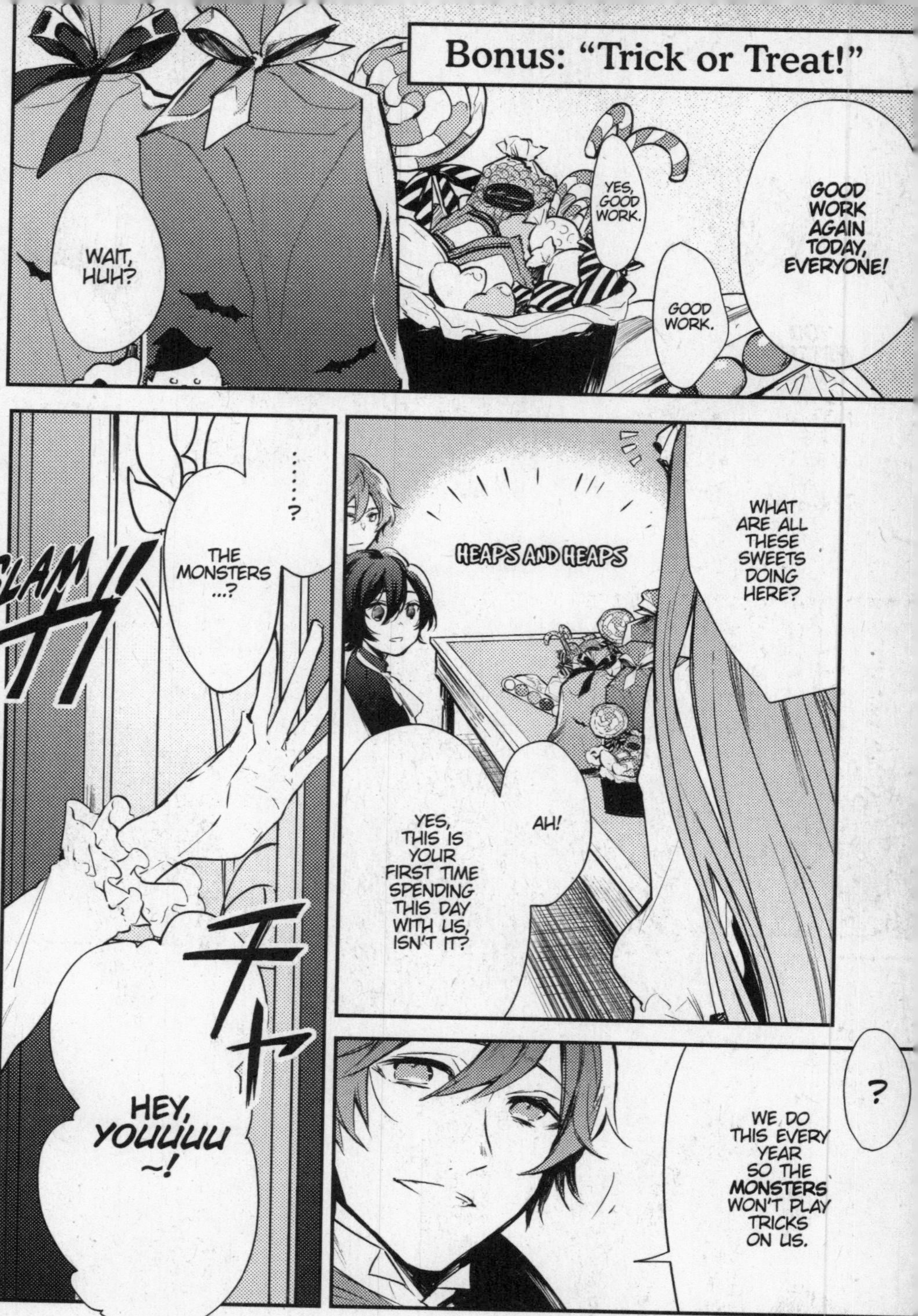
Bonus: "Trick or Treat!"
GOOD WORK AGAIN TODAY, EVERYONE!
GOOD WORK.
YES, GOOD WORK.
WAIT, HUH?
WHAT ARE ALL THESE SWEETS DOING HERE?
HEAPS AND HEAPS
AH!
YES, THIS IS YOUR FIRST TIME SPENDING THIS DAY WITH US, ISN'T IT?
?
WE DO THIS EVERY YEAR SO THE MONSTERS WON'T PLAY TRICKS ON US.
......?
THE MONSTERS ...?
SLAM
HEY, YOUUUUU ~!

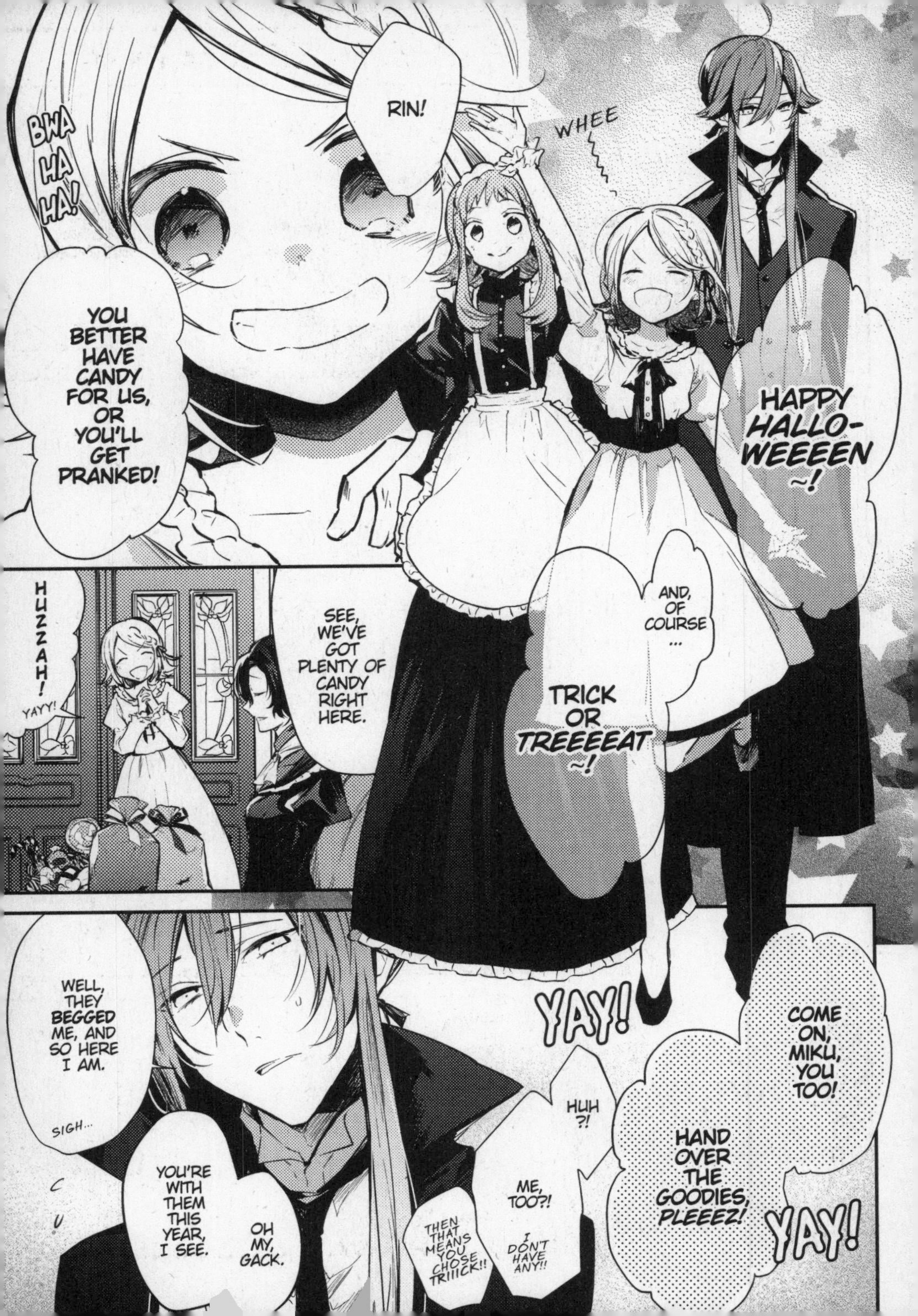
WHEE
HAPPY HALLO-WEEEEEN ~!
AND, OF COURSE ...
TRICK OR TREEEEAT ~!
RIN!
BWA HA HA HA!
YOU BETTER HAVE CANDY FOR US, OR YOU'LL GET PRANKED!
SEE, WE'VE GOT PLENTY OF CANDY RIGHT HERE.
HUZZAH!
YAYY!
YAY!
COME ON, MIKU, YOU TOO!
HAND OVER THE GOODIES, PLEEEZ!
YAY!
HUH?!
ME, TOO?!
I DON'T HAVE ANY!!
THEN THAT MEANS YOU CHOSE TRIIICK!!
WELL, THEY BEGGED ME, AND SO HERE I AM.
SIGH...
YOU'RE WITH THEM THIS YEAR, I SEE.
OH MY, GACK.

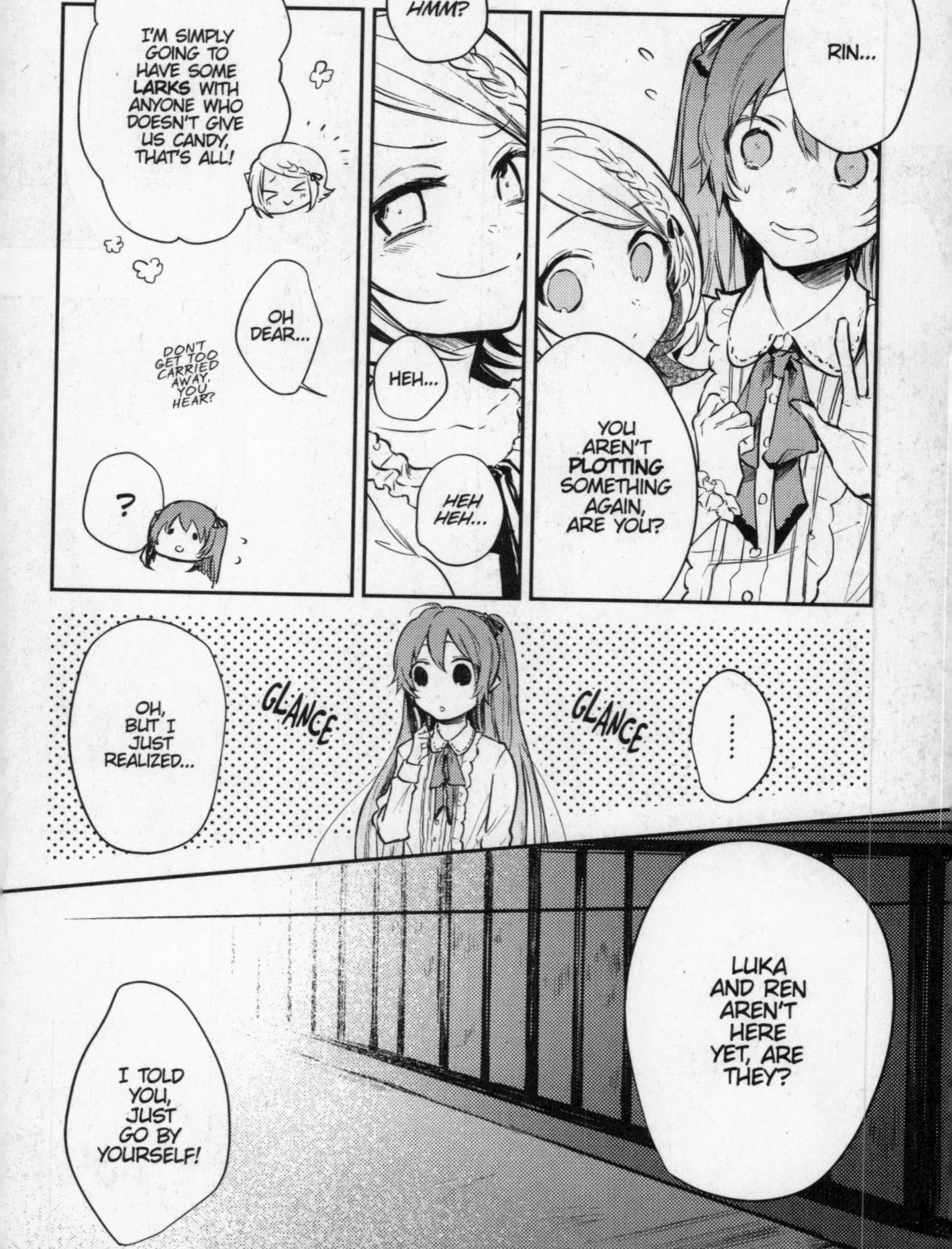
RIN...
YOU AREN'T PLOTTING SOMETHING AGAIN, ARE YOU?
HMM?
HEH...
HEH HEH...
I'M SIMPLY GOING TO HAVE SOME LARKS WITH ANYONE WHO DOESN'T GIVE US CANDY, THAT'S ALL!
OH DEAR...
DON'T GET TOO CARRIED AWAY, YOU HEAR?
?
......
GLANCE
GLANCE
OH, BUT I JUST REALIZED...
LUKA AND REN AREN'T HERE YET, ARE THEY?
I TOLD YOU, JUST GO BY YOURSELF!

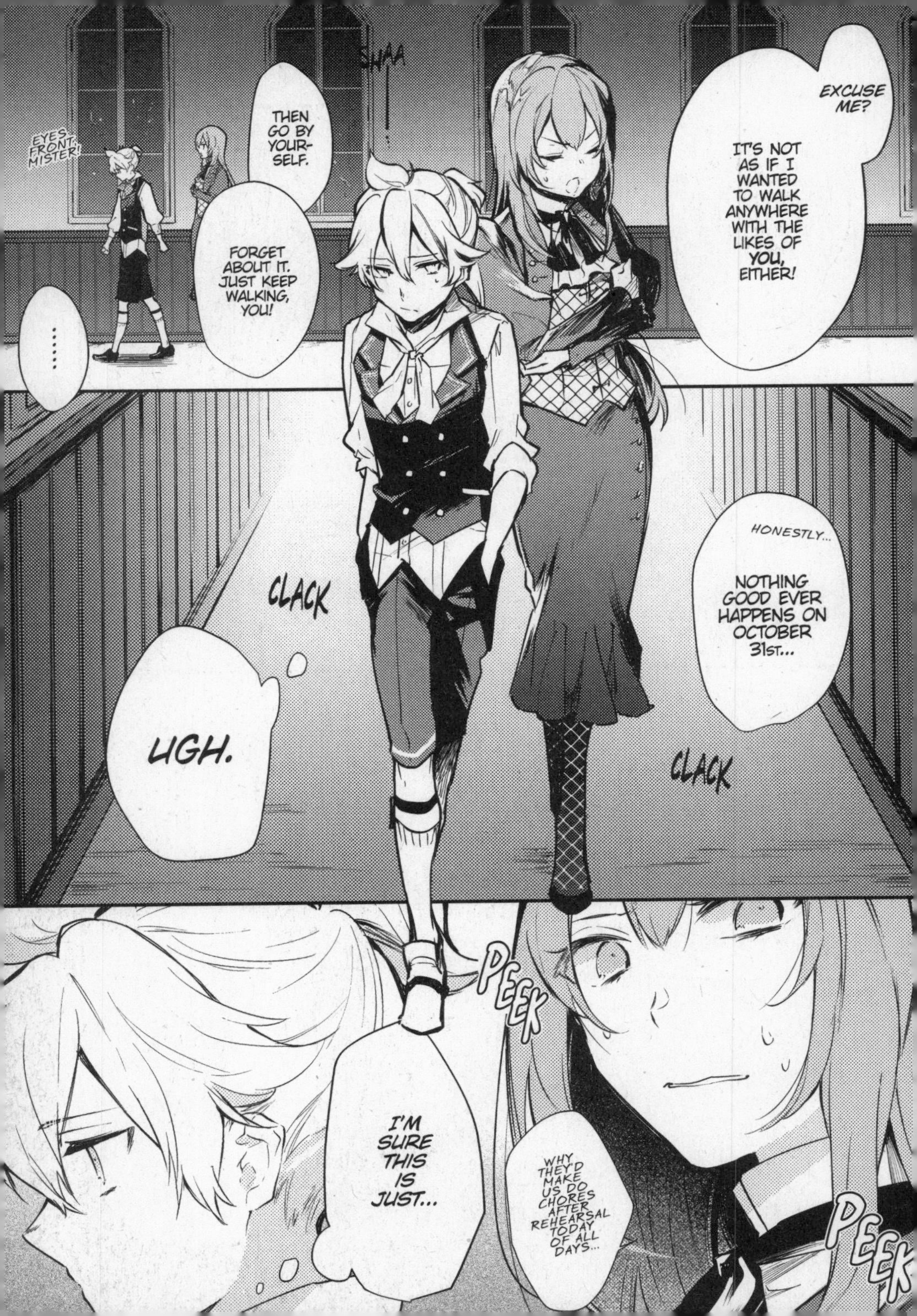

EXCUSE ME?
IT'S NOT AS IF I WANTED TO WALK ANYWHERE WITH THE LIKES OF YOU, EITHER!
SHAA
THEN GO BY YOUR-SELF.
FORGET ABOUT IT. JUST KEEP WALKING, YOU!
EYES FRONT, MISTER!
......
HONESTLY...
NOTHING GOOD EVER HAPPENS ON OCTOBER 31ST...
CLACK
CLACK
UGH.
PEEK
WHY THEY'D MAKE US DO CHORES AFTER REHEARSAL TODAY OF ALL DAYS...
PEEK
I'M SURE THIS IS JUST...

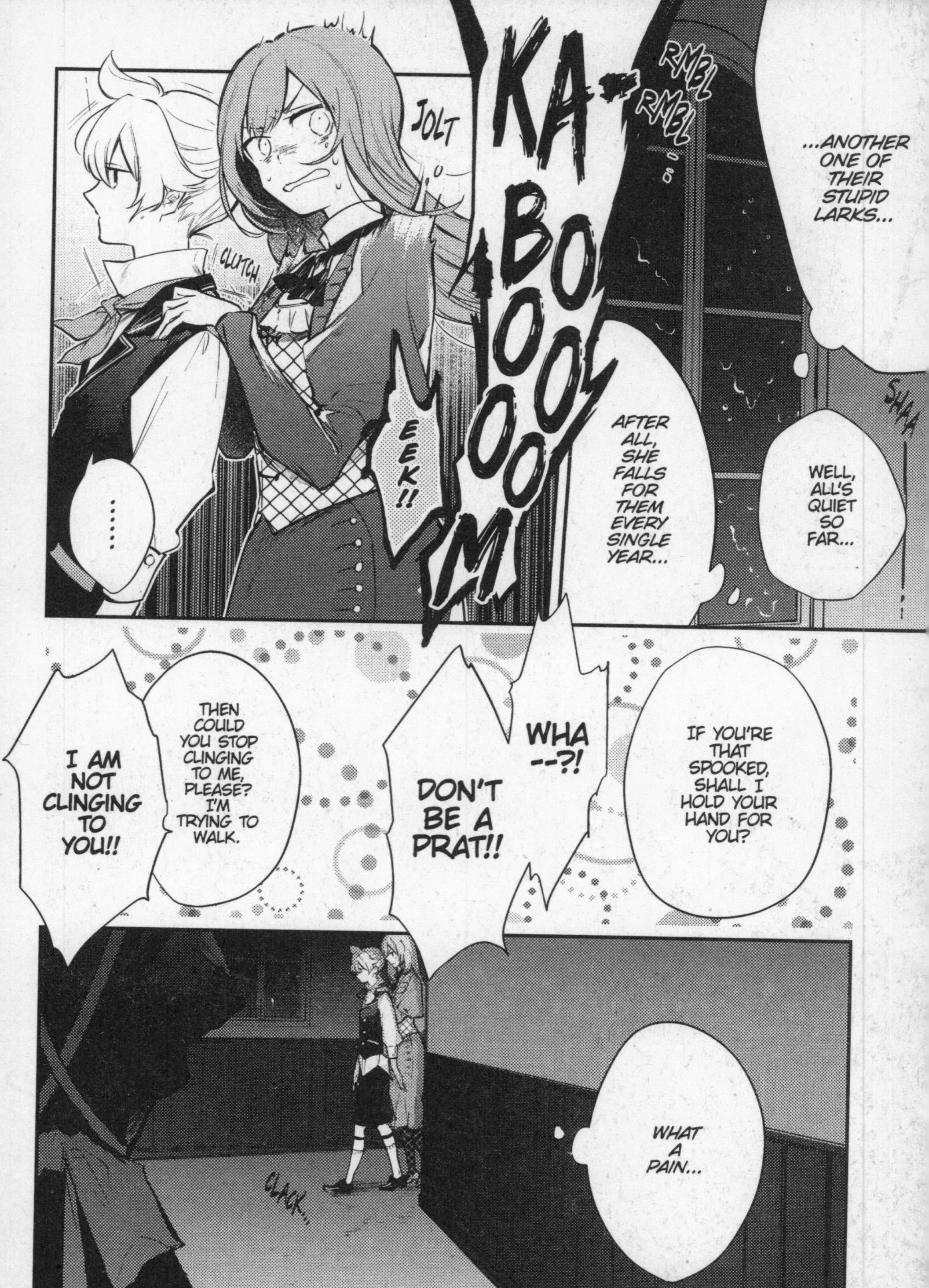
...ANOTHER ONE OF THEIR STUPID LARKS...
RMBL RMBL
KA-BOOOOOM
JOLT
SHAA
WELL, ALL'S QUIET SO FAR...
AFTER ALL, SHE FALLS FOR THEM EVERY SINGLE YEAR...
EEK!!
CLUTCH
......
IF YOU'RE THAT SPOOKED, SHALL I HOLD YOUR HAND FOR YOU?
WHA--?!
DON'T BE A PRAT!!
THEN COULD YOU STOP CLINGING TO ME, PLEASE? I'M TRYING TO WALK.
I AM NOT CLINGING TO YOU!!
WHAT A PAIN...
CLACK...

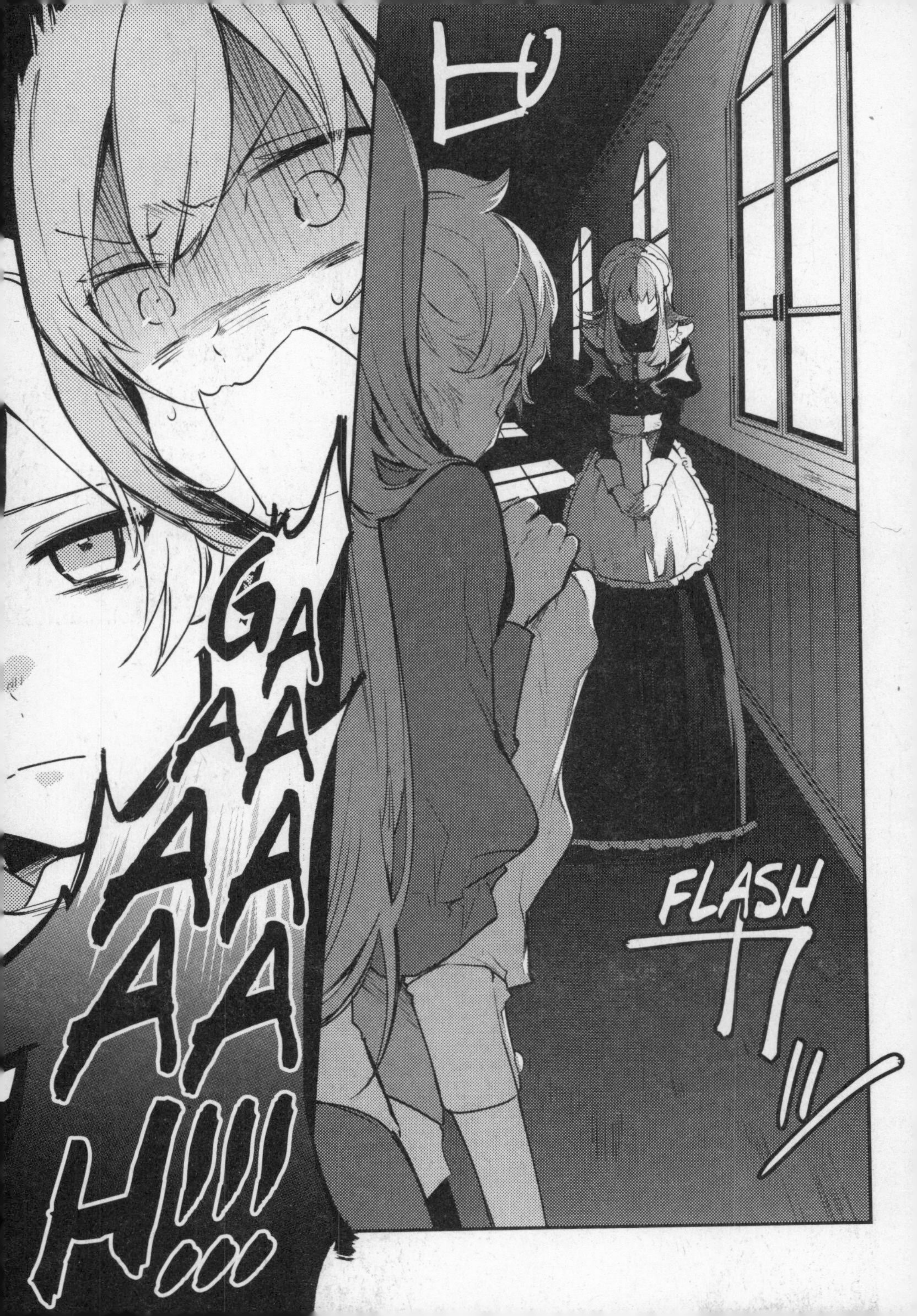
FLASH
GAAAAAAAH!!!!...

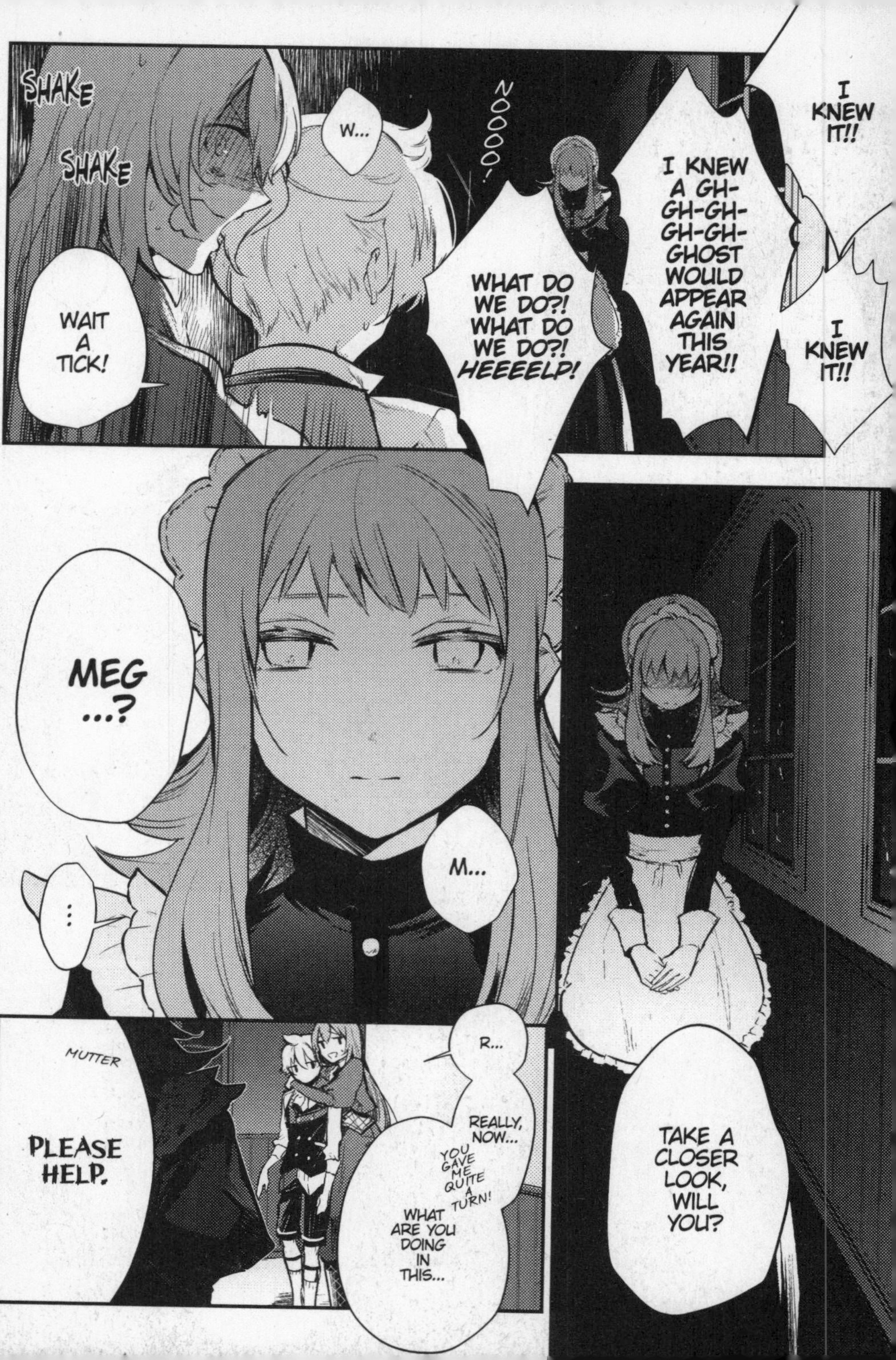
I KNEW IT!!
I KNEW IT!!
I KNEW A GH-GH-GH-GH-GH-GHOST WOULD APPEAR AGAIN THIS YEAR!!
NOOOOO!
WHAT DO WE DO?! WHAT DO WE DO?! HEEEELP!
W...
SHAKE
SHAKE
WAIT A TICK!
TAKE A CLOSER LOOK, WILL YOU?
MEG ...?
M...
...
R...
REALLY, NOW...
YOU GAVE ME QUITE A TURN!
WHAT ARE YOU DOING IN THIS...
MUTTER
PLEASE HELP.

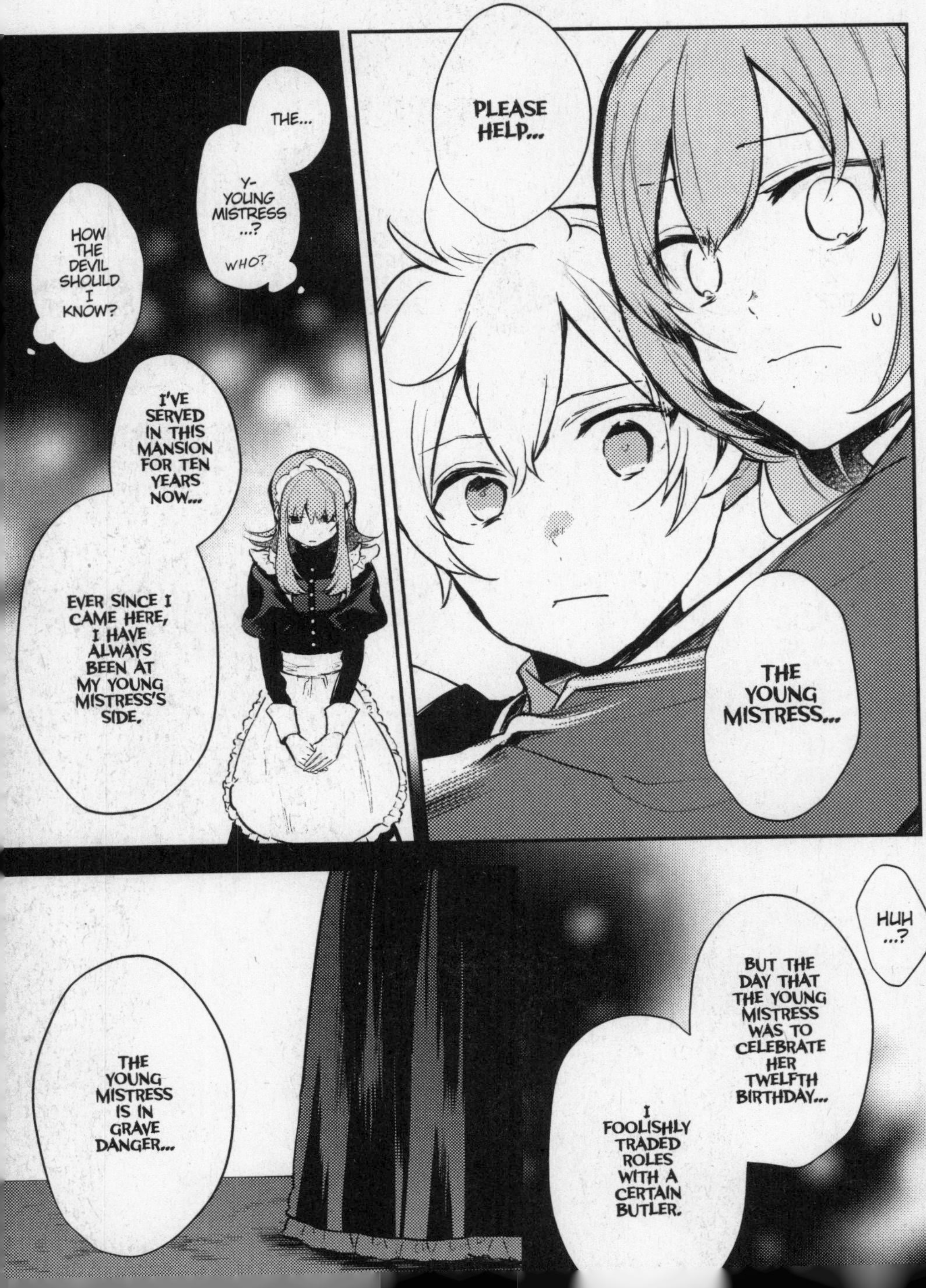
PLEASE HELP...
THE YOUNG MISTRESS...
THE...
Y-YOUNG MISTRESS ...?
WHO?
HOW THE DEVIL SHOULD I KNOW?
I'VE SERVED IN THIS MANSION FOR TEN YEARS NOW...
EVER SINCE I CAME HERE, I HAVE ALWAYS BEEN AT MY YOUNG MISTRESS'S SIDE.
HUH ...?
BUT THE DAY THAT THE YOUNG MISTRESS WAS TO CELEBRATE HER TWELFTH BIRTHDAY...
I FOOLISHLY TRADED ROLES WITH A CERTAIN BUTLER.
THE YOUNG MISTRESS IS IN GRAVE DANGER...

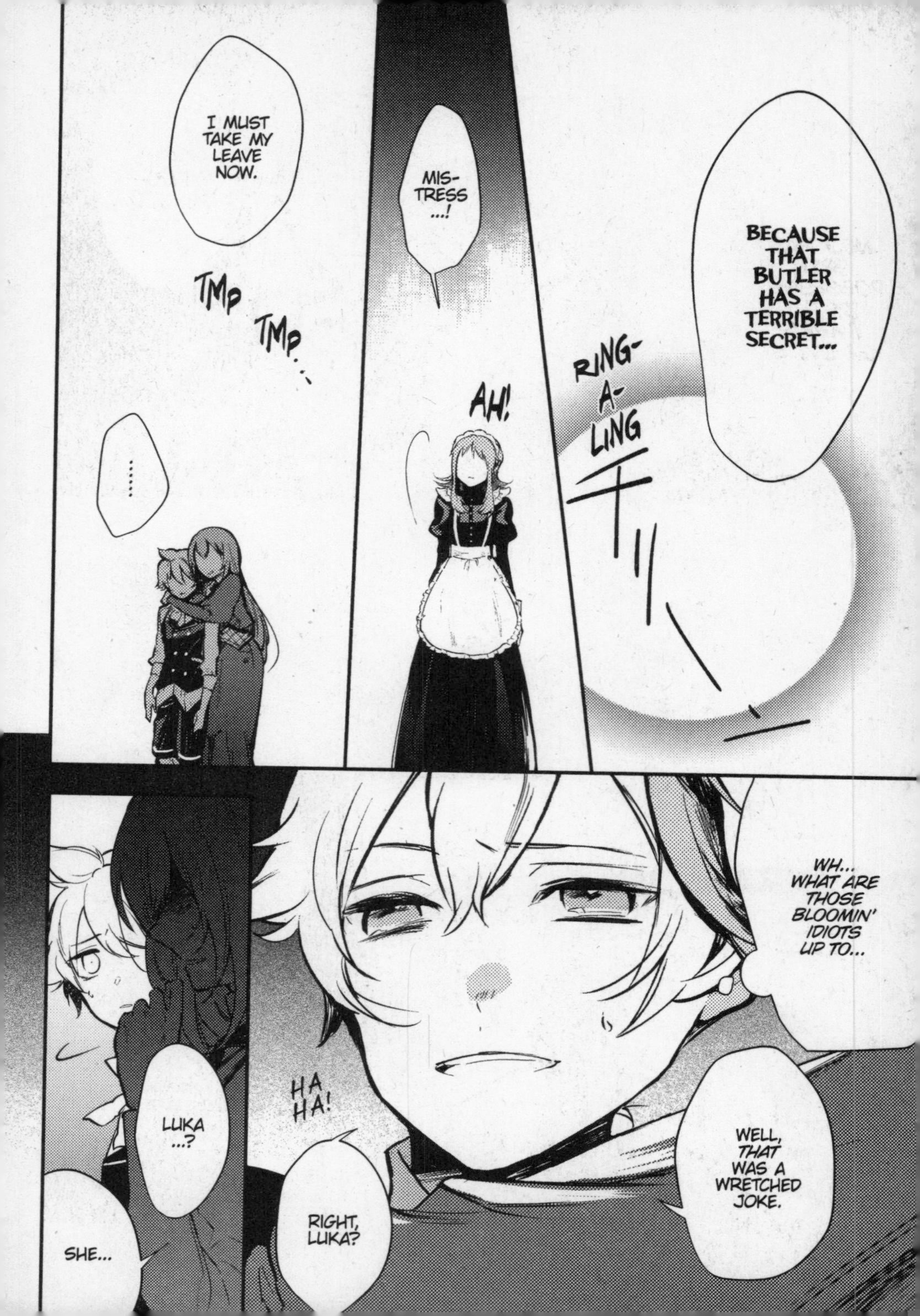

BECAUSE THAT BUTLER HAS A TERRIBLE SECRET...
RING-A-LING
MISTRESS...!
AH!
I MUST TAKE MY LEAVE NOW.
TMP TMP...
......
WH... WHAT ARE THOSE BLOOMIN' IDIOTS UP TO...
WELL, THAT WAS A WRETCHED JOKE.
HA HA!
RIGHT, LUKA?
LUKA...?
SHE...

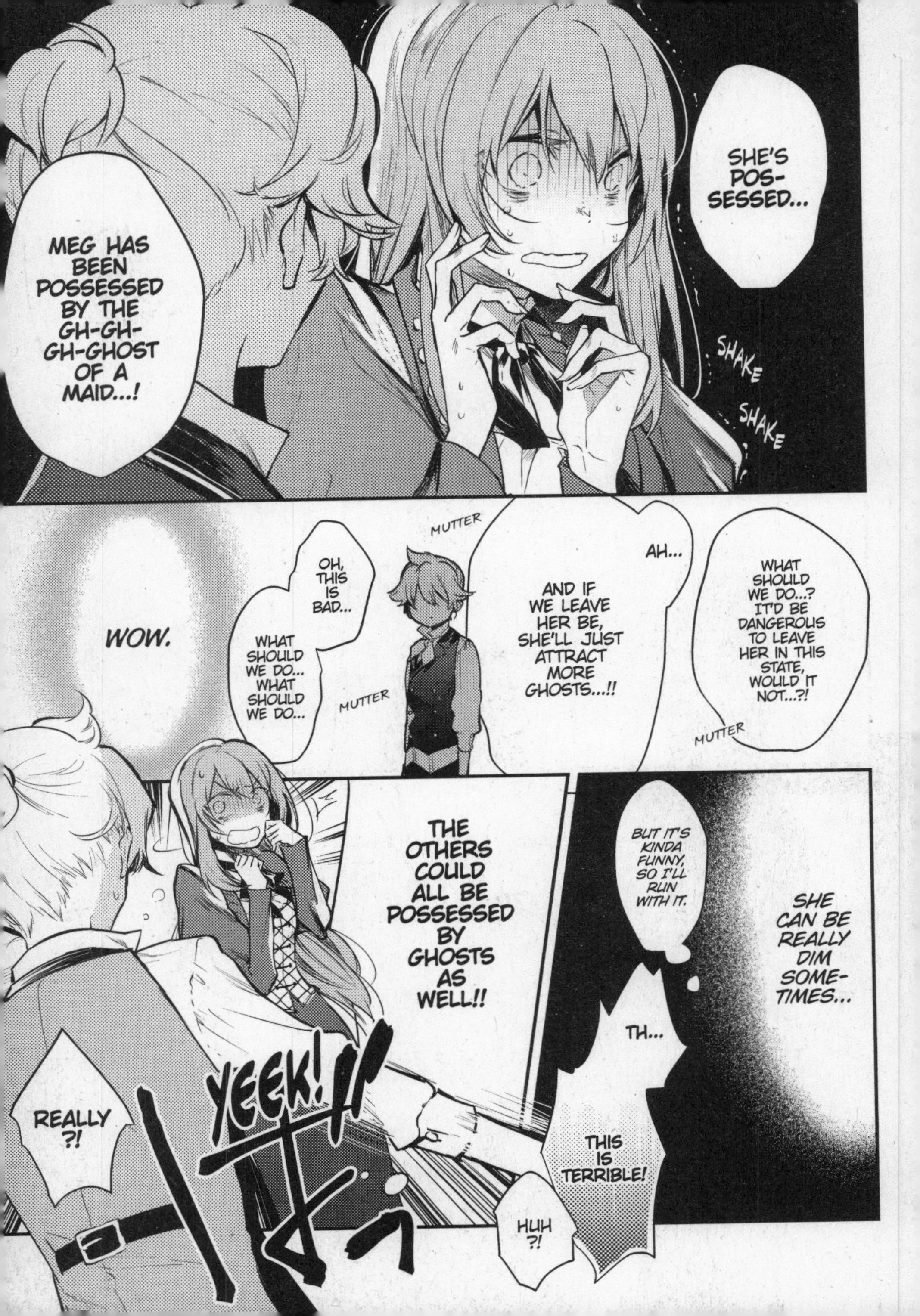
SHE'S POSSESSED...
SHAKE
SHAKE
MEG HAS BEEN POSSESSED BY THE GH-GH-GH-GHOST OF A MAID...!
WHAT SHOULD WE DO...? IT'D BE DANGEROUS TO LEAVE HER IN THIS STATE, WOULD IT NOT...?!
MUTTER
AH...
AND IF WE LEAVE HER BE, SHE'LL JUST ATTRACT MORE GHOSTS...!!
MUTTER
OH, THIS IS BAD...
WHAT SHOULD WE DO... WHAT SHOULD WE DO...
MUTTER
WOW.
SHE CAN BE REALLY DIM SOME-TIMES...
BUT IT'S KINDA FUNNY, SO I'LL RUN WITH IT.
TH...
THIS IS TERRIBLE!
THE OTHERS COULD ALL BE POSSESSED BY GHOSTS AS WELL!!
HUH?!
YEEK!!
REALLY?!

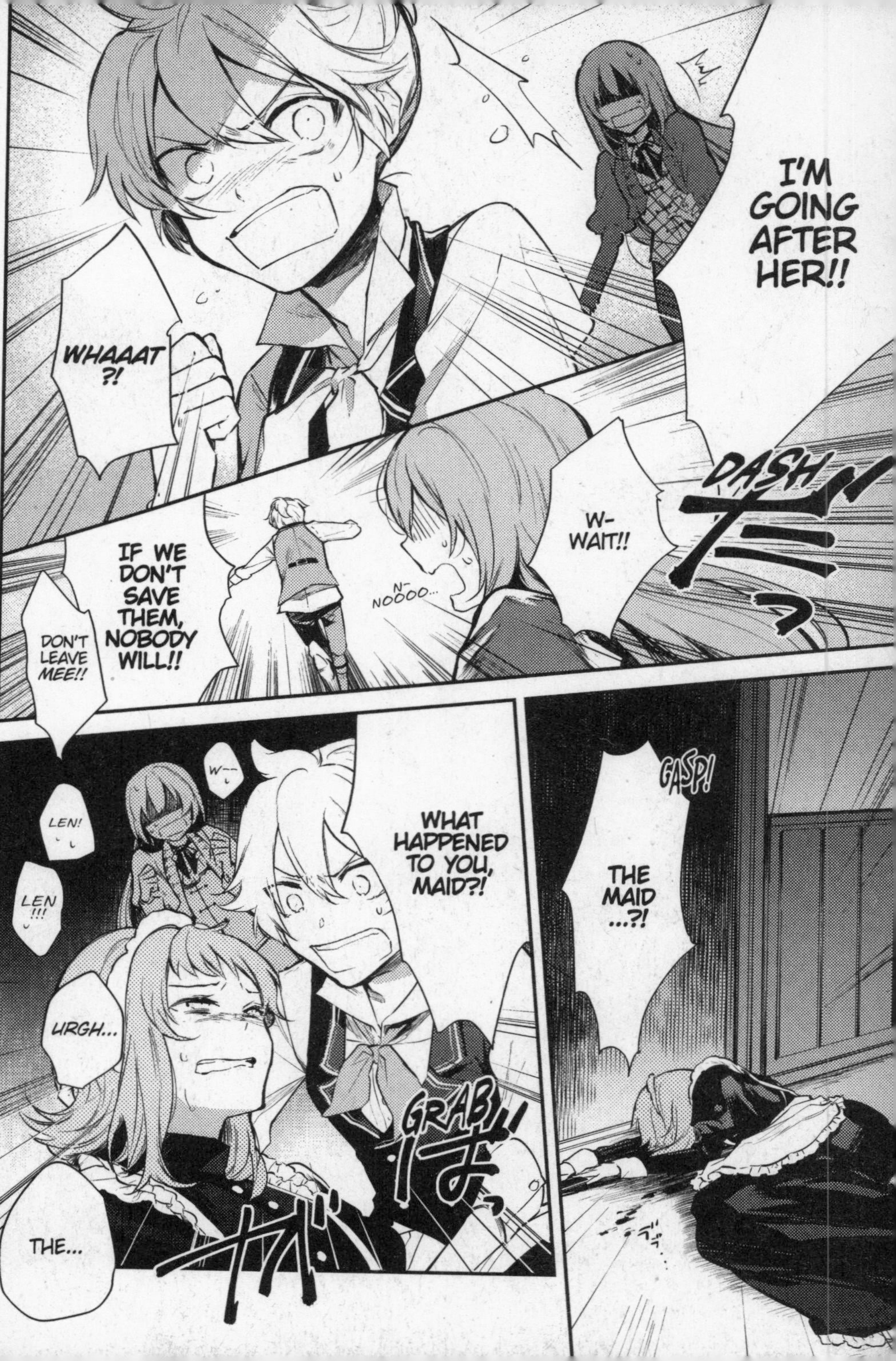
I'M GOING AFTER HER!!
WHAAAT ?!
DASH
W- WAIT!!
N- NOOOO...
IF WE DON'T SAVE THEM, NOBODY WILL!!
DON'T LEAVE MEE!!
GASP!
THE MAID ...?!
WHAT HAPPENED TO YOU, MAID?!
W--
LEN!
LEN !!!
URGH...
GRAB
THE...

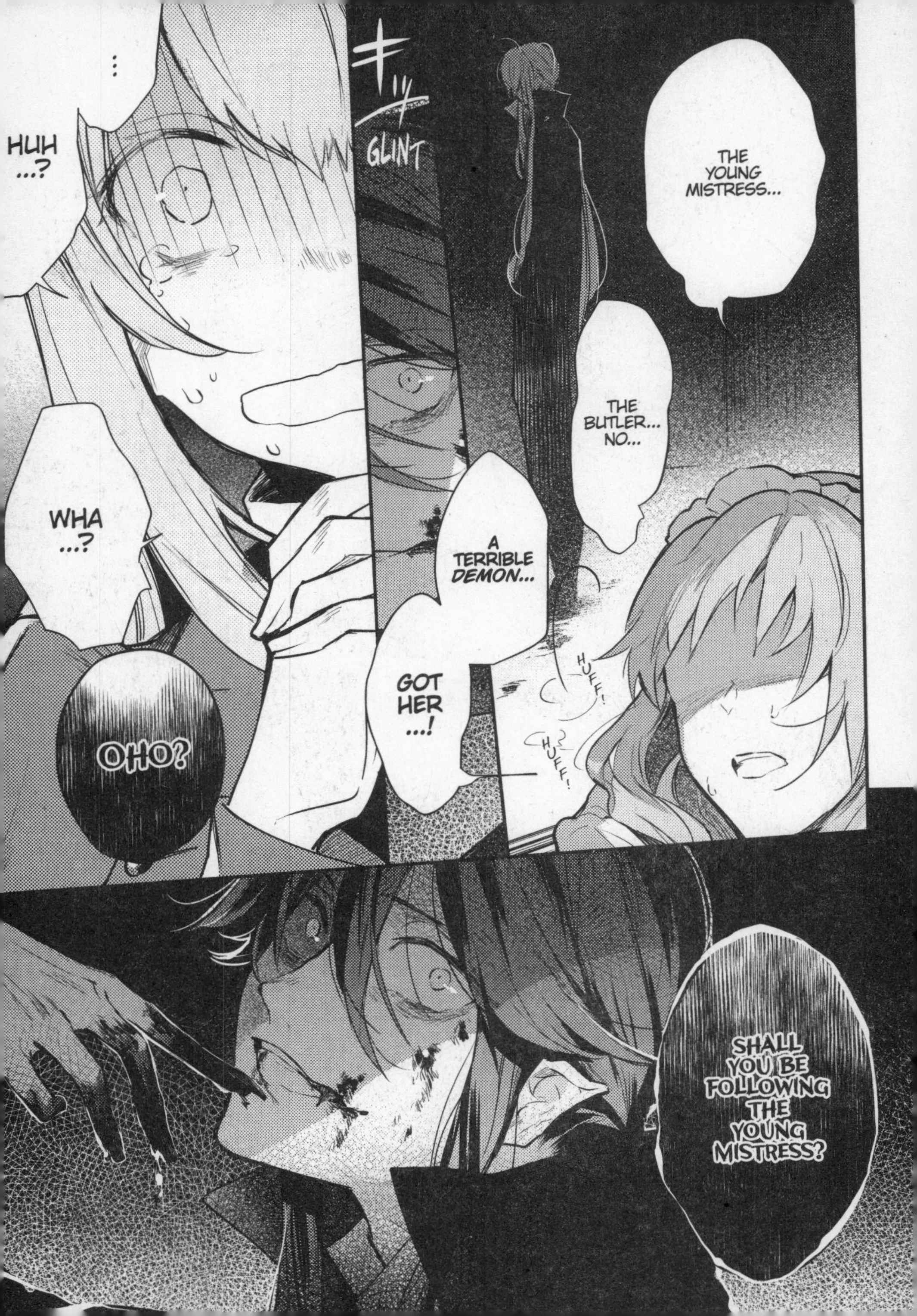
THE YOUNG MISTRESS...
THE BUTLER... NO...
HUFF! HUFF!
A TERRIBLE DEMON...
GOT HER ...!
キッ
GLINT
...
HUH ...?
WHA ...?
OHO?
SHALL YOU BE FOLLOWING THE YOUNG MISTRESS?

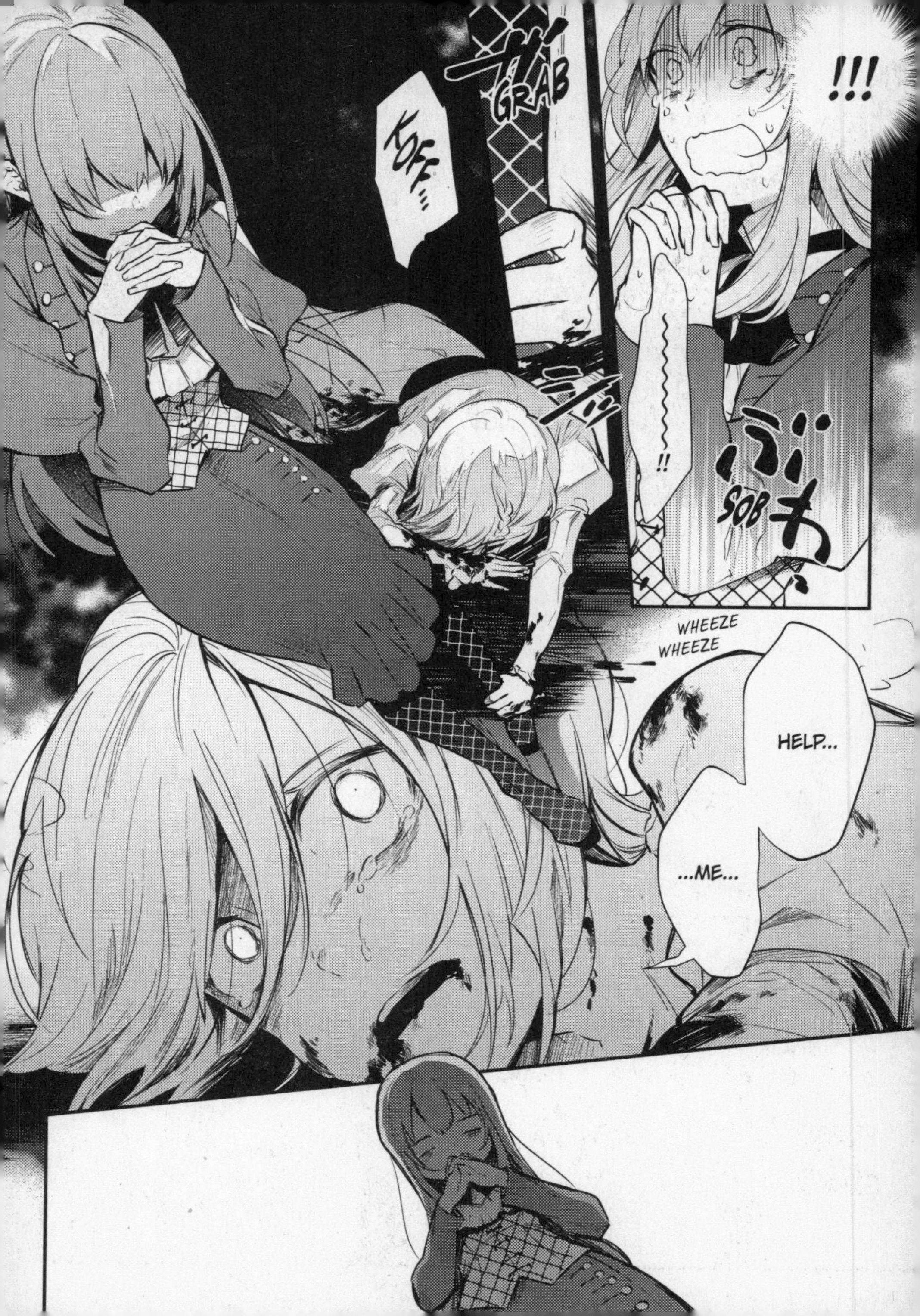

!!!
!!
SOB
GRAB
KOFF...
WHEEZE
WHEEZE
HELP...
...ME...

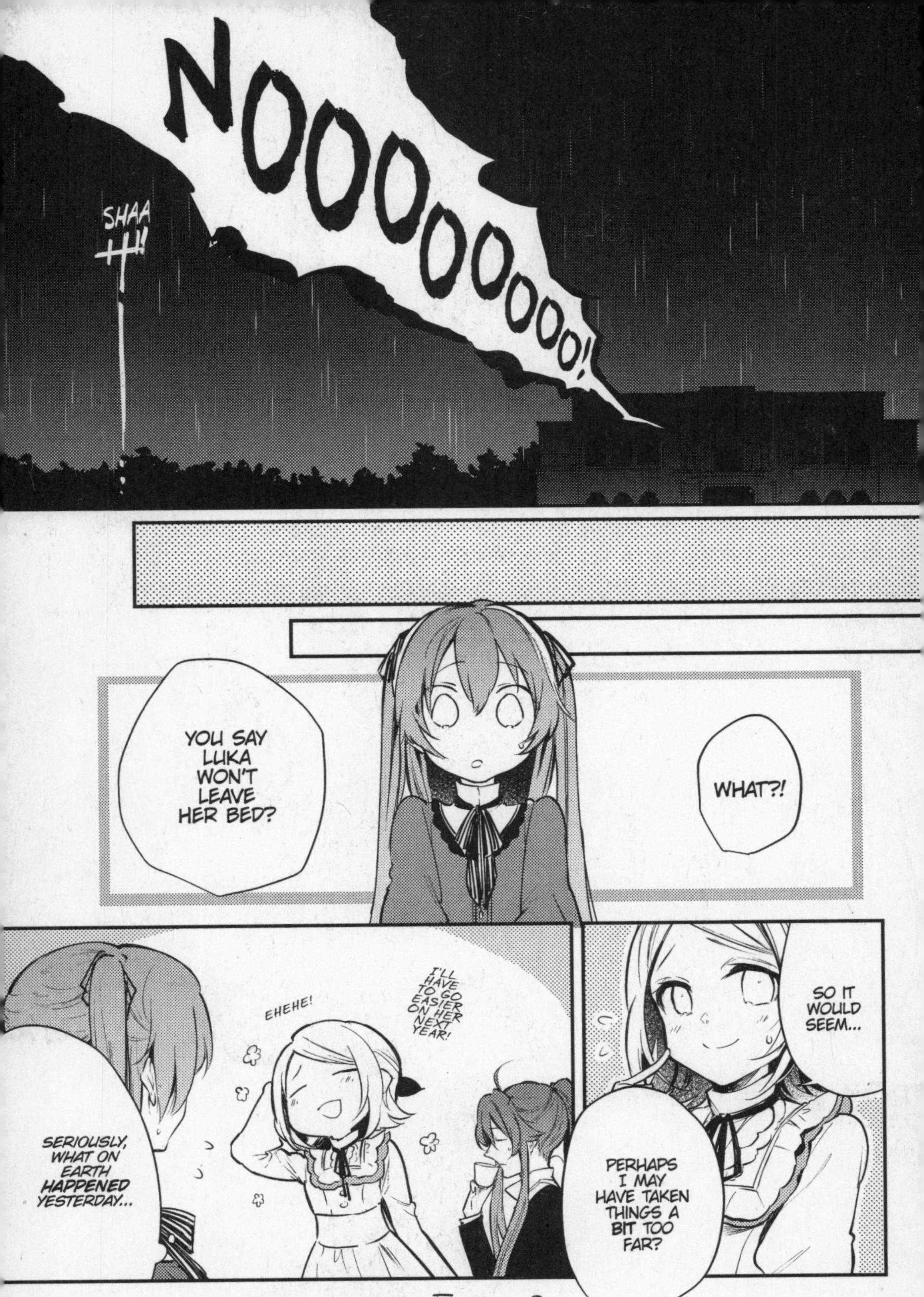
NOOOOOOOOO!
SHAA HH!
WHAT?!
YOU SAY LUKA WON'T LEAVE HER BED?
SO IT WOULD SEEM...
PERHAPS I MAY HAVE TAKEN THINGS A BIT TOO FAR?
I'LL HAVE TO GO EASIER ON HER NEXT YEAR!
EHEHE!
SERIOUSLY, WHAT ON EARTH HAPPENED YESTERDAY...

—END—

Bad∞End∞Night

～インセイン・パーティー～

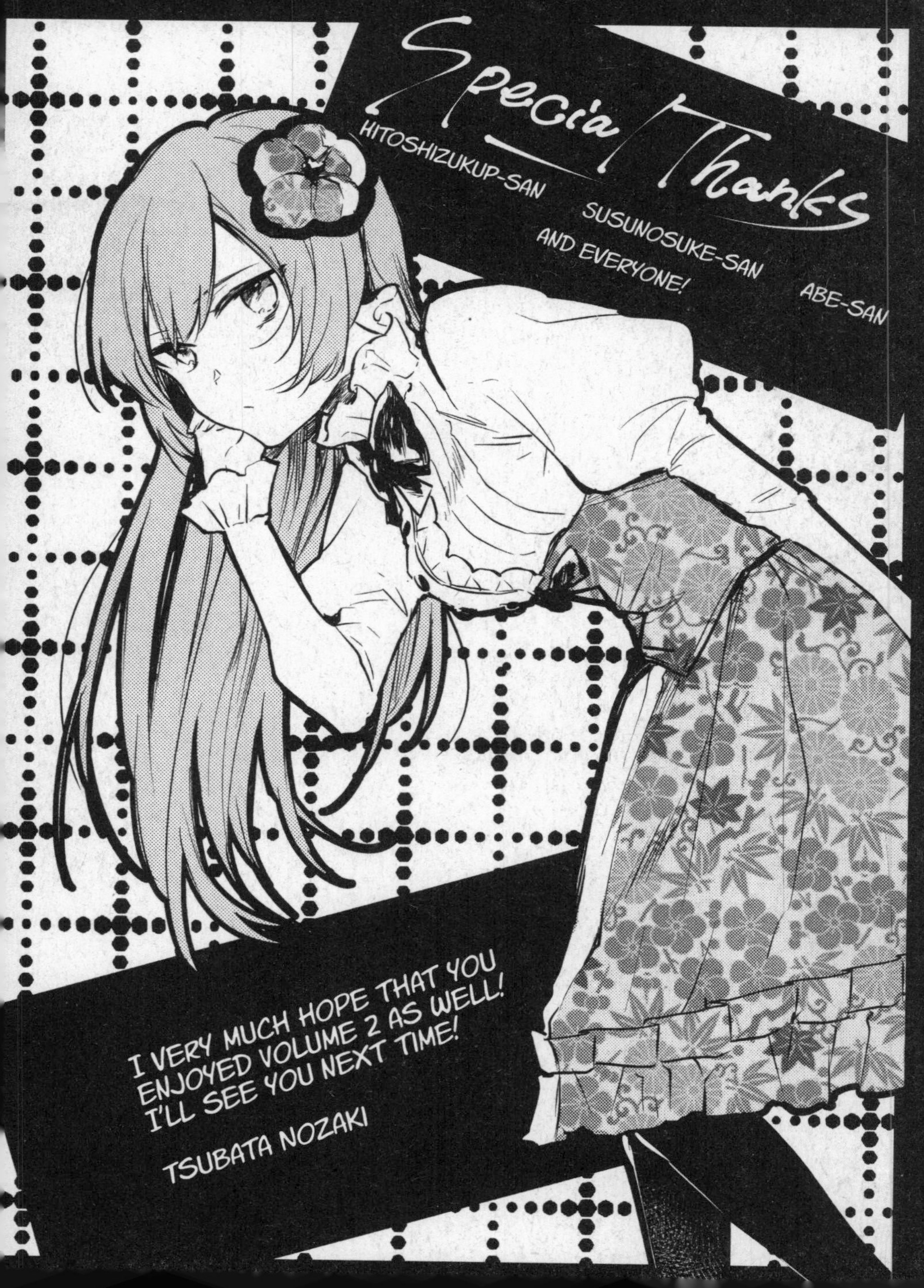
Special Thanks
HITOSHIZUKUP-SAN
SUSUNOSUKE-SAN
ABE-SAN
AND EVERYONE!
I VERY MUCH HOPE THAT YOU ENJOYED VOLUME 2 AS WELL! I'LL SEE YOU NEXT TIME!
TSUBATA NOZAKI

Bad∞End∞Night

~インセイン・パーティー~

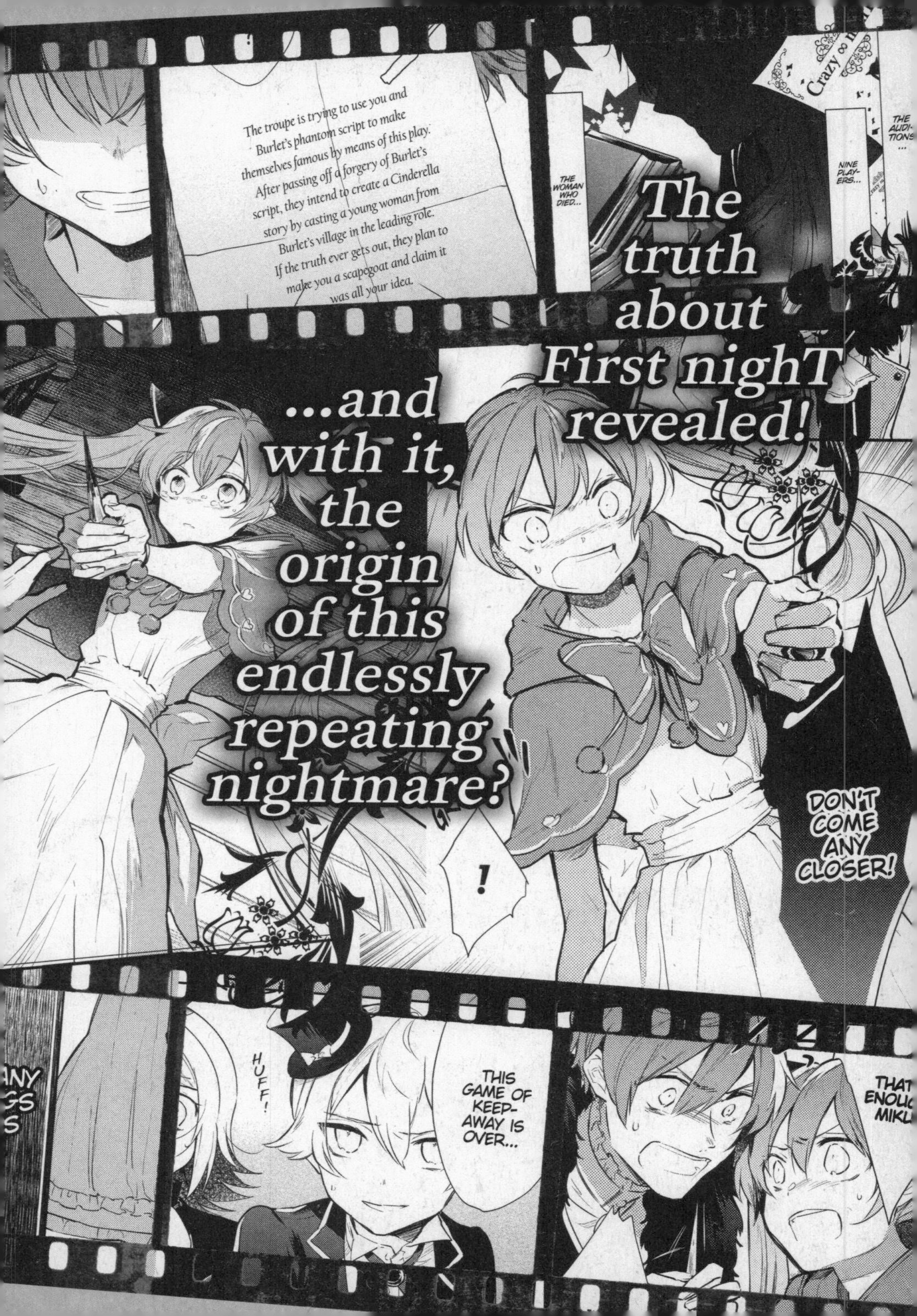
THE AUDITIONS...
NINE PLAYERS...
THE WOMAN WHO DIED...
The troupe is trying to use you and Burlet's phantom script to make themselves famous by means of this play. After passing off a forgery of Burlet's script, they intend to create a Cinderella story by casting a young woman from Burlet's village in the leading role. If the truth ever gets out, they plan to make you a scapegoat and claim it was all your idea.
The truth about First nighT revealed!
...and with it, the origin of this endlessly repeating nightmare?
DON'T COME ANY CLOSER!
!
THIS GAME OF KEEP-AWAY IS OVER...
HUFF!

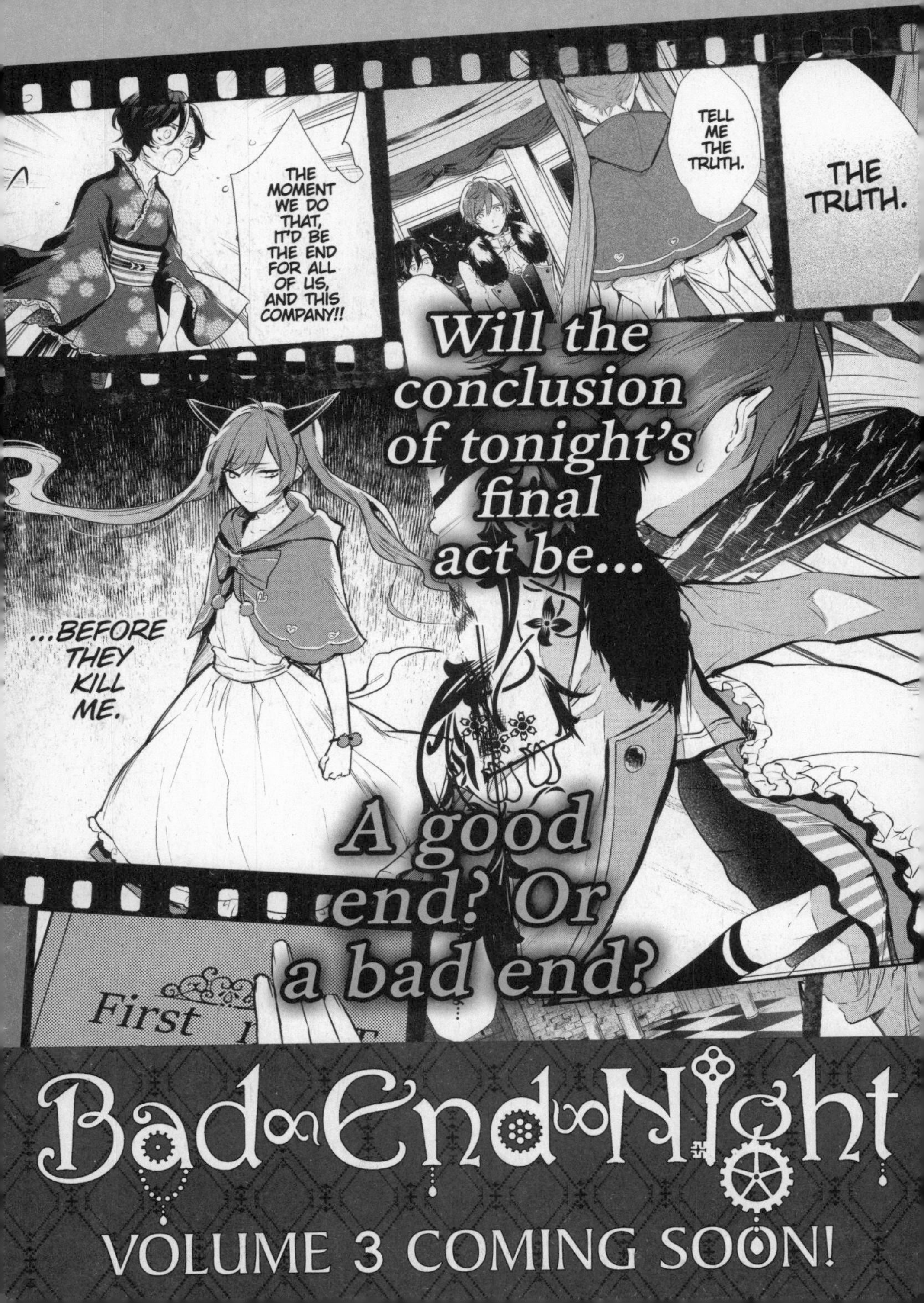
THE TRUTH.
TELL ME THE TRUTH.
THE MOMENT WE DO THAT, IT'D BE THE END FOR ALL OF US, AND THIS COMPANY!!
Will the conclusion of tonight's final act be...
...BEFORE THEY KILL ME.
A good end? Or a bad end?
First
Bad∞End∞Night
VOLUME 3 COMING SOON!

SEVEN SEAS ENTERTAINMENT PRESENTS

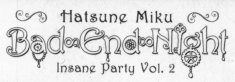

Hatsune Miku Bad∞End∞Night
Insane Party Vol. 2

story by HITOSHIZUKU-P × YAMA△ art by TSUBATA NOZAKI

TRANSLATION
Jenny McKeon

ADTAPTATION
Shanti Whitesides

LETTERING AND RETOUCH
Roland Amago
Bambi Eloriaga-Amago

COVER DESIGN
Nicky Lim

PROOFREADER
Tim Roddy

ASSISTANT EDITOR
Jenn Grunigen

PRODUCTION ASSISTANT
CK Russell

PRODUCTION MANAGER
Lissa Pattillo

EDITOR-IN-CHIEF
Adam Arnold

PUBLISHER
Jason DeAngelis

First published in Japan in 2016 by ICHIJINSHA Inc., Tokyo.
English translation rights arranged with ICHIJINSHA Inc., Tokyo, Japan.

ISBN: 978-1-626925-26-7

Printed in Canada

First Printing: July 2017

10 9 8 7 6 5 4 3 2 1

READING DIRECTIONS

This book reads from ***right to left***, Japanese style. If this is your first time reading manga, you start reading from the top right panel on each page and take it from there. If you get lost, just follow the numbered diagram here. It may seem backwards at first, but you'll get the hang of it! Have fun!!

1
2
3
4
5
6
7
8
9

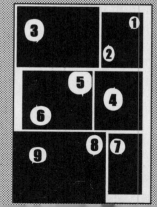